Relationality and Resilience in a Not So Relational World? Knowledge, *Chivanhu* and (De-)Coloniality in 21st Century Conflict-Torn Zimbabwe

Artwell Nhemachena

Langaa Research & Publishing CIG
Mankon, Bamenda

Publisher:
Langaa RPCIG
Langaa Research & Publishing Common Initiative Group
P.O. Box 902 Mankon
Bamenda
North West Region
Cameroon
Langaagrp@gmail.com
www.langaa-rpcig.net

Distributed in and outside N. America by African Books Collective
orders@africanbookscollective.com
www.africanbookscollective.com

ISBN-10: 9956-764-29-9

ISBN-13: 978-9956-764-29-7

© Artwell Nhemachena 2017

All rights reserved.
No part of this book may be reproduced or transmitted in any form or by any means, mechanical or electronic, including photocopying and recording, or be stored in any information storage or retrieval system, without written permission from the publisher

Table of contents

Acknowledgements..v
Abstract..vii

Introduction and background:
on matters of violence and resilience..................................1
Chivanhu and modes of resilience...28
Theoretical/conceptual frameworks..37
Chapter Outlines...46

Chapter One: Resilience or Sacrifice?
Droughts and Knowledge Translation....................................49
The Worlds, entities and knowledge practices
related to droughts and rains..59
Conclusion...80

Chapter Two: The Mhepo, Mweya and
Ruzivo: Knowing, Sensing and Resilience............................83
Brief notes on violence and matters of knowledge.............................97
Prophecies, dreaming and divination...102
Witchcraft-related violence...114
Ruzivo and resilience...119

Chapter Three: Ethics Beyond Bodies?
Ukama, Violence and Resilience..129
Brief notes on politics and violence in Zimbabwe............................141
Ukama, mhepo and mweya..146
Ukama: the coloniality of violence..170
A return to a few key issues..183

Chapter Four: On Economies of Kutenda:
Agency, Action and Resilience Against
Economic Adversities..189
A brief look at economic challenges...203

Agency, Action and Openness?
resilience in everyday life economies...206
Kutenda...223

Chapter Five: Sensing Presences?
Health, Illness and Resilience..**243**
Some brief notes on health and survival during the crisis.............. 251
Manifestations, comings and goings of everyday life..................... 254
(Hau)ontology: making sense of dreams, divination
and prophecies...263
A return to a few key issues about presences
Absences.. 273

Conclusion..**279**

Glossary of terms.. 303

Bibliography..307

Acknowledgements

My most sincere gratitude goes to Associate Professor Lesley Green (University of Cape Town) and Professor Fiona C Ross (University of Cape Town) for mentorship. To Professor Francis B Nyamnjoh, my Head of Department during PhD studies, I also say thank you for the encouragement, to become a robust African scholar, and for mentorship throughout.

I would like to thank the Andrew Mellon Foundation and the Eric Abrahams International/ Refugee Scholarship for funding research leading to this book. I also thank the University of Cape Town; Chantel Reed and Anne Wegerhof at the University of Cape Town for the professional services they offered during my studies for Ph.D. My thanks also go to the villagers in Buhera District and fellow church members with whom I have journeyed and from whom I have learnt a lot over the time.

To my fellow, Joshua Ben Cohen, with whom I have travelled all the way from the start of my PhD study and from whom I have learnt a lot also, I say thank you. The walks we had up the Table Mountain, and in the forests on the mountain slopes; the visits to the sea and the stories we shared all contributed to my latent curriculum. I would not want to forget Professor Munyaradzi Mawere, a fellow PhD student and Zimbabwean who has always encouraged me to write and publish as much as possible.

My thanks also go to my wife Esther Dhakwa-Nhemachena for all her support to me and to our children during the journey of studying, the intellectual, emotional and financial exactions thereof I initially underestimated. I say thank you for all the support; you have always been a wife and a half.

I would also want to thank Gisele Morin-Labatut for assisting with some copy-editing of this book.

Abstract

This book explores the resilience of villagers in a district within Manicaland province of Zimbabwe that was afflicted by violence particularly from the year 2000. The province was marked by conflicts partly resulting from the expropriation of farms from white farmers, by interparty violence, interpersonal violence, witchcraft related violence. There was also structural violence emanating from sanctions imposed by Euro-American countries on the country as well as the after effects of Bretton Woods institutions-imposed neoliberal economic reforms. Thus, the period posed immense challenges to life and limb. Yet institutions of welfare, security and law enforcement were not equal to the task of ensuring survival necessitating questions about the sufficiency of [colonially] established institutions of law enforcement, media, politics, economy and health in guaranteeing survival in moments of want. What modes of resilience villagers deployed in the contexts of immense want, acute shortages of cash, basic commodities, formal unemployment levels of over ninety per cent, hyperinflation which in 2008 reached over 231 million per cent, and direct physical violence is cause for wonder for scholarship on everyday life.

Based on ethnographic data gathered over a period of fifteen months, this book interrogates villagers' modes of resilience in the context of the challenges: it explores matters of knowing and ontology with respect to chivanhu, a mode of engagement which has been narrowly understood as 'tradition' of the Shona people. It explores how aspects of chivanhu such as kukumbira (to request or petition), mhepo/mweya (wind/air) and ruzivo (knowledge), ukama (relationships of interdependence), kutenda (to thank) as well as sensing/feeling (kunzwa) played out in the modes of resilience among the villagers. Having been marginalized and subalternised due to emphasis, during the colonial era, on Western epistemologies, the modes of knowing and resilience under chivanhu have not seen much resurgence and official recognition in spite of the revalorization of 'indigenous' knowledge in other realms of life. Engaging scholarship arguing for decolonization of subalternised knowledge and also critically engaging scholarship on relational ontologies, the book interfaces chivanhu and some tenets of the relational ontologies as a way to see ways in which they speak to each other. In this way it endeavours to tease out ways in which aspects of relational ontologies might be useful in enriching understandings of chivanhu and how chivanhu might be useful in enriching relational ontologies. Thus the book looks at how different kinds of entities are interconnected and interdependent in ways that can help rethink violence as well as the attendant modes of resilience.

The book underscores the fact that in chivanhu there are interconnections and interdependences among different entities. Owing to colonial boundary demarcations and rigidifications of differences, such interconnections and interdependences evident in everyday life were underplayed and dismissed in favour of epistemologies that stressed the individual. In the preference for colonial epistemologies, alternative everyday life ways of peace-building and peacemaking lost traction in the Western formal sense, resulting in official efforts that narrowly focus on the formal institutional means of surviving violence. It is by pursuing the differences and sameness of epistemologies that this book explores the modes of resilience by the villagers in rural Zimbabwe.

Introduction and Background

On Matters of Violence, Ontologies and Resilience

Such were the difficulties of living in Zimbabwe that between 2000 and 2009 the rate of inflation rose until it reached 231 million percent in 2008, over 4000 people died of cholera and the rate of formal unemployment reached over 90% in a context of acute food, cash and water shortages that attended the economic meltdown within the country (*The Zimbabwean* 22 March 2009; Tarisayi, 2009; Coltart, 2008; Gasela, 2009). Statistics produced during the period indicated that about 40,000 allegations of violations of human rights occurred including torture, arson, murder, rape, assault, threats, confiscation of property including farms and livestock belonging to opponents (Reeler *et al.*, 2009; Reeler, n.d.; Lovemore, 2003). In this context Zimbabweans braced to confront multiple forms of violence including direct physical violence in which victims were often abducted at night and marched to bases of militia or the military where they were tortured using sjamboks, rifle butts, log, sticks, booted feet, blunt objects, rubber hosing, tire strips, bicycle chains, electric cables, electricity, water and other fluids used for suffocation. Approximately 10,000 homes were allegedly destroyed and 20,000 people were displaced by the violence (Reeler n.d; Masunungure 2009). These statistics were of course contested among the various parties, that is, the Movement for Democratic Change (MDC) and the Zimbabwe African National Patriotic Front (ZANU PF) (see for instance the Zimbabwe Independent July 1-7 2011; *Biti, Chihuri in war of words*, p 1-2).

However it is important to note that in scholarship, statistics are controversial since they are often used as mechanisms to shame opponents, to deliberately create moral panics and to conduct some kinds of modern witchhunting in order to discredit political opponents (Edgerton *et al.*, 1963; Ben-Yehuda, 1985). In this respect, Ben-Yehuda (1985) argues that during conflicts some people create moral panics by deliberately generating frightening statistics in order to psychologically prepare citizens for the changes that the moral crusaders or moral entrepreneurs desire (Ben-Yehuda, 1985: 201-2). Thus, in moral panics, a condition, episode, person or group of persons emerges to become defined as a threat to societal values and interests: its nature is presented in a stylised and stereotypical fashion by the mass media in which the 'right thinking' people pronounce the diagnosis and solutions or ways of coping. For Amutabi (2006) misrepresentations, including images of self-flagellation, representing Africans as never changing and permanently vulnerable have the effect of frightening Africans making them perceive themselves as needy, poor and helpless thereby eroding any potential they might have in efforts at self-development. Similarly, Pottier *et al.* (2002) have argued that during conflicts there is a lot of deliberate disinformation as well as challenges in reaching out some areas to verify the information. In the light of these critiques it is imperative to treat statistics cautiously and with due cognisance of the existence of what Ndlovu-Gatsheni (2013) calls the "invisible global matrices of power", manifesting in the realm of global media ownership, which are often antithetical to postcolonial African states and nationhood.

Zimbabwe's economic decline and political violence began to escalate with the introduction of structural adjustment programmes that were foisted on Zimbabwe, at the behest of the International Monetary Fund (IMF) and World Bank (WB), a decade earlier than the crisis. The structural adjustment programmes that were imposed by the Bretton hood institutions resulted in deindustrialisation and attendant retrenchments of workforces, deregulation of wages, deregulation of prices and the removal of price subsidies. Such structural adjustment programmes have been blamed by some (like Bond, 2005) for worsening inequalities, unemployment, soaring inflation and trade deficit, deindustrialisation, shortages of basic commodities (McCandless, 2011: 34). The challenges in Zimbabwe were also attributed to the legacy of colonial rule, and to African nationalist politics (Raftopoulos, 2009). There was confrontation over land and property rights and over the historical meaning of nationalism and constitutional questions. There was the restructuring of the government into more authoritarian forms in the name of launching anti-imperialist struggles in Zimbabwe. Other scholars have alleged that the Zimbabwean crisis emerged due to the government's mismanagement of the economy, to the land redistribution in which farms were expropriated from White farmers, to violations of property rights and to executive lawlessness (Ndlovu-Gatsheni, 2006). Yet others have attributed the crisis to neoliberalism and incomplete decolonisation (Moyo, 2008). Moyo has argued that the escalation since 2000 of the land and political struggles reflects growing calls for land reforms and reparations on the continent. For Moyo (2008), 'the land question' has become internationalised not least because it mirrors incomplete decolonisation processes in ex-settler colonies but also because global finance capital is increasingly entangled in conflicts over land, minerals, and natural resources in Africa's rich enclaves. Yet other scholars have highlighted western governments' efforts to marginalise the country from international affairs and the ways in which President Mugabe skilfully used Pan-Africanism and nationalist discourses to frame the situation as one of on-going colonial injustice – a crisis resulting from international interference including sanctions by the United States of America, Britain and the rest of the European Union, and the imposition of the IMF and World Bank's poorly designed economic reform policies.

The crises in Zimbabwe have also been attributed to the failure by the United Kingdom to support the needed land reforms (McCandless, 2011) that the United Kingdom initially promised to fund at the time the independence of Zimbabwe was negotiated in 1979 at Lancaster House (Gono, 2008). Scholars like Gono (2008) further argue that the crises resulted from illegal economic sanctions imposed on Zimbabwe by Euro-American governments so as to generate, among the ordinary people, the view that the ZANU PF government is a very dangerous thing to have in the country. These issues are understood by scholars to have contributed to the generation of multiple crises namely a governance crisis, a leadership crisis, an economic crisis, a humanitarian crisis and a land crisis (Ndlovu-Gatsheni, 2006). The period was marked by an unprecedented fall in Gross Domestic Product, by the breakdown of law and order, by international isolation as well as conflicts between Blacks and Whites, rich and poor and between the opposition Movement for Democratic Change (MDC) party and the ruling ZANU PF. It was also marked by acrimony between the ZANU PF led government and the European governments, some of which were deemed by the Zimbabwe government to be set on blocking the on-going Zimbabwean land redistribution exercise. But there were also recurrent droughts that afflicted the country during the period (Muzondidya, 2009), which saw agricultural as well as industrial production tumbling resulting in massive inflation, unemployment and shortages of basic commodities on the market.

How Zimbabweans were resilient in such a context raises fundamental questions not only about governance but also about everyday life in the context where, as Chitando and Manyonganise (2011) noted, Zimbabweans, the region, the continent and the broader international community could not readily find institutional solutions. The parallels in the modes of violence perpetrated by the colonial and postcolonial governments (Weitzer, 1984; Zaffiro, 2002) suggest the need not to focus narrowly on conventional Western formal mechanisms in rethinking violence resilience and survival. The fact that, during both the colonial and post-colonial periods, the Western and colonial institutions that are replete with inequalities were used to perpetrated violence and repression speaks to the inadequacy of relying on formal mechanisms in the matters of surviving violence and repression. The fact that the law, premised on Western jurisprudence, is often used to repress and legitimise violence, indicates the inadequacy of focusing narrowly on the law as a guarantor of survival. In Zimbabwe for instance the colonial Law and Order Maintenance Act of 1960 enacted by the colonial Government was retained by the postcolonial government until the year 2002 (Weitzer, 1984). This underlines the insufficiency of the notion of the social contract and formal institutions, as conceived in the European sense, in guaranteeing security for citizens but as the ZANU PF government argued, what mattered was not only security in this sense but also national sovereignty. The Rhodesian Broadcasting Corporation – known since Independence as the Zimbabwe Broadcasting Corporation – became a personal mouth-piece of then-Prime Minister Ian Smith when he sought, during the Unilateral Declaration of Independence in 1964-65, to design an information sector amenable to his control and supportive of his policies (Zaffro, 2002). This suggests that when a state, whether colonial or post-colonial, considers itself under threat, it tends to assume greater control, including over the media – indicating continuities of logics of governance. Thus, the colonial and postcolonial recourse to violence and repression as modes of governance (Mbembe, 2000; 2006) has entailed dynamics of radical predation, and logics of cruelty and excess: dynamics that have effaced the distinction between war time and political time. While this observation by Mbembe is insightful, one can add – in view of structural economic violence that includes acute inequalities [cascading from the global realm] which bedevil Africa – that there has been effacement of the distinction between war time and economic time in Africa.

Such dynamics of polarisation and predation in politics necessitate thinking through matters of order and security that are presumed in the Euro-American idea of the social contract. Hobbes and Bodin assumed that the Euromodern state had territorial circumscription, political unification with one power centre and a single supreme authority called the sovereign (Gumplova, 2011). But the situation in Zimbabwe could not be understood merely in terms of political unification but also in terms of polarisation on premises of race, political party affiliation and economic inequalities. Although Hobbes presumed that the sovereign was the supreme power in society serving to prevent individuals from harming others, the sovereign in Zimbabwe was contested using a variety of means including mass protests, social media and so on. Thus Hobbes' presumption that an absolute and indivisible power in the form of the sovereign in the social contract provided the means to overcome anarchy, civil war and the plurality of authorities assumes the status of a hypothesis in situations where electoral democracy is violently contested to the extent of creating divisions within the nation. While such divisions and polarisations are viewed negatively scholars, like McCandless (2011: 5), argued that polarisation in Zimbabwe is rooted in genuine and legitimate unmet colonial and historical grievances that have meaning for people globally over centuries; the desire for political and economic justice and the desire to participate genuinely in decision making that affects society.

Though such violence has been understood to speak to the weaknesses of the sovereign, other scholars have traced violence to outside the jurisdictions of the sovereign. Mbembe (2000: 284) for instance traces some violence to the decomposition of the state in Africa, his argument being that states were decomposed with the imposition of IMF's economic structural adjustment programmes and that states became [more] prone to violence as a result of their decomposition. Linking violence to international struggles to exploit raw materials, Mbembe further argues that in the regions on the margins of the world's major contemporary technological transformations, the deconstruction of existing territorial frameworks goes hand in hand with the establishment of an economy of coercion whose objective is to destroy superfluous populations and to exploit [African] raw materials. The profitability for multinational corporations, of this kind of exploitation, Mbembe argues, requires the exit of the state, its emasculation, and its replacement by fragmented forms of sovereignty. Though some blame the governments for adopting the policies, other scholars like Bond (2005) have argued that the IMF and the World Bank imposed the ESAP policies and the attendant conditionalities on developing countries of which many countries found themselves obliged to accept the IMF and World Bank ESAP programmes that led to losses of post-independence gains in welfare which had been part of the populist nationalist programmes.

In his assumption that rationality among rational human beings undergirded the social contract, Hobbes could have gone further to consider different kinds of rationality, as is evident from contemporary scholarship on knowledge (Turnbull, 2000) and how they have played out in matters of politics resilience and survival. He was of course concerned with a form of Euro-American rationality which is understood by some contemporary scholars as having radically separated society from 'nature'. Placing great hope on such unimodal rationality as he did, he did not envisage ways in which institutions such as the legal institution could be used to perpetrate what other scholars have called lawfare (Comaroff and Comaroff, 2006) in reference to ways in which courts and the law are often used to persecute opponents (du Plessis, 2009; Mattei *et al.*, 2008). Similarly the Hobbesian conceptualisation fails to take into cognisance Chabal's (2005) observation that patrons, who can be international or local, often fuel violence in order to capitalise on the chaos, retain and grab what they need. While Bodin (1992) suggested that the sovereign can only be absolute in relation to positive law and not in relation to 'divine law and natural law', this view ignores the implications of the secularisation of politics. The failure by the churches in Zimbabwe to bring contestants to negotiate fruitfully (Chitando and Manyonganise, 2011) signified ways in which even the quests for divine intervention could not provide guarantees in the political terrain where issues of governance, sovereignty, nationhood, resilience and survival are often defined more in terms of secular expediencies, however limited in their own imports.

For these reasons, questions about how to rein in the excesses of the political conflicts need to tackle the dichotomies between the secular and the sacred. There is need to think what secular tools are available to effectively control the violence or what sacred tools are available for the same purpose or still what tools bridging the secular and the sacred aspects are available to curtail excesses. But controlling the African sovereign alone in a world where, as will be explained in Chapter Four, there are other global dictatorships [on developing countries] such as the IMF, WB and so on (Amutabi, 2006; Amin, 2011; Bond, 2005; Stiglitz, 2002) would at best bring half the results. Cyber-democracy or electronic democracy on the internet (Bryan *et al.*, 1998; Muzondidya, 2010; McGregor, 2010) has been argued to offer spaces for the control excesses. They are noted to have, through virtual spaces, offered new ways of rethinking space, time, the social, the political, the private and the public beyond the narrower assertions. However cyberspaces are also abused by networked criminals and those who foment violence and rebellions in the local spaces from afar, to deterritorialise African nation states. Along with civil society organisations, the ideological inclinations of the forms of social media are often contested in as much as they are often inaccessible in the everyday life of many in villages such as I studied, afflicted by conflict and want.

The contestations around matters of sovereignty in Zimbabwe mirrored contestations of the idea of sovereignty in scholarship. Though some scholars like Smith (2011) have written against sovereignty, others have argued that it is difficult to imagine how it could be possible to manage pressing socio-political, economic, ecological, technological and even international problems and crisis trends without institutional machinery necessitating the sovereign (Offe, 1996: 66). Others have argued that it is states that go to war not peoples, and so it is the existence of the states that allows people to know when they are at war, when war is over, and whether they have won, otherwise war would not be war but chaos. It is states that enable people to know whether they are up or down (David Runciman, cited in Bickerton *et al.*, 2007: 10). Although scholars like Saskia Sassen (1996: 1-30) cited in Hansen and Stepputat (2005) argued that sovereignty is being 'unbundled' away from the nation states and into new and partially global and supranational arenas and institutions, others have noted the persistence of sovereignty. It has for instance been argued that the war on terror and the United States of America-led attacks on Afghanistan and Iraq demonstrated that underneath the complex structures of power in modern liberal societies, territorial sovereignty and the foundational violence that gave birth to the 'truth' of the Euro-modern nation states remains the *raison d'être* in periods of crisis (Hansen and Stepputat, 2005). Still other scholars have understood sovereignty not necessarily in terms of absolute autonomy but in terms of the independence of a state interacting in a system of states (Fowler and Bunk, 1960), but some have argued that the products of state building are frail because they derive their authority from their relationships with international organisations rather than from a political relationship with own societies (Bickerton *et al.*, 2007).

But there have also been contestations about which notion of sovereignty is being critiqued in contemporary scholarship, with some arguing that the idea of sovereignty that is being critiqued is the Euro-modern one that emerged in Europe from the complex power struggles between the Vatican and the Kings of northern and western Europe (Hansen and Stepputat, 2005). So while some have argued that the idea of sovereignty that is fading today is of more recent origin – the liberal constitutional sovereign state that can be dated to the 1789 French Revolution (Bickerton *et al.*, 2007) – others have predicted anarchy in the absence of the African sovereign. Thus, scholars writing about Africa have argued that a picture of the pre-colonial period as feuding chaos is incorrect (Bourdillon, 1991: 13) as there were networks of trading links which could only have been possible in a situation of some stability. Others have in fact noted that before AD 1100 Iron Age societies in pre-colonial Rhodesia (now Zimbabwe) were stratified, with headmen and political kingdoms; and as the pre-colonial Zimbabwe state emerged, institutions of kingship and political dynasties evolved (Huffman, 1980). Despite some tensions, it has been noted that many different groups of people lived in comparative peace though Europeans stressed Ndebele raids (Beach, 1994; Ranger, 1966: 173-174). Thus scholars like Ramose (2002: 468) argue that it cannot be emphasised that there was sovereignty and sovereigns long before the terms were coined. For Ramose, the coinage was an affirmation of the historical reality of [African] sovereigns.

In spite of these contentions scholars like Bhila (1982) have noted the existence of pre-colonial wars though some of them were noted as having been fanned by the Portuguese who were interested in controlling [via divide and rule] African polities and economies. While scholars like Daneel (1970) have noted that even *Mwari* (God) in vernacular Zimbabwean Shona was God of peace, others have noted that although it was *Mwari* who ordered that the column, of what subsequently turned out to be colonial officials on the initial colonising mission, safely enter the territory, it was also *Mwari* who ordered that Black inhabitants of the territory being colonised rebel against the colonial officials (Kane, 1954: 27; Bullock, 1927: 123). The invasion of what is now Zimbabwe by Cecil Rhodes' forces gave rise to the Ndebele war of 1893 and to the first *Chimurenga* war of 1896-97 both of which risings were led by chiefs, Ndebele indunas (warriors) and some religious figures

(Ranger, 1977). Other scholars like Chitiyo (2004) have noted that the first *Chimurenga* war in Zimbabwe was against colonial land seizures and the hut tax, as well as a response to environmental calamities of rinder pest, locusts and droughts which the inhabitants believed were caused by White settlers, whom they regarded as destroying the balance of nature, including sovereignty. During the first *Chimurenga* war, colonial soldiers and police seized the crops of the inhabitants as well as their livestock in order to force capitulation of the Ndebele and Shona people. The first *Chimurenga* war claimed 8000 lives (Ranger, 1977). Bulldozers were used by colonial settlers to raze homes and armed police also rounded up the inhabitants of the African villages as ways to suppress the revolt. The second *Chimurenga* war, against colonialism, stretching from the 1960 to 1979, claimed 50,000 people, but it was mainly Africans who were tortured, beaten, murdered by the colonial Rhodesian Front (Schmidt, 2013). The second *Chimurenga* war created 250,000 refugees and 400,000 people were internally displaced while 750,000 people were kept by colonial settlers in what were called protected villages which were in effect concentration camps designed to prevent the inmates from collaborating with liberation fighters (Schmidt, 2013). In the 1980s, soon after gaining independence from Britain, there was also the *gukurahundi* (Alexander *et al.*, 2000) in which the post-independence government launched an onslaught against the Ndebele some of whom were alleged to be bent on destabilising, with the support of the South African apartheid government of that time, the new postcolonial Zimbabwean government (Zunga, 2003).

The Zimbabwean government's onslaught, in recent years, against "civil" society organisations, deemed to be agents of neoimperialism, bears testimony to the kinds of struggles civil society organisations themselves have to engage in to survive (Tarisayi, 2009; Coltart, 2008; Matyszak 2009). The hardships including risks of being arrested for activism as well as the general hardships of the Zimbabwean crisis, which members of "civil" society organisations had to survive, indicate the kind of difficulties that activists had to bear in the name of democracy and agitation for the rule of law. The frequent electricity black-outs and the acute cash shortages, both of which affected the usability of communication and information technologies, testify to the shortcomings of communication and information technologies in matters of democracy and struggles for survival. The assumption, in instituting such mechanisms of "civility", is that the mechanisms are themselves resilient and invariably equal to the challenges of survival in the contexts of hardships. But then they are often inaccessible, unaffordable and therefore out of reach in contexts such as Zimbabwe, particularly in rural peasant communities lacking not only in electricity but also in regular and sufficient incomes to run the technologies.

Though such rural communities lacked radios, mobile phones and telephones, the internet and electricity or batteries to power those technologies, they had their modes of resilience. Resilience here is taken to mean the capacity of households and communities to bounce back after a shock and also the capacity to adapt in order to be more resilient in anticipation of future shocks (Malin, 2006). In conceptualising resilience, I also borrow from Holling *et al.*, (2002) who regard resilience as the capacity to buffer change, learn and develop, as a framework to understand how to sustain and enhance adaptive capacity in a complex world of rapid transformations. But in examining the vernacular modes of resilience attention will also be paid to adages that inform it in times of hardships. The import of such adages as *pakukutu hapaurayi* (difficulties do not necessarily entail death) in the context of the challenges in Zimbabwe will be explored. The villagers whom I studied actively deployed modes of resilience in response to food shortages, unemployment and droughts. Implied in the modes of engagement are alternatives to the conventional notions of "civil" society; and in these modes there was recourse to what Kasfir (1998) calls the 'primordial public realm' which, however unorganised it may appear to outsiders, is often viewed by many Africans as far more significant than the formally organised "civil" society promoted by scholars and donors. The modes of engagement have some parallels with arguments, by some scholars, that in real life people normally seek alternative channels, sometimes subtle and masked ways for fulfilling their aspirations and protecting their interests in such situations, thereby making it necessary to look beyond formal organisations in seeking "civil" society (Nyamnjoh, 2005). But in a context with a background where colonial authorities rigidly defined domains of life in terms of private and public spheres – considering their colonial institutions to constitute the public sphere within which "civility" inhabited (Comaroff and Comaroff, 1999) – defining "civility" in postcolonial terms requires new theorisation. It implies that scholars and analysts of Africa may not always find "civil" society where they are used to looking for it and therefore there is a need to provide a theoretical space for the possibility of African civil society taking new forms (Nyamnjoh, 2005). The issue is arguably to make notions of democracy democratic, and notions of freedom free (Englund, 2006) by opening them up to alternative and conflicting definitions that do not assume that the majority of citizens are ignorant, irrational, illogical, uncivil and backward. Rethinking such modes of politics offers space to understand civic groups and engagements that operate outside the colonial Euro-modernist frame (Makumbe, 1998: 306) but which were officially treated with aversion as a result of colonial politics and epistemologies that continue to predominate. The colonial modes of engagement cannot be simply contrasted with modes of engagement prior to colonialism. For instance in European law, notions of *iustitia*, *ius* and mores were derived from goddesses, such as the goddesses *Justicia* and *Fides*, much like in enchanted pre-colonial Africa (van Zyl, 1991: 83). In this sense, it is possible that in clamouring for Western justice, Africans constantly invoke Western goddess called *Justicia* in spite of Western pretences to secularisation of Western laws.

Colonially categorised and treated as 'traditional' and 'ethnic' (Ranger, 2010; Lentz, 1995) the otherwise more flexible and inclusive modes of engagement of the inhabitants were rigidified and parochialised. In a context such as Zimbabwe, different groups of people such as Venda, Karanga, Kharutse, Ndebele, Ndau and Kalanga, straddling different contemporary nations such as Botswana, South Africa, Zimbabwe, and Mozambique, resorted to the same *Mwali* cult in the Matopo Hills (Werbner, 1989; Werbner, 1977 cited in Ranger, 1979). Although colonial settlers and scholars have portrayed Africans in ethnic and "tribal" fragments, these groups of Africans could hardly be defined in narrow ethnic or "tribal" terms since all of them had common allegiance to *Mwari* who surpassed "tribal" and ethnic cleavages, as it were. Narrowed down identities (Nyamnjoh, 2007) can aptly be understood in terms of Maldonado-Torres' (2008) conceptualisation of Euro-modernity as a paradigm of war, on the basis of the binaries it is understood to have instantiated by overly rigidifying identities.

In *chivanhu,* which has been narrowly rendered in scholarship as 'tradition' or 'traditional religion' of the Shona people of Zimbabwe (Shoko, 2012; Gelfand, 1964), distinctions do not invariably assume the salience that are rendered in 'Euro-modernist' epistemologies. Things, as I will argue below, are often assumed to be connected, or possibly or potentially connected, in many ways, one of which is via the wind or air *(mhepo or mweya* in vernacular terms). Such conceptualisations resemble findings by other scholars that the wind or air is variously understood not only in meteorological senses of natural science but also in terms of 'deities' or 'spirits' that connect things and enable life (Kuriyama, 2002; Low and Hsu, 2008).

Though such wind or air (also understood in terms of souls) has been conceived by some scholars like Bird-David (1999) in terms of animism – which presupposes immanence of the wind or air in things deemed to have souls or 'spirits' like the human ones – other scholars render different translations. Some have noted that those who have considered African modes of engagement as animism based their arguments on casual enquiries and thus missed the nuances of such African modes of engagement (Opoku, 1978: 10; Rattray, 1927: 2-3). It is argued by these scholars that in Africa, the 'spirits', which are understood to have unlimited mobility, come to attach themselves to objects which do not however become interchangeable with the 'spirits' or 'gods' simply because the 'spirits' have attached themselves to them. Opoku (1978) and Rattray (1927) challenge not only the colonial resilient anthropological portrayals of Africa in term of animism [and immanence of spirits] but they also deconstruct contemporary geographical and environmental portrayals of sacred places as "healing landscapes" that presuppose immanence of spiritual power to heal. They also challenge related portrayals [often disguised as novel and transformational] that such sacred places themselves constitute animistic juristic personhood, as contemporary scholarship on naturalising jurisprudence and ontologies endeavour to do.

Regarded by *svikiro* mediums, *n'anga* (healers or prophets) and their followers as places of recourse for supplication particularly in times of difficulties such as droughts, conflicts and illness (Gelfand, 1959; Daneel, 1970; Ranger, 1999), places where *midzimu* or ancestors and *Mwari* were deemed to manifest are revered. Such places as the mountains, including the famous Matopo Hills in south western Zimbabwe have been conceived as resting places (rather than the embodiment of the ancestors) for ancestors' spirits (Murphy and Wannenburg, 1978). But these were also places where, because the objects of reverence were not regarded as mere objects, the 'modernist nature-culture divide' (Latour, 1993; 2004), which is the basis of the modernist constitution and the social contract, is somewhat destabilised.

While Latour's conceptualisation of the modern in terms of the divides [between nature and culture] is useful in analysing the modes of engagement in this study, other scholars have argued that the growing divide between the north and the south, between Blacks and Whites across frontiers and within them emanate from the shameful past characterised by slavery and colonialism which need to be redressed (Gifford, 2012). It is also important to notice that the terms 'nature' and 'culture' are not themselves in widespread common use in everyday life (where there is rather much use of terms like *zvisikwa* (God's Creations that constitute heritages) and *chivanhu* (modes of engagement which other scholars have narrowly understood as tradition). If the body and the mind, that are used as premises by those who argue that Descartes introduced nature-culture divide, are conceived as *zvisikwa* (created by God) then both mind and body, rather than assuming separate categories, become aspects of God's Creation. In *chivanhu* there are no conceptualisations of nature, *if* nature is explained using the big bang theories that exclude *Mwari* (God) as Creator. Further, modernity, as Comaroff and Comaroff (1993) argue, cannot be defined in the singular in contexts where the cultures of industrial capitalism have never existed in the singular either in Europe or in their myriad transformations across the face of the earth. Other scholars like Schmidt (2006) and Eisenstadt (2000) have preferred to write in terms of varieties of modernity and multiple modernities respectively, but as Chirikure (2010) argues even some [educated] Africans came to erroneously believe that Africa only became modern as a result of colonialism. As I will explain in this book, in everyday life the terms modernity and tradition are not commonly used. Rather, villagers tend to speak about *chirungu,* which refers to European ways of life, including the spiritual/religious aspect of life) and *chivanhu,* which refers to the African ways of life; these terms have different valences to "modernity" and "tradition" as binaries which presume that one is contemporary and the other is past.

In this book, the concept 'Euro-modernity' is used for analytic purposes to describe the worldview that is understood to hold to those binaries between tradition and modernity. Thus, while the 'nature-culture' divide, in Latour's sense, may have been foisted on Africa by Euro-modernist epistemologies and politics, the exactions by various European governments had unforeseen outcomes as the conquered and the colonised societies were never simply transformed into the European image (Comaroff and Comaroff, 1993). In fact in everyday life, as I will show in this book, there are no presumptions in the concepts *chirungu* and *chivanhu* that *chirungu* separates nature and culture as in fact there were some villagers who considered *varungu* (Europeans) to have, with colonialism, appropriated *zvisikwa* including land using *chirungu* cultural frames. The import of this is that, contrary to scholars like Latour (2004; 2005), from the point of coloniality Euro-modernists did not separate nature from culture but they in fact attached themselves to the nature [which they appropriated] in the colonies. Evident is the fact that the rationale of colonialism was not nature-culture divides it was not to separate nature from European cultures but rather to embed European colonist culture in the nature within colonies and indeed the world over. Thus, implicit in this is the fact that assertions that Euro-modernists separated nature from culture are simplistic particularly because Euro-colonialism was about precisely the opposite-it involved colonial settlers appropriating and embedding of themselves and their cultures in nature [land/environments] in the colonies. Indeed this is the bone of contention even in contemporary African societies [such as Zimbabwe] where colonial appropriation of land and resources from Africans is at stake and is central to conflicts. For this reason, binaries in Zimbabwe are so complex that they cannot be simplistically interpreted in terms of Cartesian dualism, precisely because they also issue from colonial appropriation of African resources. Africans need not be simplistically understood in terms of Cartesianism, which many [in everyday life] haven't got the slightest knowledge about.

Such spaces of everyday life constitute, for some scholars, a heterodox mix of fluid, multiple and dense practices, and often escape the panoptic gaze of bureaucratic power (de Certeau, 1984: 60). Although the concept of everyday life has been erroneously vilified by some philosophers as confused, mystified and relying on unsubstantiated prejudices rather than on verifiable principles of objective science (Gardner, 2000: 131); for other scholars, everyday life constitutes the margins of the state or sites of practices where the state is often remade as populations struggle to secure political and economic survival (Das and Poole, 2004). While everyday life is often constituted in terms of forms of resistance (Scott, 1985); it can not necessarily be reducible to acts of resistance but rather it also involves a mixture of ways of enhancing and sustaining life. Though everyday life has been understood in terms of acts, events, happenings, meanings, worldviews, language, communication, interaction, work, imagination, consciousness and interpretations of human beings (Heller, 1990); there is an emerging corpus of literature that indicates the existence of different, if broader, conceptualisations of life in other places of the world. Scholarship on 'non-modern' ontologies (Blaser, 2009) and on animist ontologies (Viveiros de Castro, 2004, Bird-David, 1999) underscore the existence of broader understandings of life in different societies where, unlike among the Shona, objects of 'nature' are deemed to have souls in ways that often parallel human ones. The upshot of insights from such ontologies has been efforts to rethink peace not merely in terms of human cosmopolitanisms, but in terms of what has been called cosmopolitics (Latour, 2004, de la Cadena 2010) that includes 'non-human' entities in a relational ontological sense. But African scholars, as I have noted with reference to Opoku (1978), have argued that places and things do not have [animate] souls: rather, places and things temporarily become the abode or places to which spirits of the deceased humans in the form of ancestors attach themselves in order to use the objects as vehicles to exercise their influence.

While the relational ontologies posited by the scholars have been argued to be useful in rethinking what are understood in scholarship as Euro-modernist binaries such as between subject/object or nature/culture, there are shortcomings of such relational approaches at least in the ways in which they are sometimes explicated. Relational ontologies have a number of tenets as scholars like Herva (2009) have pointed out. Citing Ingold (2006), Herva notes that relational ontologies propose that all entities in the world (organisms and inanimate objects) are continuously changing or coming into being, and that the identities and properties of entities are determined by the relationship between different entities. So for Herva, the identities and properties of organisms and things are contextual and continuously being generated rather than 'inscribed' in the physical constitution of entities. The upshot of this argument is, Herva notes, that relational ontologies dissolve the boundary between organism and its environment and rejects the subject-object dualism that pervades Euro-modernist epistemologies. However, the basic contention in relational ontologies that relations between entities are ontologically more fundamental than the entities themselves (Wildman, 2006; Inwagen, 2011; Paul, n.d.), risks whittling down the significance of the substantive entities themselves. These scholars' contention that the substantive entities themselves have no essence, no inherent qualities of their own, has been critiqued by other scholars who argued for instance that denying essence to Africans explained colonialism. Vera (2001: 116) for instance has argued that to circumscribe and dominate Africa as an Edenic space depends on the elimination of the African as actual human presence; in this way the African essence [as is the case in some contemporary arguments against African essence including the essence of African indigenous knowledge] is circumscribed before it is actually encountered. The issue of the denial of African essence raised by Vera has been noted as having been central to the colonisation process in what is now Zimbabwe. In Zimbabwe, Mungazi (1996) for instance notes that after the colonial deposition of King Lobengula in the 1890s, there was the publication of the Rohn Report which presented highly negative images of the mind of the Africans, described in the report in ways that collapsed the distinctions between human beings and animals, as 'stupid animals'.

Conversely, taking substantivist ontology (as distinct from a relational ontology) in which entities are ontologically primary and relations are ontologically derivative instantiates the categories premised on delimitations of the entities. Furthermore the sheer variety of relations which can be emotional, sexual, aesthetic, spiritual, legal, moral, imaginary, financial, technical, semiotic, political, economic, linguistic, physical, pose challenges in specifying kinds of relations in operation and the values attached to them at any given time and place. So, although scholars who subscribe to animism as a relational ontology argue that animals are people too (Harvey, 2006), other scholars such as Gilhus (2006) note that humans and animals are not usually allowed to have sexual contact with each other; for example, sexual contact with an ass was considered a special punishment for female transgressors in the Roman Empire. What this implies is that the phenomenon of relations is much more complex than is often presented in scholarship that focuses on one or a few strands at the expense of others which may be equally or more valued depending on space, time and other variables. If, to be identified with an animal and to be forced to have sex with an animal constitutes punishment, then there is no cause for Africans to celebrate animism or relational ontologies that fail to separate them from animals.

This complexity of relations and connections underlies paradoxical divergences in scholarship on relational ontologies itself. Latour's (2005) Actor-Network approach that seeks to bridge binaries between humans and what he calls 'nonhumans' by considering both as actors/actants is itself premised on the application of semiotics of materiality (Law, 2006). On the other hand Ingold's idea of "meshworks of entangled lines of life is about the way in which materials of various and variable properties, enlivened by the forces of the" cosmos", mix and meld with one another in the generation of things" (Ingold, 2010). So, while Ingold (2007) points out that in animistic cosmologies there is attribution of supreme importance to the winds, as winds give shape and direction to people's lives as much as they are powerful in their own right, other scholars stress the significance of material objects in understanding life. In understanding relations, other scholars argue that what connects is the "universe" as a whole through the "energy" locked in nature (Helmoltz, 1892: 141 cited in Brown and Capdevila, 2006). Still other scholars emphasise social relations in conceptualising networks (Noble, 1973; Boissevain and Mitchel, 1973). In formulating their theories about relationality scholars such as Viveiros de Castro (2004) and Bird-David (1999) suggest the existence of similar souls in human beings and nonhuman entities. It is important to note here that though the subject-subject relations advocated for in the animist scholarship can be at least theoretically useful in rethinking violence, the challenge is that forms of violence such as torture are based precisely on the recognition of the tortured as a subject, with feelings of pain which are the basis of attempts to extract confession and other evidence. In other words, some forms of violence are precisely directed at subjects and not objects.

The ways in which different epistemologies and ontologies with different metaphysical commitments play out together, connecting and separating (Verran, 2013; Turnbull, 2000) is best considered in everyday life situations where modes of resilience and survival often necessitate tactical and strategic turns. Such modes of resilience are spaces where Euro-modern rationality and other forms of rationality co-realise themselves in processes of creative fertilisation as people navigate hardships. They offer spaces, as it were, to rethink Euro-modernity from its underside in Maldonado-Torres'

(2008) sense and to decolonise epistemologies dismissed by Euro-modernity which closed off the very possibilities that the alternative rationalities opened up (Pignarre and Stengers, 2011). To appreciate the setting of the fieldwork for this book, it is important to now look briefly at the field site.

The research site: contextualising matters of violence and resilience

Such resilience that is the subject of this book characterised the citizens of Zimbabwe broadly. But here I focus on informants in Manicaland Province, some three hundred kilometres east of the Zimbabwean capital city of Harare. Buhera District was one of those most intensely affected by violence, partly because the leader of the opposition party, the MDC, hailed from there. Buhera District was thus heavily contested between the opposition party and the ruling ZANU PF party, which historically had its strongholds in rural districts including Buhera. According to Beach (1980), Buhera was an area dominated from the pre-colonial era by people of the Shava/Hera totem dynasties in the south centre of the country, that is, the land between the main watershed in the west, the Odzi River in the east, the upper Sabi valley in the north and the Devure River in the south. The Shava/Hera totem was not exclusive in this area but the dominant dynasties of the Hera were the Mbiru of Shava totem which constituted the nucleus of the Shava/Hera area. Old Buhera in the pre-colonial period consisted of all the land from the Sabi-Odzi and Sabi-Devure confluences as far up as the Umnati River on the other side of the main watershed of the plateau. Inhabitants of the Njanja totem as well as villagers of other totems have over time, by settlement and expansion, divided the Hera territory into two. A fort on the Gombe mountain in Buhera is one of the few stone buildings on the plateau to be definitely linked by European scholars with a Shona ruler, that of Mbiru (Beach 1980: 74-5). Mbiru was seen in Buhera as the founding ancestor of the Hera/Shava/Museyamwa people and of the many Shava groups as well. He is said to have come from the Zulu, yet others say he was in Buhera from the beginning. Mbiru's place of abode shifted frequently from Gombe Mountain. In Buhera many families claim descent from Mbiru as well as from Nyashanu, the dynastic title that replaced Mbiru.

Old Gombe was abandoned by the Hera/Shava to the oncoming Njanja totem. There were raids by the Rozvi in the area, and Old Buhera was weakened by civil wars as well as by the tendency of the Hera to move away. There was settlement in Old Buhera by the Njanja who had proof of origins in the lower Zambezi (Beach 1980: 289). The origins of the Njanja have been traced to the Portuguese held territory now known as Mozambique and this has led to suggestions that the Njanja founding ancestor called Muroro was a Portuguese; however, careful examination suggests the original Njanja were Africans (Beach ibid: 291-2). Three generations after the arrival of Muroro, that is, around 1724, the Njanja expanded across Old Buhera. Muroro's family group originally settled in Bvumbura in Western Buhera under the local Shiri totem of the Chirwa ruler. For Beach (1980), it was with the support of the Rozvi ruler called Gwangwava that in about 1805 the Njanja leader Neshangwe supplanted the Chirwa ruler and became the first of a line of independent rulers named Gambiza. Moving from Bvumbura, the Njanja occupied a large tract of Hera territory in Buhera. In some cases the Hera fought back but much of the land including the Old Hera centre of Gombe Mountain was taken without a struggle. By 1857 the Njanja had acquired a reputation as iron workers, and wealth from the iron trade enabled Neshangwe to increase his following. All the available evidence on the iron industry associates it with the northern Njanja dynasties nearest to Wedza Mountain. What is lacking in these accounts by Beach (1980) is oral evidence during the fieldwork which indicated that Kuvheya, identified by Beach as Muroro, got married during one of his trips from Mozambique to Bvumbura, to King Chirwa's daughter; and this is how Muroro happened in the first instance to be given a piece of land by Chirwa. He had many children and so his requests for pieces of land were granted by the ruler to whom he had become related, and this is partly how the Njanja expanded (interview with Kotwa 3 June 2011).

As recorded in the 2005 census, Buhera District has a

population of about 30,000 grouped in 12 000 households; wards have an average of about 3 000 voters. The district is in the communal lands where villagers survive as subsistence farmers, formerly governed under the colonial Tribal Trust Lands (TTL) Act of 1930 but now governed under the Communal Lands Act of 1982. Chiefs, Headmen and Village Heads assist in governing the area in terms of the Traditional Leaders Act (Chapter 29: 17) of 1998 which defines their powers and parameters. Apart from the 'traditional' leaders, the District Council also governs under the Rural District Councils Act (Revised Edition of 1999). Although the district is predominantly populated by the Shona speaking people, there are some Ndebele speaking people in the far north who were resettled by the colonial government from Matebeleland region to Buhera in the 1930s following the enactment of the colonial Land Apportionment Act of 1930 which divided land along racial lines (Anderson, 1999; Musoni, 2005; Palmer 1977). So though initially occupied by the Hera people under Mbiru (Beach, 1980) the district is now also occupied by many groups of people including the Njanja.

Conflicts over land and over political leadership have occurred in the district since the pre-colonial era when different groups of people and even members of the same clans vied for positions (Beach, 1980). And because Buhera is where the opposition party (MDC-T) leader and Zimbabwe's Prime Minister in the inclusive government of 2009 comes from, it has been one of the hotbeds of violence in Zimbabwe's recent past. During the colonial period, conflict over land occurred between the Ndebele immigrants being resettled in the district by the colonial government and the Njanja who had settled in the area prior to colonialism (Anderson, 1999; Musoni, 2005).

The soils in the district are sandy with scattered rich red and black soil in the northern part of the district, which is located in an area with annual rainfall below 650mm. For this reason it is afflicted with droughts and therefore there is extensive and semi-extensive farming. Partly because of its location, villagers have suffered food shortages and have therefore had to supplement agriculturally based food production with gathering wild fruits and hunting small animals (Mararike, 1999). In the past they have also relied on remittances from relatives as well as on government drought relief programmes and on Non-Governmental Organisations (NGOs) such as AFRICARE and Dananai. They have also relied on other modes of engagement including *mukwerera* (rain petitioning, conventionally referred to as rainmaking) to avert droughts (Mutasa, 2010; Mararike, 1999; Vuifhuizen, 1997). Apart from relying on [alternative] epistemologies, the villagers also rely on meteorological reports to predict the weather patterns and thus agricultural cycles. Although NGOs have supplied food to the villagers, they often specified criteria for distribution that left out some individuals and families. Also sometimes the village heads or political party leaders who often mediated in the donations excluded the names of their opponents on the requisite list of would-be-beneficiaries. For these reasons, food donations were themselves causes of friction among the villagers, some of whom sought to edge others out of lists of beneficiaries. Apart from wrangles over food donations, relations among villagers were also strained by competition for land on which to establish gardens. During the period of the crisis, vegetables often supplanted maize, the basis of *sadza,* a thick maize porridge which was the staple diet of the villagers. But because of the recurrent droughts many rivers in the district dried out, resulting in competition for land close to the few rivers that continued to flow.

But the conflicts over the land in the district also involved government institutions and officials. For instance in June 2011, I attended a village meeting convoked by the Environmental Management Agency (EMA) to discuss the issue of gardens. At the meeting the EMA official insisted that the villagers move their gardens from the banks of the major rivers because the gardens were causing silting in the rivers. Villagers argued that there was nowhere else they could erect their gardens which were their source of livelihood. The EMA official threatened legal action against defiant villagers; but during the conversation I had after the meeting with one of the villagers, he averred that no one would pull down his garden, adding that he would resort to witchcraft should anyone attempt to do so.

In the cases of violence, recourse could be to the police stationed at centres such as Murambinda and Buhera offices, but villagers often alleged biases in the ways in which the police, some chiefs and village heads handled reports. In this context some resorted to prayers in the various churches within the villages as ways of coping with the violence. Branches of churches such as apostolic sects, Apostolic Faith Mission, Roman Catholic, and Methodist, are found in the district, and because the Shona predominate in Buhera it is important to put Buhera briefly in the broader context of Shona socio-economic history.

Buhera and some issues in the broader Shona context

Villagers in Buhera District made reference to the phenomenon of the *ngozi* (also reported by Bourdillon, 1976; Gelfand, 1956 and 1959), that is, the aggrieved dead who are deemed to return to afflict tormentors. Other villagers made reference to ways in which they considered the *mhondoro* territorial guardian ancestors and *Mwari* (God) punished those who tormented, exploited and killed others. References to the *mhondoro* and to *Mwari* as capable of punishing crimes such as murder, abortion and incest have been reported as widespread in parts of Zimbabwe (Gelfand, 1956; Vuifhuizen, 1997) but they also portray politics as beyond the conventional human, if narrow secular domain.

But apart from punishing offenders, *Mwari* and the *mhondoro* were deemed to be providers of food (Gelfand, 1967: 21), to protect inhabitants and guarantee their welfare provided the living obeyed rules including respect for life, sexual purity and care of the environment (Chung, 2006). The inhabitants such as the Njanja are noted not only for having produced cloth and mined and smelted iron ore, copper and gold (Bourdillon, 1991: 7,13; Ellert, 1984: 50), but to have also engaged in the production of various items (Chirikure, 2010).

Contrary to assumption in Eurocentric scholarship that there was no civility in Africa prior to colonialism, there are indications that in Zimbabwe the *mhondoro* and *Mwari* offered buffers against misrule and against narrow political interest. The *mhondoro* were deemed to be in communion and to consult together on appropriate occasions, and so their influence often transcended individual 'tribes' owing to historical links among them (Abraham, 1966: 38). Historically, the *Mwari* cult functioned at a broader level to investigate abuses following from any narrow ruling-class orientation. Individual kings who incurred the displeasure of the *Mwari* cult fled for fear of supernatural sanctions that it invoked. Thus there were indications that the highest *mhondoro* had 'transtribal' influence and power though there is some confusion as to whether these *mhondoro* were really clan ancestors or they had never had origin in mortal existence (Muphree, 1967: 44). Some noted that some *mhondoro,* whom others deemed to have actually been prophets and with power originating directly from God, such as Chaminuka, Goronga, Makwati and Nehanda, were addressed as *vana vaMwari* in Shona or as *Abatwana BoMlimo* in Ndebele, translated as Children of God (Bullock, 1950). This was because they were deemed to be emanations of *Mwari* and associated closely with the *Mwari* cult and the priest attached to the cave shrines in the Matopo Hills. And for this reason they were not appeased by sacrifice because the *mweya* that seized the mediums had never had mortal existence. As hinted above, the breadth of the influence of the *Mwari* cult was so extensive that even the Ndau and the Manyika (sub-groups of the Shona) people in the far Eastern part of Zimbabwe sent delegates to the Matopo Hills in the South West (McGonagle, 2007: 83). In this way the *Mwari* cult served to link the Ndau and the Manyika across political boundaries with others in the broader region, including inhabitants of surrounding countries such as South Africa, Mozambique, Botswana and Zambia. But other scholars have traced the *Mwari* cult as well as Chaminuka to as far as the vicinity of Lake Tanganyika and to a time before 1500, well before the colonial period (Ntholi, 2006).

But apart from connecting different people across broad geographical areas, the *Mwari* cult also serves to show ways in which some particular mountains, hills and caves were not always regarded merely as objects of "nature". *Mwari* was deemed to manifest in the skies and everywhere in the woods, or in the earth itself (Gelfand, 1967). *Mwari* was also deemed to move from cave to cave or to pass like a shooting star (Bullock, 1950). However, *Mwari* "was not a fetish god bound by some stick or stone but could pass over the breadth of the land manifesting his presence by a divine fire" (Bullock, 1927). Although other scholars and colonial officials argued that the voice, deemed to be that of *Mwari*, which was heard from the cave, could have been that of a ventriloqual 'witchdoctor' assisted by the echoes of the cave (Bullock, 1950; Chigwedere, 1991; Daneel, 1970), other scholars have questioned the notion of "witchdoctor" (Chavunduka, 1980; Gelfand, 1967). Gelfand for instance has argued that the term is wrong if it is used to denote something bad or evil since the *n'anga* is not evil; but the word may have been originally used in its wider meaning to denote one who is able to manipulate occult forces for the good of human beings. For Gelfand (1967), the Shona people believed that in nature exist powers or forces that could be manipulated to benefit or destroy.

These differences in understanding the modes of engagement can be understood in terms of epistemological and political hurdles that beset the colonial context. While some suggest that the colonial authorities, keen to establish their kind of order, would not have admitted other forms of order and power for fear that they would not have been able to mobilise the labour power of the inhabitants of the colonial territory (Simmons, 2012), other scholars have argued that the modes of engagement of the inhabitants were favourable to the state. Gelfand (1956: 168) for instance argued that the Shona, who considered the 'spirit' world as very real, feared the dead as they did policemen; and this ensured that they did not become a problem to the colonial state. But some scholars have noted that colonial officials feared that rebel locals would rely on the dead for empowerment against colonial settlers. For instance Ranger (1969: 95) noted that in November 1897, within four years of occupation of the territory by the settlers, a magistrate called Marshal Hole wrote that "the superstition of the Shona rendered the task of reducing them to submission far harder than the Ndebele" whom he deemed to be "reasonable enough to know when they were beaten".

Although Gelfand (1956: 168) argued that it was when these 'tribal' ties and rites were abandoned or became lax that the individual lost his fear of the spirits, was tempted to break the law, and thereby became a problem to the state, others such as Lyons (2004) noted that even the colonial settlers were afraid of the 'spirits'. Lyons gives the example of 1897 when colonial settlers killed mediums of *mbuya* Nehanda and *sekuru* Kaguvi who had led the first rebellion against the colonisers. Because the settlers were afraid of the resurrection of the spirits, they buried the mediums' bodies in secret graves so that their bones and spirits would hopefully not rise again and find new mediums. While the work of other scholars (Levin, 1993; Erlman, 2004; Stoller, 1989; Classen, 1993) suggest that the problem in understanding such metaphysical and "cosmological" modes of engagement premised on invisible entities could have been because of modernist epistemological privileging of the ordinary sense of vision, the challenge is that even as such modes of visions of invisibles were officially dismissed, the modern colonial government set up colonial and imperial institutions which were themselves not amenable to the ordinary [African] sense of sight.

Though Euro-modernist epistemology's emphasis on empirical observation raised the ordinary sense of sight to a supremely privileged position relative to other senses (Stoller, 1989; Levin, 1993), the development of virtual modes of communication has been understood by some in terms of the mystical and spiritual. Deleuze's approach (see Goddard, 2001) to the cinema has for instance been that mysticism can be understood as a practice which actualises a prediscursive seeing and hearing, a vision or a voice that otherwise would have remained virtual and which constitutes an ecstatic experience of the outside. For Deleuze, as in the case of the mystical, cinema is understood to become a 'spiritual' tool capable of facilitating an experience beyond the boundaries of static selves and into profound contact with the outside. Such a Deleuzean rendering has the potential to offer space to rethink the binaries between the secular/sacred, visible/invisible that Euro-modernity is understood to have instantiated: it is an approach that makes it possible to conceptualise ways in which re-enchantment of the world has taken effect in the contemporary period. However, the presuppositions of immanence in the renderings are problematic in epistemologies and ontologies that do not deem spirits to be necessarily immanent in matter whether 'natural' or artificial. This observation notwithstanding, the renderings can be useful in understanding *chivanhu* where assumptions of radical, invariable distinctions, between the visible/invisible, secular/sacred are not always sustained. A closer look at *chivanhu* shows that it is not invariably about ordinary secular ocularcentrism.

Chivanhu and modes of resilience

Chivanhu is understood by some scholars, like Shoko (2012), in terms of 'traditional' religion and by others such as Gelfand (1964; 1985) in terms of 'traditional' medicine. However *chivanhu* is the original term for the vernacular language now popularly known as *Chishona* or *Shona*. It is the term from which the vernacular word *vanhu* (people) originates. The vernacular language called *Chivanhu* or *Chishona* includes a number of dialects such as *Chikaranga, Chindau, Chizezuru, Chimanyika*. In addition, *chivanhu* also refers to *tsika* (etiquette) which includes the rules that one is expected to follow, the vernacular modes of engagement and of thought that are enshrined in what is called *hunhu*. The *tsika* (etiquette) is the criterion upon which one is classified as *munhu* (person) with *hunhu*. This *hunhu/unhu* has been understood by some scholars as the spiritual content of one's personality or the moral and ethical aspects which if one is lacking one is referred to as: *havana hunhu* (they do not have that which marks a person) or they may be referred to as *imhuka dzevanhu* (they are mere animals) (see Chivaura, n.d.). *Hunhu* is characterised by togetherness, brotherhood, sympathy, respect, tolerance, peace, sharing, oneness (Muzvidziwa and Muzvidziwa, 2012). *Hunhu* also includes politeness, civility, circumlocution, propriety (Pearce, 1990; Gelfand, 1970; Mandova and Chingombe, 2013). *Munhu* can be used to refer to an ordinary person and more significantly to one who is considered to be fully moral in the vernacular sense. Whereas Brown (2001); Coole and Frost (2010: 1) characterise things in terms of liminality and ambiguity, in the vernacular *chinhu* (thing, plural *zvinhu*) is not invariably ambiguous or liminal. In Shona *chinhu* denotes something that is distinct from a human being or person.

Apart from the moral, ethical and linguistic aspects of *chivanhu*, there is the aspect of *mweya/mhepo* (air/wind/breath) which has been translated by some scholars as 'spirit' (Kuriyama, 2002; Low and Hsu, 2008). The concepts of *mweya/mhepo* have been variously understood in the existing literature on Zimbabwe. *Mweya/mhepo* has been understood as spirits manifesting as 'breath' (Burbridge, 1924). The *mweya* as it is conceived by the Shona has been understood by scholars like Muphree (1969) to refer to the psychic entity which can roughly be translated as 'soul' – i.e. the life principle of an individual that survives the death of the body. For Zambezia (2002) *mhepo* is a metaphorical extension of the sense of *mhepo* (wind) in a meteorological sense. Other scholars like Werbner (1991) conceived *mhepo/mweya* as the soul of a person, which survives the death of the body; it also defines the character of a person and explains the changes of character. For Kramer (1993: 73) *mweya* in Shona and *muuya* in Tonga means wafts of air or breath and it is compared by the Shona to the wind. For scholars like Manyame-Tazarurwa (2011) *mhepo* in Shona refers to spirits that move about. *Mweya/mhepo* also refers to the *mhondoro* ancestors (deemed to manifest in mediums). It also refers to the *midzimu* or deceased family elders. *Mweya/mhepo* can also refer to an aggrieved dead returning in the form of *ngozi*. *Mweya/mhepo* can refer to a *shavi* or deceased foreigner. A *mweya/mhepo* can also be the spirit of a deceased human being (*chikwambo*) raised by witches (Gelfand, 1959; Crawford, 1967; Shoko, 2007). But the *mweya* also refers to the Holy spirit addressed in vernacular as '*mweya mutsvene/mudzimu unoera*'.

These various conceptualisations, or understandings, of wind/air point to some of the challenges faced in seeking to comprehend the metaphysics of *chivanhu*. Framing it, as has been done in much scholarship, simply and narrowly as tradition, loses the dynamism suggested by the idea of *mhepo* and *mweya*, which presupposes motion. Motion and time conceived in the secular Western humanistic mode is of a mechanical relentless marching from the past to the present and future (Delaney, 2004). Such conceptualisation of time ignores the motions of other kinds of beings or forces in the universe. It ignores the complexity of the universe – whether conceived in terms of the scientific "dark invisible matter" or the ether (Mackenzie, 1998) – which has similar logics to *mweya*. The conceptualisation of time also ignores the 'oecological time' or time manifesting in the 'rhythms of physical or organic nature' as argued for instance by James and Mills (2005). It hardly takes cognisance of the complexities, multiplicities and simultaneities (Mbembe, 2001; Bergson, 2002) of lived time as engendered by the (un)foldings of the "universe", if worlds, with which different kinds of entities have motley connections. A decolonisation not only of space but also of time (Mignolo 2007) entails attention to such complex metaphysical conundrums that were hardly adequately digested in the bustle for colonies.

It is by refocusing attention to such different metaphysical renderings that the colonially induced balkanisation of spaces, temporalities and species in Africa can be rethought. Through attention to such renditions, spaces can be redefined in ways that make them accommodative of connections to other spaces. Similarly, paying attention to such metaphysical renditions permits redefinition of temporalities in ways that allow for their concurrences, multiplicities, simultaneities, conjunctures, and disjunctures as defined by different connections with different aspects of the worlds. By paying attention to such metaphysics the colonial fractionation and atomisation of spatial and temporal domains can be rethought in ways that have beneficial import for peacemaking. This is not of course to argue that the colonial simply fractionated things, but the contention is also, if more, with the ways in which it *a priori* redefined and rendered the [alternative] cosmologies unfashionable, ignoring their nuances in the process. Replacing *chivanhu* with the narrower notions of culture and tradition, the colonial officials at least formally froze and humanised the otherwise more fluid modes of engagement that did not rigidly conceive time in terms of fractions belonging to the past, the present and the future. Intriguing to note in *chivanhu* are the ways in which different temporalities could sometimes cohabit in the same space in much the same way different entities could sometimes not be rigidly separated.

The vernacular term of *ukama* is useful in understanding the various connections between spaces, temporalities, species, etc. While some scholars have understood *ukama* rather narrowly in terms of blood and affinal relationships (Gelfand, 1981: 7; Mararike, 1999; Gelfand, 1987: 185-6) others have represented it in terms of broader connections and interdependence among elements in the universe (Murove, 2009). In this sense, framing *ukama* merely in terms of blood and affinal relationships unduly narrows down understanding of connections with other entities including for instance the worlds of ancestors which are deemed to play roles in *chivanhu*, such as in rain petitioning ceremonies. Such worlds and entities are not connected merely via blood or affinal relations but also via *mweya/mhepo*. The only scholar that I have been able to find grappling with the ways in which different beings were deemed to be connected in this way is Michael Gelfand (1959: 13), who wrote that

Perhaps better understood (by the Shona people) is the word '*mhepo*' or '*mweya*' which refers to the air upon which 'man', animals, insects and plants depend. The term is closely bound up with *Mwari* (God) because all living things depend on air. *Mhepo* or *mweya* is part of the 'tribal' spirits and every living being, as there is a continuous to-and-fro passage of air through the body.

Several issues can be brought to light from this explication of *ukama*. The first one concerns relational ontologies, an approach advocated for by scholars, some of whose ideas I explore in the subsection on theoretical conceptual frameworks, in an endeavour to rethink the Euro-modernist dichotomies. Another issue is whether in this metaphysical rendition primacy is given to *ukama* rather than to the substantive entities constituting the web of *ukama*. If primacy is accorded to *ukama* rather than to the substantive entities, the issue is whether this would not amount to what has been referred to as the death of the subject who has previously been denied space by structuralisms instantiated as part of modernity. If, as Paul (n.d.) points out, relational ontologists reject the notion that entities have internal structure and categorical priority, then this might well mean the death of the subject at least in so far as primacy is not accorded to the substantive entities themselves. Conversely, if primacy is accorded to the substantive entities with relations being derivative, it becomes difficult to rethink the self-centredness that often characterises the perpetration of violence. If, as Fontein (2004) noted, mediums' narratives of their own past often illustrate the blurring between the agencies of the ancestors and their own, whilst keeping the personhood of the mediums and the ancestors separate, then there is need to pay closer attention to liminal moments in *ukama*.

Though the configurations of *ukama* might be [erroneously] understood in terms of the Deleuzean Body Without Organs (BWO) by which he refers to an affective, intensive, anarchist body with zones and gradients and thresholds traversed by powerful inorganic vitality, not defined by its wholeness or its identity but by its becoming, its intensity as a power to affect and to be affected (Poxon 2001), this rendition is problematic. It is problematic in that in *ukama* the identity of the person does not necessarily appear to have been fractured beyond recognition as suggested in Poxon (2001). *Ukama* does not necessarily entail the dissolution of the person or self, even in the case of healers and spirit mediums who are sometimes "possessed" by ancestors (*midzimu*), but subsequently retain or recover their senses of personhood and self-identity. In a context where citizens engage in exorcism as well as cleansing rituals (Dube, 2011; Schmidt, 1995; Reynolds 1996) and where mediums are not necessarily possessed all the time, it is necessary to interrogate notions of immanence and transcendence in relation to the everyday life modes of resilience in Zimbabwe.

The presumption of the immanence of God in nature by other scholars (Smith, 2001; Pearson, 2001; Bryden, 2001) requires questioning in view of the vernacular references to *Mwari* as *Nyadenga/Samatenga* (owner of the skies) or *Wekumusorosoro* (the one who ranks highest above the creatures). Though there are reports that inhabitants of what is now Zimbabwe visited the Matopo Hills to consult the voice of God that manifested in it (Ranger, 1999; Daneel, 1970), other scholars have drawn similarities between the inhabitants' conceptualisation of God and the Christian one (see also Jeater, 2007). For Bullock (1950) *Mlimo* or *Mwari* is the highest God whose name is used by some mission society in translating God. In his first Anthropological textbook on Zimbabwe, Bullock (1927) noted that 'natives' referred to *denga* (heaven) in the same way Europeans did. *Mwari/Musikavanhu* was deemed to be lofty and indifferent to the prayers, wellbeing and suffering of individuals, concerning himself with communities rather than individuals (Gelfand, 1967). But there was an elaborate indirect approach to *Mwari* through mediums and the *mhondoro*; direct approach to *Mwari* was made by his priests at one of his shrines at the Matopo caves (Muphree, 1967). While some scholars argue that in animistic societies [elsewhere] nonhumans such as animals are considered to have culture, dances and other attributes paralleling human ones (Descola, 1996), the modes of engagement to avert droughts in what is conventionally understood as 'rainmaking' (Gelfand, 1959; Bourdillon, 1991; Daneel, 1970; 1998) suggest that it is the *mhondoro*, the *midzimu* and *Mwari* (rather than the lions considered for instance to be manifestations of the *mhondoro*) who are deemed to have human attributes and hence to answer to the requests for rain in the ceremonies.

Though some have found it incongruous that people who they considered primitive had the idea of a Supreme Being (Opoku, 1978), others have pointed out that the idea of a Supreme Being has nothing whatever to do with missionary influence, or with contact with Christians or even Muslims (Rattray, 1969: 140). While AB Ellis could not accept that familiar religious ideas found in Africa were 'native' in origin, holding that the idea of a Supreme Being among the Akan was a recent European importation (Chapman and Hall, 1887 cited in Opoku, 1978), others do not find the idea of a Supreme Being in precolonial Africa incongruous. For Rattray cited above, those who find it incongruous that the West African 'negro' who seemed backward in most things should have so far progressed in religious development forget that the concept of a 'Supreme Deity' was not the prerogative of minds which we commonly consider the greatest of old – those of Greeks and the Romans – but rather of 'primitive' people who lived after the pyramids were built but before the advent of Greece and Rome – the Bedouins of the North African desert. So while some date African prophesy to periods after colonialism (Aquina, 1967), others have noted that the practice existed prior to colonialism, and that African prophets were victimised and suppressed by colonial authorities anxious to forestall prophet-led rebellions against them (Anderson and Johnson, 1995; Chigwedere, 1991; Hansen, 1995; Setiloane, 1976: 92).

Though some church members where I attended services were scornful of healers and mediums, certain scholars have noted ways in which African independent churches such as Apostolic churches and Zionist churches suggest Christianised versions of tradition or traditional versions of Christianity or ways in which the independent churches are an attempt to link traditional practices and Christianity (Shoko, 2012). Other scholars have noted ways in which 'spirit' mediums who played roles in the rebellion against colonial authorities were labelled witchdoctors (Chigwedere, 1991; Nyathi, 2001; Ranger, 1969). The *midzimu* – which for Burbridge (1924) are not demons but gods, distinguishable from *mashavi* 'spirits' of deceased foreigners – were labelled as demons. Colonial authorities had difficulties translating aspects of *chivanhu*, and therefore called the African doctors *n'anga* (bone throwers), even if they threw *hakata* – which were wooden rather than bones – and even if such a title as 'bone throwers' lacked the implications of healing, knowledge of herbs and support in times of calamity which formed the mainstay of the *midzimu* and the *n'anga* (Jeater, 2007). The *n'anga* were labelled 'witchdoctors' although their main work exceeded matters of witchcraft. *Chiremba*, the vernacular term for *n'anga* in Mount Selinda, was translated back into English as 'native doctors skilful with *hakata*' even though some did not even throw *hakata* when divining (Jeater, ibid). Colonial officials sought to undermine the legitimacy of *n'anga* through mission schools, by organising professional associations which could censure colleagues who referred patients to *n'anga* and insult those who used medicines from *n'anga* (Chavunduka, 1986 cited in Waite, 2000). Through legislation such as Law and Order Maintenance Act (LOMA) of the 1960s communal gatherings were prohibited and these included the dance festivals (Hadebe, 2001 cited in Waite, 2000) which formed the basis of *chivanhu*.

On the basis of *chivanhu* and against the background that some of its modes of engagement have been formally recognised through the work of *n'anga* in matters of health (Waite, 2000; Chavunduka, 1997; Simmons 2012) and in matters of prosecuting witches (Zimbabwean Criminal Law, Codification and Reform Act of 2004), this book will explore the import of *chivanhu* in villagers' modes of resilience in Zimbabwe. The idea of surviving violence is not meant to imply that villagers always struggled as much as they did during the period of the crises in Zimbabwe. If to survive is understood, as I do here, in terms of the vernacular term *kurarama*, it assumes wider import, that is, it refers to life more broadly (whether lived well or in suffering). The vernacular term *kutambura* is narrower and refers to life lived in suffering. But in *chivanhu*, even if one is living well, one will still be enjoined to continue struggling, for the sake of other *hama* in the families. In the light of critiques of dominant epistemologies which have been argued to have resulted in the colonisation of African knowledge and to continue to take leading roles in shaping what constitutes progressive global values imposed on the African people (Ndlovu-Gatsheni, 2013: 11), this book also contributes to the debates on decoloniality. Though the focus is on *chivanhu*, the villagers' modes of engagement were also affected by other forms of knowledge including the Euro-modernist epistemologies understood as modernist by other scholars. While much of the modes of engagement offer opportunities to interrogate what are deemed as Euro-modernist epistemologies, there are instances in everyday life where villagers appear to have drawn from such epistemologies in their modes of resilience. In this sense the modernist epistemologies cannot simply be critiqued as dichotomous and therefore bad. There were indeed, among the villagers, modes of engagement which, though relying on distancing the self from others, cannot be simply assigned to Euro-modernist binaries implied in the epistemologies. Modes of resilience that involved distancing oneself from perpetrators of violence and seeking refuge elsewhere could be interpreted as reliance on dichotomisation, in evading violence, but such modes of resilience cannot simply be categorised as modernist. In this sense, victims of violence simply sought refuge in different places where they could avoid contact with perpetrators. Matters of avoiding contact with others are also traceable in *chivanhu* where during rain petitioning ceremonies (*mukwerera*) breast feeding women were not allowed to attend (Gelfand, 1959); so *chivanhu* cannot be romanticised as absolutely free of modes of engagement that could at least approximate dichotomies, however less rigid as indicated by the reflexivity in the everyday life modes of engagement.

Aims and objectives

The broad aim of this book is to explore villagers' modes of resilience, in the District of Buhera, and the kinds of ontologies and epistemologies implied therein. In the following chapters, we will first seek to explore villagers' modes of resilience to recurrent droughts and to examine the ways in which these populations related the droughts to broader violence in Zimbabwe's past and present. We will then explore these modes of resilience to discover the ways in which villagers sensed and knew about the likelihood of outbreaks of violence, and the ethical issues that undergirded their society's relations of *ukama*. And finally, we will relate these modes of resilience to economic hardships as well as ways in which this resilience manifested and still manifests itself in the face of illness in the context of the hardships.

Beginning with a chapter on ways in which villagers understood and responded to the recurrent droughts which were also interpreted in terms of violence allows us to explore how different entities in the environment were considered to be connected in ways that help re-engage ideas on the "social contract" in discourses on governance. But in so far as the villagers' modes of responding to the droughts also entailed engagement with different epistemologies, the chapter also offers opportunities to explore connections between different epistemologies bearing on matters of rains and droughts. To appreciate the theoretical orientation of the book, it is important to outline the approaches that inform it.

Theoretical/conceptual framework

In thinking through the issues raised in this book, we rely on explications from literature on relational ontologies in so far as they offer tools to understand modes of resilience. I also rely on the field data that I collected to explore ways in which the theories can be informed by the ethnography. The concerns raised by some scholars about the ambiguity of relations (in relational ontologies), which could be sexual, aesthetic, mechanical, technical, theological, logical, moral, imaginary, physical (Wildman, 2006), are important to factor into the analysis of modes of engagement in *chivanhu* among the villagers in rural Zimbabwe. Further concerns are that if we say relations are ontologically primary, then we need to specify what kind of relations are ontologically primary because there are a host of decisions to make on the basis of whether the relations are axiological, logical, perceptual, causal, or conceptual (Wildman, ibid.). The third concern of Wildman is that there is need to know whether relations between entities are more fundamental than the entities themselves and whether they are not mere attributions made by conscious entities capable of expressing them in language.

Animistic relational ontologies presuppose the immanence of power to matter (Albert, 2001), but the doctrine of univocity which explains the cosmologies (presupposing immanence) have been critiqued by some scholars. The critique has been that if 'being' is said in one and the same sense of everything, there is need to explain what constitutes the differences between things (Smith, 2001). This can in essence be read to refer to the question that if God for instance is deemed to be immanent in every creature, then what would constitute the differences among these creatures? Relational ontologies in this sense are useful in thinking through issues of difference and sameness as well as of hierarchy in respect of *chivanhu*. While some scholars have posited that relational ontologies are rhizomatic, that is, with no hierarchies (Law, 2006; Latour, 2005), other scholars writing on Africa have suggested that there are hierarchies and boundaries, for instance not only with respect to different epistemologies but in matters of citizenship and belonging, often resulting in xenophobia (see for instance Nyamnjoh, 2005; 2006; 2007; 2012).

In this book, I draw insights from Ingold's (2006; 2007; 2011; 2012) work particularly his rendering of life in terms of meshworks of entangled lines, his explications on becomings and his ideas on things and material objects including the need to shift focus from congealed objects to fluxes and flows of life. But Ingold's (1993; 2010) argument that we live in an open world with no inside and outside, and that knowing is a matter of wayfaring, that is, going along an open ended road, needs to be interpreted against restrictions on movement particularly in contexts of violence. The limitations on movement imply restrictions to flows as well as limitations to connections in such contexts of violence and in a world separated by borders. I also draw on insights from literature on animism, particularly from Descola (1996); Garuba (2013) and Bird-David (1999); but this literature will be interpreted against African cosmologies as they appear in ethnography as well as in the field site where I carried out research. Some insights will also be drawn from Latour's (2005) Actor-Network Theory but I will be mindful of the fact that he developed his theory for tracing normativity in techno-scientific networks (Waelbers, 2011); there may therefore be some differences with my own context in rural Zimbabwe. As is evident in Ingold's and Latour's work on meshworks and Actor-Networks respectively, there are some differences in that while Ingold emphasises not the materialities but fluxes and flows, Latour's Actor-Network Theory (ANT) was built from semiotics of materiality (Law, 2006). Though thinking with the idea of networks is useful, it has been argued by some that the network metaphor impoverishes our understanding of power (Prey, 2012). It is blind to relationships of exploitation that require attention in a world that is increasingly connected but remains wedded to the exploitation of surplus value. Other scholars such as Castells (2000); Hardt and Negri (2004), cited in Prey (2012), posit the network as the dominant form power takes in contemporary society. Yet other scholars like Brown and Capdevila (2006) have argued that the concept of force underpins networks because networks are assemblages of forces: they emerge from and dissolve into the play of power, which makes networks what they are, and is eventually responsible for their collapse. Still others have argued that Latour's ideas are rich, yet poor from an ethical point of view (Waelbers and Dorstewitz, 2013). For these scholars, the 'doings of things' and people are, in Latour's work, couched in one and the same behaviourist (third person) vocabulary without giving due recognition to the ethical relevance of human intelligence, sympathy and reflection in the making of responsible choices. For this reason Latour (2006: 16) points out that the ANT has been critiqued for proposing the 'death of man' involving dissolving humanity into a field of forces where morality, ethics and psychology are absent. In spite of Actor-Network Approach attempts to bridge the binaries between subjects and objects, other scholars have pointed out that the hypothesis in this approach is not universally applicable. Callon (2006) for instance has argued that a market opposes buyers and sellers, and that a market is a challenge to the ANT because it introduces a strict separation between what circulates (goods which are inert, passive and classified as non-human) and human agents who are active and capable of making complex decisions. Whereas Latour focuses on action, other scholars have argued that life experiences do not refer merely to acts, events and happenings, but also to general frameworks of meaning, world views and institutions which guide, synthesise and order the process of experiencing itself (Heller, 1990: 44). It is important to note for the purposes of this book that while the work of other scholars on animism suggests immanence of, for instance, souls in entities, Ingold's (2007; 2008) open world (being a world of becomings, fluxes and flows) is more open and accommodative of processes in the world-in-formation. However whereas flows and fluxes are emphasised by some, other scholars have argued that everyday life consists of intertwined constant and variable features (Heller 1990). Indeed Ingold (2011) recognised the limits of fluidity when he argued that in an "animate" world everything is movement and nothing is certain, but fluidity also has its limits, its stoppages and its moments of consolidation. Also, assumptions of openness in the capitalist world market, with no inside and outside, have been critiqued as a model for imperial sovereignty (Maurer, 2004: 63) that stresses openness of the world for capital even as citizens in various parts of the world are obsessed with and confined by borders and boundaries occasioning xenophobic tendencies as indicated above (Nyamnjoh, 2006).

This book borrows insights from Latin American scholarship on modernity/coloniality, notably from Anibal Quijano (see Mignolo, 2007: 4) who defined coloniality as the invisible constitutive side of modernity involving the coloniality of power, of being and of knowledge. The coloniality of being is the ontological dimension of coloniality that points to the excess occurring when particular beings impose on others (Escobar, 2002). For scholars of decoloniality, liberation and decolonisation point towards conceptual projects of delinking from the colonial matrix of power. Mignolo (2007: 16-7) points out that decoloniality means working towards a vision of human life that is not dependent upon or structured by the forced imposition of one ideal of society over others, which is what modernity/coloniality does and hence where decolonisation of the mind should begin.

Before engaging the substantive chapter in the book, it is important to explicate methodological matters.

Methodology

Lefebvre's (2000) assertion – that ambiguity is a category of everyday life of which reality is never exhausted since from everyday life situations springs forth actions, events and results without warning – could not have been more apt to a field site where the eruption of violence was part of the possibilities of everyday life. Scholars who have researched violence have characterised such sites where social relationships and cultural realities are critically modified by the pervasion of fear, the threat of force or irregular application of violence, as dangerous fields (Pottier *et al,*. 2011). Researching such dangerous fields carries multiple risks that necessitate the consideration of calculated strategies whereby the gain of credible information outweighs the risks of personal harm to the researcher and informants.

Such risks attendant to entering a field site of violence appeared just before I headed off from Harare, the capital city of Zimbabwe. I received an sms (text message on my mobile phone), from one of my brothers, indicating that, if I was heading off to Buhera, I should be careful because there was political violence in the villages. But carefulness was not easily exercised as it entailed postponing the fieldwork indefinitely, as long as the violence was on. But it meant that I had to redefine and re-plan my fieldwork so as to minimise the possibilities of encountering violence while I worked in the site. For this reason I spent the first two months of my fieldwork period outside the context of the field site. When I eventually entered the field site I decided to spend some time watching processes as well as establishing networks with a few villagers, allowing me some fall back positions. Beginning by watching processes in everyday life allowed me to gain some acceptance as well as information about the villagers' own modes of surviving the risks of violence, which could be useful in my own case. As Pottier *et al.* cited above noted, researchers of conflict do not control the setting they work in but rather rely on 'local' intelligence, knowhow and protection. Eventually I was invited by some of the villagers to their churches, to divination sessions, ceremonies and sessions where they received donations from NGOs. Some even invited me to village meetings such as the one with the Environmental Management Agency (EMA) where issues about the villagers' gardens were discussed. In this way, I was able to begin some participant observation where I relied on jotting short notes that enabled me to reconstruct the interactions, conversations and events much in the way explicated by Field and Morse (1995: 112).

Participant observation

Participant observation included prayers in the African Independent Churches as well as visits to such places as mountains for prayers with church members. Such visits involved sharing dreams with church members, often during sessions when prophets in the churches interpreted the dreams. Participant observation also included my attendance in prayer sessions when I was taken ill toward the end of my fieldwork. Much as in van Binsbergen's (2003) case, where he allowed himself to be captured as a patient of Southern African *sangomas*, I became a patient of the apostolic churches, one of which had incidentally prophesied my illness eighteen months before it occurred. On the day of the first prophesy about the illness, I had visited an old man in the village whom I had previously met and with whom I had established a relationship. Twenty minutes into our conversation, I saw apostolic church members arriving at his homestead. After the old man had informed me that there was going to be a church service there, I expressed my keenness to participate; it was during this service that it was prophesied that I would fall ill a year and a half later. Prophecies about the illness were made in the different apostolic churches in which I participated during the course of the fieldwork. The *n'anga* and *svikiro* mediums whom I met during interviews in the fieldwork also warned that I would be afflicted by an illness, the particulars of which tallied with one another and with the illness itself, when it finally hit me. Participation in this sense allowed me to understand how witchcraft-related violence was conceptualised and dealt with in advance in the churches and by *n'anga* and mediums.

Such a reflexive moment can be understood in terms of Hastrup's (1995) argument that the reality of fieldwork is a liminal phase for both subject and object in which the distinction between them is dissolved. While reflexivity can be effected by using observation and other methods in which interaction is kept to a minimum, thus reducing the effects of researchers on their results, reflexivity can also be enhanced on the basis of a very high level of interaction based on complete participation (Davies, 2009). The negative side of my complete participation in the sessions was that it deepened my sense of loss of control of a situation that involved grappling with witchcraft-related issues. However the experience shifted me to different realities and practices of the field site. It allowed me, as Marcus (1998) argues, to have a sense of a world different from the one which is accessible to common sense. Participating in my informants' world of dreams is one such way of joining them, from which I learnt about their modes of engagement.

Sampling and unstructured interviews

The sampling was mainly purposive with a focus more on information-rich cases from Apostolic churches, healers and medium, as well as villagers who had encountered violence. Four *n'anga* were interviewed, two male and two female. One *svikiro* medium was also interviewed about surviving drought and the ceremonies conducted in this context. Interviewees ranged in age from eighteen to ninety years. These interviewees were drawn from a total of six villages in selected wards in Buhera District. A total of ninety three interviewees, of which fifty were male and forty three female, were selected. Among the interviewees were village school teachers and Agricultural Extensions Services officers, carpenters, builders, nurses, vendors, weavers and peasant farmers. As well, five prophets of Apostolic churches were interviewed. Three Meteorological Services officers were interviewed in connection with Meteorological Services interventions in times of droughts. I also conducted participant observation, including viewing and interpreting the synoptic charts, statistics by meteorological officers, their apparatus including rain gauges, radiosondes and processes of electrolysis to produce hydrogen which was used in radiosondes.

The villagers' interviews were unstructured, which permitted the respondents to freely narrate their encounters with intermittent sub-questions being asked by the researcher so as to clarify issues. Sometimes the respondents offered to connect the researcher with their colleagues who had also encountered violence.

Other sources of data

Useful information was also accessed from the media and the Zimbabwe Parliamentary Debates in Hansard as well as the Zimbabwe National Archives. I also walked across mountains such as the Gombe, and along some rivers and to villagers' fields.

Ethics

As Pottier *et al.* (2011: 12) argue, researching in conflict situations requires the researcher to think on his/her feet, changing research plans, designs and developing *ad hoc* solutions to minimise risk and damage on a day by day, sometimes moment by moment, basis. In my own research in the conflict-ridden villages, research plans constantly had to be adjusted on account of refusal by informants to give consent, or because the moments proved too risky. One example was when I intended in the early part of my fieldwork to interview an elderly female healer I had heard about in the village. Upon arriving at her village, I found her sitting in her yard with her husband. They received me well and she asked me whether I wanted to interview her or her ancestor who possessed her. I requested to speak to her as well as her ancestor whereupon she responded that speaking to her ancestor required an intermediary. Unable to locate her daughter-in-law whom she considered good at playing this role, she fetched her son, who arrived thirty minutes later. Upon arrival her son, who appeared ill-tempered even with his parents, rather rudely asked me what I wanted, a question which was perfectly in order. When I replied that I wanted to interview his mother's ancestor, he rudely asked me what for. I responded indicating that I was a student researching on matters of surviving violence, to which he asked me what I would want to do with that information. I explained that I was going to write a PhD thesis on the basis of the information, to which he countered with, '*handizvigoni*' (I cannot do that). His parents tried to persuade him saying that his role would be simply to intermediate and nothing else but he answered by asking his parents, '*ndati kudiiko nhai baba?*' (What have I said to you, father?).

This incident would not have been so surprising in a context where villagers and families had been divided along political lines resulting in ill-temper even amongst family members; but it is quite another thing for a researcher to be in a situation in which one would be at a loss as to how to mediate between parents and children. Wanting to interview members of different political parties in a context of conflict is itself tricky in that the researcher can unknowingly be deemed to have taken one side when seen interviewing or wanting to interview opponents. There is a lot of suspicion in such contexts and it is therefore often tricky to do interviews. I decided to resolve the heated argument between the son and his parents by informing them that it was perfectly acceptable to decline to participate and bidding them good bye. Another incident occurred in which I requested a villager for an interview after which request the man and I withdrew to a place away from the earshot of other villagers for the interview. However, after the interview I met the villager together with other men. Rather than maintain reticence about my previous interview with him, the former interviewee informed me that the men with whom he was at the same place were his opponents. He stated that they were his opponents who had wanted to kill him so if they had anything to say about their violence they could say it to me so that I could record the views of both sides. In spite of my having informed him that I was more interested in how villagers survived violence than in identifying who engaged in violence against whom, the man hinted that if his opponents saw me with him, they would harass me. Because my intention was not to worsen relations between villagers but rather to conduct research on how violence was survived, I quickly decided on a way that would bring the opposing villagers together so that they could at least have something to share and realise that it was possible for them to cooperate rather than oppose each other. My decision was to buy them two litres' worth of beer that they could share. My former informant then smiled and remarked that he would even share his cigarette with the opponents even though they wanted to kill him.

Such ethical issues can be understood in terms of riddles about how to maintain a position of neutrality in a politically and emotionally charged environment (Pottier *et al.*, 2011) as well as how to think beyond the often legalistic protocols in research ethics which often offer inadequate guarantees of ethical research (Ross, 2005). My approach was to cultivate sensitivity including the capacity to suspend a particular approach and (re)configure when to listen, speak and when to maintain silence (see also Henderson, 2005), how to defuse potential outbreaks of violence and what tools to use in so doing. In a context pervaded by apprehensiveness of danger from the use of pieces of technology such as cameras and voice recorders which were also used by some civil society organisation and villagers to record and send report of violence, I had to desist from using the same. My decision was partly because it risked my being identified with other people and organisations simply fishing for incidences of violence to circulate in the world. In a place where such technologies as voice recorders and cameras were not so common, using them generated the apprehension by villagers about the identification of their voices and persons beyond the contexts of the villages and the interviews.

Though some of the villagers indicated that I could reveal their names, I have retained anonymity by using pseudonyms. In writing up, I have also avoided disclosing [intimate] geographical and personal data that would make it possible to trace the informants. During the fieldwork I took care to keep my research notes out of the field site so as to prevent the risk of opponents' stumbling on them and using them to fan violence. To enhance my own safety, I maintained contact with my PhD supervisors in Cape Town via mobile phone. Although it was not easy to maintain contact in an area with poor or inexistent network coverage and no electricity, the moments of contact I did have proved useful emotionally and intellectually.

Chapter outlines

In Chapter One I look at how villagers engaged in *kukumbira mvura* (petitioning) for rain, focusing on villagers' modes of resilience to the recurrent droughts in Zimbabwe through the performance of rituals conventionally but erroneously understood as 'rainmaking ceremonies'. It situates the droughts in the context of the violence by drawing on ways in which villagers connected the occurrences of droughts to violence in the past and the present. Drawing on the fieldwork, I will refer to the ceremonies as rain petitioning ceremonies instead of 'rainmaking' because the villagers asserted that they request for, rather than make rain, as portrayed in existing literature. Drawing on some theoretical debates on relational ontologies, I explicate the webs of connections of different elements in the rain petitioning ceremonies. I follow up these partial connections in Chapter Three where I explore the vernacular idea of *ukama* modes of relating.

Chapter Two focuses on matters of knowing and sensing violence. It looks at how villagers knew and sensed violence in a context of dearth of newspapers, radios, television sets, internet and such other kinds of media. It explores how villagers relied on dreams, divination and prophecies to sense and know about violence at a distance, that is, without actually physically involving themselves in it. In this sense it interrogates matters of 'formal' truth, reality, objectivity and rationality. It argues that much more than these epistemic 'formalities' is required to navigate violence in everyday life. Drawing on the vernacular conceptualisations of *mhepo/mweya* (wind/air) as central to matters of knowing through dreams, divination and prophecies, I challenge the notions that their knowledge can simply and narrowly be defined as local and traditional.

Chapter Three examines *ukama* (relationships) as modes of resilience. It argues, using the notions of (*mhepo/mweya*), that portrayals of *ukama* in terms of blood and affinal kinship are too narrow. What circulates in *ukama* is not only blood and marriage-related elements, but also the *mweya/mhepo* which connects different kinds of elements or beings, and temporalities. In view of the broader connections via the *mweya/mhepo* between different beings in the world, the chapter then considers matters of ethics where *ukama* is understood more broadly than has been portrayed in literature. It examines what an ethics based on notions of the *mweya/mhepo* might contribute to rethinking violence, particularly in a context where the rule of law has broken down and can no longer guarantee security of citizens. This idea of *ukama* is discussed in the context of issues arising from debates on ontologies including the nature-culture and subject-object divides that have been traced to modernist epistemologies and ontologies.

Chapter Four looks at what I call Economies of *kutenda* (to thank), which is crucial in the giving and receiving within *ukama*. The chapter focuses on villagers' modes of resilience economically or materially and how their modes might be used to rethink matters of openness in economies. It explores the villagers' understanding of matters of the economy in relation to the environment upon which they survived.

Chapter Five examines Sensing Presences: Illness, Health and Survival. Drawing on some theoretical debates on senses and sensing, the chapter problematises the categorisation of senses in Western thinking as invariably five, and the attendant privileging of ordinary ways of sensing. It argues that there are different ways of sensing the presence of events such as illness and illness causing factors, and that it is necessary to take into cognizance different ways of sensing things that may themselves be engaged in complex processes of comings and goings. Privileging the ordinary sense of sight as modernist epistemologies do assumes that things always render themselves to the gaze; but in a world of complex manifestations, comings and goings, elements are also elusive to the gaze yet nevertheless retain their presence. The conclusion refocuses on *chivanhu* and ways in which it plays out with selected tenets in theorizations on relational ontologies. It spells out the partial connections between *chivanhu* and relational ontologies, and then suggests how the modes of engagement in *chivanhu* can be theorized.

Chapter One

Resilience or Sacrifice?
Droughts and Knowledge Translation

In recurrent drought-afflicted-Zimbabwe, the universality of meteorological 'scientific' facts explaining droughts has been open to contestations. The contestations occurred in a context where citizens were enjoined to exercise resilience in view of both the ongoing droughts and the conflicts over land, as a resource. Resilience as I will explain below is understood in Holling *et al.*'s (2002) sense of the capacity to rebounce, resist shock and adapt in a world in transformation. In the media, the recurrent droughts were explained partly in terms of the violence that characterised Zimbabwe's history, including the most recent violence associated with elections after the year 2000 as well as with the expropriation of huge tracts of land owned by about 4000 White commercial farmers who controlled the fertile and well-watered Highveld. The majority of Black Zimbabweans (constituting about fifteen million) were crammed in sandy-soiled, drier parts of the country to which they were pushed by the colonial government, for a century.

Whereas the 1896 ecological crisis of cattle plague, droughts and locusts was explained in terms of political crisis caused by the inception of colonialism – deemed to have threatened the sovereignty of Black Africans whose cattle were confiscated and whose land was expropriated by the White colonial settlers (Ranger, 1979) – the recent recurrent droughts had many more explanations. Though scholars have written quite a lot on droughts in Zimbabwe, the issue of droughts will be dealt with in this chapter with reference to *chivanhu* ontologies which have not been attended to in existing scholarly works. It has been argued that ontology involves not simply the abstract study of the nature of being but also the underlying beliefs about existence that shape our everyday relationships to ourselves, to others and to the world: ontological commitments are therefore tied to questions of identity and history, with how we articulate the meaning of our lives, both individually and collectively (Coole and Frost, 2010: 5).

Explanations of the droughts which appeared in the media not only showed that matters of causation of the droughts were far from having been settled among the citizens of Zimbabwe, but they also underscored the fact that before engaging in relevant actions by way of resilience strategies people first have to make sense of the adversities in their midst. This chapter will argue that resilience to droughts is partly a matter of drawing on available "cosmological" and metaphysical resources. But before people engage in such modes of engagements to survive adversities, the processes are preceded by reflection and thought processes which explain the contestation about the causes of the droughts in Zimbabwe. In other words, individuals engage in thought processes that would belie contemporary critiques of Cartesian cogito, as alien to Africans. In short, the fact of the contestations is at the core also the fact of processes of thought or cogitation by African people, before they engage in actions to avert or alleviate adversities that befell them. In other words, to presuppose that thinking or cogitation processes started and perhaps also ended in Europe, with Rene Descartes, is to erroneously presume that Africans did not think or cogitate prior to the advent of colonialism. Thus, efforts by some scholars at [a variant of] decoloniality that is blindly premised on an indiscriminate deconstruction of cogitation and thinking, coupled with erroneous underlying assumptions that Africa inherited abilities to think from Rene Descartes are arguably counterproductive and unfaithful to the epistemologies and ontologies of Africa that show that Africans were indeed great thinkers well before the advent of colonialism.

One comment in the media explained the droughts in terms of *El Niño* building up in the Pacific: *"Zimbabwe: Experts predict drought"* (The Herald, Harare, 20 July 2009). But this explanation was contested by other accounts premised on the linkages between the droughts and the perpetration of violence in the country. Other explanations were that the droughts could only be averted by recourse to traditional ceremonies including *mukwerera* and traditional cleansing ceremonies to cleanse the nation of blood spilt during the liberation war fought in the 1970s: *Negation of Traditional Values Blasted* (The Herald, Harare 20 January 2003; *Zim 'needs' cleansing ritual* (News 24.com AFP Special Report, 28 April 2009: 13: 19). And yet another explanation by the Zimbabwe Government was that the droughts were being caused by neoimperialist Britain and the United States of America, that were opposed to the land redistribution in Zimbabwe, and were thus alleged to be chemically doctoring the weather so as to arm twist governments in the Southern African region so that they would capitulate to the whims of the world's super powers (BBC News, 28 June 2005: 15: 13; *UK, US caused Zimbabwe Droughts*). As will be shown throughout the rest of the book, even in the light of these different explanations of the droughts everyday life has taken for granted worlds that constitute facts from the points of view of informants.

While the explanations of the droughts in terms of the *El Niño* offered conventional 'scientific' accounts, literature on Zimbabwean ethnography indicates that there are other ways of accounting for droughts which link the everyday life of human beings to the environment and to politics. As hinted above, droughts have long been explained by some citizens in terms of political and other conflicts deemed to disrupt the relations between human beings and entities held to be guardians (such as the *mhondoro*) of the environment (Vujfhuizen, 1997; Daneel, 1998). Although *mhondoro* are understood as opposed to violence, other scholars have reported that the expropriation of land such as from the [minority] Whites for purposes of redistribution to Blacks was supported by 'spirit mediums' and the *mhondoro* guardians of the land, as well as *Mwari* (God) (Sadomba, 2008; Daneel, 1970). Droughts have also been explained in terms of Zimbabwean national leaders neglecting the rain shrines after they came to power in postindependence dispensation. There are allegations (Alexander *et al*, 2000) that the leaders failed to report to shrines to thank 'spirits' and *Mwari* for their support in the liberation struggle and that the leaders failed to lead the way in cleansing the nation of the effects of war. The leaders have been charged with failing to offer apologies for violence, but this argument ignores the fact that the war was understood in the first place as sanctioned by the *mhondoro* and by

Mwari (Daneel, 1970; Bullock, 1927; 1950). In such cases of war other scholars like Schmidt (1997) have noted remarks by the Shona that '*hondo haina pfukwa*' (war does not lead to haunting).

Allegations that famine originated from conducts of governments have a long historical record, but as indicated in the Zimbabwe government's allegation that the weather was being doctored by Euro-America, there is also the perception that invisible distant others sanction droughts by chemically doctoring the weather. Historically, colonial rule coincided with severe food shortages, droughts, locust invasions and animal diseases including rinderpest that culminated in the 1896 Chimurenga war (Chigodora, 1997: 23-4, 29). The Ndebele people in the south western part of Zimbabwe blamed the European settlers [considered to have disrupted the spiritual metaphysical order] in the 1890s for these catastrophes (Kane, 1954: 101-102). But as Iliffe (1990: 21) notes, the Europeans who were deemed to have caused the famine and other evils claimed instead that the six years since their invasion had witnessed an environmental disaster and that Africans blamed their hunger on their rulers and had risen to put an end to both hunger and colonialism out of despair. With respect to the control of rinderpest, colonial authorities were accused of bias by Africans insofar as they enforced the regulations unevenly as they killed more of African cattle (Mutowo, 2001).

Supplying the motivation by colonial settlers who profited from African [meteorological, climatological and other] crises, Chigodora (1997: 23-24, 29) noted that preventing the Ndebele inhabitants from harvesting was a vital military objective of the colonists who wanted to subdue them. All 'native' supplies of corn were therefore destroyed, by the colonial settlers, throughout the country including in the eastern districts where the war had raged on and where locusts had also destroyed crops. The European colonists are also noted as having destroyed the stores of Ndebele and Shona corn that they could find, and they burnt the crops (Illiffe, 1990). Indeed the first *Chimurenga* war of liberation from colonial rule in the 1890s was to protest against land seizures and the hut tax, but the war was also a response to the environmental calamities mentioned above (Chitiyo, 2004).

During the early colonial era, God's oracular voice [which helped with advice in times of crises] was consulted by African inhabitants at Matopo Hills in south western Zimbabwe. As a result, the calamities were deemed by some African inhabitants to be visited on the land by *Mwari* (God) who was displeased with colonial settlers' oppressive rule involving expropriation of land and cattle belonging to the Africans. The Shona people (who constitute the majority of inhabitants of Zimbabwe) were historically informed of offences that occasioned droughts, by the *mhondoro* (and by *Mwari*'s oracular voice) speaking through the mediums (Bourdillon, 1976) but in the contemporary era it is also via Western science that citizens are informed of greenhouse effects, climate change and so on, including the need to reduce gaseous emissions. It was a requirement to atone in order to abate the droughts, but atonement involved sacrifice (Bourdillon, 1976). While this sacrifice may appear to be surpassed by the 'modern' era, there are parallels in the logics and approaches to matters of climate change and greenhouse emissions particularly with respect to the fact that some in the Global South have raised questions about why gaseous emissions by others in the Global North should affect them more.

In *chivanhu* metaphysics, offences were held not merely as against the state but also against the *mhondoro* guardians of the environment as well as against God as the Creator. *Mwari* and the *mhondoro* were concerned not only with direct blood-shedding but also with oppressive and expropriative structural violence by the colonial or imperial administration for instance. In this logic *Mwari* and *mhondoro* were deemed to be against structural violence and oppression such as arising from expropriations of property as well as direct violence. Thus, in a world of structural violence and inequalities at various levels, explanations of droughts that demonise the postcolonial states should go beyond merely assuming that it is only direct violence that occasions sanctions with droughts. Structural and symbolic violence from within the states as well as from outside, such as violence that originates from the invisible global matrices of power, can also be understood as occasioning sanctions with droughts.

As Das (2004) contends, violence in the local or in the margins of the state is induced not only by the national but also by global structures and strictures. The global [understood here in terms of the hegemonic West] can be seen as increasingly usurping the logics of mediums and divinities understood here as transcendental and less bounded by space and time than ordinary human beings. This is especially so in contexts where the internet and other forms of media have displaced and replaced conventional oracles while at the same time facilitating global cascades of oracular messages and voices that penetrate the peripheries. Thus, the physically absent presences, the visible invisibles, by way of the global cascades continue to influence Africa, in the logics of the numinous persona. Writing about ICTs that are increasingly replacing spirit mediums in forecasting weather, scholars like Kroker (2004) have argued on the basis of metaphysical renditions that the ICTs encompass 'gods of speed' that circulate in net space and connect spaces, places and people. Thus the technologies facilitate the interventions in the local by distant global invisible others who invisibly influence the quotidian, yet paradoxically continue to regard indigenous epistemologies similarly premised on the nexus between the visible and invisible realms to be irrational, nonrational, illogical and other such derogatory terms.

But the logics of divinities that are often played by the global virtualities have also often been contested from both Christian and indigenous perspectives. For instance from a 'human rights' perspective, donors including the World Bank and the IMF have advocated for the legalisation of homosexuality in Africa to such an extent that in the case of Uganda, they withdrew aid as a protest against the enactment of legislation penalising homosexuals ("Zimbabwe style 'Finesse' for Uganda: Silent Over Museveni, Government Now Wants Talks About Rights" *Sunday Times*, 2 March 2014: 10). However, Christians have traditionally held that homosexuality is against the Heavenly God's law. African cultural arguments have also been advanced that homosexuality is contrary to African cultures, norms and values, to the laws of the *mhondoro*s and of *Mwari* and that the practice of homosexuality [as that of incest and murder] leads to sanctions including droughts from *mhondoro* guardians of the land. These arguments are especially apposite where African cultures, norms and values are held to be controlled by the ancestors such as *mhondoro* in concert with *Mwari*, who, when displeased, are deemed to visit droughts. Such contentions that environmental disasters resulted from acts of witchcraft, incest, abortion, conflicts, and disrespect for ancestors and disobedience of the *mhondoro* (Ranger, 2003) appear to be contrary to the 'secular' renderings of contracts and law. In *chivanhu*, *mhondoro* are not [immanently] locked up in nature and other objects as is presumed in naturalistic theology and in the presumptions of postmodern re-enchantment. The laws of the *mhondoro* and *Mwari* appear to clash with the secular naturalistic laws of the hegemonic Western world and it appears that it is partly as a result of these clashes that droughts are explained in indigenous epistemologies and ontologies.

However it is important to take into cognisance Bodin's (1992) argument that, as for 'divine' and 'natural' law, every prince on earth is subject to them and it is not in their power to contravene them unless they wish to be guilty of treason against God and to wage war against Him. One can therefore argue, from an indigenous knowledge point of view, that Western secular laws wherein humanity is expected to contravene divine law effectively set humanity up against God. Thus, while secular laws are conventionally portrayed as heralding freedom from God and the meddlesomeness [including the imperatives of sacrifices] of spiritual deities, setting humanity up against God can be interpreted as effectively sacrificing humanity in so far as it sets that humanity up against God, for judgement and perhaps execution. Even though the Hobbesian law of nature, as the law of God that is beyond the social contract, can be understood as implying that only the law of God surpasses the social contract, other scholars like Hardt and Negri (Passavant and Dean, 2004; Buchanan and Pahuja, 2004) have argued that emperors also operate beyond the social contracts of nation states which they transcend. In this sense, inhabitants of peripheral nation states are subject both to the laws of God and the laws of empire [both transcendental] that they struggle to keep and reconcile lest they suffer sanctions and sacrifices from either God or empire, or both of them.

The challenge in so far as indigenous explanations of droughts are concerned is that often the laws of God and the *mhondoro*, that have come to be considered as superstition in Western epistemologies, have been suspended for centuries because the West has increasingly set itself up in the place of godly supremacy over the world (Nhemachena, 2016; Nhemachena, 2017).

The context within which Zimbabweans survived during the crises underscores modes of sacrifice and resilience. Keen to relieve the majority of citizens that had been crammed in infertile and dry regions of the country since the colonial era, the government of Zimbabwe risked the ire not necessarily of God but of empire when it signalled that it would appropriate land from the minority White farmers. The White farmers many of whom had ceased growing maize, the staple, [and shifted with the inception of economic structural adjustment to horticulture] needed the protection of the resilient British Empire that was unwilling to fund for orderly land redistribution in terms of the earlier agreements as per the Lancaster House Constitution. Thus, the British Labour Government that was latter alleged by the Zimbabwean government to be doctoring the weather to create droughts in the country and in the southern African region had in 1997 refused to meet the costs of land redistribution to Blacks as agreed in the 1979 Lancaster House Agreement (between the liberation fighters, the colonial regime and Britain). The British official, Clare Short, wrote to the Zimbabwean government in 1997 thus: "I should make it clear that we do not accept that Britain has a special obligation to meet the costs of land purchase in Zimbabwe. We are a new government from diverse backgrounds without links to former colonial interests. My own origins are Irish and, as you know, we were colonised not colonisers" (Gono, 2008: 91).

The Western sanctions, including those that emanated from the U.S.A's Zimbabwe Democracy Recovery Act 2001 (ZIDERA), coincided with recurrent droughts in the country; much like the inception of colonisation in various African countries (Feuerman, 1990; Chitiyo, 2004; Chigodora, 1997) coincided with droughts, diseases, that is, famine and epidemics. As if there was collusion, the refusal, during the period of the crises, by the German company Giesecke and Devrient (G & D) to sell paper for printing money to the government of Zimbabwe, which had relied on it for 43 years (Gono, 2008), coincided with the recurrent droughts that would otherwise be explicable in terms of *mhondoro* and *Mwari*. The point here is that during Zimbabwe's recent crises, the West appeared to withdraw together with *mhondoro* and *Mwari* from nourishing the country yet during the inception of colonialism, the West appeared together with famine and epidemics that ravaged Africans and their livestock forcing them to rely on colonial settlers.

The important question in this instance is whether empire has conflated itself with African nature, *mhondoro* and God in such ways that when empire's interests are threatened by local revolts and re-appropriations of land, it conjures up droughts as part of the sanctions against the recalcitrant people? Put in another way, the question is whether empire has become so immanent in African nature that opposing imperial domination conjures up sanctions including recurrent droughts? One would also be interested to see the connections between these questions and the discourses on animism and immanence that are increasingly being popularised in academies across the world. If animistic societies liberally engaged in sacrifices, the worship of earthly divinities that explained the popularity of witchcraft and sorcery activities, how might scholars understand recurrent droughts in view of discourses on such animism, witchcraft, sorcery and recognition of multitudes of divinities [in this sense sacred and secular] in the world? In other words, might the contemporary popularisation of animism, presupposing polytheism, be intended to legitimise the West as one of the envisaged immanent deities controlling [including invisibly controlling from a distance] the environments and resources across the whole planet?

Sacrifice in times of environmental crises, calls for placating the powers that control nature [in Africa] (Reid, 1999: 99) and such sacrifice requires drawing of [internal or external] victims close before sacrificing them (Girard, 1977: 10). It is such sacrifice that underlies the violence to which the recurrent droughts were attributed. While the Zimbabwean state exhorted citizens to be resilient and to sacrifice in the name of the struggle for restitution of land [from equally resilient colonial structures of ownership] to the Black majority, Western driven "civil" society organisations exhorted their members and followers to be resilient and to sacrifice in the name of human rights and the rule of law. Sacrifice in this instance has transmogrified from sacrifice to divinities to sacrifice to the states and to ideologies including (neo-)imperial ones. If sacrifice results from denial of essence (Vera, 2001) including by collapsing or conflating human beings to be sacrificed together with animals, African metaphysics of *chivanhu* are arguably less prone to sacrificing human beings [particularly because *mhondoro* that bring rain are held to detest spilling human blood] than would animistic epistemologies and ontologies (Frazer, 1926; Descola, 1996; 2005) that efface distinctions between human beings and animals. In other words, it is not necessarily the presence of distinctions that cause violence rather it is the absence of distinctions that result in one being sacrificed in place of the other.

If naturalised [relational] metaphysics is traced to Western scholars such as Ludwig Feuerbach and others, including those that conflated God with nature (Oliver, 1981; Chakravartty, 2013); Evensky, 2005; Kincaid, 2013) or with European hylozoic cosmologies that presume God to be immanent in nature (Bryden, 2001), one witnesses the effacements of distinctions between human beings and God that made colonisation less disgusting for colonisers who elevated themselves to "God". Similarly, if animistic ideologies are traced to such European scholars on immanence and naturalistic metaphysics, it becomes easier to see how effacing distinctions between human colonised others and animals made colonisation and enslavement of others less disgusting for Westerners (Boonzaier *et al*, 2000: 10; Magubane, 2007: 10). For others like Gifford (2012), Brennan (2012) and Mungazi (1996), enslavement and colonisation were legitimised by Western ideologies holding that the enslaved and colonised were beasts of burdens to be driven like cattle or that they were horses to carry the imperial burdens. While animism has been attributed to cosmologies of the colonised, scholars like Opoku (1978); Rattray

(1927: 2-3); Fontein (2006: 88); Bullock (1927) and Gelfand (1970) underscore the fact that Africans have never been animists. For Opoku (1978), Africans do not believe that every object without exception has a soul but rather that 'spirits' of deceased humans can have certain objects as their habitat or abode and can temporarily be embodied or attached to material objects. Writing specifically about the Shona people whom I have researched for this book, Bullock (1927) noted that the Shona people do not consider rivers and mountains themselves to be animate; and they do not pray to animals even though they believe that spirits of the deceased humans may temporarily rest in or attach or use certain trees as their vehicles (Gelfand, 1970).

A closer look at the ontologies and epistemologies of *chivanhu* helps understand the everyday life modes of engagement, in relation to droughts, of the Shona villagers in Buhera.

The worlds, entities and knowledge practices related to droughts and rains

Villagers in Buhera District related with entities of different kinds in their everyday life, at metaphysical or cosmological levels. Everyday life among the healers and mediums was based on relations between human beings and other entities in the environment, and these entities such as the *mhondoro* ancestor guardians of the land and their mediums have been noted by scholars as having been instrumental in Zimbabwe's land redistribution exercise (Sadomba, 2008). My own interviews with village heads Samuel and Bere, *mbuya* Magoge (a healer) and Monica (a villager under Samuel) indicated that some human beings were connected and related not only to other human beings but also to the *njuzu/madzimudzangara*, ancestors deemed to live in an underworld below pools and rivers (see also Burbridge, 1923, 1924; Bernard, 2003, 2007; McGregor, 2003). The human beings were also considered by such villagers to be connected to other invisible ancestors. For Burbridge (1924: 98) the *madzimudzangara* occupy the realm of the immortal dead clothed in the imperishable flesh of their second bodies beneath selected pools and hills away from human scrutiny. They conduct members of their clan to their realm to teach them to be doctors. However for Gelfand (1959: 106, 121) members of the present generation have generally forgotten that one of their ancestors was once a pool doctor (see also Zvarevashe, 1997). Yet other scholars such as Daneel (1970: 50) note that the *jukwa/njuzu* are deemed by the Shona to be close to God, and to have never had mortal existence (see also Bullock, 1950: 162). In spite of these observations portraying the *njuzu* realm as beneath selected pools and rivers, Gelfand (1959: 6) notes that during the time it does not possess its medium, the spirit is believed to be living in space. Other scholars have argued that the Shona people do not believe that people die but rather that they pass on to the next world (Chavunduka, 2001: 6). Some of the villagers including the healers and mediums pointed out that humans got *ruzivo*, a form of expertise for healing ailments; from the *njuzu*. The *njuzu* were also considered to be present under some streams, rivers, pools and springs which did not dry out even in the years of severe droughts. However, when humans violated the *njuzu* by using chemicals including soap, dirty, sooty or metal containers to fetch water from such rivers, springs, pools or streams, the *njuzu* moved away in the form of localized whirlwinds and the places subsequently would run dry. The springs, rivers, pools and streams were considered to be '*pamisha*', that is, the villages or headquarters of the *njuzu*. Villagers reported hearing sounds of cows mooing, sounds of drumming, singing and whistling under such bodies of water which were home to the *njuzu* beings. It is the character of *ukama* relations, as I will explain later in this chapter, with both the *njuzu* and other ancestors, which were considered to affect rains or to bring on droughts.

Encounters in the early colonial period in Africa saw challenges of translation of different modes of engaging with the world and what transpired during these early encounters helped shape contemporary understandings of the world. Endfield and Nash's (2002) paper for instance explores interactions and reactions, in the early colonial period, of missionaries and the people they encountered in areas affected by frequent droughts. The missionaries considered the introduction of irrigation technology and agricultural settlement as both moral and practical solutions to droughts, even if irrigation and other technologies already existed in Zimbabwe prior to the arrival of Europeans (Posselt, 1935; Manzungu, 1997; Ellert, 1984; Chirikure, 2010). In spite of these observations, missionaries are noted to have sexualised African landscapes using images such as penetrating, opening up, cutting into an area, virgin ground (Schmidt, 1995). It is pointed out in Endfield and Nash (2002) that the missionaries regarded the work of the 'rainmaker' as a folly and a curse, with the result that 'rainmaking' was ridiculed and scorned as a simple absurdity too ridiculous for sober argument. But this critique notwithstanding, the missionaries themselves prayed for rain (see Comaroff and Comaroff, 2005), oblivious of the fact that their logic was similar to that of the people they scornfully called 'rainmakers'. In turn, the people encountered in the region by the missionaries associated the droughts with the arrival of Europeans, some of whom were alleged to have killed the Kings' animals such as the leopards associated with rains.

The missionaries came into contact in many areas of Africa with societies that adhered to the concept of a single deity, such as *Mwari* among the Shona (Daneel, 1970), manifested in the environment rather than in the Bible. The misunderstandings between the missionaries and the people they encountered in this case arose from the challenges of translation of the different modes of engagement with the world. This is not to disregard the case of Ethiopia, where Christianity and the Bible had spread hundreds of years before African colonisation. Nor does it disregard observations that in Africa, writing had been known before Christianity and that the writing and sciences were understood to have originated from Ancient Egyptian gods (Ackroyd, 2005; James, 2009) who taught human beings. Visiting Greek philosophers like Plato, Socrates, Pythagoras and Thales are noted to have been initiated into the Egyptian mystery system and taught by priests for many years before returning to Europe.

Understanding God only in terms of the word in the Bible implied efforts to make God portable and appropriable by those who carried the Bible, that is the Word, as they could always erroneously conflate carrying the Bible with having God on their side and vice versa. Equally erroneous representations of Africans in terms of the immanence of animism and fetishism implied efforts to portray Africans as having no knowledge of the Creator God in Heaven, and in the process to view Africans as the 'heathen others' of Europeans.

The identification of air/wind as a manifestation of the divine has been noted elsewhere and is widespread in Africa. Setiloane (1976) notes that among the Tswana people *Modimo* (God) is understood as supreme, invisible and intangible. Among the Nuer, it is noted by Evans-Pritchard (1967) citing James (1957: 207) that God is *kwoth*, a being of pure spirit who is like air everywhere, in the sky yet present on the earth which he created and sustains. As well, Colson (2006: 49) notes that among the Tonga people the term *muuya* (air) is specific to human beings and carries the implication of breath and movement; and neither plants nor other natural beings have *muuya* although they may have power/force. Such representations of God in terms of wind/air pose an important distinction with European perceptions where God is monopolised as European. If God is, as African "cosmologies" hold, represented as air/wind, it means that God is not monopolisable, but is everywhere and has always been everywhere including in Africa. This is contrary to European perceptions that God was brought to Africa by missionaries.

The missionaries' perceptions legitimised the view that there was no connection between *mhondoro* and God yet Africans have since pre-colonial times known God as *Mwari, Musikavanhu, Nyadenga, Mutangakugara, Dzivaguru, Chikara* (Bourdillon, 1976). Though some missionaries regarded the ways of the people they met in early colonial Zimbabwe as heathen and sought to reduce God to the word (see Jeater, 2007), other missionaries noted that *Mwari*'s attributes were those of God (Bullock, 1927). Indeed, the notion of Supreme Being has been traced to the earliest dictionary of a Bantu language compiled in 1650, as well as in Bosman's description of West Africa in 1705 (Parrinder, 1967: 19). For the precolonial Rwandese, God as Supreme Being has been known as *Nyamurunga* (Jahn, 1961: 105). With respect to the Tonga people, *Leza* (God) is a term traced back to 1000 BCE by Ehret (Colson,

2006: 5). The *Mwali* (God) worship in Zimbabwe has also been traced to precolonial 1500th century (Ntholi, 2006: 41). It is important to underscore the fact that all these observations by the different scholars dispel notions of the existence of animism in Africa given the animistic presumptions of polytheism and absence of a Supreme God. Also notwithstanding the different names they gave to God, it is clear that Africans had notions of one Supreme God and that they did not, as is presumed in animism and scientific naturalism, regard things and human beings in the world as having originated by some Big Bang.

Much of existing literature appears to ignore the African conceptualisations of God as they pre-existed colonialism assuming in the process that Africans got to know God only via the colonial officials and missionaries. Yet Abraham (1966: 37) cites Manuel de Faria e Sousa, who as a Portuguese traveller stated in 1674 that the subjects of Mutapa kingdom believed in one God and they called upon the royal *muzimos* (*mhondoro*) as Europeans did the saints. Kings among the precolonial Shona were understood to go to Heaven as Antonio Bocarro (1635), another Portuguese traveller cited by Abraham (1966), noted of Mutapa Kingdom; but the kings did not transform, as noted about other places in the world, into stars, the sun or other features. Posselt (1935: 137) for instance notes that investigations have not shown that any of the 'tribes' of Southern Rhodesia ever had any form of sun worship or solar cult or that the sun was an object of veneration. These observations are supported by Garbett (1977: 57) who noted that "some of the most important local spirits such as Chaminuka and Nehanda were held never to have been mortal. They mediated between human beings, the lesser spirits and *Mwari* (God) and they were referred to as lions of the Heaven (*mhondoro dzematenga*). In ways that also indicated that the *mhondoro* resided in the heavens, in rain petitioning ceremonies of the Shona there were addresses such as "…..*Dzivaguru, Ambuya Nehanda tipeiwo mvura, imi vari kumatenga musatifuratire, musatikangamwe mhuri yenyu, tipeiwo mvura nyika yenyu yaparara……*": this is translated as "grandmother (honorific) Nehanda give us rain, you who are in the Heavens do not turn your backs on us your family, give us rain, your country is in trouble" (Chitehwe, 1954). While some scholars have interpreted *mbuya* Nehanda and *sekuru* Chaminuka as mortal human beings, other scholars such as Mutswairo (1983) and Gelfand (1959) have noted that Nehanda and Chaminuka referred to *mweya/mhepo* rather than to living human beings who were mere mediums. Nehanda and Chaminuka were 'transtribal' in the sense that mediums were not defined or delimited by lineages: mediums could be of different lineages in the same way mediums of spirits (prophets) in apostolic sects can be of different lineages. In this sense the terms *ambuya* and *sekuru* were merely honorific rather than references to particular lineages. In this way Chaminuka and Nehanda were titles and not references to individual mortal persons or lineages. With regards to Mwari, some scholars like Werbner (1977: 209) have even noted trinity in the precolonial Zimbabwean cardinal *Mwari* oracles at Njelele, Matonjeni and Dula [shrines at Matopo Hills] that stand in relation to each other as do the Beings in the *Mwari* cult's trinity of Father, Mother and Son: the south is the realm of the father whose oracle is at Njelele, the east is the realm of the mother whose oracle is at Matonjeni and the west is the realm of the son whose oracle is at Dula shrine. Other scholars such as Bullock (1950: 145, 147) also noted the existence, at Matopo Hills in south western Zimbabwe, of precolonial priests of *Mwari* who were called *wahosana* or *Bantwana boMlimo* or children of God who included Makwati, Nehanda, Kaguwe and Gororo. These children of God were considered by the Shona people to be direct emanations from the godhead and as not having had mortal existence; they were not subject to sacrifice or *kupira* in the same way as lower ranking ancestral spirits. Incidentally *wahosana* and *izihosana* (for the female virgin vestal entourages at Matopo Hills) appear to have the same roots with *hosana,* commonly used throughout Christian churches. It is these hierarchies and connections from the lower level ancestors to the higher level *mhondoro* and to God that were destroyed during colonialism. The colonial distortion and destruction resulted not only in erroneous and narrow notions that Africans worshipped ancestors but they also resulted in disjunctures between ancestors, *mhondoro* and God.

We shall now consider the categories 'rainmaking' and 'rainmaker' as used by some missionaries cited in Endfield and

Nash (2002) above and seek to demonstrate that they do not accurately describe *mukwerera* ceremonies in Buhera. These Western categories erroneously imply that there is production or manufacturing of rain by the *svikiro* mediums. They further imply that the people who perform the ceremonies can put together or assemble all the ingredients to produce the rain much like how manufacturers might make things or objects. As I will argue below, the *mukwerera* ceremonies involved petitions for rain via the *mhondoro* entities understood to manifest in the form of wind. Although mention is scantily made in some literature of requests for rain to the *mweya/mhepo* (air/wind) (Gelfand, 1962), emphasis has often been placed on material 'objects' such as rain stones used to make such requests (Dah-Lokonon, 1997). The emphasis, I contend should not be merely on the 'objects' but on the *mweya/mhepo* of the *mhondoro* (considered to have similar subjectivities as humans) as understood by the petitioners for rain.

The *svikiro* medium in Buhera did not profess to be a 'rainmaker' or to engage in 'rainmaking' as portrayed by other scholars (Chitehwe, 1954; Vuifhuizen, 1997), elsewhere in Zimbabwe. In response to my question about what is commonly understood as 'rainmaking' ceremonies, the *svikiro* said: *tinokumbira mvura kubva kumhepo* (we request rain from the wind, that is, from the *mhondoro*) in this sense referring to ancestors who are understood in both African and Catholic theology (Daneel, 1970) as intermediaries between God and humans. In this book it is to *midzimu* and *mhondoro* as mediators between the living descendants and God that the term ancestor is applied. It is not all the deceased who become *midzimu/mhondoro* and therefore ancestors in *chivanhu*. In the *mukwerera* ceremonies for rain, villagers gathered under the *muchakata* tree to petition the *mhondoro* for rain. A petition being subject to action or inaction (delayed or otherwise) by the petitioned appears closer to the requests for rain. These modes of engagement with the weather world were an acknowledgement of different forms of life of and in the *mweya/mhepo*, deemed as manifestations of the *mhondoro*, capable of heeding petitions and intervening to make life possible with rain. Much as Heidegger argues (Zahavi, 2008), experiential everyday life is not necessarily incomprehensible, or without inner logic and rationality, but it is on the contrary imbued with meaning, rationality and self-understanding. This implies that understandings of the world are necessarily partial depending on time and the place one begins to make an inquiry about it.

Interesting ideas emerging from the sciences and related to the weather suggest that the wind, the clouds and the rain are not merely physical phenomena but that they are also biological and full of life in that in the wind, the clouds and rain there are bacteria which are understood as 'rainmaking bacteria' (National Geographic News, 12 January 2009; Rainmaking Bacteria Ride Clouds to 'Colonise' the Earth1; Lousiana State University, 29 February 2008; Evidence of Rainmaking Bacteria Discovered in Atmosphere and Snow2) underline varieties of life related to rains and droughts. Both the scientists and the *svikiro* mediums reveal that there are ordinarily invisible life forms which are crucial for precipitation though they envisage different kinds of invisible life forms. As will be explained below the fact that both envisage ordinarily invisible life forms does not entail that the *mhondoro* is immanent as or translatable as bacteria; it is merely to note that the logics of invisibles in Western science and *chivanhu* share similar planes. Whereas naturalistic theology presumes that revelation comes from nature, in *chivanhu* revelation and prophecies are deemed to come from spiritual planes. Therefore in *chivanhu* the *mhondoro* is not synonymous with invisible objects of sciences.

To petition for rainfall, the villagers in Buhera gathered under a particular *muchakata* tree. There were many *michakata* (plural of *muchakata*) trees in the villages in spite of deforestation because villagers shied away from cutting them for reasons I will explain shortly. The *muchakata* tree under which villagers assembled to petition the *mhondoro* was not just a tree or sacred place, but rather a village of the *mhondoro* ancestral beings. For instance the *svikiro* said: "*panzvimbo idzodzi pamisha yevamwe vanhu saka panotogara pachitsvairwa*" (such places are the villages of other people [referring to *mhondoro* ancestral beings] so we regularly sweep them). It is these trees which seem to have been translated by others like Bourdillon (1976) as shrines. The medium swept under the particular *muchakata* tree where the *mukwerera* was held and so all other *michakata* were treated differently. It appears that such petitions interweave worlds. During the performances the entities of the supposed past in the form of the *mhondoro* ancestral founders and guardians of the territories were regarded as present, petitionable and as manifesting their presence by speaking through the mediums or by appearing in the form of lions.

The *mukwerera* ceremonies do not involve prayers to objects or to the earth as some have argued in the case of Gaia, the goddess of Earth in Ancient Greece. Morgan (1901: 91) for instance notes that opinion which began to prevail in Greece was that prayers for rain were sometimes offered in Athens to or through Gaia. Gaia was in the classical period regarded as among the Greek chthonic (underworld) divinities and it was not until the Roman times that she appeared to have lost that earlier personality and to have come to be a personification of the ground. But contrary to other scholars, Morgan argues that in prayers the usual conception was that the winds and clouds did not act independently but under the orders of the god Zeus. While scholars like Lovelock (see Smith, 2011) would want to perceive the earth in terms of Gaia, such perceptions simply recycle colonial ways of sexualising and animating the landscapes which colonists wanted [as a precursor] to 'penetrate' and occupy (Schmidt, 1995).

Although the ceremonies to petition for the rains were open to all villagers, not all of them took part as expected by the *mhondoro*. Christians such as Brian and Maria who belonged to the Apostolic Faith Mission and the Apostolic sect of Masowe did not want to participate as they described the ceremonies as *zvinhu zvemweya yetsvina* (things that are related to ill winds) so they preferred to pray for rain. Such statements by church members notwithstanding, healers, mediums and prophets all insist on purity/*kuchena*/*kucheneswa*/ *kushambidzwa*/*kugeza*. Healers and mediums insist that the deceased have to be cleansed/ *kuchenurwa* so that they become ancestors/*mudzimu*. The cleansing is meant to separate the deceased from the ritual dirt and from witchcraft that would have killed them. But sometimes villagers do not perform the rituals due to absence of resources, or because they prefer to join churches rather than bother with cleansing their deceased relatives. While in the churches there is condemnation of the deceased as polluting and dirty, in *chivanhu* there is recognition of uncleanliness resulting from association with death. But there is also cognisance of the fact that the uncleanliness and pollution may emanate not from the fault of the dead but from witches who would have killed the deceased by planting polluting herbs and *zvikwambo* in the deceased's body. So, in *chivanhu* care is taken to cleanse the dead without invariably blaming them for pollution associated with death. In such religions as *chivanhu*, taboos are meant to maintain ritual cleanliness and avoid pollution which is associated with danger. The *mudzimu*, as Gelfand (1959: 121) rightly notes, are family spirits and, among the Shona, they are recognized as being of Shona origin; they are therefore distinct from *mashave*, which are spirits of foreign origin that settle on innocent, unsuspecting Mashona who are thereby forced to accept them and come to terms with them. Although the some church members argued that they relied only on the Bible to pray, they also placed significance on place in the sense that their prayers for rains were done on the Gombe Mountain which, as will be explained below, was considered by some villagers as inhabited by the deceased people of the *hera* totem. In this way they sought to break from the mediums' modes of engagement but only succeeded partially: they remained connected in some way. While the Pentecostals contended that they talk to God directly without using intermediaries such as ancestors, the *svikiro* medium and *mbuya* Magaya, a healer, had different views. From their points of view the church members simply replaced ancestors by preferring to use their leaders and prophets as intermediaries between them and God.

Creating disjunctures was one of the objectives of the colonists who wanted to open up African metaphysical realms so as to expose Africans and force them to seek shelter, so to speak, in the colonists' metaphysical sheds. Breaking the African metaphysical hierarchies opened up spaces for *mashave* (foreign spirits) to which, as Colson (1971) notes, many subsequently became vulnerable. Yet the colonial dispossession of land, of cattle and labour as well as the separations from relatives that resulted from the forcible resettlement of Africans to reserve areas incapacitated the latter. The Africans who were increasingly becoming victims of *mashavi* possession no longer had resources, the unity and cohesion with which to perform rituals for their ancestors to protect them from *mashavi* possession. Some villagers whose two members had succumbed to illness shortly before I began fieldwork stated that they lacked resources to consult a healer or go to hospital to try and save a third member of the household who was bedridden when I began fieldwork. The point here is that colonists celebrated rendering Africans vulnerable in material senses, psychological and metaphysical-spiritual senses and these exposures rendered Africans amenable to possession by *mashavi* spirits, rather than by their ancestors whose rituals they could no longer afford to perform after their resources including livestock were expropriated by colonists. It can be argued that the colonial ideologies that demonised African rituals as evil were meant to facilitate the dispossession of Africans It is conceivable that colonists would have had difficulties expropriating those African cattle that were sanctified through *chivanhu* rituals and therefore dissuading Africans from performing rituals was a way to ease the challenge of expropriating their livestock and other resources. It is thus argued here that Africans might have believed that their rituals were devilish, in the sense of being against God, when in fact colonists meant that African rituals were evil in the sense that they prevented the colonists from expropriating the Africans' resources, so protected via *chivanhu* rituals.

Owing to the connections between *Mwari* and *mhondoro*, *svikiro* mediums were considered by some scholars to have been prophets (Mutswairo, 1983; Gelfand, 1956) and to be likened by scholars such as Gelfand (1956: 17) to the Bishops and Archbishops in a Christian society. Thus Crawford (1967: 87) argued: "For a person who believes in the *mhondoro*, the possession of a prophet of the Pentecostal churches by the spirit of God, Christ or the Apostles, appears in no way untoward". These views by Crawford have been supported recently by Heathcote-James (2009: 13, 32, 182-3, 186) who noted that Jesus is seen as Black in Ethiopian visions and White in Caucasian ones. For Heathcote-James, some European informants reported seeing loved deceased family members as their guardian angels, whom they now believed served as angelic influences. Heathcote-James further noted that ghosts, guides, angels, energies all theoretically separate entities with own descriptions and connotations became merged into one when people attempted to define what an angel represented to them as some even saw deceased parents including mothers and grandmothers, dressed as angels in white with white wings. In Zimbabwe, (see for instance *The Sunday Mail* 26 April 2015 p 4, "*Debunking the Word Christian*"), others have argued that the word Christ is English deriving from the Greek *Christos*, Latin *Christus* and old English *Crist* where *Christus* is a title of the highest achievement so that one is aware of divinity. It is argued that the word *Christos* is derived from ancient Egyptian *KRST*, *Karest* or *Karustin* where *KRST* was the immortalisation condition through mummification first achieved by *Asar* (*Osiris* in Greek) and that *KRST* or *Karest* later became *Krishna* as an adoption of Indus civilisation (see also Magubane, 2007: 25, 34). On a similar point, Bloom (1997: 75) has argued that it is an ancient pattern that gods of other faiths and nations are demoted to the status of demons: as guardian angels of rival states these former gods could be easily and conveniently associated by colonists with evil and pestilence.

These views are supported by Daneel's (2007) observation that in Catholic theology those ancestors who obeyed 'natural law' are with God and therefore can be mediators, be they Christian or non-Christian ancestors. This observation by Daneel is supported by Gelfand (1959: 7) who notes that there did not appear among the Shona to be an ethical code, written or committed to memory comparable to the Ten Commandments, but there were legends and histories comparable to some passages to be found in the Bible. Daneel's (2007) as well as Gelfand's (1959) observations notwithstanding, due to their participation in leading the anticolonial rebellion at the inception of colonialism in 1896, *mhondoro*s and their mediums were labelled as devilish and as powers of darkness and witchdoctors by the colonial establishment. Though church members claim that they pray to God directly, it is important to consider whether God in His greatness would after hearing prayers not instead still send one's ancestors as His emissaries, at least those that have observed His laws.

What both the Pentecostals and the rest of the villagers at the *mukwerera* ceremonies did appeared to me to be petitioning for rain; rather, they indicated that they were praying (which is arguably a way of requesting also) and *kukumbira* or requesting for rain. The practices are separated or different but related. They rely on relations between the visible and invisible entities and beings such as ancestors for those who perform *mukwerera*, *ngirozi* deemed to be from the heavenly world for those who pray for rain from God. However the challenge in such a village where members had different ways of engaging with the weather world was to democratise the practices, to make space in order for the different knowledge practices to be considered without a priori dismissals.

Altering modes of engagement in the world including relations within the human domain without petitioning other entities in domains beyond but connected to the human often resulted in reprisals and disruption of relations of reciprocity among the beings and entities in the environment. It was not just the relations between the visible entities and beings that mattered in the wellbeing of human beings in Africa but the relations with the invisible entities also such as ancestors (see also White, 2001) and for this reason the past is often played in the present as ways to honour the ancestors. In this sense, an emphasis on the linearity of time fractures relations of reciprocity within the environment and as Garuba (2013) argues, "There is need to recognise the complex embeddedness of different temporalities, different discordant formations and different epistemological perspectives within the same historical moment". But in Zimbabwe, and Buhera in particular, rethinking Euro-modernity implies not only a focus on its notions of time but also of work: invisible entities such as *mhondoro* ancestors were regarded as working during some days to ensure that humans and other entities had rains and they rested on other days. Normally each *mhondoro* has a rest day during which he is honoured and villagers are not permitted to work during the particular day when the *mhondoro* will also be resting. Failure to observe the *chisi* rest-day resulted in reprimands from the *mhondoro*.

This idea that days and even months are associated with the dead forefathers may be understood in terms of the 'traditional' as opposed to the 'modern' but then even in the 'modern' era months are also associated with the dead, but they have been so internalised them that most people often do not realise the associations (Richard *et al.*, 1982). For example, in the modern Western calendar, based on the Julian calendar established by Julius Caesar, January, the first month of the year, is dedicated to *Janus*, the two-faced god of doors, and March to the Roman god of war Mars, etc. July and August celebrate the Roman Emperors Julius Caesar and Caesar Augustus. Similarly, the days of the week in the Anglo-Saxon tradition are named in honour of gods of the Norse and Greco-Roman mythologies: Tuesday honours the Norse God of war Tyr (or Tiw in Old English). Wednesday is dedicated to Woden or Oden, the god associated with healing, death, royalty, knowledge, battle, sorcery, etc. Thursday is dedicated to the god of thunder called Thor or Thunor, hence Thor's day.

These implantations of the Western gods, after whom week days and months are named, belie the assertions that Westerners separated nature from culture. In fact they underscore the fact that Westerners since colonialism have implanted and embedded themselves and their gods onto African continent and it is such embedments and implantations that are the causes of conflicts over land and other resources in countries such as Zimbabwe. Colonisers therefore did not necessarily come with separations between nature and culture since they conflated themselves and their cultures with African environments. The challenge is not simplistically about Cartesian *separations* and Western science as purported by others; the challenge is also to do with gods and goddesses that have been *conflated*, superimposed and "implanted" in African landscapes.

The association of some months with European Emperors speak to ways in which the forebears of Africa have been replaced with the forebears of Europe in conceptualisations of temporality. Equally, the dedication of most of the days of the week to ancient European mythology (Delaney, 2004) speaks to mere replacement of African deities by European traditional ones rather than to a qualitative change resulting from the imposition of Euro-modernity on Africa. The issue then is not about whether Africans follow traditions and Europeans follow modernity but it is about which and whose traditions are in question, even if some may appear new when actually they are old. The implications of the translation by colonial missionaries of African ancestors as 'demons' had, as Comaroff and Comaroff (2005: 505) argue, unfortunate results in the form of the long term colonisation of the consciousness of Africans who continue to regard their ancestors as demons.

During *mukwerera*, some of the villagers did not even request recusal and for this reason the *svikiro* medium was often dejected by the poor attendance or nonattendance in the ceremonies, which she contended benefited every villager when the rain eventually fell in the area. Attendance at the *mukwerera* was therefore so variable that when I intended and had agreed with the *svikiro* that I would attend one near her homestead in 2011, it was according to the *svikiro* medium aborted because villagers did not come in their numbers to partake. Instead the *svikiro* went on a different day to another village a distance away to assist in their *mukwerera*. To me she narrated how the *mukwerera* is done. The following is therefore an account based on what village headmen Samuel and Bere, the *svikiro* medium and her brothers Paul and Anton said of how the *mukwerera* is conducted. The *svikiro* and her brothers maintained that *mukwerera* is being misunderstood and unnecessarily opposed by some villagers out of lack of knowledge and they lamented that knowledge about such *mukwerera* is being lost because it is not written in books or other texts. The following is an account of how the *mukwerera* was performed.

After the *matakapona*, which is a gathering for thanks giving following harvests, people begin to prepare for the *mukwerera* which involves petitioning of the *mhondoro* for rains for the next season. Mature and married nephews on the medium's paternal side cut firewood for the brewing of the beer. *Rapoko* grain is collected from the villages and the *mhondoro* is informed of the impending *mukwerera*. Elderly women soak the *rapoko* grain which is used for beer brewing. The people who cut the firewood have to abstain from sexual intercourse until the end of the *mukwerera* for the *mhondoro* considers sexual intercourse impure. Women who are breastfeeding are also not allowed to partake because breastfeeding is also considered to be impure because the *mhondoro* detests milk. After the beer has been brewed the *mhondoro* is informed that his beer is ready for consumption. During the *mukwerera* there is drumming, singing and clapping of hands. People have to kneel down and clap their hands when making the petitions, speaking exclusively in Shona. Headmen Samuel and Bere as well as the *svikiro* medium pointed out that it often rained even as people were about to leave the *rushanga*, at the *mukwerera* tree, for the homes.

During the *mukwerera* one clay pot full of beer reserved for the people of the *mhondoro's* clan is placed into the *rushanga* (an enclosure of spaced poles which I saw around the *muchakata* tree where the ceremony is held). A nephew of the clan pours a little of the beer in four directions around the *rushanga* and then gives the remaining beer to the elders of the clan. The rest of the people then form a circle around the *rushanga* and each one is given a *mukombe* (a gourd container) full of beer. As participants drink, they sit down. The remaining beer is left in the *rushanga*. Clay pots and the *mukombe* are left in the *rushanga* and they are collected by elderly women the following morning. The elderly women have to ululate / *kupururudza* as they collect the items, and they have to shrill even though there may not be anyone else visibly present since they regard the *mhondoro* beings to be present, albeit invisible.

The above account shows that the *mukwerera* was conducted through forms of relatedness understood as *ukama* between human beings and invisible entities such as ancestors. It is also necessary that villagers relate well together during the *mukwerera* and from the point of view of some villagers, even before and after the *mukwerera*, relations among different beings and entities if upset would result in droughts. For instance Martin, an elderly man whom I met when he was taking a rest at the shopping centre in the village, contended that the violence in which some villagers and citizens of Zimbabwe had died during the decade starting in 2000, angered God who then visited the recurrent droughts on Zimbabwe. Martin had just cycled some 20 km from a school where his son teaches. He had gone there to seek his son's assistance with money for food, having harvested only five kilograms of maize grain that year. It is important to note here that the God envisaged in *chivanhu* indigenous knowledge is not the naturalistic or naturalised God that Eurocentric epistemologies consider to be immanent in nature (Artigas, 2001). Even though there are traces of implicate order metaphysics in indigenous knowledge, villagers tend to separate causes in such a way that causal power is sometimes attributed to ancestors and other time it is attributed to God and so on. This is the reason why droughts, famines, disasters and illnesses are often interpreted differently even if the agents may try to evade apprehension.

Perhaps one related good illustration of how people often look beyond the [discernible] obvious to discern causes is found in Feuerman's (1990: 127) work in Tanzania. The years 1897-99 had witnessed disasters including rinderpest, locusts, very long droughts, diseases and violence at the inception of colonialism in Tanzania. It was a period when jiggers or chigoe fleas first spread to the Tanzanian Shambaai and brought illness that the Shambaai had not previously known. These tropical fleas burrow into the skin of humans and cattle and feed on their blood, causing irritation and serious infections. Although some people interpreted the disaster in terms of God's punishment, others remembered the plagues as punishments meted out by the Europeans including a German planter who, faced with local refusal to work on his farm, sent to Germany for an earthen pot full of jigger eggs. They remembered him breaking the pot in a village adjacent to his estate to punish recalcitrant workers. This example from Feuerman (1990) underscores the fact that disasters are not merely interpreted in terms of God's or ancestors' punishment but are also linked to human beings responsible for the occurrences. In this sense anthropocentric explanations are not entirely dispensed with but are part of the corpus of explanations.

Although the *ukama* among the villagers I studied involve human beings, they are not restricted to connections via biological kinship as suggested by Gelfand (1981); nor is *ukama* limited to bodily forms or to marriage or affinal kinship. Rather, *ukama* is broader than kinship in the sense that it encompasses relations with the *mhondoro* ancestral beings that connected them to the environment which they are understood to own and control. *Ukama* is open in the sense that the ancestors are considered to connect their descendants with entities and landscapes within their jurisdiction.

In *ukama* a radical distinction between human life and the lives of other entities such as the *mhondoro* is not invariable; however, the *ukama* is not necessarily animistic for a number of reasons. The first is that animism emerged as a category from within Euro-modernist ontologies which presumed radical separation between human beings and other entities. Animism has been defined in many but related ways as noted by Bird-David (1999: S67): it is defined as the belief that inside ordinary visible tangible bodies there is a normally invisible, intangible being – the spirit. The second reason is that animism is a religious belief involving the attribution of life or divinity to such natural phenomena as trees, thunder, or celestial bodies. Third, animism is defined as the belief that all life is produced by a spiritual force, or that all natural phenomena have souls. Fourth, animism is defined as the belief in the existence of a separable soul-entity, potentially distinct and apart from any concrete embodiment in a living individual or material organism. Fifth, animism is defined as the system of beliefs about souls and spirits typically found among many preliterate societies. As pointed out above, the *svikiro* medium did not consider the *mhondoro* ancestor that spoke through her as a mere spirit, a soul or divinity but also as a relative – her grandfather. In Buhera, the villagers related to their ancestors who, as in other parts of Africa, are considered to be dead but alive, in that their *mweya/mhepo* (air/wind) continue to live and to influence the human world (Nyathi, 2001). They related with them not merely through the category of belief but through *kutenda* which also means to be thankful or to be grateful for the harvests and for the rains, or for anything good that is done including by fellow villagers. Animism understood as the attribution of life by human beings to inanimate things misses an important point in that it presumes that it is always the visible human beings who will be speaking and making the attributions whereas when the female *svikiro* medium spoke about different worlds inhabited by different ancestors, it was the deep male voice of the *mhondoro* (conceived as wind) inhabiting her that was heard. And as in other parts of Zimbabwe, what such mediums say is not attributed to them but to the *mhondoro* that speak through them (Lan, 1986).

The fact that the *mhondoro* is deemed to move in and out of his medium allowing the medium to recover her personality after the possession session has significant implications for understanding the idea of resilience and sacrifice in Shona indigenous knowledge. The movements imply that the personality of the medium is not incapacitated or mortified by the *mhondoro* but the medium's personality has room to rebound, to return to the initial position when she recovers after the sessions. But because the *mhondoro* moves in and out, there are no presumptions of animism in such Shona epistemologies and ontologies where ancestors such as the *mhondoro* are deemed to attach themselves temporarily to entities or objects which they use periodically as vehicles to exert their influence. In *chivanhu* sessions of possession there is no complete annihilation of the personality of the medium but rather such personality is given the chance to rebound or recover.

From the study among the villagers, it can be argued that the beings and entities are not invariably reducible to their morphological appearances as on the one hand, they can be what they look like but on the other hand – on the basis of cyclicity similar to those in possession sessions – they may be what they do not look like. A mountain, a lion, or even *mhepo/mweya* (wind/air) can be what they appear to be on the basis of their morphological or meteorological features, but they can be more than that because of the invisible entities such as the *mhondoro* manifesting in them, albeit temporarily.

As pointed out above, the *mhondoro* is also understood by the *svikiro* to manifest as *mhepo*/wind, but he was not mere *mhepo* when he manifested in his human medium or when manifesting as a lion. And the *svikiro* medium can be a mere human being but she can be more when the *mhondoro* is manifesting in her. Such African metaphysics are neither presumptions of animism, entailing the turning of the *mhondoro*s into the physical features to which they temporarily attach themselves, nor claims that God is interchangeable with physical features in the environment. What this means is that binaries between nature and culture are sometimes rendered fuzzy without implying that nature becomes a subject as a human being; rather, it is merely visited by spirits of deceased human beings that come and go. If baboons, lions and *every* other being or natural phenomenon were interchangeable with *mhondoro* or with God, as implied in Frazer's (1926) and Tylor's (1871) notion of animism, there would not have been room in African metaphysics for sacrifice *to* the ancestors, an argument that is made by other writers on Africa. If beings used to sacrifice were interchangeable with the ancestors to whom the sacrifices are made this would amount to sacrifice *of* rather than *to* ancestors. *Ukama* relations among the villagers maintain some openness for possibilities for such switches, as noted above. This is to say that the entities can be merely what they appear to be, animals, mountains and nothing more. The openness of the relations bears some resonance with Ingold's (2007) argument that in 'animistic' cosmologies there is attribution of supreme importance to the winds and such: "animism is not a system of beliefs about the world but a way of being in it characterised by openness rather than closure" – and by openness he alludes to sensitivity and responsiveness to an environment that is in flux. As noted with reference to Zimbabwean villagers, the notion that entities such as the *mhondoro* temporarily attach themselves to objects is not a way of life but such occurrences are rare: for the *mhondoro* to attach himself to an object or even to his medium is an exception rather than a rule since the *mhondoro* is free also to detach himself from a particular object or even from his medium and move back and forth. Yet for Ingold (2007), "there is no separation between the substances and the medium since the wind, rain and other weather phenomena enter into substances and the substances are in the wind, in the weather: that is substances and the medium are mingled in an open world with no insides and outsides but comings and goings". In Buhera the *mhondoro who hosted by the svikiro medium* comes and goes away, that is he appears, disappears and reappears; and the njuzu entities also appear and disappear.

But openness has to be qualified because it is not always the case that human beings and even fauna are in the open or want to be in the open. This is why even in the precolonial past inhabitants of Buhera built a fortress on Gombe Mountain which now stands in ruins. This is also why the enclosures at Great Zimbabwe were made in the precolonial past: villagers often ran into huts and houses for shelter when it was cold or when it was about to rain. Even the corpses of the dead in *chivanhu* must never be kept in the open, and must be buried or hidden (*kuvigwa*). Fauna such as birds seek enclosures in the nests. The vernacular statement that '*dzvinyu kuzambira zuva huona bako*' (for a lizard to bask in the sun is to have a cave in view) underlines the fact that one should have somewhere to hide in case of danger. In this sense the world is not invariably open, and of course openness is not always celebrated as indeed it may entail vulnerability when one is away from enclosures. Openness may entail risks of invasions such as occurred with respect to farms in Zimbabwe and such as the vulnerability that occurred during the colonial era when Africa was portrayed by European travellers and scholars as open, empty and vacant.

While Ingold's (2007) use of the notion of becomings presupposes absolute openness, the world is not necessarily absolutely open. Thus, to designate the existence of closures, boundaries and delimitations I use the term 'unbecomings'. The deportations of Zimbabweans who had migrated to other countries during the crises, and the structural violence as well as direct violence from the local and global realms all effectively speak to closures rather than openness in the world. Some villagers pointed out that because their *ukama* had been ruptured by interparty violence in Zimbabwe, they could not attend ceremonial parties and other gatherings together as they no longer saw eye to eye with their assailants. While the violence can be understood in terms of the local and the national boundaries, if one conceived it in terms of theoretical approaches that argue that the distinction between the local and the global are being eroded, one is apt to envisage the violence as explicable in terms of broader global cascades on the local and national moral geographies. Though Ingold (1993) stressed openness of the world, other scholars writing about

Southern African "cosmologies" have noted ways in which during petitioning for rain villagers often fenced off or pegged up the villages as ways to protect themselves against witchcraft practices that affected rains; and yet some chiefdoms often hired 'rainmakers' from outside their localities (Schapera, 1971; Krige *et al.*, 1956). Thus unqualified assumptions of openness and becomings can entail vulnerability and the risks of being sacrificed. In fact in *chivanhu,* becomings that entail going without returning are derided as *kuita chitototo/kuita gumbo mutsvairo/swera kuenda,* all this implies that one can go but should remember to return to the origins.

Conclusion

The fact that in Zimbabwe, spirits can temporarily attach themselves to objects without becoming interchangeable with those objects, supports Temples' (1959: 23-4) assertion that the foundation of religion in Africa has been erroneously accepted as consisting of ancestor worship, animism, cosmic mythology, totemism and magic. Temples' observation that worship of the Supreme Being is very old in Africa similarly dismisses erroneous assertions that Africans are animists. If objects are properly understood as vehicles or seats of spirits, as in African metaphysics, it would become easy to understand why contemporary efforts to revive 18th century Western teleology (Jones, 1997: 371-4) have no foundations in African ontologies and epistemologies. While African ontologies show that spirits cannot be conflated with objects that they use as vehicles or seats, it is 18th century Western teleology that has replaced the wisdom of the Creator with the wisdom of teleology, evolution that moralises nature itself while dismissing the existence of God as Creator ex nihilo. This Western teleological thinking, which is foundational to Western animistic thinking is closely linked to the development of Western science (Artigas, 2001) and *a fortiori* to Greek natural science which was based on the principle that the world of nature is saturated or permeated by mind and therefore alive, intelligent, orderly. Although animism [often also considered part of relational ontologies] is touted by some scholars as heralding cosmopolitical peace (Latour, 2004), this chapter underscored the fact that animism in fact explains violence in context where human beings are likened to animals and therefore denied human essence. This supports Yahya' (2001) argument that animism and the attendant social Darwinism underpinned violence and legitimised colonisation, enslavement, dispossession and impoverishment of others deemed to be so similar to animals that they had no human essence, no institutions, and no notions of ownership of resources.

It has been argued in this chapter that to conflate Africans with animals repeats the logics of the colonial and enslavement eras that served as precursors to the sacrifice of Africans in the interests of empire. As Feuerman (1990: 126) observed in Tanzania, it was colonial settlers who reduced 'rainmakers' to ridicule so that they were called pigs in their subjects' songs and this led them to stop performing the ceremonies including fertility rites of the land. Similarly, in the context of *chivanhu* and the attendant insistence on *hunhu*, that distinguishes a human being from an animal, to address villagers as pigs or as indistinct from animals would be a profound insult to them. The fact that in *hunhu* villagers are expected to observe ethics, morals and laws against murdering other human beings, the fact that they are enjoined by *hunhu* against prostitution, abortion, incest and so on distinguishes them from animals that do not have such constraints. Thus even though Zimbabwean liberation fighters, who were scurrilously addressed by the colonial settlers as guerrillas and terrorists with tails, considered themselves to be *vana vevhu* (sons of the soil), this must be understood as an assertion resolve to be free. Lan (1987: 163, 171-2) rightly argues that this was a clarion call to all those who were denied their full rights and freedoms in their own native land; it was a rallying point, a political doctrine of self-realisation, self-assertion, of determinacy, of hope, of resolve to be free; it had militancy and to divorce it from this would be to miss its true meaning and relevance. This argument by Lan speaks to the need to pay close attention to exercises in translation, separating literal from metaphoric statements in order to do epistemic and ontological justice to African people. As Stelladi (2000: 234, 248, 249) argues it is important not to trust a metaphor and even theory blindly since they always have unsizeable parts that remain hidden .In this sense, metaphorical statements by the liberation fighters need not be interpreted literally since they have unsizeable parts that are lost sight of when literal meanings are unduly privileged. In fact, to privilege literal meanings even where there is a risk of ignoring metaphorical depth is to deny epistemic and ontological justice to African epistemologies that are not always as superficial as (neo-)colonial animistic translations have rendered them. To fail to separate metaphor from literal meanings, or to fail to separate resilience from sacrifice, or to fail to separate human from animal replicate colonial logics that also failed to distinguish [rain] *making* from [rain] *petitioning*.

Chapter Two

The *Mhepo*, *Mweya* and *Ruzivo*: Knowing, Sensing and Resilience

> "*A day before my daughter was beaten by a policeman working at the nearby police station, I had a dream. In that dream, there was a fence and just outside it there was a dog and a snake. I somehow felt pity for these creatures. In the dream, I also saw some people wanting to get into the fence around my homestead. However the fence moved up and down in a way that made it difficult for the people to enter it. I knew during the dreaming that there was going to be trouble in my family. The man was drunk when he met my daughter who was on her way back from school. The man asked her which school she went to. Upon responding, the man accused my daughter of being boisterous and then he slapped her on the head. He was detained in the cells for a day and upon his release he came to my homestead intending to pay damages including fees for my daughter's medication. I felt pity for him because I saw that in his family there is mhepo (wind) that creates problems for him so that he would misconduct himself, get detained and lose his job. I told him about the mhepo but I declined his damages*" (Noreen, a healer, 6 August 2011).

Within the variety of means of surviving violence that gripped Zimbabwe, dreams such as Noreen's offered some villagers ways of sensing violence ahead of time, as will be shown in this chapter. In a context where the villagers lacked access to media such as newspapers, radios, television and the internet, they often relied on ways of sensing violence such as dreams, divination, prophecy as well as personal tips. While there is often, as in the case in Zimbabwe, emphasis on the significance of conventional media which played important roles in modes of resilience, this chapter argues for the need to consider also the significance of alternative modes of engagement among the villagers. Though such modes of engagement often escape the attention of policy makers, they offer alternative ways of resilience during crises at least at the level of everyday life, and in this sense it is useful to consider them in peace building and democratization initiatives. Considering such modes of engagement entails paying attention to everyday modes of knowing and sensing as well as ways in which they may be understood in relation to ordinary modes of knowing and sensing. In other words, the relation between such everyday modes of engagement and the ordinary modes of knowing is one of translation and rethinking ways in which different knowledge heritages play out together, their differences notwithstanding. Thus by bringing together different knowledge heritages in this book and particularly this chapter, I seek to grapple with ways in which they can be understood not merely in terms of opposition but also in terms of differences and sameness (Verran, 2013) that cross-fertilise across space and time.

Knowing things via such modes as dreams (Reynolds, 1996; Okazaki, 2003; Auge, 2012; Bernard, 2007; Freud, 1999; Friedson, 1996; Krog *et al.*, 2009; Wiseman, 2008; and Campbell, 2008) raises issues about what it means to know things in the world. Although epistemologies have in history tended to privilege direct physical observation in their modes of knowing (Levin, 1993), which has also facilitated colonial and postcolonial power relations hinging on the direct gaze (Erlman, 2004), what it means to know has increasingly become a contentious issue particularly in the light of arguments that even writing itself was originally a sacred activity (Barnes, 1984: 188). While some scholars and philosophers such as Socrates, Pythagoras, Empedocles and Faraday (Snell, 148: 153; Bloom, 1996: 62, 137; Wiseman, 2011: 150; Campbell, 2008) are known to have relied on spirits that served as their warning voices, by the 1620s Francis Bacon had established a binary between science and mysticism (Fudge, 2008).

Though some scholars have linked philosophy and scientific knowledge to European, and in particular Greek origins, others have contended that philosophy and scientific knowledge originated in Egypt. Geometry, for instance, first came to be known in Egypt and subsequently passed into Greece. Hence it is argued that the Ancient Greeks inherited from other people many of their techniques such as farming, metalworking and writing, altering and transforming this knowledge (Herodotus, 1948: 142, 167; Starr, 1984: 3; McKay *et al.*, 1983: 16; Jahn, 1961: 187). Greek

Philosophers Thales, Pythagoras, Plato and Aristotle are believed to have journeyed to Northern Africa, notably Egypt, where they benefitted from the scientific and technical knowledge of this country (Onyewuenyi, 2006; Asante, 2000; George, 2009). For George (2009: 10, 24, 34, 91 100), Egyptians taught Pythagoras and other Greeks what mathematics they knew; and the Egyptian mystery system included geometry and arithmetic sciences of transcendental space and engineering, land surveying, astronomy and mensuration, and numeration logic. And when the Greeks subsequently colonized Egypt, they looted numerous books of learning. Centuries later, when Napoleon Bonaparte invaded Egypt, he took historians, astronomers, mathematicians, engineers, naturalists, artist and painters on his expedition, to study everything they encountered in Egypt, where they remained for two years (Reid, 1999: 129).

While some have considered precolonial peoples to have lacked scientific knowledge, there are records from different parts of the world that show advanced knowledge of science. Berlitz (1975: 164) for instance refers to the *Mahabharata,* the great Hindu epic considered by some to have been written as early as 1500 BCE, which deals with actions of gods and ancient peoples. It contains a wealth of details of a scientific nature with references to aircraft and rocket propulsions. It has verses devoted to flying machines called *vimanas* with details of their construction. In another ancient Indian text, the *Samarangana Sutradhara,* the advantages and disadvantages of different types of aircraft are discussed, including their capabilities of ascent, cruising speed, descent, descriptions of mercury as the fuel power source, recommendations regarding types of wood and light-heat absorbing metals suitable for aircraft construction. Berlitz (1975: 161) notes that though there are pictorial representations of aircraft on rock etchings found in ancient American cultures, most of the written or pictorial records of the ancient civilised nations were destroyed by the Spaniards during the conquest. Observations by Berlitz (1975) are similar to Ellert's (1984: 57) who argues that the precolonial Shona people were innovative and had developed mining, smelting, agriculture, textiles from wild cotton, the manufacture of *magudza* (blankets) and of *zvigidi* (guns), in addition to a democratic way of life and all these were destroyed by incoming colonists in efforts to stem competition from Africans. Yet colonial political and racist propaganda portrayed the Shona as helplessly primitive and needing protection and civilisation. Also similar to Berlitz (ibid.) Schmidt (2013) notes that immediately before the Independence of Zimbabwe in 1980, some records were destroyed by the colonial government.

Although certain scholars subsequently discredited some kinds of knowledge as based on mysticism – such as the Egyptian knowledge originating from the god Osiris who taught his subjects agriculture, architecture and other skills (Reid, 1999: 109) – others such as Crosson (2013) argued that Euro-modernity has not seen a retreat of spirits but has translated the dead into visible and audible presences through modern mediums. For Levin (1993), modernity under late capitalism has been noted, by thinkers like Benjamin, as dominated and haunted by dream images and commodified fetishes, visual processes that re-enchant the world. Thus, while it has long been keen to hide the sources of its knowledge, modern Western science has been shown to rely on knowledge inherited from societies and people all over the world. For instance Harding (1994: 3) has argued that many non-Western knowledge traditions were appropriated and fully integrated into modern science without acknowledgement of their sources. Examples include pre-Columbian principles of agricultural production, mathematical achievements of Indian and Arabic cultures; and the magnetic needle, the rudder, gunpowder and many other techniques discovered by the Chinese. In short, significant amounts of knowledge of local geographies, geologies, animals, plants classification schemes, medicines, pharmacologies, agriculture, navigational techniques and local cultures that informed European sciences were provided by traditions of non-Western peoples who are sadly not acknowledged as sources of such knowledge. This for Mengara (2001: 5) was meant to make the imperial process effective so the knowledge that Africans had of themselves and of their environments had to be obliterated. The various 'discoveries' of African peoples, including lands, mountains and rivers, were presented by the various explorers as happening for the first time, thanks to their unfaltering courage. The Africans who lived around these areas and who had names for all these paradoxically newly 'discovered' places were seen as insignificant presences whose knowledge of the existence of these things did not count. And despite the fact that the European explorers travelling across and throughout Africa used African informants who usually took them to these 'undiscovered' places, native knowledge was not considered valuable by Europeans.

As far as processes of knowing are concerned, it has been noted that some peoples have different ways of making sense of the world on the basis of odour, heat, audition and sight (Classen, 1993). For some, the senses are not limited to conventional physical perceptions but include the spiritual senses considered to constitute 'inward' senses. Still other scholars have sought to understand matters of knowledge not in terms of 'inward' spiritual senses but in terms of immortal souls or spirits considered to shuttle back and forth in their cosmic peregrinations and transformations (Conford, 1964; Frede, 1996; Nightingale, 2010).

While such views of the mind in terms of the peregrinating soul rather than merely of the physical features of the brain has been vogue in the history of knowledge (Snell, 1948; Yolton, 2000; Pargament, 2007), the mind has come to be understood merely in terms of functional features supported by the physicality of neurophysiological aspects. According to Bloom (1996: 96), Berger discovered during the 1920s that sleep is accompanied by the rise of electrical brain waves. But an understanding of the mind merely in terms of functional features neglects other dimensions of sensing and knowing. While eminent leaders in psychology took the root meaning of the word psychology from psyche (soul), psychology distinguished itself, with the rise of positivism in the early twentieth century, from theology and religion which were deemed to be impediments to the scientific search for enlightenment and rationality. But as is clear from the forms of violence that are perpetrated using Euro-modern institutions (Maldonado-Torres, 2008; McLean, 2004), Euro-modern rationality has an underside that may not have been adequately attended to given the reverence paid to the Euro-enlightenment.

But even as the Euro-modernist epistemologies defined away the soul in the quest for positivism, thereby narrowing down the cosmological resources that could be drawn from to survive, they paradoxically continued to engage with some immaterial, invisible and incorporeal phenomena even in the sciences. Differently understood, such immaterial, invisible phenomena seem to share space with everyday representations of how things are connected in the world. While in everyday life the wind, differently understood in terms of meteorology and in 'spiritual' terms (Low and Hsu, 2008; Kuriyama, 2002; Ingold, 2006; Zysk, 2008), is deemed to connect things in the world, 19th Century Western science conceived the invisible ether, believed to pervade the universe and to be of significance in orthodox physics, chemistry, biology as well as theology (Mackenzie, 1998). The ether, deemed to be composed of particles that move in particular ways so as to produce the forces found in the phenomena of electricity and magnetism, predicted in the 1880s the existence and means of producing radio waves (Dear, 2006: 3), which later facilitated the kind of long-distance communication that is central in this chapter. So while in the sciences, the universe is conceived as constituted by tiny waves (Thompson, 2009) and electrical energy as a 'universal fluid' that permeates and connects all forms of animate and inanimate things (Stolow, 2009: 89), the ways in which they connect and differ need attention in the interest of forging decolonial epistemologies (Turnbull, 2000; Verran, 2013).

Connections and differences between the modes of engagement have been understood differently, with some scholars like Gelfand (1956: 43) arguing that the Shona people in Zimbabwe took dreams much more seriously than Europeans did. According to him, if dreams were frightening for the Shona, they were taken as warnings that the dreamer should seek the advice of a healer; and the inference made was that the ancestors were warning of imminent danger. Yet according to Campbell (2008: 26) René Descartes' scientific discoveries were also based on his dreams on 10 November 1619. At the time, Descartes felt himself at the edge of a theoretical breakthrough to a new science. One of his dreams was of a whirlwind with thunder and sparks; he then dreamt of two books, one a compilation of poems and the other a dictionary representing all the sciences gathered together. A stranger appeared in his dreams and recited a poem beginning with the words *Est et Non*, which Descartes recognized as composed by the Roman poet Ausonius. His interpretation of this dream was that the dictionary represented the sciences, and the book of poetry represented revelation and inspiration, or the union of philosophy and wisdom. *Est et Non*, he decided, corresponded to the Pythagorean yes and no, or truth and falsehood, in human knowledge. He attributed these dreams to the spirit of truth that had decided to open for him the treasures of all the sciences.

In dreams, the air is deemed to attach and detach from the body as Colson (2006: 49) observes among the Tonga, where during life the *muuya* may leave the body and travel about. This is thought to explain dream experiences; and in sleep one also receives visits from other kinds of spirits. For Freud (1999) what mattered in the relay of information was not 'deities' such as ancestors but the "neural" or "mental energy" which circulated in a system in contact with the external world through the self or ego imagined as an organisation of "neurones" constantly charged with "energy" and able to receive or inhibit stimuli from outside. It can also be noted that while notions of *mweya/mhepo* are dismissed in psychology, the psychological notion of stream of consciousness also presupposes circulation or movement. Although more contemporary scholars like Ingold (2007) have argued that the wind makes us hear by transmitting sound waves, they have not adequately attended to the connections between different modes of engagement such as between those deemed secular and the sacred. The ways in which the secular and the sacred connect and separate are explicated by scholars such as Deleuze who argued for instance that as in the case of the mystic, cinema can become a 'spiritual' tool capable of facilitating an experience of ecstatic subjectivation in which spectators experience cinema as an optical, sound situation, a voice or a vision and a scattering of time crystals that lead them beyond the boundaries of their static selves and into profound contact with the outside (Goddard, 2001).

Although this Deleuzean rendering of the cinema and mysticism offers ways in which to rethink the divide between the sacred and the secular, the inside and the outside, truth and falseness, virtuality and actuality, the realm of the virtual is presented differently in scholarship with some arguing that it is the universe itself that is a virtual reality (Whitworth, 2007). The significance of such virtualities herein is that they too facilitate communication at a distance and so foregrounding them helps in understanding ways in which the virtualities or the logics of different virtualities, in time and space, play out in everyday modes of resilience via communication at a distance. Deleuze for instance understands events as virtual, neither inside nor outside the world, but actualised in a state of affairs in the body and in the lived world without assuming identity with them but enjoying a secret and shadowy path that is either subtracted or added to any actualisation. Others have argued on the basis of naturalist theology that God can be said to be a 'metaphor' for the universe and to be virtual reality, as contrasted to physical sensible reality. They argue that God's presence is enhanced by suppression of disbelief in the same way that immersion in a computer graphic virtual environment is enhanced (Sheridan, 1998).

However these arguments do not auger well with cosmologies where God is deemed to have created the world *ex nihilo*. Besides, using the metaphor of virtual environments to understand God has the risk of mistranslating the African cosmologies where God is deemed to manifest as air/wind (Mbiti, 1970: 141, 142; James, 1957: 207; Setiloane, 1976). The Shona people understand God/*Mwari* as too great to be approached personally and even to be contained in a house: this Shona conceptualisation of God contrasts with scholars who presuppose that God is containable in netspace, in wires or technologies. Although science is understood to have progressively dispensed with God in its understanding of the world, it has designed ways albeit naturalistic by which to communicate and act at a distance, and such ways of acting at a distance are interpreted by some scholars in terms of the logics of gods. Ophir (1991: 18,

21) for instance argues that the person who can occupy invisible space, such as virtualities, can invade and control any space enclosed by and for others such that spatial demarcations have no hold over the person, so the person can act dangerously just like a god who can traverse any enclosed social space and meddle in human affairs and manipulate them according to his/her own will, seldom seen and if seen, usually disguised and rarely identified. In this sense electronic democracy that uses networked computers as a way of bypassing national media (Bryan *et al.*, 1998) is a method of acting at a distance and meddling like gods in other people's domains without being seen, as Ophir argues. For this reason other scholars have argued that posthumanist and poststructuralist ethics premised on technological capacitation is an ethics that avoids face to face contact with the other, it is therefore deemed to be an antihumanist ethics (Weinstone, 2004; Bryant, 2013).

Though virtualities [that like dreams enable communication at a distance] are considered to decentre the human by its imbrication in technical networks (Wolfe, 2010); Atwood's (2010) observation that human beings sometimes jam devices underscores the fact that human beings are far from being decentred. For scholars such as Dean (2004: 273) the extension in opportunity for communication that carries the postmodern economy and that restructure global relations into decentred and deterritorialised networks themselves justify imperial order. While the global virtualities facilitate such deterritorialisation, that is dissolution of the association of territory with land (Shapiro, 2004: 294), other scholars such as Baron (2005: 12) have argued that deterritorialisation, and associated processes, is the old practice of conquest and plunder repeated for the umpteenth time by the same old actors wearing new costumes and showing some technical innovations. Some have pointed out that such virtualities constitute anti-politics and can be used to bypass the nation-states where citizens are unhappy with state violent politics. Kaldor (2003: 56) for instance argues that the realm of anti-politics or the parallel *polis* is one where the individual would refuse collaboration with the state. Though it has been argued (Dean, 2004: 270) that such virtualities create rhizomatic, horizontal, deterritorialised and democratic images where an indeterminate and potentially unlimited number of interconnected nodes communicate with no central point of control, it has also been noted that the virtualities result in a pyramid with Euro-America at the top and the deterritorialised nations constituting the multitude beneath.

While Deleuze (Goddard, 2001) makes connections between the virtual and the actual, this view necessitates the recognition of types of multiplicities such as the actual states and the virtual events which presuppose questions about immanence and transcendence in the ways in which things are conceived in everyday life such as I studied in Buhera. If as is suggested in Deleuze, (Norris, 2010) and Bergson (2002), events including recollection have the character of arriving, passing from the virtual to the actual, then at least some forms of reality and truth [such as in Shona dreams noted in this book] instead of taking the form of correspondences and coherences of things also assume the character of arriving and congealing into actuality.

Though the arrival of virtual events is conventionally understood in terms of communication and information technology (Harper, 2002; Horst and Miller, 2006), bodies as mediums (Stolow, 2009) whether of events as recollections, dreams, divinations and prophecies can also be understood as sites where such arriving events condense, actualise and disperse. While this rendition of the body parallels the Deleuzean body without organs (BWO) which he understood as open and traversed by powerful non-organic vitality that destroys personal or self-identity beyond recognition (Poxon, 2001), [spirit] mediums have been noted as retaining their personal identities even though they also assume the identities of the ancestors 'possessing' them (Fontein, 2004; Lambek, 2009: 16). Even though mediums maintain openness of their bodies to the ancestors possessing them, they foreclose visitations by the wind/air (conventionally understood as spirits) of *mashavi* (spirits from strangers) and the *ngozi* (aggrieved dead that are thought to bring suffering on the living) (Gelfand, 1966; Zambezia, 2002; and Bourdillon 1976). Questioning openness, other scholars such as Mararike (2009: 28) have noted that foreign spiritual attachment figures that claim to be attachment figures to the Shona people are regarded as *midzimu yaka bereka ngozi* (spirits which came carrying behind them dangerous foreign spirits). Yet Pentecostals (Maxwell, 2006; Marshal, 2009) are also reported to adopt techniques to foreclose visitations by African ancestral figures, erroneously regarded as *mashavi* or foreign spirits, as well as by *ngozi,* and effects of witchcraft. On the other hand Crawford (1967: 83) argues that *mashavi* cult resembles that of the Pentecostal churches in some ways because both are cults of spirit possession. For Hugh (1934) cited in Bullock (1950: 121,137,158) possession by the *shave* appears to be no more than the genuine thrill of complete abandon to religious ecstasy, in other words the non-physical orgasm of psychic abandon or release. While it has been noted by Gelfand (1959: 121) that those possessed by *shave* may speak English, Afrikaans, Portuguese or any other foreign language, a *shave* is the restless spirit of foreigners who died in Zimbabwe and then settled on innocent unsuspecting victims. Psychologists like Jung (Moreno, 1970) consider such phenomena in terms of archetypes conceived as bringing to contemporary human beings the mind of ancestors, their modes of thinking, feeling and experiences of life. For Jung, more primitive deeper forces and structures of the archetypical psyche act like psychic magnets and pull the conscious mind into their orbits.

While the increase in *mashavi* possession has been noted at the inception of colonialism (Colson, 1971) this can be connected to struggles by colonists to open up the spiritual spaces of Africans that had historically been occupied and protected by their African ancestral figures. For instance Hansen (1995: 150) observes that Nyabingi religious group's opposition to colonial rule in Uganda caused colonial disillusionment and so there was a mass production of Christians that would provide an alternative to the Nyabingi. For Hansen, colonial officials deliberately employed missionaries and Christians to stem the tide of Nyabingi and the colonial officials echoed this by labelling the followers of African religion as 'traditionalist' or people without religion and so 'traditional' religion came to be held in low esteem. Equally among the Tswana, Setiloane (1976: 207) notes that Whites looked with suspicion on everything that had to do with dramatic revelation and so official Western colonial opinion hardened, 'for the people's own good', against African prophecy. For Mararike (2009: 30) such opening up and tampering with African spiritual faculties meant that Africans found themselves in a 'zone that had no network coverage': when they tried to communicate with ancestors the response was 'no network coverage or the number you have dialled is not available'; but those who introduced Christianity created new network zones with new numbers for those Shona people who wanted to be answered. Yet other scholars have noted that from 1966 the Roman Catholic and other Christian Churches have had burial ceremonies that emphasise communication with the spirits of the family's ancestors and in the ceremony there is explicit acknowledgement of the role of ancestors as mediators between the deceased and the Christian God (Daneel, 1987: 260).

Such perceptions, as noted above, of *mhepo/mweya* (wind/air) as differentiated in terms of meteorological air/wind, of ancestors (*midzimu*), of the aggrieved dead (*ngozi*) (Gelfand, 1956; Engelke, 2007; Werbner, 1995; Zambezia 2002; Muphree, 1969; Werbner 1991), and of heavenly *ngirozi*, underscore some differences and sameness in everyday modes of engagement. In the context of Buhera some villagers, like Samuel, commented thus: "*Vanhu vanodzora mudzimu asi mudzimu hauoneki, mudzimu mweya. Saka kana munhu afa anoenda kumadzitateguru, anoenda kumhepo*" (Villagers conduct ceremonies for ancestors so that they return to the living but the ancestors are invisible, the ancestors are air. So the dead go to their ancestors, they go to the wind). In other contexts comments noted included *musha wapinda mhepo* (a wind has got into a village) in reference to a quick spreading disease or problem (*Zambezia*, 2002) and in reference to a *ngozi* called *mhepo*, deemed to arrive in a village in the form of a whirlwind (Gelfand, 1956). In yet other contexts, the *mhepo* or *mweya* (Gelfand, 1956: 13) has been understood, entirely in a meteorological sense, as the air upon which 'man', animals, insects and plants depend. But Gelfand proceeds to state that among the Shona the term *mhepo/mweya* is closely bound up with *Mwari* because all living things depend on air. Such formulations, as well as his remark that *mhepo* or *mweya* is part of the 'tribal' spirits and every living being, given the continuous to-and-fro passage of air through the body, generalise the terms *mhepo/mweya* and lose the nuances including the ways in which the *mhepo/mweya* is differentiated in everyday life.

Despite noting the ways in which *mhepo/mweya* is deemed to connect things, Gelfand did not explore the implications of such connections on matters of time, space and on matters of knowing. If, as Low and Hsu (2008) argue, wind connects wilderness to the hearth, moving from beyond the body to within the body, from the dead to the living, from the quotidian to the divine, connecting people to people and people with the environment, then understanding things via the wind/air has implication for time and space. If the wind is understood to collapse space between things it can also offer tools to rethink ways in which multiple temporalities between the spaces and things get collapsed in ways that permit not only synchronisation or diachronisation but also moments when simultaneities of temporalities (Mbembe, 2001; Bergson, 2002) share the same space. Understanding *chivanhu* in term of the traditional or the past as some scholars do ignores the ways in which the cosmologies often bring different spaces, time and things into compositional unity (Devisch, 2001: 105; Farriss, 1987; Kapferer, 2006) and differences that defy the tyranny of evolutionary linearity of time. If, in Africa, spiritual realities are not limited by ordinary categories of time and space (Richards, 1990) then there is need to think beyond the rigid binaries of the 'modern' and the 'traditional' in ways that parallel the virtual modes of reality as explicated by scholars such as Whitworth (2007) and Bergson (2002).

Whitworth's argument that the universe is a virtual reality with the world being an information simulation running on a multi-dimensional space-time screen support results of quantum physics that each quantum choice divides the universe into parallel universes. This means that everything that can happen does happen somewhere in an inconceivable multi-verse of parallel universes. The results of modern physics experiments showing that time dilates, space curves, entities teleport and objects exist in many places at once also help to underscore, in this sense, the ways in which complexity exposes the tyranny of narrowing down life, including everyday life such as I studied, to time as mechanical linearity. Conceptualising things in the world as partially connected, if via the medium of the *mhepo/mweya*, makes it possible to conceive time as shared, allowing for simultaneities, for singularities as well as pluralities in the experiencing of time. But while Bergson understands such temporal complexities in terms of the unfolding of the universe, in everyday life in the villages I studied significance was often placed on the *mhepo/mweya* which, through rituals (see also Shoko, 2012; Farriss, 1987), could be manipulated by human beings. Unlike Euro-modern epistemologies that have for instance sought knowledge of the past by exhuming bodies and disinterring them from ancient graves, the epistemologies of *chivanhu* are partly premised on knowledge via *mweya/mhepo*. In this sense the cosmologies implicated are human centric (see also Kapferer, 2006; Devisch, 2001: 105; Burbridge, 1925) at least in the ways in which human beings mobilise other things via rituals.

Ruzivo, which is the Shona term that encompasses knowledge and wisdom, does not refer only to knowledge and wisdom via the *mhepo/mweya* as there are other ways of gaining knowledge (Mangena and Mukova, 2013). In *ruzivo*, there is also orature through which knowledge is shared and passed from one generation to the next (Hadebe 2001), and knowledge gained simply by being attentive to changes in the environment to predict weather patterns (Mararike, 1999; Mutasa, 2010). Ellert (1984: 72-4) and others have noted that Shona distance communication and information sharing also relied on *pembe*/whistles, *Hwamanda*/wind instruments/trumpets, *humbe/chigufe*/blowing into *matamba* shells by manipulating fingers over the stops, *mutoriro*/flutes from a piece of cane or hollow wood sealed at both ends, *kanyenge* or *kanyenje*/flutes of the aerophone class, *mikwati yenyere*/wind instruments and *chiporiwa*/mouth instruments. The Shona are also noted as having relied on a signal fire system to share information and knowledge (Beach, 1994). Experiential knowledge is underlined in *chivanhu* by the adage that *muzivi wenzira yeparuware ndiye mufambi wayo* (the knower of a path on a rock is one who has walked on it). There is also knowledge gained through schools and the mass media occasioning 'hybrid' realities that dictate the need to straddle the worlds of *chivanhu* and Euro-modern media as villagers often creatively draw on both to negotiate communication hurdles (see also Nyamnjoh, 2005). Though the different ways of sensing and knowing violence were important in their various respects, the thrust of this chapter is more on those that allowed for engagements at a distance without actually being involved or engaged in the scenes of violence.

The violence about which I write and which the villagers had to survive spanned more than a decade beginning in the late 1990s. By focusing on this period I do not mean that there was no violence prior to it, but simply that villagers, as will be indicated below, noted that it was with the formation of the opposition MDC party at this time that the ruling ZANU PF became as violent in the villages. But also at the beginning of the year 2000, the ZANU PF government-sponsored Constitutional Draft, meant *inter alia* to compulsorily acquire land from White farmers, lost the referendum vote. To account for this loss the government blamed White farmers who, it alleged, had ordered their farm workers to vote against it; it also blamed the opposition MDC as well as some civil society organizations alleged to have campaigned for the 'No' vote (Raftopoulos, 2009). In light of these developments the country descended into an abyss of violence and repression. To get a sense of the contours of the violence it is imperative to focus on it, however briefly.

Brief notes on violence and matters of knowledge

The magnitude of the violence that ensued was such that between July 2001 and August 2008 the Human Rights Forum reported 4,765 allegations of torture and 39,000 violations of human rights (Reeler *et al*., 2009). The violations included abductions, assaults, rape, murder and damage to as well as confiscation of property. In the majority of the cases of violation reported, the law enforcement agents did not act because of their alleged biases towards the ruling party. The law enforcement agencies were reported to be corrupt and biased towards the ruling ZANU PF (Reeler *et al*, 2009).

In suppressing dissent the government used colonial legislation such as the Law and Order Maintenance Act (LOMA) which was enacted by the colonial government keen to stem the liberation war uprisings in 1960. Weitzer (1984) has noted such continuities between the colonial and postcolonial apparatuses of repression including the LOMA and the Emergency Powers Act of the 1960. In colonial Zimbabwe of the 1960s there was also frequent use of notions of 'national interest' and 'state security' to suppress dissent: during this colonial era, Parliament delegated a wealth of its powers to the Executive and there was formal and informal censorship on the media coupled with virulent attacks on organizations with the potential to wreak havoc upon the official government line. The media in postcolonial Zimbabwe were controlled using legislation such as the Public Order and Security Act (POSA) and Access to Information and Protection of Privacy Act (AIPPA). Parallels, including the bombing of some media houses, also existed between the colonial and postcolonial periods (Thondhlana, 2011; Weinrich, 1981). The media houses were themselves polarised with the state media blaming private media for purveying Western ideologies and lies that dented the image of Zimbabwe. On the other hand the private media alleged that the state media were biased toward the ruling party and purveying its ideologies. In this polarised context it was not easy to distinguish truth from falsehoods.

Much in the same way that Pottier *et al.* (2010) argue that in situations of conflict there is often disinformation with statistics generated to support latent causes, the polarisation in Zimbabwe can be understood to have generated statistics that were often meant to generate moral panics, and even modern witch hunts. Though such mathematical and statistical processes are often understood as secular, other scholars, notably Pythagoreans have argued that numbers have been attributed with special powers that make them fit for magical conjurations and for astrological prognostications (Schimmel, 1993: 10). Others like Amutabi (2006) have likened those who generate frightening statistics to 'witchdoctors' and 'magicians' who prey on the vulnerabilities of their patients by diagnosing bizarre ailments designed to force them to seek treatment, as an alternative to death, even if the treatments do not ultimately cure the ailments. In *chivanhu*, these observations are supported by the adage that *avengwa anhuhwa* (he/she who is hated becomes smelly) which is similar to the English proverb "give a dog a bad name and then hang him".

During the fieldwork it was also stated by some informants that some villagers who wanted to be transported to Harvest House where victims were sheltered and fed in the capital city, burnt down their own huts so that they would be taken care of free of charge by their political party and by donors of their party. Thus, in a context of recurrent droughts and threats of starvation, some villagers burnt down their own huts, and accused members of other parties, so that they would attract the sympathy of their parties' donors. Furthermore, the fact that some citizens wore clothes similar to police uniforms complicated matters around allegations of police brutality including allegation that police confiscated villagers' radios. Similar to allegations of police confiscating radios, some villagers in fact pointed out that fellow villagers besieged by hunger waylaid their fellow villagers in order to rob them of their maize meal.

Narrating about the confiscation of villagers' radios, Pal noted during an interview on 6 June 2011 that he and his colleagues who were MDC members listened to rechargeable solar radios; but when violence reached its climax in 2008 these radios were confiscated by the police who patrolled the villages with the intention of apprehending the villagers who had such shortwave radios over which news about violence in the country was beamed every evening. Many radios were confiscated and those who possessed them were beaten up. Pal and his colleagues used to listen to Voice of America (VOA) Studio Seven on the radio every evening, aware that it was risky to do so. According to Pal, the police patrolled the villages even during the night on foot, on a bicycle or in a vehicle. This resembled complaints about what happened in the liberation war against colonialism where, as Lan (1987: 132-3) notes, some people complained that they were kept in keeps or concentration camps and their property such as radios, beds, chairs and maize were all destroyed; yet if one complained one was hit by the colonial authorities.

The confiscation of the radios and the controls placed on listening to radio stations such as the Voice of America (VOA) can be understood in the context of the government's efforts to 'localize' media content. The Access to Information and Protection of Privacy Act (AIPPA) had as one of its provisions the 'localization' of such media content. It may also be understood in the context of the government's efforts to control the influence of NGOs, some of which had donated the radios that were being used by villagers such as Pal. While there were complaints about lack of enforcement of the rule of law in Zimbabwe, Mattei and Nader (2008: 1) argue that law has a role in imperialism and colonialism: because the rule of law has a dark side, law has been used to justify, administer and sanction Western conquest and plunder, resulting in the massive global inequalities that we see today.

In the context of the violence and the government's repression of the media, some villagers relied on prophets and healers as well as on their own dreams to sense violence. Five different apostolic sects were located in the villages though there were also churches such as Roman Catholic and the Methodist that do not rely on prophecies. Four healers were also located among the villagers, offering their services to those who relied on them. Although some apostolic sects have been noted as averse to using the Bible in their services (Engelke, 2007), many sects in Buhera relied on prophecies as well as the Bible. Even the healers such as Noreen and the medium, both of whom attended the Roman Catholic Church, also relied on the Bible though back home they relied on divination. In spite of the antipathy displayed by members of Apostolic churches towards healers and mediums, the latter on their part asserted that they owed their allegiance to *Mwari*, whose voice they consulted at the Matopo Hills in the past (see also Ranger, 1999; Daneel, 1970; Gelfand, 1959; Bullock, 1950) and whose name has been translated by some mission societies as God (Bullock, 1927; 1950; Jeater, 2007).

Although understandings of *Mwari* have been contested, with some scholars referring to the voice at the Matopo Hills to be that of witchdoctors (Bullock, 1950), other scholars and even Bullock himself pointed out that *Mwari* was not understood as having anthropomorphic attributes (Bullock, 1950: 150). He noted for instance that *Mwari* was neither a fetish god bound by some stick or stone, nor a totem/fetish, nor yet an apotheosis of an ancient (Bullock, 1927). Still other scholars, as hinted in the previous chapter, have gone so far as to liken the mediums of principal *mhondoro* with the Archbishops and Bishops in Christian society (Gelfand, 1956: 17). Others noted ways in which the *Mwari* cult offered buffers at the national level against misrule by individual chiefs and kings whose powers were neutralised by the fear of supernatural punishment that the cult could invoke (Abraham, 1966: 38-39). Thus despite the elaborate indirect approach to *Mwari* through mediums and direct approach by the priests at the cave shrines (Muphree, 1969); *Mwari/Nyadenga* was considered to be in the *denga* (heaven) as is the Christians' God (Bullock, 1927; 1950). Thus, in her research among the Tonga people of Northern Zimbabwe, Colson (1971: 210) notes that they [the Tonga] argued that before Europeans came and outmoded the need for prophets, great prophets had been possessed, in the precolonial era, by wonderful powers, unlike the present crop of deceivers.

Attention to such metaphysical issues would have shown that far from being merely matters of tradition and locality, the cosmologies, at least in so far as they were premised on *mhepo/mweya* and the manifold connections it facilitated, spoke more of diversity and unity of things, space and time notwithstanding. The mobile phones upon which villagers partly relied have also been argued to constitute a striking conjunction of remote co-present communication (Cooper *et al.*, 2002: 281) and for this reason Campbell (2008: 21) argues that dreams including the logics of instantaneous knowledge have been realised again at the end of the modern period via new technologies of communication. The metaphysics in prophecies, dreams and divination speaks to logics of modes of virtuality by which connections are understood to be forged in everyday life despite distance and time. Instead of understanding democracy simply in terms of e-democracy or e-governance, there is need to incorporate everyday life modes of resilience since this will offer space to rethink the marginalisation of the poor. The poor as Englund (2006: 6, 9) argues are marginalised in the evocations of participation and empowerment; in the rhetoric of freedom and democracy they do not get opportunities to participate in defining what freedom, human rights and democracy mean in their contexts. For Englund, the starting points in defining democracy, freedom and human rights as abstract values has not been the actual concerns and aspirations of the people, their particular situations in life and experiences. Such modes of engagement as prophecies and divination among the villagers indicate different conceptualisations of politics.

Prophesy, dreaming and divination

Ways in which connections at a distance were deemed possible featured in matters of dreaming, divination and prophecy throughout the fieldwork. The matters relating to dreaming and prophecy came to the fore in April 2011. I had missed the annual church gathering for Pascal which was held in April 2011, being in Cape Town at the time, so I was keen to attend the Pentecost gathering scheduled for June 2011. This gathering was to span a period of five day from the 10th to the 14th so we had to prepare adequate food to cover the time. A bus was hired to take us to the district of Murewa (about 80 km from Harare). We arrived at about 9pm of the 9th of June and immediately unloaded our belongings and put them in the tents where we would be staying. We spent the entire five days singing, preaching and praying, breaking only to eat, bathe and fetch firewood. It was winter time in Zimbabwe so we had to keep the fire alight to keep us warm.

At about 2am of the last day of the gathering we felt rather tired and sleepy, and I had to struggle to stay awake in order to observe all the proceedings. The leader and founder of the church had earlier on noted that it would be on the last day of the gathering that some of the members were going to receive their gifts of the *mweya* for which they had gathered. I was requested by one of the leaders to preach so I summoned the remaining strength and courage I had to stand before the crowd. I welcomed the invitation, but then as I preached I could see with frustration many of the church members dozing. So I decided to make the sermon as brief as possible. After the preaching I receded to the fireplace and dozed off while other preachers took the stage. It was at about 4am that I was shaken to full wakefulness by the shrilling of some church members. They spoke in unintelligible language, moved about all at the same time in different directions around the place of the gathering. It was my first time to attend such an event and so I was most astonished. I shifted my position in order to sit close to one of the church members who appeared to know something about what was happening. He offered some interpretation of what was being said. Then he hinted that they were speaking the language of the Holy Spirit (*mweya*/air) and that they had received the *mweya* in their bodies for the first time. But in all this they seemed to be overpowered and to have lost control of themselves. The church founder just looked on as if nothing strange was happening. After the commotion was over he rose to the stage and handed over some earthen ware plates to mark the church members, who had by then returned to calm, as prophets.

In a context where villagers and other citizens were engaged in modes of resilience against extraordinary challenges, the events at the church gathering could be conventionally understood in term of psychiatric disturbances to their minds (see also Patel *et al.*, 1995; Jackson, 2005), particularly given the series of sleepless nights that we had spent. But then, if the events are interpreted this way the multiple modes of virtualities such as those anticipated by the church members throughout their gathering would appear marginal. In such cases where prophecies and dreams are understood to be coming from outside the mind there is need to focus not merely on the mind but rather on the interlinkages between the body and the outside in order to see the envisaged connections at least from the point of view of the congregants. If the events are considered in the context where, because of the government's drive towards localisation of the media content, some citizens erected satellite dishes in order to evade the localised media, then prophecy and dreaming can be understood as efforts to establish contact with the outside beyond static bodies and minds. The fasting and confessions that preceded the gathering can be interpreted in terms of the broader need, particularly of citizens in urban areas during the crisis period, to connect with others near/far, visible/invisible. This need led to purchasing satellite dishes even in times of acute cash shortages and hyperinflation, and despite the risk of reprisals from the government which often ordered the pulling down of these satellite dishes; it speaks to the broader efforts in the population to overcome loneliness and isolation from the world, to actively seek connection and information from the outside world.

But the world with which prophets sought to connect was not just the human world about which they prophesied but also what they understood as the heavenly world. Similarly, healers sought to connect with not just the human world but often the [underworld] of *njuzu* to which some healers such as Noreen above claimed they had been in order to acquire healing *ruzivo* (see also Gelfand, 1956; Burbridge, 1924; Bernard, 2003; 2007; McGregor, 2003; Mawere and Wilson, 1995). Conjured by such understandings of worlds is an image that is the direct opposite of conventional portrayals of villages as remote and isolated from the world. Though it was mainly prophets, healers and mediums rather than the rest of the villagers who were held to commune with the worlds, their modes of engagement with them suggest the presence of ontologies distinct from the colonial modernist ones. Whereas the colonial modernist epistemologies and ontologies privileged kinds of knowledge in the human world that could be accessed via the direct observation methods, *ruzivo* was gathered from multiple connected worlds. And whereas such direct observation-based epistemologies privileged the individual self as a knower, knowing at least via such *mhepo/mweya* among villagers was sometimes considered to be impersonal particularly in the churches where it was deemed to be from God.

Looked at from the point of view of the colonial modernist epistemologies that privilege ocularcentrism and the metaphysics of presence, the worlds envisaged by the prophets would appear little more than subjective assertions. However, if considered in the context of everyday life affected not only by distant places but also by invisible state institutions, it is easy to understand the everyday life logics of connections between the visible/invisible, near/far. The distant invisible state and global institutions understood to have been visiting violent events on the villages did not render themselves to the sense of sight in everyday life but they were considered to nevertheless have presence in the villages. In this sense the visible/invisible, near/far occupied the same spaces, necessitating ways of sensing and knowing that could not privilege direct physical sight.

I had an interview with a prophetess I will call Tra on 9 March 2011 at her homestead, located about ten kilometres away from the Harare-Murambinda highway. Tra bemoaned the troubles she had had from the year 1999 when her husband joined the opposition MDC party. Her husband, she alleged, was being hunted by members of the ruling ZANU PF on account of his membership in an opposition party. She noted that during the period of violence her *mweya/mhepo* (wind/air) showed (*kuonesa*) her problems even before they happened. Through her dreams, her wind/air, revealed wars in which her husband was involved. Each time such wars were revealed in her dreams she knew that trouble was impending and so she duly warned her husband, who would then take flight and seek refuge in the capital. When peace resumed in the village (indicated to her via dreams that did not portray wars), Tra informed him using her mobile phone. With joy Tra stated: "My wind/air always informed me when there was trouble. I had dreams about wars. The wind/air helped a lot. During the period of political violence, church members like us saw visions about the state of things in the country".

Tra's claim that she was given visions and dreams is interesting to note in the context of the violence. Interpreted in such a context, her obvious inclination to decentre herself from the modes of sensing and knowing underscores the apprehensions of villagers in claiming to and operating alternative sources of information in a situation where the government was averse to any media but those it controlled. Where the government confiscated sources of information such as radios, decentring herself and asserting that the visions and dreams originated from the *mweya/mhepo* may be understood as a device to forestall possible victimisation. In fact, within the churches of which services I participated, there were members addressed as *varoti* (dreamers) and *varatidzwi* (those who are rendered visions) who, with the assistance of prophets, shared their dreams and visions with the rest of the members. Prophets within the churches not only interpret the dreams but they also determine if the dreams are originating from *Mwari* or from demons that are deemed to relay dreams in mockery of church members. Sometimes the dreams are interpreted as *hopewo zvadzo* or mere dreams not originating from *mweya/mhepo* and therefore without prophetic meaning. If decentring of the self is understood in the context of similar findings in different African situations (see for instance Friedson, 1996; Reynolds, 1996) it may not be explicable simply in terms of the fears of reprisals in the context of the ongoing violence within the villages. Besides, if it was simply for fear of reprisals that Tra decentred herself by claiming that the dreams and visions were coming from another source, I would have expected her not to recentre herself during the interview that I subsequently had with her. For these reasons, the decentring of the self, even if at the moment of dreaming, can be understood in terms of connections, not only in everyday village life but also in relation to post enlightenment modernity, where technologies, be they physical or otherwise, are often deployed to connect things that may not necessarily be within sight.

In such a time of violence, the preoccupation among villagers was to endeavour to have *ruzivo* about oncoming events and find ways to evade the violence. Villagers could ill afford to wait for violent moments to actualise. For instance Tra noted that in the period immediately preceding the 2008 rerun of Presidential elections, her husband refused to take flight and seek refuge. She had warned him that party members were on their way to the homestead to look for and to assault him. But he reasoned that he had stayed away from home too much and had resolved to remain at home this time. Four days after he ignored the warning to flee, the assailants arrived at his homestead at around midnight. They were armed with guns, and because it was dark Tra did not manage to identify them. They knocked on the door with force. Before Tra and her husband could respond, the door was struck with more force and swung open:

I then felt like I was filled with '*mhepo/mweya*' and I started *kurira nendimi* [literary translated to sound with the tongue in reference to what is understood as the language of the air/wind] as I moved out of the house. I walked around the house and then headed for the forest. When I was in the middle of the forest which is at the foot of the mountain, I heard gunshots. The shots went thrice. I knelt down and prayed: I was filled with fear because I thought someone had been gunned down. After the prayer, I walked back home and on arrival I was informed by one young boy that the assailants had taken my husband with them. He informed me that they had taken him to Rusape Police Station on trumped-up allegations that he was causing violence in Buhera District.

Dreams and prophecies can thus be considered to offer modes of resilience; but Tra alleged that she and other prophets were sometimes harassed by party supporters on allegations that they were forewarning intended victims. Tra for instance noted that at one time she was summoned to a ZANU PF night political gathering called *pungwe* where she was harassed and ordered to provide a cow, which was slaughtered and consumed by supporters, on allegations that she was forewarning the intended victims.

But dreams also pertain to matters outside the realm of politics. I had dreams during the fieldwork, some of which referred to other people including church members. Sometimes I did not relay them partly because I considered them my own trivial experiences and partly because I was often too busy and forgot even to write them down. In one of my dreams I visited one of the church leaders but unfortunately when I arrived some men I did not know were busy unroofing his house and they had also ploughed his garden. In the dream I was unhappy about what the men had done and asked them why they had done so. They did not respond so I walked to a place nearby where I saw the church leader I had visited. He was lying down on a flat rock looking sickly. At a nearby homestead many people were gathered and my sense in the dream was that it was a funeral gathering. I watched them carry a coffin and proceed to a graveyard which I sensed in the dream was close to the church leader's home. I followed them to the graveyard for a while but all this time I was complaining and saying, "but these people should not have done what they were doing to the church leader". I woke up before reaching the graveyard but my sense was that it was close. About a month after the dream the church leader was taken critically ill. I paid him a visit and found him lying down barely able to rise and walk. He had missed two weeks of church services. I asked him why he had not sent a message to the church and he pointed out that he had sent his step-son to relay the message. Although I saw this young man at the recent church service, he had not said anything about his step-father's illness, keeping quiet for some reason about the illness.

Feeling bad that I had not reported this earlier dream as required in the church, to the rest of the church members and to the leader who was now ill, I phoned two prophets who arrived immediately to conduct prayers. I was censured for not reporting the dream, and reminded that the dreams were not mine to keep. With my participation in the churches my dreams had become clear and I was often surprised by how they often accurately portrayed the wakeful world.

Dreams provided the villagers with tools to make sense of their environment but they also underscored ways in which things were connected beyond the sense of ordinary sight. By treating wakeful and dream events similarly, villagers can be understood to shun the radical distinction that is often assumed to exist between them. But they can also be understood to shun radical distinctions between day and night events that are emphasised in ocularcentric epistemologies. Even though some dreams were considered to have hidden and elusive meanings, day time as well as wakeful events were also often elusive in the context of the violence. This made elusiveness an insufficient ground upon which to dismiss dreams. Perpetrators of violence for instance often visited their victims wearing masks and in the cover of the darkness of the nights, also rendering their identities elusive.

In light of their elusiveness, dreams can be understood in terms of the broader events of everyday village life. The news for instance about the interparty negotiations and the possible abatement of suffering with a political settlement arrived in the villages as exciting and promising events even though the political settlement did not subsequently actualise as an abatement of suffering among villagers. Equally, news about the National Healing Programme that was instituted by the unity government just after its inception arrived in the villages as good news, but because only a few participated the events did not actualise in everyday village life. Similarly in a broader African context where promises of development and betterment of life have not materialised, they can be understood in terms of dreams that have failed to actualise or virtualities without actualisation. In this sense, events in everyday wakeful life are not always radically distinguishable from dream time events, some of which actualised while others failed to materialise. Understanding matters of sensing and knowing in terms of the wind characterised village life; but it may also be a metaphorical reference to events that are yet to actualise in the context of the ambiguities and prevarications in life.

Such references to the ambiguities and prevarication in life in terms of the wind are made for instance with respect to individuals who are unpredictable. Statements such as '*ane mamhepo*' (he/she has winds) are often made in reference to individuals who prevaricate including in ways deemed harmful to others. But such statements are also made in reference to individuals deemed to be afflicted by bad winds/*mhepo dzakaipa* which are considered to explain their prevarications. For this reason the *mhepo* that enter and connect with the body are controlled via rituals such as exorcism and appeasement in the churches and by healers (see also Reynolds, 1996; Schmidt, 1995; and Dube, 2011). Because winds are often associated with such prevarications, I noticed that within the churches the terms *mweya* (air) is preferred when referring to stable and nonviolent flows.

The salience of connections between things in such cosmologies has led to their different interpretations. While Kapferer (2006) has argued that the 'cosmologies' involve processes whereby events, objects and practices are brought into compositional unity in which they are conceived as existing together and in mutual relations has some support, his other arguments are contested. His view that witchcraft and sorcery constitute the 'metacosmologies' (ways of patterning or bringing together acts, events or practices that may normally be expected to exist in different or separate cosmological frames) (see also Devisch, 2001: 105) is amenable to definitional contestations of witchcraft and sorcery. Though others have used the term witch in the context of Zimbabwe, some have argued that the Shona had no vernacular words for witchcraft, sorcery, magic and magicians as used in Europe (see for instance Gelfand, 1967). Others like Burbridge (1925) have argued that 'witchdoctors' tap psychic energy in certain natural objects which they annex to their drugs and persons. For him, the *n'anga* (erroneously understood as witchdoctor) originally meant one who was able to manipulate the occult forces for the good of human beings. Still for other Zimbabwean scholars like Chavunduka (1980: 132), *muroyi/umthakathi* (conventionally translated as witch/sorcerer) included people who poisoned others, those who failed to carry out necessary rituals for their dead relatives, people who committed antisocial acts or trouble makers, arsonists, deviants, eccentrics and incest committers (see also Hallen, 2006: 202).

Among the villagers in Buhera where healers and mediums for instance considered their ancestors as immortal, alive albeit in different forms and interacting with the living (see also Colson, 1971; McGregor 2003), Chavunduka may well be right to include failure to perform rituals as an aspect of witchcraft by the living. But as Bullock (1927) observes, witches could have no *mudzimu*, and also unmarried youths and wizards could have no *mudzimu*, and so no funeral obsequies were performed for members of these groups if they died. It is important to note here that though churches separate *Mwari* and *vadzimu*, *Mwari* has historically been concerned with the welfare and honour of the ancestral spirits and so those who consulted *Mwari*'s shrine at Matopo hills were admonished to maintain the rituals due to ancestors (Muphree, 1969: 49-50). But Lan (1987: 170) also states that during the liberation war, individuals with malice, who did not cooperate with the liberation fighters, individuals who were politically untrustworthy, treacherous, who acted against the interests of the peasants as a whole or anyone who opposed the altruistic and benevolent *mhondoro* and their protégés, the 'guerrillas', for selfishly individualistic purposes, were placed in the category of those that the ancestors opposed, i.e. that of the witch. Equally, in the 1890s the Ndebele in south western Zimbabwe referred to Rochefort Maguire [one of the three members of the Cecil Rhodes' party who tricked King Lobengula to sign the concession which was the basis of the subsequent colonisation] as an *umtagati* (wizard/witch). The Ndebele reputed Maguire as *umtagati* with the story that he was wont to ride about at night on a hyena, making him a wizard (Kane, 1954: 40-1). Apparent in this is the fact that witchcraft and sorcery apply as much to the occult as to those that trick and colonise others deviating in the process from the ways of the ancestors including *chivanhu*. Thus, if witches and sorcerers are celebrated, as some scholars do, merely for bringing things into assemblages, the question, with respect to colonialism as witchcraft is, whether colonists must be celebrated for bringing colonies into assemblages with (neo-)colonial imperial centres that have ushered in violence, dispossession and exploitation to Africans?

But beyond analysing witchcraft in terms of either failure to perform rituals or in terms of performing rituals that brings things from different cosmological frames together, it is necessary to look more closely at its metaphysical implications in relation to violence and survival.

The significance of performing rituals including for purposes of gaining *ruzivo* from ancestors was underscored by Godobori, whom I interviewed on 6 August 2011. In his words,

In the Gombe the booster has collapsed again which means that the medium did not perform the rituals well because he only wanted money from the Econet. Money is what has caused a lot of problems, *hama* no longer have harmonious relations due to money. There is intense competition within families and also *hama* do not want their family members to become rich, they paradoxically tolerate it when outsiders become rich or are rich in their eyes. Churches also cause divisions within families since because of the influence of churches, members can no longer perform *chivanhu* rituals together. In my case, I say that Jesus of Nazareth is for the Europeans, I have doubts about him though I have no doubts about *Mwari*, the Creator of human beings (*musikavanhu*) because we [meaning Black inhabitants of Zimbabwe] have always known Him. *Musikavanhu takagara tichimuziva* (we have always known the Creator of human beings). *Vatema havasivo vakarovera* Jesus *saka vane mhosva yeyi uye vanopinda papi munyaya iyi, havasi kuchekereswa vasina kutadza here apa? Ini ndinomboti vakaparidza vachishora chivanhu ndinodzoka kumba kwangu ndoti handichadi kudzokera ku*Church *iyo iri pedyo ne*door *rakatarisa kuno. Vamwe ma*Bishop *vanouya pano vachida kusimbisirwa zvinhu zvavo ndoti vatange vagadzira chivanhu, vonogadzira nekubika doro vozokumbira kusunungurwa ku*Church *kwavo (*The Black people are not the ones who killed Jesus so what crime did they commit and why are they included in the story of the killing of Jesus, are they not being sacrificed for the crime that they did not commit in this case? Sometimes I feel like returning home in the middle of church services when preachers begin to vilify *chivanhu*. I feel like I do not have to continue attending the church services in that church of which door is facing this direction. Some Bishops consult me wanting to be fortified, I tell them to go and perform *chivanhu* including brewing beer and after performing *chivanhu*, they go back to their churches and confess so that *vanosunungurwa* (they are released from association with *chivanhu*).

*Vamwe vanopiwa hope nemidzimu. Kushopera kwakafanana nehope. Hope dzinokunda kushopera chete dzimwe hope dzinouya dzakahwanda. Vamwe vanhu vanotsipika hope vaona kuti munhu uyu anoona. Kana watsipikirwa hope unotoenda wogeza nekunwa mvura yemuti wesunungura vadzimu. Mabira emudzimu kuti utaure panouya n'anga nemasvikiro votamba vochohwera vachiti 'iwe haugoni' voita kuti mudzimu uite shungu wobuda wotaura. Iye zvino masabhuku ave kungoita mikwerera pasina masvikiro pamwe kusvora kana kusada kutongwa. Zviyo zvinounganidzwa zvopiwa mukadzi wasabhuku zvimwe anenge achiyamwisa, sadza rave kubikirwa kumba kwake roendeswa pamuchakata, zviyo zvave kunyikwa muma*dish. *Tinofara kuti tine vanotitsigira vemuma*University *nokuti kwatiri kuenda kwakaoma nekusaziva.*

Pamabira vana babamunini vangu vaitotiza nokuti vaive nezvavaive nazvo. Vakazofa vachitambura. Mudzimu kurwadza unenge wakatsipikwa, pakasoswa wopinda zvekumanikidzira. Umwe unenge uine zvinotevera kana wosvika vanhu vaya vakauvhara vanozoti atenga mudzimu, atorera umwe. Mudzimu hausiye munhu nyangwe akaenda kuchurch.

*Vema*church *vanoti chivanhu hakuna asi kana munhu afa ndipo patinosangana nokuti rukao runotemwa newedzinza kwete mufundisi. Panenge munhu ofa vanoti ave kurotomoka apo anenge ave kuona vedzinza rake, vedzinza rake ndivo vanomutambira* (Some villagers are given dreams by their ancestors. Divining is like dreaming. Dreams are better than divining, only that some dreams are vague. Some envious people can block (*kutsipika*) other people's dreams when they realise that, for instance their intended victim is seeing too much during the dreaming. When your dreams have been blocked you have to drink and bath using water and an herb called *sunungura vadzimu* (release the ancestors). At the *biras* that are conducted so that *midzimu* can talk, *n'anga* and mediums have to attend, they sing, dance and joke with the *mudzimu* claiming that the particular *mudzimu* cannot talk. This is meant to motivate the *mudzimu* to begin talking. Nowadays village heads cannot conduct ceremonies well. This is probably because they do not want mediums to assume power over them. I am happy that there are people like you who are in university and come to support us; the direction we are heading to because of ignorance is not good at all. My uncle never attended *biras* in our family because he had *zvikwambo* that he wanted to hide and about which he was apprehensive that if he attended the *bira* they would be revealed by *vadzimu*. But the *zvikwambo* eventually killed him in a very miserable way. When the *mudzimu* manifest in its host with a lot of troubles on the host, it is because some living human beings will have blocked, or denied voice, (*kutsipikwa*) or the opening for the *mudzimu* to visit the host with comfort. Other *midzimu* may manifest with a lot of troubles on the host because there will be witches who will be blocking its entrance to the family or to its descendants. The *mudzimu* does not abandon its medium even if one becomes a church member.)

Church members do not agree that *chivanhu* exists but then when one of their members dies that is when we meet with the church members because the preburial ritual of *rukau* (to mark the grave site using a hoe) is always done by a member of one's family and not by the pastor or some other church member. When a person is dying they say that he/she has insanity when he/she begins to talk about things that they do not understand. In fact the dying individual will be seeing and communicating with his/her forefathers. It is one's forefathers who receive the dying individual into *Nyikadzimu*.

While Godobori's statement might be interpreted, if read on the surface, in terms of Deleuze's instantiation of the order of Antichrist (Poxon, 2001), he is not necessarily Antichrist but simply prefers to deal with *Mwari* that he and other Black Zimbabweans have always known, as mediated by the *mhondoro*. As indicated elsewhere in this book, an order of Antichrist that instantiates an inclusive body permeated by non-organic vitalities is not supported in *chivanhu* where even healers and mediums select the forces that possess them and where they also insist on ritual purity in which forces that are ritually impure are excluded. It is in fact colonists that promoted ritual uncleanliness among Africans by dissuading Africans from performing their cleansing rituals. Thus, I would argue here that the impurities that afflict Africans are a result not necessarily of Africans' faults but of the colonists that sought to hybridise Africans with impurities [from colonists' own nonorganic vitalities] by dissuading their cleansing rituals, which were meant for purity.

This interview with Godobori underscored the significance of retaining *ruzivo* about rituals in *chivanhu,* yet some rituals associated with witchcraft were understood to bring a lot of suffering for villagers. Bearing in mind, as noted above, the fact that witchcraft is not only about the use of concoctions against others but also about the perpetration of various forms of mischief including colonisation, cheating, exploiting, dispossessing and perpetrating violence against others, a look at issues of witchcraft would reveal the challenges faced by villagers with respect to the witches.

Knowledge and witchcraft-related violence

Matters relating to witchcraft were raised when, as part of my efforts to create connections in the village during my preliminary fieldwork in 2010, I was visiting an old man who had the same totem as I. My chat with him was cut short when he informed me that there was going to be a church service in his house that morning. After the usual greetings, we moved with the church members into the hut where the church service was to be conducted. It was one of those moments during fieldwork when an event offers itself for the taking, so I decided immediately to join the church members in the prayer without knowing what was in store. Towards the end of the service the prophet pointed at me and prophesied that I would experience acute pain in my feet at some point. According to the prophet, some *varoyi* [ordinarily understood as witches] who were envious of me had gathered soil from my footprints, mixed it with herbs, needles and other substances. In ways that suggested that the *varoyi* had the capability to activate the environment to harm me, the prophets intimated that they had placed the concoctions under cover on one path on which they knew I would walk.

I did not seek the prophet's assistance after the service because I considered his utterances somewhat trivial since I did not experience anything amiss with respect to my health at that time. I merely took note of his utterance and also informed my supervisors about it. Similar warnings were issued to me by the *svikiro* medium, healers and different prophets whom I subsequently met throughout the fieldwork. It was only in December 2011 that I started feeling acute pain in my feet. The pain moved all the way up my legs and to my head. It was so acute that at some point I could not walk and I felt that the top of my head was slowly becoming very hot. I felt weak and some thickness in my head as if it was inflated. Sometimes I felt soft wafts of wind blowing only over my head even as I was sleeping. The illness persisted into my year of writing up and forced me to prolong the fieldwork, during which I consulted the prophets to learn more about the illness and how from their point of view it could be resolved.

I could have fallen ill because of the stress that attended studying violence, but what surprised me was that prophets, healers and mediums foretold the illness a year and a half before it struck me. Among the villagers, time is conceived in terms of the conventional linear trajectory with the future. For instance, underscoring *chivanhu* mathematics and calculus, the future is conceived in terms of *makore mashanu anotevera* (in the next five years), *makore zana anotevera* (in the next hundred years), *makore mazana mapfumbamwe anotevera* (in the next nine hundred years) *makore chiuru anotevera* (in the next one thousand years) or *zviuru zvipfumbamwe* (nine thousand years) and so on. Equally the past is conceived for instance in terms of *makore mashanu apfuura* (the past five years), *makore chiuru apfuura* (the last one thousand years) and so on. These specific perceptions of time are contrary to erroneous views that there was no science, mathematics, or any ideas of linear time in such epistemologies as *chivanhu* in Africa. But time among the villagers, as indicated by their attention to the environment in predicting weather patterns, was also gauged on the basis of changes in other elements of the environment. The changes in the foliation of plants and in the behaviour of animals and birds provided ways in which time could be read even as the villagers also relied on the conventional clocks. The prophets, healers and mediums such as those who forewarned me also relied on the *mhepo/mweya* in their vocations. The primacy of the *mhepo/mweya* in this sense was underscored by the medium who, when I interviewed her in connection with rain petitioning ceremonies, asked whether those who regarded her vocation as merely traditional knew when the *mweya* that is in them was born: "*ivo vanoti zvatinoita tichikumbira mvura ndizvakare vanoziva here kuti mweya uri mavari wakazvarwa riini?*" (Do those who say what we do is traditional and belongs to the past know when the air that is in them was born?).

This comment raised by the medium indicated that villagers did not only rely on what has been understood as oecological time in reference to time measured in terms of the cycles of seasons, the plant and animal behaviours, yearly cycles all of which would render notions of time simply cyclical on the basis of the rhythms. Time is also understood in terms of *mweya/mhepo* that in terms of back and forth movements complicates the conventional ideas of time As there are phrases in Shona such as *kudyiwa nenguva/mwaka/* to be overtaken by time, there are also notions of time in a linear sense as they are in a cyclical sense. Taking into cognisance these connections via the *mhepo/mweya*, the body can be conceived as one and several, singular and plural, uniting yet also differentiating perceptions of time. This appears to explain ways in which healers, mediums and prophets could bring different events lying in different temporal and spatial domains into the kind of simultaneities that characterised the forewarnings about my illness.

Suggested in the above is the existence of other senses in addition to the physical senses of contiguous space and time. Such senses may be understood to be activated by the singing and dancing that often precede the healing and prophetic sessions. Noreen for instance remarked: "*madzimudzangara taive nawowo, waiti ukaridza ngoma waiona zvimwe zvinhu uyevanhu. Rudzi nerudzi rune mapiriro arwo nzira haingaiti imwechete. Varungu vamwe vaitevedzera chivanhu pakutanga, kana Rhodes aitokumbira pavaiisa mireza pasingaiti vosiya*" (We had the likes of television sets and radios. When we beat drums we saw some spiritual manifestations. People have different ways of engagement, the way can't be singular. Some Europeans initially followed the ways of the inhabitants, even Rhodes requested places to erect flags, and where it was not permitted they did not erect them).

Noreen may well have been referring to instances such as in the early periods of contact where European traders made requests for land to set up stations and *feiras* (markets) which were granted after discussions amongst the Africans and libation ceremonies to protect traders at the *feiras* (see for instance Bhila, 1982; Burbridge 1923). Inferable from Noreen's remark are ways in which *chivanhu* was often mobilised in matters that could be characterised as 'modern' thereby collapsing the temporal binaries between the past and the present. Within the villages for instance, I was greeted with stories about the ceremonies conducted over the previous two years by the Econet Wireless Company, which sought the aid of the medium and the chief to erect a booster on the Gombe Mountain, regarded as sacred. Many other stories about different mountains were recounted, but it is important to note the way in which different epistemologies and ontologies with different metaphysical commitments were brought into unity in spite of their differences. Rituals, as ways of bringing together different realities, temporalities and spaces could explain the absence of radical distinctions between different modes of engagement (see also Nyamnjoh, 2012) in Africa. But they also explain the characterisation of some as simply 'traditional' and or 'local', highlighting points of difference yet ignoring moments of unity.

In a postcolonial state understood as visiting forms of violence that replicated those of colonial times, the radical distinction between the new and the old can hardly be sustained. Similarly, where the exigencies of Euro-American democracy required sacrifices that replicated the sacrifices attributed to the so called traditional societies, the radical distinction between the new and the old is not always sustainable. Such manifestations of democracy sacrifice not only individual Africans who suffer at the hands of (neo)liberalisation and the attendant structural violence; they also sacrifice African cultures and socio-political institutions that are destroyed in the name of Euro-American liberalisation. In a situation where education requires immense sacrifices it can hardly be distinguished from the sacrifices of that which is conventionally regarded as old and past. What changes, so to speak, are not necessarily the games but the pitches and the balls in the epistemic and ontological engagements.

While my illness could be explained in terms of witchcraft as well as in terms of the stress from the violence that I studied, it also resembled a rheumatic state which Gelfand (1985: 32, 36) likened to *chipotswa*. In *chipotswa* Gelfand noted that the witch plants poison on a victim's path so that when he/she steps on it or comes into contact with it, it enters the body within which it circulates to other parts. Whichever way the illness is looked at, it signifies that bodies are receptive and permeable even to that which may be harmful to life; and among the villagers steps were taken to restore the bodies to their normal states. But efforts to get cured constitute resistance to the flows that Ingold (2006; 2007) writes about: people select what could be received by their bodies. Although all forms of knowledge have their forms of rationality and ways of establishing objectivity (Turnbull, 2001) the risks in studying witchcraft make it difficult to work with disparate knowledge systems to create a shared knowledge space in which equivalences and connections between the rationalities can be constructed.

As a mode of prehension, of reaching into each other or grasping, witchcraft (*uroyi*) was deemed among the villagers as destructive not only of lives of individuals but also of the connections among them. The witch hunts and ordeals administered to suspected witches (Reynolds, 1996; Gelfand, 1967) as well as the exorcism rituals and protective devices to which the villagers resorted underscore the general antipathy to witchcraft. They also underscore the fact that witchcraft has never been an accepted or inherent part of *chivanhu* as intimated by some scholars who characterise African modes of engagement with the occult as merely another form of witchcraft. The prosecutions of witches through the Zimbabwean Criminal Law (Codification and Reform) Act of 2004 wherein witches were deemed to have been unduly protected by colonial legislation (Chavunduka, 1980; Simmons, 2012) officially underscore such aversions to witchcraft. But by relying on healers to render evidence in witchcraft prosecutions (Geschiere, 1997; Geschiere and Fisiy 1994) the latter also underlines ways in which different epistemologies and ontologies have been brought together in the litigations against witchcraft and sorcery. Such official recognition of healers' knowledge in the postcolonial courts necessitates a close look at ways in which the kinds of knowledge that escaped the radar screen of colonial modernity play out in the postcolonial context. *Ruzivo*, the vernacular kind of knowledge, is one such type, some features of which eluded Euro-modernist epistemologies.

Ruzivo and resilience

Some of the ways in which *ruzivo* is acquired in *chivanhu* were underscored in the following experiences. One of these involved an interview with a villager named Hoko, born in 1924. During the interview on 1 July 2010, he said,

> "*Vadzimu vanonzi mhepo nekuti vakaita semhepo havaoneki*" (ancestors are called *mhepo* because they are like wind: they cannot be seen). They can possess *mhondoro* lions. *Mhondoro* may not be seen but villagers will see its hooves. "*Vadzimu vanobuda pavanhuzve. Kana vanhu vasvikirwa zvinoreva kuti mhondoro iri pedyo. Vanorima nechisi vanoona mhondoro inovachisidzira.*" (The *midzimu* also manifest in human beings also.

When people have been reached by the *mhondoro* it means that the *mhondoro* is close to the human beings. Those who work in the fields during *chisi* days can see the *mhondoro* and that frightens them away). Other villagers who work on *chisi* day can see *chapungu* (bateleur eagle) that signifies *midzimu* and it frightens them if they work during *chisi*. He said villagers take *rapoko* to places such as under *michakata* trees and they clap their hands and inform *midzimu* thus, "*tinokumbira mvura nyika yaoma tisvitsireiwo kuna Mwari*" (we request for rain because the country is now dry, may you forward our request to *Mwari*). They use the *rapoko* to brew beer for *mukwerera* but now other villagers are young children who do not know what to do. Europeans wanted *kupingudza vanhu* (to change the ways of life of the inhabitants) that is why they altered our *chivanhu*. They did not want *vanhu* to compete for money with European institutions (*zvechirungu*). "*Vakuru vaiziva chivanhu vainzi nevarungu havazivi saka vakadzvanyirira ruzivo rwechivanhu. Varungu vakaramba chivanhu vasingachizivi vasati vapinda mazviri kana machiri, vaiti midzimu ma*demon *zvisizvo.*" (Our elders who knew *chivanhu* were labelled as ignorant and this suppressed *chivanhu* ways of knowing. Europeans could not accept the validity of *chivanhu* yet they did not know it and had not entered the lives of the bearers sufficiently to know *chivanhu*; they labelled *vadzimu* as demons yet this is not correct). Now it no longer rains much because "*vanhu vave kubata bata nekuda mari. Mwari nevadzimu vaisada mishonga yakaipa. Kubva kare vaida vanhu vakachena misha yakachena uye nzvimbo dzakachena. Vanhu vave kunamata zvikwambo senyoka dzinorutsa mari saka havachaoni kukosha kwemikwerera. Kunze kwekubatana nevamwe mumikwerera vave kunotsvaga zvikwambo zvinovaunzira mari yavanoshandisa kutenga chikafu kunze kwenyika panguva yenzara saka vanoti mukwerera haishandi. Vanhu vaikumbira chekudya pasi pemichakata vachipiwa. Mikwerera yaiitwa nevanhu vemisha, misha yaive nevedzinza rumwe chete. N'anga dzemazuvano dzinonyepa chadzinoda imari chete.*" (Some villagers rely on *mushonga* concoctions, which are harmful to others, because they want money. *Mwari* and *vadzimu* have never wanted anything to do with such harmful concoctions that people rely on especially these days. They have always insisted on the cleanliness of people, of homesteads and other places. But these days some villagers are no longer as clean because they rely on their *zvikwambo*, for instance those who rely on snakes that they use to steal money from others, so they no longer consider the relevance of *mukwerera*. Instead of joining others in *mukwerera* they now look for *zvikwambo* that give them money which they then use to import food in periods of drought so they allege that *mukwerera* does not work).

These views underscore the ways in which the ancestors, instead of being heroic for African descendants, have unfortunately come to be associated instead with 'demons' and with evil, often merely because they are no longer alive. But on the other hand the dead in the Western sense continue to be regarded as saints, as heroes or, if they have written books and articles, their voices continue to be heard in the shrines of universities, where the word 'libraries' has effectively replaced the conventional notion of shrine. In Africa, where the shrines of ancestors used to be places of resort to acquire *ruzivo* so that descendants would know their grandmothers, as in the vernacular saying *kuziva mbuya huudzwa*, the marginalisation of such African archiving results in the loss of one's origins and history, creating in the process people who do not know their grandmothers, so to speak. The resort in such cases will then be to colonial epistemologies, rather than to archives of *chivanhu*, that have historically promised more than they have delivered particularly in terms of alleviating the plight of the poor and guaranteeing employment in the modern sector in the light of shrinking industries and deindustrialisation.

As part of *ruzivo*, in the processes of *mukwerera* on which I dwelt in the previous chapter, villagers were expected to remember the ways in which rituals were done. Hoko noted for instance:

> *Pfungwa dzinofanira kubata nekuchengetedza zvinhu. Ikozvino vobikira doro remukwerera mumba zvisingabvumirwi. Ikozvino vobikisa vazvere zvisingabvumurwi, kana kubikisa pfambi kana asina kuwanikwa. Ikozvino voreverera vakamira, kana vari pazvituru vakapfeka bhutsu. Vanhu vanofanira kurova makuva, kuremekedza midzimu nevakuru. Zvese izvi zvinofanira kuchengetwa mupfungwa. Pfungwa dzakafanana nema*book *dzinochengetedza ruzivo.*" (The mind should grasp and retain issues. Nowadays villagers brew the beer for *mukwerera* in the houses, not under *muchakata* trees

as required, but then this is not allowed. Nowadays the villagers ask breastfeeding mothers to brew the beer for *mukwerera,* but this is not allowed in *chivanhu*; they also ask prostitutes in the village to brew the beer for *mukwerera,* but this is not allowed. Nowadays they inform the ancestors about *mukwerera* while they stand on their feet, sit on stools or wear their shoes, but this is also not allowed in *chivanhu*. Villagers should conduct ceremonies to ensure that the dead do not remain in the bush but join others in the *Nyikadzimu*; villagers should respect *midzimu* and other elders. All these things should be retained in the mind. The mind is like a book because it also retains knowledge).

Hoko proceeded to indicate how mediums and *mhondoro* used to teach villagers. He explained that at *banya* [special huts made for rituals, excluding *mukwerera,* associated with the *mhondoro*] villagers were taught, by the *mhondoro* speaking through the medium, how to retain knowledge so that rituals could continue and so that villagers could learn to carry on the ritual processes. Churches are disturbing *chivanhu* because the church members allege that *midzimu* are demons, but the latter are not demons: they are holy spirits. The *midzimu* are still alive. For the teachings in the *banya,* elderly women and men and all those who are married attend. The *svikiro* mediums teach villagers in the *banya.* Villagers are reminded how to perform which rituals at what time. They are told to preserve *dambo*/wet areas and to protect them from cattle. Villagers who are deemed impure for various reasons including prostitution, incest and infanticide are admonished in the *banya.* It always rained when the ceremonies were performed. Often it would rain on the same day even if initially there were no clouds. During the *mukwerera* the villagers were often told by the *mhondoro* to hurry back home before the rain started falling. There is need for more villagers to perform the ceremonies so that the rain can be more widespread.

As a popular epistemology, *ruzivo* does not invariably radically distinguish between visible/invisible, near/far. In this ways the violence that is occasioned by visible/invisible, near/far including institutions and witchcraft can be understood as not radically distinguishable. The dreams, divination and prophecies, in so far as they are deemed to bridge space and time, can be read as popular technologies to collapse time and space in ways that resemble the effects of communication technologies and other modes of virtualities. Although the information society is often presented as having been created by technology and individual entrepreneurs immersed in innovating (see for instance Burnett *et al.* 2009), dreams among the villagers (see also Reynolds, 1996; Gelfand, 1956, Okazaki 2003; Krog *et al.*, 2009) can also been considered as 'alternative' everyday mediums of communication. In the light of rationalist Euro-Enlightenment philosophies that displaced the spirit world to the realm of psychology, dreams may have been understood as hallucinatory thoughts; but with the development of virtual modes of communication, enabling communication with the near/far, visible/invisible, modes of rationality premised on a metaphysics of presence have been attenuated.

Though healers, mediums and prophets have privilege in the modes of engagement, some villagers like Tito, whom I met at a beer hall when I attended an NGO food distributing session, doubted the *ruzivo* that healers, mediums and prophets claimed to have. Tito asserted that healers, prophets and mediums are liars. Giving an example of his own consultation of a healer two years back in connection with his mother's funeral ceremonies, he indicated that he had been lied to when the healer incorrectly stated the purpose of Tito's visit.

In *ruzivo*, knowledge is acquired in many ways: by observing things, by physical movement in the environment, in the form of experiential knowledge as underscored in the statement *chakachenjedza ndechakatanga* (experiences of the past inform the present and future), by the movement of the *mweya/mhepo* [conventionally understood as soul/spirit] as well as, in terms of the vernacular idiom '*kuziva mbuya huudzwa*' mentioned above, through being taught or told. In *chivanhu* there is insistence on *kuva nenjere/kuve neungwaru* (to have intelligence), *kuve nepfungwa* (to have a working mind), *kuve nemunyati* (to be witty/clever) and there is the notion of *uropi* (physical brain) as seen for instance in animals slaughtered. There are also notions of *unyanzvi* and *umhizha* which refer to skills and expertise in for instance smithing, making hoes, baskets and axes. By physically moving in the environment villagers acquired *ruzivo* about plants, fruits, animals, the weather and soils. And, as implied in the rituals that healers, mediums, prophets and church members underwent the *mweya* also had to be freed to move beyond the bounds of the body. This significance of linkages between movement and knowing is increasingly gaining attention in scholarship but it is hardly considered in much of the scholarship that focuses on bodily movements in times of violence. In *ruzivo*, to know one is sometimes also to know the invisible that accompany the presence of the visible one. As indicated by the ways in which healers, mediums and prophets treated my presence during the fieldwork, sensing the physically present is deemed to tell barely half of the story about one. I was moving in and out of their lives but they paid attention to invisible things including the illness that they foresaw. The significance of the freedom of *mweya* to circulate was indicated by some of the prophets who explained my inability to even dream about my oncoming illness in terms of the need for prayers which involved bathing using milk and water from waterfalls to free my *mweya* and enhance my dreams.

Rituals and prayers can thus be understood as ways of releasing one for circulation, not only in the physical sense as in wayfaring (Ingold, 2007), but also in the *mhepo/mweya* sense. The phrase often used in apostolic churches to refer to such release, *kusunungura mweya* (to release or unbind the air/soul) is similarly used to refer to releasing bodies from bondage. This suggests multiple ways of circulating knowledge, some via physical movement in the environment and others via the *mweya*. It also suggests different ways of moving and assembling knowledge in the world with some doing so through rituals, art, ceremonies, while others do so through writing, building and other techniques (Turnbull, 2001). But more importantly, it suggests lack of prioritisation of the kind of stasis that is often used to define epistemologies that differ from the formal Euro-modernist ones. But in *chivanhu* there are also injunctions against openness, particularly via adages such as *usafukure hapwa pane vanhu* (do not expose your armpits to other people), similar to the English injunction against washing one's dirty linen in public, *usashaye hana* (you should have a heart that keeps secrets), *chiri mumoyo chirimuninga* (what is in the heart is in a cave), *usavhiyire chidembo pane vanhu* (do not skin a polecate where there are other people), *chakafukidza dzimba matenga* (houses are covered by roofs).

This chapter has shown African modes of resilience premised on *chivanhu* and ways in which they play out with other knowledge heritages. Ways in which *chivanhu* separates and connects with other knowledge heritages have been discussed. Scholars such as Kroker (2004), citing Heidegger, argue that technology is the new language of revelation entailing the liquidation of subjectivity and signifying the territory of the 'posthuman' where bodies and minds are mobilised. This chapter, on the other hand, has argued with some support for pluriversality in which what matters is not only technology in the Euro-modern sense.

Along with decolonial scholarship such as Escobar (2002: 8, 11, 12) and Mignolo (2007), the chapter has argued for border thinking that engages epistemology with a view to surfacing other epistemologies and the coloniality of Western epistemology from the perspective of the epistemic forces that have been turned into subaltern. In tandem with decolonial scholarship that views decoloniality as a means of working towards a vision of human life that is not dependent upon or structured by the forced imposition of one ideal of society over those that differ, this chapter has surfaced ways in which modes of resilience in *chivanhu* offer spaces for alternative democracy and modes of political being by bringing other epistemologies to the fore. While technology is important in modes of resilience, the modes of resilience in *chivanhu* do not presuppose the kind of 'posthumanism' advocated by other scholars (Bryant, 2012; Viveiros de Castro, 2013; Halberstam and Livingston, 1995; Clarke, 2003). In this regard, in *chivanhu* there is no shifting of attention away from human beings to animality or to technology since attention is rather focused on *vanhu/bantu* that are deemed to be different from *zvinhu* (things). Similarly, contrary to Halberstam and Livingston's (1995) postmodern contaminated bodies and Deleuzean 'bodies without organs' (Poxon, 2001), bodies in African metaphysics such as *chivanhu*, even if they function as receptacles for ancestors, are not conceived as fractured beyond recognition and beyond the identity of the self. In fact care is always taken to ensure one is not overtaken by forces around: this accounts for the African modes of resilience discussed here. In the context of *chivanhu*, posthumanism as presented by other scholars as a shift of attention away from humanity would not speak to decoloniality of Africans who have suffered violence, colonial and postcolonial. While posthumanism, encompassing virtual technologies, would presuppose the bypassing of the African states as the overarching goals of communication at a distance, evidence from the history of Africa and from *chivanhu* modes of resilience indicates that African states and the modes of communication at a distance coexisted and enriched each other. For this reason it was only with the colonial state that what some scholars have called 'talking drums' or 'drum language' to convey messages over great distances in short spaces of time (Rattray, 1969) were considered by colonial authorities as aversive, because these methods were also used by Africans to evade taxes by alerting others to flee from the colonial taxman (Carrington, 1949). Such African modes of knowing, communication and resilience were opposed by colonial governments not because they were irrational but because they provided means of escape from the strictures of colonial oppression.

The fact that the African modes of engagement were labelled as secret societies (Bourdillon, 1990) even as colonists set up their own schools, colleges and universities to which they did not admit Africans, means that colonial damnations were only meant to facilitate replacement of African institutions with colonial institutions. Equally, while knowledge emanating from *chivanhu* has been interpreted by others in terms of the occult, other scholars like Posselt (1935) and Ellert (1984) have noted practices by European archaeologists that would be interpreted in *chivanhu* as occult and infringing taboos. The digging up of graves and the looting of corpses have been relied upon by European archaeologists as ways of knowing the African past; yet touching and looting the dead is taboo in *chivanhu*. These observations call for questioning the application of labels such as 'occult' to African ways of knowing and the categorisation of some African ways of knowing as [unnecessary] 'superstition', while conversely, European ways of knowing are characterised as [essential] 'scepticism'. The use of technologies and the reliance on connections in *chivanhu* does not entail posthumanism, as in fact to say of another human being *hausi munhu/haasi munhu* (he/she is not a human being/person) is a serious insult that could result in serious violence. Thus, it is imperative in thinking through violence and peace to consider matters of ethics that will be dwelt on in the next chapter.

Chapter Three

Ethics Beyond Bodies?
Ukama, Violence and Resilience

The procession walked up the mountain. At the top, groups of members of other churches had also camped for days. When our group reached the top of the mountain, we all knelt down to pray before a huge cross made of stones. I was informed that it had been erected by the founder of the church. After the prayers, we proceeded to a spot where we lit fires to keep warm overnight. Two of the prophets walked around the mountain looking for a cave in which members of our group would pray. It had been agreed while at the church premises that everyone would go into the cave at three in the morning so that they could pray and be sanctified in the cave. There was singing and praying by the fireside until three o'clock in the morning. The procession of church members then went into the cave. The two prophets entered first so that they could help everyone pray. It was very difficult to see in the dark where to sit down or even find standing space. It reminded me of the dark cave at the Chinhoyi tourist resort in Zimbabwe where I had gone earlier and where inhabitants of the district had found sanctuary from raids during the pre-colonial periods. Men and women in the group held one another's hands as they fumbled their way deep into the cave. After the prayers we all crawled out in a procession. Just after sunset, the prophets recommended that we get into another cave not far from the first one. Again, every member was expected to enter the cave. From the mountain we went to a waterfall where everyone in our group was prayed for and bathed using the water at the base of the waterfall. Groups of members from different churches were again present and busy conducting their own prayers at the same waterfall.

Trips to such places as the mountains for purposes of supplication to God appear not to be new in Zimbabwe, where scholars have noted such visits for instance to the Matopo Hills where inhabitants made pilgrimages to consult the voice of *Mwari*

(God) in times of difficulty such as hunger and droughts, as well as succession conflicts (Ranger, 1999; Daneel, 1970; Gelfand, 1956; Bullock, 1927; 1950). Although the literature on Zimbabwe does not adequately grapple with the questions, scholars elsewhere in the world have interpreted such places and features in a number of ways using the lenses of immanence where for instance some cosmologies (that presume immanence of God) presuppose that in matter there is immanent power explaining the univocity of Being in all things (Pearson, 2001; Albert, 2001; Smith, 2001). These views premised as they are on immanence unfortunately presume pantheism and polygenesis that do not exist in Zimbabwe. Thus, in Africa, Parrinder (1967: 18) has noted that God, the Supreme Being, is considered the greatest power of all, the strong one who possesses life and strength in himself and from which every creaturely force is derived. For Parrinder, few if any African peoples have been without belief in the Supreme Creator; and even where that belief has been influenced by Islam or Christianity, the original idea may still be traced to pre-colonial Africa. Parrinder notes that a Supreme God is named in the earliest dictionary of a Bantu language compiled in pre-colonial 1650, and in Bosman's description of West Africa published in 1705. And Manuel de Faria e Sousa (Abraham, 1966: 37) wrote in 1674, well before the Zimbabwean colonial era, that the people subject to Mutapa acknowledged only one God, adding that they called upon the royal *muzimo*s in the same way as Europeans did the saints.

Further, scholarship premised on the assumption that God is immanent in all things is challenged by scholars who argue that in other societies the whole of materiality is thought *not* to be overruled by spiritual authority, such that doctrines of animatism and animism are not justified since there are many things in the environment that are merely objects (Stanner, 2005: 95). Some West African scholars have also argued that Africans do not consider every object to have its own soul; rather, they believe that spirits inhabit or attach themselves to some objects while retaining their own freedom to move (Opoku (1978: 3, 10). So for Opoku some of these spirits are associated with certain features of the environment such as trees, rivers, mountains, rocks, but such palpable objects are not, as some scholars think, the 'gods' themselves. The palpable objects are "only dwelling places of the 'deities', for the 'deities' are essentially 'spirits' and have unlimited mobility, able to come and go at will".

Similar contentions have been aired by Hornung (1983) who noted that Egyptian gods may be encountered in liminal spaces where the worlds of the humans and the worlds of the gods come into contact. The individual animals are not gods: the god only temporarily takes his abode in them, making them his vessels. For Hornung (1983) gods were not restricted to a single place or aspect of nature as they could move about freely. Also, writing about the Tonga people in Zimbabwe, Colson (2006: 48-49) observes that the term *muuya* (air/spirits of humans) is more specific, carrying the implication of breath and movement; neither plants nor natural features are thought to have *muuya*, though spirits of ancestors are thought to be associated with some places which serve as their natural shrines. So Tonga people, appealing for rain at deep pools, springs or rock faces said to be sites of spiritual power, direct their appeal to ancestral spirits because neither plants nor pools nor rock faces had *muuya*. For Bullock (1927) the Shona people do not practice animism since they do not consider the rivers, mountains and pools themselves to be animate.

While scholars such as Viveiros de Castro (2013) argue for the need to abandon the anthropocentric perspective for a posthumanism that involves turning away from the human in the sense of turning towards animals, others like Gelfand (1970) have argued that a person with *hunhu* [which animals do not have] shows respect for the stranger *munhu* (human being), thinks rationally and in a responsible way, and can control his passions, instincts and desires. The Shona people differentiate between human being and animal because an animal does not possess *hunhu*. For this reason, *ukama* and other humanely connections are a function not of animism but of *hunhu* as explicated in *chivanhu*. It is on the basis of *hunhu* that early European travellers to Africa were treated with hospitality by Africans. Jahn (1961: 117, 192) notes for instance that the reports of the first Europeans to come to Africa agree that they were received everywhere with friendliness and good will. For

Parrinder (1967: 123), kindness and hospitality are part of ordinary African people, and travellers like David Livingstone journeyed practically unarmed across the entire continent. When Mungo Park 'discovered' the upper Niger he was alone and a stranger in Western Sudan, and it was an old woman who had pity on the stranger, took him in and fed him like a child. Jahn argues that the European discoverers were received with friendliness, yet the Europeans repaid the friendship badly because they subsequently enslaved the Africans.

In pre-colonial and early colonial Zimbabwe a number of scholars have also mentioned the same kind of hospitality. Kane (1954: 40) pointed out that when Charles Rudd and his two companions left the capital of Matabeleland on an exploration mission on behalf of Cecil Rhodes, they took with them a written document, known as the Rudd Concession, wherein King Lobengula granted them exclusive mining rights in Matabeleland, Mashonaland and other adjoining territories. The explorers nearly died of thirst when traveling through the Kalahari wastes and Rudd, thinking that his days were numbered, buried the valuables including the Concession. They subsequently chanced upon a party of 'natives' camping for the night, who gave them water, thereby saving both their lives and the Rudd Concession. Also, Samkange (1973, 34) cites Ranger who states shown that the Mashona people in fact welcomed the 1890 European invaders, believing that their stay was temporary. Ranger notes that it had never occurred to them that their land could be taken away from them by strangers. According to Hromnik (1980), Lobengula had a tolerant attitude towards outsiders, a typical attitude of the Bantu in general. For Posselt (1935: 111, 150, 183) when the Portuguese missionary João Dos Santos was residing at Sofala in Mozambique in about 1587, he noted that King Monomotapa of the time, who also bore the title of *mambo*, was well disposed towards the Portuguese. Posselt writes that Mzilikazi, father of Lobengula and founder of the Matabele kingdom, also received visiting missionaries in a friendly manner, allowing them to reside at his residence, treating them kindly and giving them land for their missionary activities. So for Posselt, hospitality has always been a shining virtue of the Bantu, and is readily extended to visitors in addition to members of the family or clan. The stranger, provided he did not belong to a hostile community, will always receive shelter and food. As Palmer (1977) notes, Kings and chiefs knew their borders, but Europeans were often confused about them. Palmer (1977) cites Ranger's (1967: 274-5) quotation of Rhodes' apprehensions about the dangers of ignoring borders thus: "I saw at once the danger of our position if a series of articles appeared in the papers from a man of Selous' position claiming that Mashonaland was independent of Lobengula...I gave him personally 2000 (British) pounds out of my own private fund....I consider I did the right thing with Selous." In this case Cecil John Rhodes sought to paint a wrong picture about [the otherwise cordial] relations among Africans in Zimbabwe. Selous [the precolonial traveller to what is now Zimbabwe] had witnessed these cordial relations among the Ndebele and the Shona [both of whom observed ethics and etiquettes of *hunhu*] but Rhodes paid him so that he would lie that relations between the two were acrimonious. Thus, Palmer proceeds to state (citing F C Selous, 1893, Travel and Adventure in South-East Africa, London) that after this, Selous went on to write extravagantly about the devastating effects of Ndebele raids on the Shona and about the consequent depopulation of the country.

Thus, while in other parts of the world the inhabitants have been noted to practice 'nature based religion' which focuses on immanence of the sacred and presumes that God is right here in the natural world – in the rocks, trees, mountains, animals, human beings (Klassen, 2003) – some Zimbabwean scholars have noted that 'spirits' such as ancestors do not habitually live in human beings or other features of the landscape, but come occasionally for some purpose (Hugo, 1925). Others have noted the existence of a hierarchy of mediums and *mhondoros* facilitating an elaborate indirect approach to *Mwari/Musikavanhu/Wekumusorosoro* who is deemed to be in Heaven (Muphree, 1968; Abraham, 1966). Although Black inhabitants of Zimbabwe were noted as pilgrimaging to the Matopo Hills to seek *Mwari*'s advice, scholars have underscored that *Mwari* is "not a fetish God bound by some stick or stone but often passes like a shooting star over the breath of the land, manifesting his presence by a divine fire" (Bullock, 1927; 1950). For Bullock, Black inhabitants of Zimbabwe had the idea of *denga*/heavens just like Europeans did and they also understood *Mwari* as *Nyadenga* (owner of the heavens). While for some scholars, plants and animals have 'spirits' which can take a variety of shapes manifesting themselves as different kinds of beings (Descola, 1996: 158), scholars have noted that it is 'spirits' of the deceased humans that stay in the bush and other places such as rivers until homecoming rituals have been performed (Fontein, 2010; Colson, 1971; MacGregor, 2003) so that the spirit of the deceased joins the ancestral world called *Nyikadzimu*.

These variations among scholars underline differences in metaphysical and ontological commitments among groups of people in the world. As Brown (2001: 5) argues, though beings in the world tend to index a certain limit or liminality, and to hover over the threshold between the nameable and the unnameable, the figurable and the unfigurable, the identifiable and the unidentifiable, the trips to mountains were nameable and even 'spirits' in everyday life were, as will be argued, nameable and identifiable. And in *chivanhu*, a *chinhu* (thing) is not by definition liminal or ambiguous, as assumed in Brown (2001) as well as in Coole and Frost (2010), but it denotes something that can be distinguished from *munhu*/human being (Jahn, 1961). In *chivanhu*, God and spirits do not transform into landforms, animals or trees as is assumed to be the case in eighteenth century European deism that Evensky (2005) writes about. *Chivanhu* shares some aspects with Ingold's (2010: 4, 5) observation that a focus on life processes requires us to attend not to materiality as such but to the fluxes and flows of materials; however, in the metaphysics of *chivanhu* fluxes and flows are often controlled as will be indicated in this chapter with reference to certain spiritual forces considered harmful. As underscored by his argument that the inhabited world is not composed of objects but of things, and that life is generative capacity of that encompassing field of relationships within which forms arise and are held in place, Ingold writes within a relational ontological rendition.

However, relational ontologies have not been found unproblematic in scholarship as a number of concerns have been raised about them. Some scholars have argued that we need to know what relations are in order to decide what we mean by the phrase 'relational ontology' (Wildman, 2006). Many kinds of relations have been noted and so the importance of identifying what relations one will be writing about has been underlined. Relations can be logical, emotional, physical, axiological, mechanical, technological, cultural, moral, sexual, aesthetic, physical, imaginary, and theological, and so there is a need to specify the kinds of relations one writes about and the values that attach to them. Scholars have also questioned relational ontologies on the premise that if, as in relational ontologies, relations are regarded as ontologically primary, and the substantive entities derivative, it is necessary to specify what kinds of relations are ontologically primary. It has been argued that we also need to know if relations are not mere attributions made by human beings, even if the relations may not be in real existence. While relational ontology presupposes that relations are ontologically more fundamental than the substantive entities themselves, substantivist ontologies, on the other hand, hold that substantive entities are primary and relations are derivative (Paul, 2013; Wildman, 2006). Although it has been noted that relational ontology holds that objects have no internal constituent structure and no essence or own being, but agglomerations of relations (Paul (2013); Wildman (2006), studies of the experience of violence and pain underscore the experience of pain as essentially internal and subjectivist such that they validate substantivist ontologies rather than relational ones.

Notwithstanding these critiques, life has been shown to be underpinned by different ways of connecting with others. Some scholars have stressed blood and affinal relationships within families (Mararike, 1999; Gelfand, 1981), but others have underlined rituals that explain connections beyond kinship groups and among many different kinship groups as well as across territorial ties (Turner, 1968; White, 1994; Chatters et al., 1994). Other scholars have noted ways in which connections are forged via exchanges between different groups (Levi-Strauss, 1970; Keane, 1994; Chigodora, 1997). Still others have underlined connections via state organisations which welded together different groups of people (Ranger, 1966). Others still have noted ways in which the colonial experience emphasised biological kinship in many parts of Africa even where kinship extended beyond blood ties (Chanock, 1982 cited in White, 1994). The resulting narrow and arbitrary colonial 'tribalisation' and 'ethnicisation' [with erroneous implications noted by Lentz, 1995 of heathenism, barbarianism and lack of civilisation] of identities presupposed more closed autonomous societies even where, as in Africa realities, there were often interlocking, overlapping, multiple and alternative collective identities defined by mobility, overlapping networks, multiple group membership and flexible context-dependent drawing of boundaries (Lentz, 1995; Ranger, 2010; 1984).

Belying colonial labels of rigid 'tribal' and ethnic' identities in Africa, the *Mwari/Mwali* cult at the Matopo Hills in Zimbabwe has been noted as having extended even beyond the Ndebele and Rozvi states, and beyond the colonial state (Werbner, 1977 cited in Ranger, 1979). The *Mwari/Mwali* cult had influence from Botswana's eastern border district across the south of Zimbabwe and into Mozambique and the South African Transvaal, with Venda, Ndebele, Kalanga, Karanga, Kharutse, Ndau supplicants (Werbner, 1989; MacGonagle, 2007). Although the *mhondoro* were noted by some as 'tribal', other scholars have indicated that the *mhondoro* were ranked and the highest *mhondoro* had influence beyond the 'tribal' confines acting in communion and consulting together on appropriate occasions as the *mhondoro* did (Muphree, 1969; Abraham, 1966; Garbett, 1966). While the 'intertribal' networks of *mhondoro* relationships were broken down with the creation of reserves which reduced mobility and eliminated the necessity of 'intertribal' alliances (Muphree, 1969: 45), the fact that the *mhondoro* were considered to be *mweya/mhepo* (Gelfand, 1956) presupposes mobility on their part.

As in other places where wind has different ways of being known, as meteorological or natural phenomenon, as breath, as spirit or deities (Low and Hsu, 2008: 3) the wind/air in Zimbabwe is variously conceived in terms of 'spirits' and in terms of the meteorological senses (for the various conceptualisations of *mweya/mhepo* see for instance (Engelke, 2007; Kramer, 1993;

Werbner, 1991; Muphree, 1969; Gelfand, 1966; 1985). The fact that wind is understood to connect wilderness to hearth, to move from beyond the body to within the body, from the dead to the living, from the quotidian to the divine, connecting people to people, people to environment, near and far (Low and Hsu, 2008), underscores the logics of cosmologies and metaphysics underpinning some modes of engagement in *ukama*.

In Zimbabwe, where children were taught to address a whole range of persons as *baba* (father), grandfather (*sekuru*), *amai* (mother), *ambuya* (grandmother) (Pearce 1990), modes of relating could not have been limited to blood or affinal ties. Though the predominant mode of relating was conceived in terms of blood and affinal family relationships (Mararike 1999: 156, Gelfand 1981) not only the circulation of blood among the members was important but also the circulation of other things such as resources defined the contours of *ukama*. In villages where totems are commonly used in greetings, where family members stay in small groups in the households, where villagers have rules of succession and inheritance based on ancestry, the observations by Mararike (1999) and by Gelfand (1981) have validity. But disruptions in the environment deemed to result from conflicts between human beings (Vuifhuizen, 1997; Fontein, 2010; Ranger, 2003) portend broader connections and circulations among different things. From the point of view of "implicate-order-metaphysics" (see Wildman, 2010: 66; 2006) where a wave-like entity is thought to link objects behind the scenes in ways not registered by ordinary experience until it emerges as "explicate-order of consciousness", some scholars suggest that *mhepo/mweya* (wind/air) is considered to connect different things as it moves to and fro (Gelfand, 1956: 13). In this way it is possible to rethink the Shona *ukama* not only in terms of blood and affinal ties (Mararike, 1999; Gelfand, 1981) but also in terms of an ethical outlook that suggests that human beings are "interdependent with all that exists" (Murove, 1999). For Mararike (2009: 22, 28) *ukama* is a relationship in which members of the family or group are expected to share with one another and find peace through the love of all. *Ukama* does not end when one dies, so each *mhuri* looks up to *midzimu* as attachment. Each person owes his or her *hunhu* to *mudzimu*. *Ukama* is blood and spiritual relationship. Mararike notes further that no outsider is converted into *ukama*, no insider can be deregistered from this *ukama*. Therefore all objects and entities of the natural order are not divided from one another but are so united in a bond that each participates in the other, making it what it is not and enabling the same entity to be simultaneously in many places.

The breadth and the openness of *ukama* and of the relationality implied in Levy-Bruhl's rendition as noted above differ in that Levy-Bruhl conceptualises very broad relationality/ connections while Mararike's explication of *ukama* is narrower. Both the narrower and the broader versions appear to be explicable partly in terms of material circumstances in that while on the one hand some would want to define connections narrowly in order to protect resources, others might equally want to define connections broadly in order to access and expropriate resources from others on the pretences of *ukama*. A recent book by Francis Nyamnjoh (2015) on cul-de-sac Ubuntuism graphically shows how Ubuntu and other related African logics are used to exploit others; including how Westerners who paradoxically benefited from African hospitality for centuries are now sadly shipping African migrants back to the continent and denying many Africans entry into Euro-American territories.

Therefore ethics and hospitality to the other need not translate to folly with one's resources as indeed in *chivanhu* it is stated; "*chawawana idya nehama mutorwa anehanganwa*" (eat what you get with your relative, a stranger will easily forget the generosity you offer them). Thus, in Zimbabwe, Manungo (2014: 289, 292, 293) notes that the war cry during the liberation struggle was *ivhu redu ngaridzoke kuvanhu varidzi varo* (the soil must be returned to its owners) and the salutation was hello *mwana wevhu* (son of the soil). Underscoring the salience of guarding against loss of ownership of resources in spite of connection in the world, Manungo proceeds to state that the Shona say *nyika ino ndeye madzitateguru edu* (the land belongs to our forefathers). Similarly, Mangena (2014: 83) states that the Shona point out that *rukuhute ruri muivhu re*Zimbabwe (the umbilical cord is in the soil of Zimbabwe), so we are sons and daughters of the soil. On the other hand Weaver (2006: 134) observes that since resource exploitation figured centrally in all colonial empires recognition of native property rights was universally eroded by colonists. Underlining how colonists related with Africans, Bredekamp and Newton-King (1984: 3, 4, 5, 11) observe that the European travellers to Africa held that if the Khoisan were to become useful servants they had first to be broken in, like newly captured slaves, and weaned of inappropriate aspirations towards independence and territorial possession: for this reason mediators among the peninsulars were sought and acquired, but their collaboration with the Europeans who expropriated land and cattle from the mediators' kin earned them disapprobation. Underscored here is the issue of the extent to which human beings can be open to connections with the others without risking exploitation, dispossession, colonisation and abuse in the emergent networks of relationships.

Though others have celebrated secular ethics and civic engagements often premised on metaphysics of presence (Davetian, 2009; Curry, 2006) others have pointed out that it is when rites and fears of the invisible are lax that the individual is tempted to break the law and to become a problem (Gelfand, 1956; Bourdillon, 1976: 234; Marongwe, 2005: 197, 219). While some have argued for a posthuman and poststructuralist ethics as sensitive to openness and difference, holding equally to those who are distant and near, to things other than human (Popke, 2003; Waelbers *et al.*, 2013; Weinstone, 2004; Garner, 1997; Bryant, 2012) others have noted different ethical and civic engagements. Parekh's (1995) and Weaver's (2006) work for example suggest that openness does not guarantee ethics and decoloniality since Early European portrayals about African and other colonial territories as open territory, (informed by John Locke's and Stuart Mill's ideas) as vacant, empty territory or *terra nullius* accounted for colonisation. Portrayals of openness prepared the way for colonists to move in without regard to original occupants who were often treated as non-existent in the *terra nullius*. For Parekh (1995), John Locke's erroneous portrayal of inhabitants of colonies, in contrast to Europe, as not having societies, polities, or any distinctions about who was an insider and who was an outsider served to open the way for colonists to move in and to disregard existing forms of closure and definitions of the colonised's property rights. In this way openness is shown to be neither in support of ethics nor of decoloniality. Writing about precolonial African borders, Moyana (1984: 172) notes that the European traveller Frederick Selous knew about boundaries between the Ndebele and Shona chiefdoms but Rhodes did not want him to reveal this and so he bought his silence with a gift of 2000 British pounds. The antithesis between notions of openness and decoloniality also underlies Parekh's (1995) view that early colonial portrayals of openness as well as the intermingling of colonial inhabitants and their environments were erroneously taken as indicating that the colonial inhabitants did not distinguish [in other word did not have borders] between themselves and animals: so the colonists held that they could not be treated as human beings in the eyes of the law.

Placing significance not so much on the 'laws of nature' (Dobos, 2012) that presuppose God is reducible to 'nature', but on 'spirits'/wind/air, people in various places (Kwon, 2010; Fontein, 2010; Perera, 2001; Lambek, 2008; Boddy, 1989; Lawrence, 2000; Abraham, 1966; Schmidt, 1997; Mbofana, 2011) can be understood as fashioning their ethical – or variants of civic – engagements. Though mediums have erroneously been understood in the colonial era as 'witchdoctors' (Chigwedere, 1991), the mediums and the *mhondoro* possessing them have been noted as providing space for villagers in the northern part of Zimbabwe to resist unpopular government imposed projects (Spierenburg, 2004).

While such ordinary ethics of everyday life (Lambek, 2010) are hardly considered in formal political discourses, they open politics to alternative competing conceptualisations in Englund's (2006) terms where he argues for the need to open up notions of democracy and human rights to alternative African understandings. The metaphysics of *chivanhu* differ from the Andes where mountains are considered to be 'sentient earth beings' deemed to challenge modern politics and hegemonic antagonisms (de la Cadena, 2010). The ethics of *chivanhu* are based on *hunhu/unhu*, tsika and other etiquette (Muzvidziwa and Muzvidziwa, 2012; Mandova and Chingombe, 2013; Gelfand, 1970; Chivaura, 2006; Pearce, 1990; Samkange and Samkange, 1980). In this sense, *hunhu/unhu* are aspects of human beings and they serve to distinguish them from animals, birds, soil, and flora as conceived in *ukama* and in *chivanhu* more generally.

This chapter discusses ethics, morality and *ukama* in the context of the violence that gripped Zimbabwe for more than a decade. To get a sense of the violence, it is important to outline some of its salient features that help ground the chapter.

Brief notes on politics of violence and the violence of politics

Zimbabwean politics during the period under consideration was founded on polarization on the bases of race, political party affiliation and often also on the basis of gender. The opposition Movement for Democratic Change (MDC) party and the ruling Zimbabwe African National Union Patriotic Front (ZANU PF) party were also polarized, and so their members were engaged in interparty violence. There was also polarisation on racial lines as well as between Zimbabwe and Britain, the former colonial master, which the Zimbabwean government accused of trying to prop up the interests of white commercial farmers whose farms were being expropriated. The violence which ensued saw about 40,000 violations of human rights including torture, assault, threats, rape, murder, arson, confiscation of property (Reeler, 2003). Victims were often visited at night, taken from their homes, abducted to bases of party activists where they were tortured (Lovemore, 2003). A number of apparatuses were used such as rifle butts, logs, sticks, buttons, booted feet, blunt objects, sjamboks, rubber hosing, tire strips, bicycle chains, electric cables, electricity from the main or from car batteries, water and other fluids for partial suffocation. In this context eighty six party activists died in the period preceding the 2008 rerun of the Presidential elections. Ten thousand homes were destroyed, 200,000 people were displaced, 1.3 million violations were reported (Reeler, 2009; Masunungure, 2009). But as reflected in the Zimbabwe *Parliamentary Debates,* 22 June 2004, vol. 30(58) there were complaints by Members of Parliament of underfunding by the treasury such that police officers were poorly remunerated, had no vehicles or no fuel to run them, as a result of sanctions imposed by Euro-America. There were also complaints that some ordinary citizens were using uniforms that resemble those of the police.

The rule of law which is often assumed to offer protection, at least to those who could afford the legal costs, vanished from the scene; in fact the rule of law as Mattei *et al.* (2011) argue was portrayed as a tool of the empire, serving to forestall redistribution of land to Zimbabweans, together with "civil" society organisations (CSOs) deemed moral crusaders creating panics as some of them produced the statistics that were used to demonise government and the ruling party. So the majority of the violations of human rights were not processed by the courts partly because some lawyers were also targeted, arrested, beaten and tortured by officials and militias of the ruling party (Pigou, 2003). Prosecutors, magistrate and judges were also allegedly threatened, intimidated and harassed by the officials and war veterans (former fighters in the liberation struggle which started in the 1960s and ended in 1980), if they handed down judgments which were not in favour of the government. It was also alleged that some judges were forced to resign and that the courts were stacked with judges sympathetic to the government (Pigou, 2003). In this context the situation became desperate for those who could not afford or could not get the protection of the law. The desperate situation in Zimbabwe was well captured by Freeth (2011: 189) who noted that: "...the law, the law enforcement agencies, our judges, our neighbours, our own abilities, the human rights agencies, the international community and the church – everything that we believed should protect us seemed to have evaporated. All that was left was God". But it was not all about victimhood for Freeth and other White farmers who engaged in gun battles with those who moved on their farms.

While Nancy Scheper-Hughes (2007: 192-202) observed citing Hannah Arendt (1969) that she grappled with the terrible burden of irreversibility with deeds that can never be undone, considering the only escape from the predicament of irreversibility as coming unbidden, in the form of grace expressed in unconditional forgiveness, the resilience among the villagers also shows tremendous fortitude. So while grappling with the burden of irreversibility, Arendt resorts to Derrida's argument that calls for forgiving the unforgivable accompanied by the ability to make and keep new promises; forgiveness and forging new social contracts seem to offer the only possibility for overcoming past horrors. In line with these arguments it is important to note that among the Shona, troubles are always expected to settle at some time or other. This is expressed in the Shona statements: *chaitemura chave kuseva/mvura bvongodzeki ndiyo garani* (troubled waters soon settle). Such modes of resilience during the troubles constitute the focus of this chapter as indeed the whole book. But it is also worth noting that in *chivanhu* it is not assumed that troubles come only from troubled waters: there are also idioms like *chidziva chakadzikama ndicho chinogara ngwena* (The quiet pool is the one that harbours crocodiles).

It was in the context of such desperation that some villagers engaged in visits to the places I mentioned above for prayers to help them evade violence or at least bear with it. Though some visited such places, others simply prayed within their church buildings. While others relied entirely on the Bible for their sermons, others also relied on prophetic utterances from *mweya mutsvene* (literally translated, air of the Holy). Yet other villagers relied on healers and mediums who performed ceremonies and provided advice to overcome want. These strategies are all fairly common where populations are seeking to survive violence (Lawrence, 2000). The churches, healers and mediums did not only offer spaces for villagers to express their challenges; through prayers and rituals, they hoped to demarcate spaces of safety for the villagers. The mountains and other places visited for prayers can also be understood in terms of places of safety where supplicants could express their challenges privately, and often in the middle of the night. These visits can be understood in terms of pilgrimages to holy places. In situations where church members were found gathering they were allegedly harassed by state agencies suspicious that the gatherings could be used by the opposition party, it is possible also to interpret the withdrawals to mountains and other secluded places as efforts to escape the gaze of the state. The fact that even nonchurch members often withdrew and sought refuge in mountains and other secluded places underscores the security that such places were deemed to offer.

But it was not only the physical aspects that offered security: church members also addressed one another as *hama* (people in *ukama* relationships), *baba* (father), *amai* (mother), *bhudhi* (brother) and *sisi* (sister). Healers and mediums were addressed as *mbuya* (grandmother) or *sekuru* (grandfather) irrespective of the existence of blood or affinal relations. Although mountains and other places can be understood to have offered physical security, the villagers sometimes looked specifically for places that they considered sacred. During my participation in church activities, I sometimes heard members commenting that they felt that some of the mountains we had visited were no longer sacred because they had been desecrated or because the *mweya/mhepo* had moved away from them. During the violence, other villagers hid in the mountains simply for the sake of the physical security that they offered. The experiences of Jac underscore such reliance on the physical security of the mountains.

Jac recounted his experiences as follows: "In 2002 when I was sitting, clad in my party (MDC) T-shirt, at the shopping centre where I was drinking beer, some unidentified men arrived in a car and started beating up villagers at the shopping centre. I did not run away so they asked me why I did not do so. One of them kicked me and another threw a brick which fortunately missed me. Some young men from the nearby Chikomba District who arrived at the shopping centre to pick up a bus to Harare helped me; they found me surrounded by seven people who were beating me up. We eventually won the battle and then my new found friends wanted to burn the assailants' car but I advised them to desist and to observe the law instead. In 2002 they (assailants) came to my homestead wanting twenty eight other members of my party in connection with various charges including rape, murder and arson: I ran away. My mother was beaten up by the angry assailants who had missed my house. So while they were beating up my mother, I ran away. I slept in the forest together with colleagues in my party but early the following morning the troubles resumed. I was subsequently assisted by my friends to move to Chikomba district where I secured some employment with an NGO. I had stayed in a mountain for a month, where I hid together with my other party members. We had food including cabbages supplied and delivered by the United States of America Agency for International Development (USAID) which also gave us blankets. I was responsible for writing down the names of the beneficiaries who were with me on the mountain. The USAID vehicle came with deliveries and it would stop by the roadside where we went to pick up the deliveries once in a while. I also carried with me to the mountain my small radio over which I listened to Voice of America (VOA) Studio Seven. I also had phone calls with VOA staff that were based in Washington who I updated daily with information on violence in Buhera. In 2004 my mother died.

As I will explain below, some mountains which were sacred were considered by villagers like *mbuya* Noreen, a *n'anga*, to be places for manifestations of *hama* on account of their forefathers having been buried in them. Other villagers like Jac considered the Gombe Mountain as just a mountain where they sought physical refuge. But church members who endeavoured to break links with *chivanhu* and with ancestors did not share the same such "cosmologies" with *mbuya* Noreen. Nevertheless, church members and the rest of the villagers including healers and mediums intersected in considering human beings as *hama*. And apostolic church members intersected with healers and mediums in considering *mweya/mhepo* (air/wind), variously conceived though, as connecting/separating beings, including people. In their modes of engagement, villagers often sought to establish *ukama* even with strangers. For this reason I did not find it very difficult to fit into the matrix of the village context during the fieldwork because the villagers I met endeavoured to establish *ukama* with me as I did with them.

Ukama, mhepo and *mweya*

When I visited *mbuya* Noreen on 5 November 2011, I found her seated outside her house shelling nuts. I greeted her, addressing her as *mai* (mother) since during our previous encounters she addressed me as *mwanangu* (my son). I gave her some snuff from Harare which she had requested during our previous interview. As I looked for a place to sit on her veranda, she asked her daughter-in-law to bring food for Pil (her son's friend) and me. While the food was being served she considered it important introduce me to Pil whom she mistakenly thought I had not met before. When she began the introductions, Pil smiled in a way that betrayed his acquaintance with me. Noreen then posed a question to Pil and me: *"asi munozivana?"* (do you already know each other?). Pil's answered *"ndisekuru vangu"* (he is my uncle). Noreen then asked me, *"saka pese paunouya kuno ndiko kwaunenge uchibva?"* (so have you been staying at his place all this time you have been visiting me?). I nodded and then to Pil she said, "When he (referring to me) first visited me I thought he was a spy. So after his first visit I asked my ancestors, who informed me that he is just interested in knowing about *chivanhu*. My ancestors informed me that he is interested in the ways in which we survive and in *chivanhu*". Implicit in the statement by *mbuya* Noreen is that *ukama* and totems act as cement and basis of solidarity and autonomy in communities. The fact that totems such as the crocodile *ngwenya* in Zimbabwe, *kwena* (crocodile) in Botswana and South Africa, span across Africa shows *ukama* among Africans irrespective of national borders. These totems coupled with periodic visits from Mozambique, Botswana, Zambia, and South Africa to the *Mwari* shrine in the Matopo Hills underscore solidarity at different levels among them. Yet the groupings and organisations in terms of *madzinza* based on totems as well as the *Mwari* shrine suffered disruption during the colonial era resettlement, labour migrations and naming conventions, wherein individuals were no longer addressed by their totems as occurs in *chivanhu* when one intends to invoke connections of *ukama*.

These colonial processes weakened the basis of solidarity among Africans who via *ukama* were reminded not to engage with *hama* in the savagery borne of the naturalistic and animistic Darwinist survival of the fittest. This will be examined later in this chapter. While colonists portrayed Africans as belonging to 'tribes' lacking organisation and society, the *chimurenga* wars of liberation in the 1890s and 1970s surprised the Europeans because they entailed a major organising force and collective memory transcending the 'tribal' boundaries they set. Social organisation has always been present in Africa. Rather it is Euro-liberalism, paradoxically accompanied by dispossession in the colonial and postcolonial neo-colonial era, that has rendered the African organisations fractious by insisting on individualism.

The notion of *hama* is variously understood by the villagers. One way in which it was understood was apparent in Nota's narrative. I had an interview with Nota on 31 May 2011 where she told me: "*Ndakabatsirwa nevatorwa panguva yekutambudzika. Hama hadzina kundibatsira panguva yekutambura. Vamwene vaitondiseka pakarwara mwana wangu vainditi achafa nenzara. Vaifurira vavakidzani kuti vasawirirane neni. Ini ndakati handina kuvinga shamwari pandakaroorwa, handingasiyi imba yangu nekuda kwekuti ndashaya shamwari. Ivo vaiti handifaniri kunyorwa kumadonor kuti nditambire. Imwe nguva ndakati nzara yaruma ndisina chekubata vana endai munopiwa porridge nambuya vaitambira kuDananai. Vana vakadzorwa vasina kupiwa kana chinhu. Ndaiita maricho. Ndakatambura ndikati vekumusha kwangu veukama havanga tumirewo umwe here kundibatsira.*" (I was assisted by strangers during the time of suffering. *Hama* did not come to my assistance during the time of troubles. My mother-in-law laughed at me and said I would starve during the crisis. She influenced other villagers to be unfriendly to me but I told them that I was not married in order to have friends in the village. I said I would not abandon my marital household for the sake of friends. My mother-in-law did not want me even to be included on the list of donor beneficiaries. At one time when we absolutely had nothing to eat in the house I advised my children to seek food from my mother-in-law who was on the list of donor beneficiaries and was receiving porridge meal. My mother-in-law however sent back my children without giving them anything by way of food. I survived on piece jobs. I suffered and wondered why not even a single person of *ukama* from my natal home came to assist.)

The other conceptualisation of *hama* was evident in Ruru's account. When I met Ruru on 23 August 2011 she said, with respect to the challenges during the crises period: "*Mwanangu iyi nyaya yekutambura yakaoma iyi uye inondirwadza. Takaoneswa nhamo nehama dzedu chaidzo pa rerun. Ini pano mombe yangu vakauya zvikanzi tinokumbirawo muriwo ini ndikati handina mombe. Ndakafuma mombe yatorwa mudanga ndikaudzwa nevamwe kuti mombe yakatourayiwa. Zvinondibaya moyo wangu. Takarwadziswa nehondo yaSmith, vowedzerazve vatinoti ndivo hama dzedu. Mwanangu chokwadi chaicho ndechekuti muungano dzakaita se matare epamusha, parufu kana padoro chaipo tinoita se paraffin nemvura zvinoti nyangwe ukazvidira mubhotoro rimwe chete paraffin inotizira pamusoro.*" (My son this story about violence makes me sad. Villagers like me were troubled by our own *hama* during the rerun of Presidential elections in 2008. My cow was forcibly taken away to be slaughtered by youths. When I woke up one morning, I discovered that one of my cows was missing. It pains my heart. We suffered during Smith's war in the colonial period; now we have suffered again because of the fellow villagers that we call our *hama*. The truth is that in the village gatherings including funerals and beer parties we members of different parties are like water and paraffin – the paraffin will rise to the top while the water sinks to the bottom when mixed together.)

Those who confiscated other villagers' belongings (including my own) should be made to return them and to restitute. If the belongings are not returned, like in my case, there will not be peace in the village until I get back my cow. I have told even the village head; I told him but he did nothing to help. If my cow is returned or compensated, then we can reconcile. If you attend beer parties even if for a short time, in the village you will notice that there are members of different political parties because the villagers will only be opposing and shouting at one another. Even this village was divided into two in 2008 with members of different political parties occupying one or the other side. All this is widening the rift between the villagers who have been failing to reconcile for a long time. In my case, even though I am old, I am not included by the village head on the list of beneficiaries from donors because I belong to the opposition party so I am not given food like is done for other elderly people.")

Although *mbuya* Noreen, who remarked above that Gombe Mountain is *hama yeva*Hera, and her husband were not of the dominant Njanja totem, they managed to settle within the part of Buhera which is dominated by the people of the Njanja totem. Her husband is of the Hera totem which is possibly the reason why she stressed that the Gombe Mountain was *hama* yevaHera. As a healer, she was shunned by apostolic church members but among the villagers, her vocation earned her the title *mbuya* (grandmother), and in her own engagements she forged *ukama* with others by addressing and treating them as *hama*. True to the vernacular saying that "*ukama igasva hunozadziswa nekudya*" (*ukama* is half empty, it can only be filled by eating), she offered food to visitors including strangers like me. In fact in the interviews she remarked that "*hakuna musha usina muenzi*" (there is no household that has no visitors) underlining the need to treat visitors well and to offer them a place to stay. She then narrated her own history in which she noted that she was originally from Mutoko but was given a place in Buhera not only to stay but also to practise her vocation as a healer. In highlighting her place as a healer, she noted that healers fell under *masvikiro* (mediums) who could assume the ascending order of *masvikiro edzinza* (mediums of the clans), *masvikiro enzvimbo* (mediums of the areas) and *masvikiro enyika* (mediums of the country). In her view the *masvikiro* were entitled to control the activities of healers in their territories and to ensure that *nzvimbo dzinoera* (sacred places) were not desecrated by villagers. She placed herself under the *masvikiro enzvimbo* as well as the *masvikiro enyika* in accordance with the Shona saying that "*mwana washe muranda kumwe*" (a chief/king's child is a subject in another chiefdom/kingdom).

Her views support Gelfand's (1959: 5) observation that the hierarchy of *mhondoro* spirits is comparable to the structures of a government department in a civil service with the chief secretary at its head, below him a few provincial officers, under them a larger number of district officers, and finally assistant district officers in large numbers. But it is such hierarchies, as noted above by

Gelfand, that were disrupted by colonial processes aimed to unhinge not only the power of mediums and *mhondoro*s but also the chiefs' powers over the land, property and their subjects. And in this way *ukama* was narrowly portrayed by colonists in terms of blood relationships yet it extended right through the hierarchy into the breadth of African territory and cosmologies via the notion of *mweya/mhepo*. If *ukama* is understood in terms not only of blood but also in terms of *mweya/mhepo* and if as in the Shona it is said that *ukama haugezwe nemvura hukabva* (*ukama* cannot be effectively washed away using water), attempts to separate descendants from their *mhondoro* ancestors can be understood as not having been completely done away with though it may have been weakened or broken down. In connection with violence and peace, Werbner (1989) has argued that they are manifestations of the awakening of divinities. In a similar vein Colson (1962) argued that naming a child after a bad *muzimu* results in the child also becoming bad; so if the deceased after whom the child is named was a murderer the child will also become a murderer. However, in contemporary Zimbabwe many have named their children after foreigners even though they know very little about these foreigners' histories. Some church members also paradoxically refuse to wear clothing having belonged to their deceased *hama,* particularly if they were not church members, while on the other hand they buy second hand clothing known as *mazitye* from overseas, knowing strictly nothing about the original owner. This reflects how at a psychological level coloniality has turned Africans inside out, so to speak, resulting in unwarranted self-denial and self-pity.

The foregoing narratives imply that *ukama* is understood in terms of affinal and blood relationships such as in Nota's account. The conceptualisation of *ukama* by Nota resonates with Mararike's (1999: 165) observation that *ukama* is 'brotherhood' in which members of the group are expected to share with one another and find peace of mind through the love of all in the extended family group or kin. Nota's account also corroborates observations by scholars like Holleman (1952) and Bourdillon (1976) that kinship involves patrilineal kin, mother's kin and that patrilineage includes *chizvarwa* family groups and lineages, which regulate the production of unilineal and exogamous kin groups with respect to 'native' conceptions of incest. But Mararike above notes that *ukama* has no English equivalence; his observation can be understood also in connection with Turner's (1968) comment about another part of Africa where "all Ndembu ritual posits the ultimate unity of all Ndembu in a single moral community". For Turner, the dominant social element in the composition of ritual assemblies is not kinship group but an association of adepts who belong to many kinship groups. For this reason, relations formed by ritual cut across 'tribal' affiliation. Though such extended relations have been understood in terms of fictive kinship relations that are deemed to extend kinship status to friend relationships in which members are unrelated either by blood or marriage but regard one another in kinship terms and employ a standard cultural typology likened to blood, sociolegal or marriage ties and parenthood (Chatters *et al.*, 1994), the idea of fictive kinship has no precise equivalence in vernacular terms. However such an idea may have been derived from what are termed *usahwira*, where people unrelated by blood can act as if they are so related because rituals will have been performed to link them via other means of establishing *ukama*. But this *usahwira* translates to *ukama* in the absence of connections via *mweya*; in *chivanhu* this is clear in the adages such as *zizi kurungwa munyu roti ndava hukuwo* (if an owl is seasoned with salt it does not have to think it is chicken too, that is to say that a person is out of place in the company of people with whom he/she has nothing in common, though striving to appear as one of them). Such distinctions are underscored in the practice of *kupira vadzimu* (to inform ancestors) which is always done by a patrilineal descendent of the ancestor. Also, in the *kutema rukau* (to mark a grave site for the deceased) it is always one of the same blood as the deceased who performs the ritual. Further distinctions are marked in rules about *makunakuna* (incest) where related individuals are not supposed to mate. For this reason, marriages in *chivanhu* are exogamous in the sense that one is expected to marry from outside one's totem.

Ukama can best be understood in terms of the blood and affinal ties as well as the *mweya/mhepo* ties.. The idea of *mweya/mhepo* ties shares some logics of the implicate order metaphysics, mentioned above, where things are considered to be connected in ways that may not be immediately apparent. While some sacred places such as the spring which I saw during my walk up the Gombe Mountain had been protected using logs erected around it, other such places indicated by the villagers were not protected physically. Even though some villagers such as village headman Behm did not explain how it was possible in view of the sacredness and the power deemed to be possessed by *mweya* that some places were considered to have been desecrated by villagers. He noted for instance that when he was still a young man he used to see and hear *madzimudzangara* (spiritual manifestations) in the vlei three hundred metres away from his homestead, but because villagers bathed and washed their clothes at the place using soap the *madzimudzangara* disappeared and now the river was running dry. Similar stories were narrated by *mbuya* Noreen and the medium of the area who lamented that villagers no longer cared about sacred places which the medium stated to be villages of entities such as *mhondoro*.

The protection of the places and the lamentations by the headmen, healers and mediums may well have been attempts to assert their power and relevance in a village where many members had turned to churches. But one may also note that, in view of their cosmologies, which presuppose that the dead continue to interact with the living, their lamentations underscore their senses of continuing obligations to the deceased deemed to manifest in other forms albeit invisible to others. While such an ethics can be open to abuse for instance by those who purport to sense what others cannot sense (Fontein, 2006), the ethics also signal challenges to the kind of conventional metaphysics of presence undergirded by the hegemony of vision. The remarks can be understood in this sense in terms of the significance of ethics to the visible/invisible, the near/distant others who may not be seen or spoken to by everyone. Similarly the kind of ethics challenges the out-of-sight out-of-mind mode of engagement that often accounted for violence under the conviction that no obligations were owed to the out-of-sight others.

In *chivanhu* metaphysics where, as noted in the chapter on rain, entities such as the *mhondoro* can be deemed to manifest and morph into other forms in order to punish offenders who desecrate the places for instance, the possibility of evasion can be more uncertain, at least cognitively. Whereas remarks by the mediums and healers that the *mhondoro* can manifest in a python (*shato*), an eagle (*chapungu*), a baboon (*gudo*) or other such forms in order to scare off and punish offenders might appear to attenuate the possibilities of chancy occurrences, they also diffuse and multiply ways in which offenders can envisage reprisals. However the *mhondoro* merely manifests on fauna without actually turning into the animals or birds for instance. In *chivanhu* different pronouns are used to refer to fauna and to human beings for instance in phrases like *gudo iri* (this baboon), *shato iyi* (this python), *chapungu ichi* (this eagle) and on the other hand *munhu uyu* (this person).

Such forms of metaphysics explicated by the healers and mediums appear not to sharply delineate between the humans and the entities like *midzimu* and *mhondoro* that are deemed to manifest in the human world. But because the *mhondoro* is deemed to manifest in or attach to such entities, much like the *mhondoro* is deemed to manifest in the medium at least for a while in order to exert influence, the other entities themselves were not considered to be humans or persons merely because the *mhondoro* manifested on them.

The fact that the *mhondoro* had moments when he visited and manifested in the medium was indicated by the medium when during my visits to request for interviews she remarked that: "*sekuru havauyi masikati, vanouya makuseniseni nezuva radoka*" (great grandfather or the *mhondoro* does not come in the afternoon; he comes in the early mornings and from evening onwards). As with healers, the medium's willingness to let the *mhondoro* enter her body suggests a kind of ethics where *hama* are accommodated even within the bodies of the individuals. Much as in White's (2001) study in Zululand, South Africa, accommodating the deceased others often involved bearing hardships: healers among the villagers such as *mbuya* Noreen endured a long period of illness as a prelude to her vocation. She was afflicted by an illness when she was in grade three at a Dutch Mission School; because it did not abate in spite of treatment in the hospitals, her parents took her to a healer who diagnosed the condition as a calling to be a healer. She remained a healer, while others left their vocations to join the Apostolic Churches.

Though such accommodation of others was frowned upon by other villagers who considered it risky and devilish to have one's mind or body entered by ancestors or other spirits, it is possible to notice many other ways in which human beings accommodate others, albeit subtly. The ways in which villagers accommodated others, in manners that had subtle but similar logics to possession by others, were apparent in Mid's narrative. She explained:

It is good to forgive and reconcile but it depends on what was done to you. I want all those who did wrong such as beating other villagers, killing other villagers, confiscating other villagers' property, destroying other villagers' houses to publicly apologise in the presence of all villagers who suffered. They should not approach their victims individually and privately because when they victimized them they moved in groups. Meeting with these assailants at parties like *nhimbe* does not make me happy. I agree with the villagers who want to go and consult *n'anga* or prophets so that those who beat up and killed other villagers can experience retribution. That way they will be forced to approach their victims to seek reconciliation. As we talk, there are two brothers who are failing to work together in their family because the elder brother pulled out the younger brother's eye. They cannot even talk to each other, and so reconciliation and forgiveness are impossible.

Even if the villagers who stole other villagers' livestock are ordered to return or restitute, they haven't got the means any more. So they should be beaten in the same way they beat up other villagers. That way they can be forced to go and look for means to return what they stole. In my case, it is because I can't find a good *n'anga* that I haven't reacted to the violence in the way I want. I would want to consult a *n'anga* who can paralyse the assailants and those who stole property like livestock, destroyed homesteads, beat up and killed others. They should rebuild the houses they destroyed. What is painful is that no single victim has had his or her house rebuilt by the assailants and no property has been returned or restituted. Some villagers are no longer attending churches because of fears of meeting their political opponents. *Chokwadi chinhu chokuita wakaputirwa chinonyadzisa. Paunozo pengenuka unotanga kuona kushata kwekuita kwako kwese* (It is true that when you do things whilst under the influence/possession by other people's ideas it is shameful. When you recover from the influence/possession you begin to see the offensiveness of all your actions). There is a family I know in which members support different political parties. The sons and daughters in that family have since stopped to materially assist their father who is of a different party.

The remarks by Mid above about *kuputirwa* (to be covered/possessed by other people whose ideas or ideologies grip and overwhelm one's mind) and *kupengenuka* (to recover from the influence or possession by the ideas of others) suggest that ideas purveyed by other people assume the logics of possessing other villagers in similar ways that some villagers were deemed to be possessed by *mweya/mhepo*. It is possible in this sense to argue that the public and private media which purveyed ideologies, including about violence against others, entered the minds and bodies of those who were thereby influenced by it. It is equally possible to argue that the ideas that villagers shared entered minds and bodies in ways that unhinged or exacerbated dichotomies between the self and the other, at least temporarily. The ideologies of the political parties, of Euro-modern binary politics, of liberty, humanitarianism, human rights, democracy all possess human beings who subsequently act on the basis of these ideological forms of possession. Mutli-party democracy as an ideological form of possession saw members and supporters of different political parties clashing within the villages and throughout the country. They can be understood to have used the bodies and minds of the activists as vehicles to play politics. They may be understood to have possessed the ideas but in the light of regrets which were subsequently expressed by some who perpetrated violence, they can also be understood to have been possessed by the ideas instead. Narratives, as I will note below, about villagers who took to staying, often lonely, in the mountains out of the shame for having perpetrated violence against their fellow villagers, can be understood to indicate moments when ideas take hold of individuals' minds and bodies followed by recovery from such possession by the ideas of others.

Although attempts have been made over time to secularise notions of civility, which had origins in the church (Davetian, 2009), and in spite of attempts to demarcate the public and private spheres during the colonial era (Comaroff and Comaroff, 1999), the partial connections between possession by ancestors and *mashavi*, and possession for instance of activists by ideas, underscore the arbitrariness of such dichotomies. In Shona modes of engagement, if one behaves in strange ways there are questions such as *wapindwa nei?* (what has entered you?), and this could be a spirit such as *shave* or *ngozi* for *kuuraya* (killing) others, for *kupomba* (prostitution), for *kuroya* (witchcraft), for *kuvenga* (hatred) for *kureva nhema* (lying), *kushora* (to despise/disrespect) for *ngochani* (homosexuality) and so on. In other words the questions reflect Shona wonderings about what might have penetrated and overborne the mind and body of people who behave in ways that do not reflect *hunhu*. This is particularly so where those individuals who are summarily defined by Euro-modern forms of politics as uncivil have not been asked to agree to the narrower versions of such civility. The contestations about civil society in Zimbabwe (Helliker *et al.*, 2008) can be understood in terms of the binaries it arbitrarily presupposes between state and society, civil and uncivil, traditional and modern as well as in terms of its own internal contradictions and conflicts. The sacrifices that "civil" society organisations (CSOs) exhort citizens to make in their confrontations with the state apparatuses can hardly be distinguished from the sacrifices in what 'civil society' often wishes away as 'traditional' societies, oblivious of the fact that time as lived is not invariably linear. The CSOs are premised on binaries between the state and society. The organisations exhort citizens, who are also often victims of the narrow "civil" society ideologies of freedom and emancipation that speak more to (neo)colonial liberalisms than to Afrocentric forms of decoloniality, to confront the state. CSOs offer critiques of Euro-modernity from within that kind of modernity; yet projects on decoloniality recognise the need to critique Euro-modernity from its underside, from the side of the subaltern in Maldonado-Torres' (2008) sense.

The exhortations by CSOs to confront the state run counter to *chivanhu* where those who are wearing rugged clothing are urged to desist from jumping over fire (*ane marengenya haacharike moto*). In this case the citizens, particularly rural folk not only wearing rugged clothes in the literal sense but whose institutions, upon which they relied on for alternative modes of resilience, have been destroyed since the colonial era, are sadly exhorted to confront the state using binary logics. But as Englund (2006) argues, CSOs have their ideologies of freedom and democracy that differ from popular notions of freedom and democracy; so those who are coopted by these organisations become prisoners of the versions of freedom and democracy that they purvey. The emancipatory frames relied on by such organisations rely on the same Euro-modernist binaries that account for violence and in this way CSOs do not provide means of flight from Euro-modernist epistemic and ontological territory where freedom and democracy are defined for the world by a few.

On the other hand, blind and absolute reliance [for action] on other people's ideas is discouraged in *chivanhu* via the adage that *zano pangwa uine rako* (before you listen to other people's ideas you should have your own ideas). The indications among villagers [who needed advice on how to handle their conflicts] that they would resort to *n'anga* and other nonconventional ways of coping with violence confound the conventional notion of civility as is evident in Tsaki's experiences below; but consulting *n'anga*s also entailed costs for the impoverished would-be clients.

Tsaki, whom I interviewed on 4 June 2011 told me that

> I can't forgive those who assaulted me in 2008; it does not work because there are certain things one cannot forgive. My daughter was raped and infected with HIV/AIDS so I do not know how to forgive in these instances. Yes the assailants should return the things that they stole, but who is going to do so when the things were stolen by so many assailants. Even if you apprehend one of the assailants, he/she will simply say 'I was being sent' by other assailants but if you ask the people who they claim sent them, they will simply ask if you saw them steal your things. I will go to a *n'anga* to look for *mushonga* (herbs) that will help inflict pain or bring the assailant to negotiation. With respect

to those who stole my things, the *n'anga* can make them insane or they can kill them because they also killed. Villagers should look for ways (*mhindu*) for retribution or restitution because for villagers to live together without negotiating for the return of stolen things or without the rebuilding of houses is difficult. But during the negotiations there is the likelihood of conflicts arising. I am looking for a *n'anga* secretly and I am retributing secretly. Up to now I have managed to kill three herds of cattle, belonging to my opponents, using cotton pesticides which are concentrated. I dip the leaves of maize into the pesticide, I get into the kraals and I give them to cattle. The cow that I give, I know it is dead. *Izvi ndinozviita pasi pechirongwa chandinoti* 'operation *chipoko/chidhoma*'. *Chipoko chinonetsa vanhu vavata uye vakamuka* (I do all this under what I call operation *chipoko/chidhoma* (witch familiars). The *chipoko/chidhoma* troubles people when they are asleep). The cattle that I fed with the poisonous cotton pesticide were found dead the following morning and the owners threw away the carcasses because they did not want to consume the meat from the cattle that died mysteriously. I do not want to attend village parties with the assailants. Some of the assailants stopped attending church services because during the sermons we often gave examples which they felt verged on calling them names. So, to end the troubles villagers who are members of different parties can part ways and not attend village parties. In cases where family members are members of different parties, this is a sign of lack of order in the families concerned; it is a sign of lack of foresight.

It is important to note for purposes of this chapter that civility can hardly remain civil if it retains the tyranny of linear time as well as of evolution that defines others as belonging to the past and some to the present. As is evident in the case above, some villagers often relied on *n'anga* to resolve and or cope with present day challenges. As evidenced also in the case of Econet Wireless, referred to in the preceding chapter, which sought to set up a booster on the Gombe Mountain, the past and the present are often played together. The medium, healers and village heads informed me during interviews that subsequent to challenges in setting up the booster on the Gombe Mountain considered by the villagers to be sacred, Econet Wireless eventually approached the chief who consulted his medium. The medium then advised Econet to provide goats and a cow so that propitiatory rituals could be performed. The Gombe Mountain was considered sacred on account of some deceased inhabitants, that is, forefathers of the Hera people, who were buried in it and whose *mweya/mhepo* were deemed to have abode in the mountain. *Mbuya* Noreen commented that "*Gombe rinozi hama yevahera, vana Mbiru na Mutekedza vakavigwa imomo*" (the Gombe Mountain is called a *hama* of the Hera people, their deceased ancestors such as Mbiru and Mutekedza were hidden in it). But other mountains in the area further away from my fieldwork site were referred to as '*homwe yeva*Hera' (pocket of the Hera). Other villagers simply refer to such mountains as *makomo anoera* or sacred mountains.

Mbuya Noreen's remarks that some mountains are *hama* while others are pockets of Hera people need not be taken literally though but they need to be situated within the broader context of *chivanhu* that distinguishes between *munhu* and *chinhu* as noted in the introduction. *Mbuya* Noreen's other complaint, cited in Chapter Four, that NGOs were donating food suitable for animals to African human beings underscores the need to consider her remarks about Gombe in the broader context of *chivanhu*. Her remarks do not imply parallels between human beings and mountains, because in *chivanhu* mountains are *zvinhu* (things) and not *vanhu* (human beings) and this is why people in Zimbabwe connect with mountains, animals, birds, trees and so on differently from the way they do with other people. For instance the Catholic Commission (1997: 7) cited in Chait (2004) observe that forced sex with animals or having logs pushed into sexual organs are ways in which opponents have been assaulted during conflicts. Rather, her remarks can be understood to mean that the ancestors of the Hera people take the Gombe Mountain and other mountains she mentioned as their abode and that therefore they are the owners/*varidzi* in her view of the mountain. In *chivanhu* mountains are for instance referred to as *gomo raNehanda* and *gomo raChaminuka* (*Nehanda's* mountain and *Chaminuka's* mountain) and some caves are referred to as *ninga dzemadzitateguru* (caves belonging to forefathers) (Matikiti, 2007). As Garbett (1977: 66) notes the "chthonic beings" are considered to be the owners of the land subject to the qualification of *Mwari* (see also Abraham 1966: 40). For this reason *mbuya* Noreen should not be understood as dispensing with matters of ownership (*huridzi*): just as the Spanish XVIth Century Spanish jurist Juan López de Palacios Rubios argued that ownership is a mark of humanity (Pagden 1993: 303), in *chivanhu* ownership is part of the mark of *munhu*. In *chivanhu* there are distinctions between *huridzi* (ownership) and *kupakatiswa/kupakata* (to possess, which can be the case even in the absence of ownership/*huridzi*). It is arguably these nuances that European colonists did not understand when they assumed that Lobengula had given them the land to own (*huridzi*) when in fact he may merely have *kupakatisa* (to possess). So instead of *kupakata* (possessing) those who fail to distinguish the two begin to *ridza* (own and use). It is also important to note that *mbuya* Noreen's reference to the Hera in contrast to the Njanja people is based on totems rather than on animistic frames; and in *chivanhu* referring to a totem does not mean that the thing referenced is personified in the same way as a human being. It can be further noted that while other scholars have understood African people in terms of totemism, the Shona people do not base their modes of engagement simply on totems as they also refer to Supreme Being, *Mwari* as the Creator: this is in contrast to animism that presumes polygenesis and pantheism. Furthermore, when I made trips together with church members to mountains, the idea was not that the mountains were animate persons with whom we could interact but rather that they were shrines where we could pray. It was the human prophets who made prophesies while on the mountains; and this was also the case in the Matopo Hills where as Daneel (1970) notes, the priest's wife became the voice of the oracle in the cave, after child bearing (Ranger, 1999).

Such places as the Gombe Mountain have been burial sites for ancestors and they often marked out the territories of chiefs (Ranger, 2003: 73). With respect to the Gombe Mountain Mbiru, the forefather of the villagers of the Hera totem was reported to have also used it as *guta* (city) and for this reason it is marked by ruins (Beach, 1980). Though *mbuya* Noreen remarked that it was *hama yevaHera*, church members went there to pray despite the fact that they did not subscribe to the perceptions of the healers and mediums. Though healers and mediums on the one hand and church members on the other differ in that the former claim to operate through ancestors while the latter claim to appeal to *Mwari*. Healers and mediums also hold that ancestors are mediators to *Mwari*. While in both ·cases *Mwari* was understood to be *Musiki* (Creator) and *Nyadenga* (the one who resides in heaven) there were important differences in terms of ways to appeal to Him. But *mbuya* Noreen's assertion that Gombe Mountain is *hama* yevaHera can also be interpreted against the contestations by mediums of the Njanja and of the Hera to perform rituals on behalf of Econet Wireless. Though in my earlier meeting with her, the medium of the Njanja stated that she was entitled to perform the rituals, *mbuya* Noreen held that it was the medium of the Hera who was supposed to perform the rituals as according to her the mountain was a *hama* of the Hera whose ancestors were buried in it. The Econet Wireless is best viewed in terms of European eighteenth century deism, which has similar logics to the idea of animism, where God was conceived in terms of nature (see for instance Evensky 2005). But to the extent that the eighteenth century European deism is premised on naturalist ontologies and naturalistic theology, it differs from churches, healers and mediums who did not conceive God and ancestors as immanent in the mountain and in nature but rather as temporarily manifesting in the mountain and other features in the environment.

During one of my interviews with the medium, to which I referred at length in the chapter on droughts, I was convinced that I was talking to her but when I later interviewed her during possession by the *mhondoro*, the *mhondoro* informed me that he was present during my earlier interview and that he had told his medium what to tell me from the background. For this reason the *mhondoro* asked me what else I wanted to ask him since he had been present during the earlier interview. It was after my insistence that there was more that I wanted to know that he agreed to the interview but he started by forewarning me about the oncoming illness which I dwelt on in the previous chapter. What this suggests is that in such metaphysics *mweya/mhepo* do not necessarily possess only in the conventional sense of being embodied, but that they can also exert their influence by attaching themselves to mediums from without.

Nevertheless, *mweya/mhepo* is understood as sometimes 'possessing' human beings by taking over their faculties and bodies. Apart from the 'possession' sessions I witnessed, there were stories among the villagers to the effect that those who desecrated sacred places were visited by mental illnesses on account of reprisals from *mweya/mhepo* (see also Matikiti, 2007; Marongwe, 2005). There were also narratives about *ngozi*, that is, the deceased deemed to return from the dead to afflict the living by way of reprisals (Gelfand, 1970; Gelfand, 1966; Bourdillon, 1976: 234; Fontein, 2010; Schmidt, 1997; Reynolds, 1996; and Mbofana, 2011). Such claims about the dead being witnessed (Perera, 2001; Honwana 2005), returning, lodging in human bodies (Boddy, 1989) and being rendered attention by the living (Kwon, 2010) are widespread in many parts of the world including Sri Lanka, Vietnam, Mozambique and other parts of Africa. Although it has been noted that fear of such spirits could act as a sanction for ethical behaviour (Bourdillon, 1976: 234) and that conceptions of such spirits apart from influencing ethical behaviour and virtues of the Shona, also influences their attitude to *hama* (Gelfand, 1970), such dead have been noted to visit a lot of suffering onto women. Spirits of deceased, including deceased males, are deemed to lodge in women's bodies (Boddy, 1989). Such avenging spirits demand compensation in the form of livestock and young girls for wives or so that they become mothers of children who replace the deceased (Schmidt, 1997). The deceased met collective punishment within the families of offenders necessitating collective responses among the *hama*.

If interpreted in terms of the conventional psychoanalytic notions of the unconscious, possession by such deceased assume the hue of individual mental illness; but if the possession is interpreted in terms of the emerging field of relational psychoanalysis (Mills, 2005; 2012) the presumed connectedness of issues becomes easier to surface. Relational psychoanalysis makes it possible to envisage the emotional transmutations, meaning construction and the connectedness of the individuals and families afflicted to their contexts of violence. Insisting on possession merely as a manifestation of the unconscious, against the villagers' own interpretations of it as conscious afflictions by deceased who have been wronged would amount to appropriation of their voices. Yet as Das (2012) persuasively argues, it is important to hear the voices of sufferers of violence, some of whom may be averse to appropriations of their voices (Ross, 2003). Yet again, insisting on relational ontology in the way relational psychoanalysis does fails to account adequately for violence, in this case among the villagers, (see also Butler and Cavarero, 2009, cited in Clercq, 2013: 134). Butler argues that the relational ontology proposed by Cavarero gave a model of the human to aspire to, but that ontology could not tell why nations went to war and why they deprived others of their humanity. In this sense, Butler's remark underscores the fact that as much as the formation of the subject is dependent on others it is also constituted through foreclosures that explain the emergence of the 'I'. But this 'I' is not necessarily oppositional to others and it does not imply a form of civility that privileges such an 'I' or even a group. There are undertones of imbrications in which civility is not even oppositional to leaders who are conceived, in *chivanhu*, as interwoven with their subjects rather than separated in the ways CSOs presume in their binary logics. It is often said that *panodya ishe varanda vanodyawo, kukokwa kwasamusha kukokwa kwevagere naye* and also *matukirwo ababa kunema mwana* (reproof is best conveyed indirectly so that it may appear that it is the father who is targeted when actually it is the child and vice versa, it may appear to be the leader when in fact it is the subject and so on.

The villagers' perceptions underscore the absence of decomposition of subjectivity, the psyche and personal identity in relation to possession, even by vengeful deceased (who temporarily possess victims); but they also highlight the liminality of the subjectivities of the possessed. I met Hum on 30 June 2011 at his homestead, not far from the village shopping centre. I had been informed that he and his family had recently consulted a healer to resolve afflictions of his family by what is known in vernacular as *ngozi*. I asked him to share his views of the *ngozi*. Hum began by noting that he understood it as the *mweya* (air) of a person, who has been innocently killed, that returns to afflict the murderers and their families. Hum noted that one of his daughters appeared to be beside herself because one of his family members killed another man whose *mweya/mhepo* had returned to haunt the family and that this was manifesting in his daughter. He noted that there were moments when his daughter manifested 'possession' when the voice of a man who claimed to have been murdered spoke through her narrating how he was killed. Hum pointed out that his daughter was considered by other villagers as insane because they could not understand what she was narrating and why she spoke in a male voice. The voice of the murdered man informed Hum's family that the murdered wanted compensation consisting of a number of cows to be paid to a relative of the deceased.

Although Hum's daughter was married before the *ngozi* allegedly started afflicting her, she was returned to her family home following her affliction with the *ngozi* who was understood to have been claiming her for a wife in compensation for the murder. Hum and his family were subsequently advised by an elderly villager, who suspected it could be *ngozi*, to consult prophets and healers. Although his daughter returned to normal after the interventions of the prophets, after about a year the *ngozi* returned and started afflicting her again. So one day she severely beat up her husband for no apparent reason. Just after the beating she spoke again in a male voice accusing her husband of having 'snatched' his wife away. While some scholars consider Africans as not having had ideas about the future, it can be argued here that the fact that they knew about *ngozi* and guarded against future risks of affliction among descendants indicates that notions of the future pre-existed colonialism. In fact, it is in the contemporary era that future afflictions by *ngozi* are summarily dismissed particularly before one is afflicted or experiences the visitations by the *ngozi*. So it is in the contemporary era that people can afford to mess around so to speak without fear of being haunted by the *ngozi* in the future: though hauntings are often explained today merely in terms of intrusive ideas or mere mental disturbances.

Such cases where 'spirits' of the deceased, including males who after dying in war are understood to possess women thereby reversing gendered bodies, are widespread in Africa (Boddy, 1989). But as in the case of Hum, they can be understood to signal some connections which may or may not be at the conscious level. But in cosmologies where changes in behaviour are explained in terms of *mweya/mhepo,* understood to move in and out of bodies, things that one may be (un)conscious of lie as much inside the body/mind as outside. Underscoring ways in which violence is understood as infectious, *mbuya* Noreen, the healer, remarked that: *vanhu vanopfekwa nemweya, ngozi indwise chero mumhuri* (literally, people are worn by the air, the air of the aggrieved deceased cause conflicts even in the families). But if looked at in the context of the political violence marking the villages and the country, Hum's daughter can be understood to have been violent with her husband because ideologies of violence had become a way to address grievances, however petty. However the logic in both instances is about where the individual is understood to have been infected by connections to others, making violence a function of such connections. If Euro-modernity is understood as Maldonado-Torres (2008) does as a paradigm of war, and if violence is also understood in terms of Darwinism that privileges not cooperation but individualism, competition and strife while at the same time dismissing the notions of the sacred, it can be argued that violence has been normalised in the world where disorder and destruction is profitable, while at the same time inhibitions to violence are weakened. Therefore, people are first possessed by ideas generating or normalising violence, before the spirits possess them.

This implies that it is not merely connections that matter in addressing violence, but rather the quality and character of those connections. In this sense it was not just the marriage that mattered for Hum's daughter but the quality of that marriage. Equally for Hum it was not just his daughter who mattered, but also the quality of the daughter, which explains his attempts to have the *ngozi* exorcised so that his daughter could be freed from the perceived connections with the *mweya* of the aggrieved dead man. If the fact that the *ngozi* was understood to be going away and coming back is interpreted in the broader political context where citizens made efforts to vote away some political officials, it portends the wider concerns about quality in their connections with others who could not have simply accepted valedictions. Similarly the arguments in scholarship on coloniality (Ndlovu-Gatsheni, 2013; Mignolo, 2007) underscore the refusal of the colonists to leave the former colonies alone; instead, they enmesh the colonies in 'networks' with the 'global' in ways that perpetuate the old colonial hegemonic relations. The new in the global relations thus implied the return of the old. Equally, the new male voice in Hum's daughter implied the return of the old prior encounter with the murdered man: the voice in Hum's daughter took him and his family backwards even as the voice appeared as new in Hum's family. The ways in which people in *ukama* assist one another can be understood in terms of the adage that *nhasi chineni mangwana chinewe/chawana hama hachisekanwi* (one should not laugh at a relative who has fallen into trouble because the trouble will haunt the next in the chain of relationships unless it is resolved). But as will be explained below, this chain of relationships is not synonymous with the chain of existence, presupposing immanence and animism, that was relied upon by colonists to colonise and exploit Africans whom they erroneously conceived as the lower rungs of the chain of existence.

Such everyday life where troubles kept coming, going, returning, often in disguises as underscored in accounts of perpetrators of violence who sometimes wore masks, in spite of efforts to keep them at bay, can best be understood in terms of what I call (hau)ontology as I will explain below. Tsaki's assertions above that he surreptitiously poisoned the cows belonging to his opponents using cotton pesticides, in his "operation *chidhoma/chipoko*", underscores the salience of the notion of (hau)ontology among the villagers. (Hau)ontology is also useful in explaining what Simmon (2012) has noted as chemical and biological weapons that are used by governments as devices for killing opponents. Some governments have for instance used substances that are difficult to detect, such as polycarbonate in South Africa during apartheid. It will also be useful in making sense of (hau)ontology to think in terms of the Southern Rhodesian government's use of anthrax, cholera, bubonic plague and viruses during the liberation war.

Borrowing insights from Derrida's (1993; 2006) notion that hauntology supplants its near homonym in ontology, replacing the priority of being and presence with the figure of the ghost as that which is neither present nor absent, neither dead nor alive, (hau)ntology is useful in explaining the realm of everyday life among the villagers. While Derrida wrote about hauntology with reference to what he called the spectre of Marx which he understood to haunt Europe at the end of the Cold War, I use the term (hau)ontology in understanding ways in which everyday life ethics are often premised on the possibilities of being haunted by the other. But what I call (hau)ontology does not prioritise deconstruction as in the Derridean hauntology; instead, it encompasses ways in which social figures, ideas and other presences haunt us whether with the effect of deconstruction or (re)construction, that is whether with positive or negative outcomes, which are not necessarily always predictable or foreseeable. In (hau)ontology the haunted's ontology is not necessarily effaced or deconstructed as entities often have the capacity to recoil and withstand shocks and other adversities, which is to say that entities devise modes of resilience.

The spectre being for Derrida a deconstructive figure hovering between life and death, presence and absence, in ways that make established certainty vacilate, speaks to the modes of life in everyday contexts where the dead are conceived as not so dead and as coming back in ways that unsettle certainties about death and life. But such a spectre also speaks to the ways in which in everyday life violence and war kept coming back even though the war of independence that ended in 1980 was deemed to have ushered in a period of peace. The violence post independence can be understood to have generated a spectre that haunted its victims, former victims, different places in the worlds that received images of the violence. In a context where secular systems of justice and coping were not available and where trust in them had deteriorated or was absent (see also Perera 2001), the law itself became a spectre hovering between presence/absence, life/death. Indeed the law itself has been understood as the spectre of the empire and imperialism that keeps coming back to the former colonies to perpetuate imperial control, independence notwithstanding. So although claims of having been visited by the dead characterised village life there is more to (hau)ontology than narratives of encountering the dead in the conventional sense. As Gordon (2004: 190) argues there are often constellations of forces that coincide in various ways in life; organised forces and systematic structure that appear removed from everyday life make themselves felt in ways that confound some separations.

So on a broader level, the illegibility, caprices and invisibility of the state as well as other institutions (that failed to curb violence among the villagers) in everyday village life (Das, 2004; Das *et al.*, 2000; West, 2003) can be understood to have instantiated their spectral presence. Yet as underscored in accounts of pain and suffering, such spectral presence did not necessarily render subjectivities decomposed as intimated in scholarship on the death of the subject. In the context of the spectral presence of citizens in the diaspora who communicated via the internet and other media offering support for those back home, it can be argued that some spectral presence actually propped up the subject by creating spaces for resilience. In this sense what I call (hau)ontology does not privilege deconstructive figures. There are also (re)constructive figures in it: in this sense (hau)ontology presupposes that the figures of the ghosts of the spectral presences can be deconstructive or (re)constructive. Such (hau)ontology does not however presume that one is always haunted, for people are not always looking over their shoulders in everyday life. But, whether viewed as spectral presences that visited healers and mediums or in terms of other forms of spectres, (hau)ontology presupposes an ethics that is attentive to the other, near and far, yet it is often the near and visible that is targeted in violence. (Hau)ontology does not presuppose incessant haunting which is why people are not always looking over their shoulders even in everyday life. However not to look over one's shoulders from time to time would be to disregard scepticism and doubt in a world that is replete with duplicities and latency; it would be, as it were, to go to sleep without even dreaming of spectres; in a way, it would be death in a world where there is latent and manifest violence. Looking over one's shoulders from time to time is a kind of evaluative mechanism that reconciles the past, the present and the future; yet it is such kind of evaluative processes that Euro-modernity dissuaded Africans from doing, even as the Europeans referred to their own archives.

The privileging of the visible in violence coupled with rebellion against *masvikiro* mediums was suggested in a remark by Ked, a young opposition party member, who noted during a conversation, rather emotionally, that: *"Kana masvikiro akapindira mberi munhu anoti ndingatye zvandisingaoni ini ndichida kuuraya wandiri kuona here. Vangatourayiwe masvikiro acho"*. (If *svikiro* mediums dissuade murderers from killing, the murderers would want to know why they should fear the *ngozi* which they cannot see when they want to kill those they can see. The mediums themselves will be killed if they intervene in such ways). Viewed in the context where mediums and the *Mwari* Cult used to provide not only 'transtribal' connections but also buffers against misrule by individual chiefs and kings (Abraham, 1966; Muphree, 1969), this remark suggests ways in which secularisation of politics explains some forms of violence. But the disposition of Ked, as well as the operation *chidhoma/chipoko* noted above by some members of the opposition party, also underscore that in (hau)ontology what may appear as a mere victim may in fact also be an assailant and vice versa; what appears to be good may in fact be bad and what appears to be the future may in fact be the past, and vice versa. Equally duplicitous were villagers who demonised *chivanhu* modes of engagements while paradoxically accepting benefits of *chivanhu* such as marriage payments. Such prevarications and duplicities have as hinted elsewhere been interpreted by the medium in terms of rejecting ancestors by people who have become 'modern', but because they have offended ancestors and are afraid to perform rituals to enable the ancestors to speak and disclose their crimes. In this sense it is not only the dead who haunt; the dead are also haunted by those that have committed crimes against them and who thereby seek to hide and avoid apprehension by manipulating the dead and by dissuading the descendants from performing rituals to let the dead [ancestors] speak.

The need in *chivanhu* to be sceptical about appearances is underscored in Shona proverbs such as *matende mashava anovaza doro* (pretty calabashes sour the beer/attractive appearances conceal inner flaws); *chinonyenga chinokotama chinosumudza musoro chawana/Zino irema rinosekerera newarisingadi* (both of which mean appearances hide inner intentions). *Ziriwo rechembere ramba waraira* (the unattractive relish of an old woman is refused only after tasting, so do not be put off even by bad appearances). All these statements underline the need to be careful about appearances that hide real intentions or dispositions, and to beware of being haunted by those who hide their true intentions.

Although attempts to re-enchant the world can be inferred from scholarship that claims that God has been virtualised in net space (Kroker, 2004) and that gods are present in every object in the cosmos, the situation in the everyday village life is more nuanced; even spirits of the dead are not deemed to be immanent in objects. Such nuances were apparent in the violence and in the accounts of it as shown in the section below on coloniality of violence.

Ukama and the coloniality of violence

I met Peel on 8 June 2011. After a sigh, she noted that the violence in the country caused her great wounds in her heart. She then stated

> My daughter was killed as if they were killing an animal of the forest (*mhuka yesango*). She had not done anything wrong. How can I forget all this when the murderers are freely walking up and down the village right in my eyes? I cannot work together anymore with the murderers. For this reason, I now do not even attend funerals for family members of the murderers in my village. I do not care even if they also do not come to attend funerals in my own family. I do not even go to church anymore because one of the church leaders is father to one of my daughter's killers. So how can I pray and get

responses from God whilst the murderers are right in my face. The murderer's father also gets very angry when he sees me. He gets angry with me on the allegation that I have exposed his son for killing my daughter. Although his son was eventually traced and apprehended in connection with the murder, he only stayed in the cells for three months.

Peel went on to state that "*mushonga wengozi kuripa nokuti mweya wemunhu wakasiyana newembwa yaunongouraya zvopera zvakadaro*" (the offenders' only way is to pay compensation because a person's wind/air is different from that of a dog that one can kill without facing the possibility of being afflicted by the wind/air). While the remarks may be read to suggest that only human beings have such wind/air, villagers like Nuh also noted for instance in relation to consecrated cows that: "*mweya unoti uri pamombe uku uri pamunhu*" (the air alternates between using the human body and the cow's body as a receptacle). Similarly noting the ways in which *mweya* can be present on some places and things albeit not necessarily assuming immanence, *mbuya* Noreen noted that "*mweya wevasina kurohwa makuva uri kumashizha*" (the wind/air of people for whom ceremonies have not yet been conducted is in the forest).

Peel's experiences underscore ways in which resilience is often based on distancing oneself from perpetrators much in the same way other citizens fled the country. Yet in spite of distancing herself physically and emotionally from the perpetrators, she hoped that her deceased daughter would retain connections with the perpetrator and take revenge against him.

Violence within the villages is contrary to *Mwari* oracles that were historically consulted at the Matopo Hills because, as Bourdillon (1990: 124, 125) rightly notes, the *Mwari* oracle did not like fighting between people in its realm of influence and it did not favour bloodshed. The *Mwari* cult had no boundaries and included all people from all nations and 'ethnic' groups. So other scholars explain the pervasiveness of such violence in terms of Euromodernity being a paradigm of war premised on binaries (Maldonado-Torres, 2008). Still others explain the violence in terms of European ideologies of social Darwinism that have become widespread over time in realms such as politics, society, economic and environment where competition and matters of survival of the fittest are stressed (Yahya, 2001). This Darwinism has been traced to European ideas about laws of nature or natural law where it is held that such laws enjoin pitiless fighting or competition for survival at the risk of extinction of weaker species or those who fail to compete. Such laws and social Darwinism can also be traced to ideas of multiple origins, that is polygenesis, evolution, rejection of God as a common Creator and attendant creation and uptake of animistic ideas where for instance colonists treated the other as animal and as dispensable to be killed, enslaved and colonised (Pinfold, 2007; Eliav-Feldon, 2009; Isaac *et al.*, 2009; Fanon, 1963; Debenham, 1960; Pagden, 2009; Bredekamp *et al.*, 1984). In such Darwinist and colonial animist renditions, colonised others were treated as swines, wolf-whelps, cockroaches, gorillas, rats, cattle, dogs, apes, beasts of burden and nonhumans with the effect of justifying mercilessness in colonial conquest and enslavement. Such animistic portrayals also justified European encouragement of, and participation in, wars in Africa as ways to acquire slaves and land in what were then termed frontiers of violence (Pinfold, 2007; Weaver, 2006; Parekh, 1995).

Encouragement of friction between African rulers and their subjects is noted to have continued into the colonial period: for instance Feuerman (1990: 124) observes that Germans forced chiefs in the colonies to confiscate land and to recruit forced labour among their subjects, earning the latters' contempt and destroying the loyalty which made them useful. In similar observation to Feuerman's (1990), Mandela (2013: 71, 105) noted that in South Africa chiefs had to submit to European colonists and risked being deposed if they sought the interests of their people. The colonists hoped by this measure that the wrath of the people would, in time, be directed not at the colonial authorities but at the Bantu authorities who were forced to carry out direct collection of taxes and exert other measures on their subjects. It is held that the European nations subsequently and paradoxically justified their colonial projects by claiming that it was the African societies that were socially anomalous, committing unthinkable crimes, cannibalism, incest, bestiality and so on (Pagden, 2009: 305). It has been further noted that Europeans then argued that in Africa there were no laws, people had no property as despots claimed everything, there was bloodshed and oppression, magnificence of murder and cruelty, and that cruelty alone proclaimed the power of African rulers (Pinfold, 2007: 308-9).

These views are also portrayed by Robert B. Cunninghame Graham, a Scottish aristocrat, politician, writer, journalist and adventurer in an article entitled "Bloody Niggers" in *The Social Democrat* (1897) noting European remarks thus:

> Niggers have no guns, so no rights. Their land is ours. Their cattle and fields, their wretched household utensils and all they possess is ours – just as their women are ours to have as concubines, to thrash or exchange, ours to infect with syphilis, leave with child, outrage, torment, and make by contact with 'the vilest of vile, more vile than beasts' (cited in Magubane, 2007: 49).

Darwinist ideologies were also clear in Weinrich's comments to the effect that the British relegated the African Kings to the role of chiefs (Mupepi, 2010: 253); their argument was based on the British monarchy where there was only one King or Queen (Weaver, 2006: 169). As well, Robinson (1983: 98) cited in Magubane (2007: 13) notes that Hume proclaimed that the colonised people had no history, no knowledge of ancient times, no writing, no gods and no heroes, no legends, not even simple traditions, no organised government, no hierarchy. In spite of colonists' statements that there were no notions of property ownership in colonial Zimbabwe, the Queen of England argued that: the 'natives' are probably in law and equity the real owners of the land they occupy and that the tax on the 'natives' proposed by the colonial settlers amounted to a charge for occupying their land and that it would result in great antagonism on the part of the 'natives' (Palmer 1977: 43).

Notwithstanding colonial scholarship to the effect that there was no justice in pre-colonial Zimbabwe, Posselt (1935: 157) noted that the *Mambo* (King) was assisted in administration of justice by a number of privy councillors. For Posselt, even captives of war were not treated as slaves in the ordinary sense, since the patron could not kill or maim slaves, who enjoyed certain privileges. It has been noted that the King had checks and balances to despotism and all important matters were dealt with by the *umpakati* or inner council. For this reason Carl Mauch, who 'discovered' Great Zimbabwe and visited Mzilikazi in 1867, testified to the unusual degree of justice which characterised the King's judgements (Posselt, 1935: 184; Child, 1965: 157).

So in spite of colonial vilification of pre-colonial peoples as violent and barbaric, scholars like WP Snow noted that pre-colonial people were peaceful with ingenious artefacts and who recognised some rights over property (Yahya, 2001: 25). Herman Melville (1846) cited in Jacobson (2000: 128-9) stated that

> The hospitality of the 'wild' Arabs, the courage of the North American Indians and the faithful friendships of some of the Polynesian nations far surpass anything of a similar kind among the polished communities of Europe: if truth and justice and the better principles of European nature cannot exist unless enforced through statute books how are we to account for the social conditions of the Typees [the name Melville gave to some Polynesians in the South Pacific Marquesas Islands]? So pure and upright were they in all relations of life that I was soon led to exclaim in amazement: 'Are these the ferocious savages, the blood thirsty cannibals of whom I have heard such frightful tales? They deal more kindly with each other, and are more humane, than many who study essays on virtue and benevolence and who repeat every night that beautiful prayer breathed first by the lips of the divine and gentle Jesus'.

The ways in which portrayals of Africans as animals were used to justify colonialism are underscored by Bredekamp *et al.* (1984: 28) who noted one colonist Sparrman saying thus: "Does a colonist at any time get sight of the Boshies-man, he takes fire immediately and spirits up his horse and dogs, in order to hunt him with more ardour and fury than he would a wolf or any other wild beast". In the same vein Fanon (1963: 6, 7, 8) noted that the colonised were reduced to an animal and so when the colonist spoke of the colonised he used zoological terms. However, for Fanon, the colonised knew all that and roared with laughter every time they heard themselves referred to as animals by the other for they knew that they were human. So for instance while the self-designation of the livestock breeders in the Khoi language (*khoikhoi*, *Kwena*) means human, i.e. human being *par excellence*, Africans were colonially portrayed in animistic terms as animals in order to render them and their assets dispensable (Bredekamp *et al.*, 1984: 16). As Bernard Magubane (2007: 41) puts it, "slavery was not born of racism: rather, racism was a consequence of slavery". In this way portrayals of Africans in terms of animism did not help bridge binaries between colonised and colonisers as it in fact justified and legitimised the binaries as it did the attendant colonial violence. It can be argued rather that the lack widespread violence in pre-colonial societies was due to such Shona injunctions as *chafamba kamwe hachiteiwe* (serious account is not taken of a single transgression) and *potsi haarwirwi asi piri* (you cannot fight over a single wrong doing but if it is repeated the second time). Other vernacular adages such as *mwoyo murefu* that enjoin the exercise of patience with wrong doers also account for tolerance in pre-colonial societies. Though Kaplan (1994) explains what he calls 'New Barbarism' on the basis of inadequate connections to the global, everyday life shows that violence is explained in terms of loss of *hunhu* and the weakening of connections to institutions of *chivanhu* including the worlds envisages in it. In this sense, rethinking violence need not focus on the global as a solution, because it in fact perpetuates coloniality (Ndlovu-Gatsheni 2013) by foisting institutions that often conflict with African modes of resilience and militates against decoloniality. It is by destroying the ethics of *hunhu* in *chivanhu* that coloniality sought to make animals out of Africans which is to say that they sought to animalise Africans by destroying their institutions, including mores, laws, *hunhu*, *ukama*, knowledge, families, polities and economies. Yet these efforts at animalising Africans appeared in the guise of a civilisation that knew no patience in engaging with the other.

Similar sentiments to Peel's, about the dead acting on the living offenders, were vented by Hoto. I met and interviewed Hoto on 2

June 2011. Hoto alleged that his wife had been killed in violence. In his account he said that

> Villagers in my ward were the first victims of violence in the year 2000. One day in 2007 villagers like me who supported the opposition party had to run away just after sun rise because assailants were approaching. Other villagers who could not run away were beaten up. My wife could not run away so she was beaten up and trampled upon as we watched helplessly from a distance. At her funeral, my in-laws charged the marriage payments they wanted and we agreed. But among the assailants was one of my cousins. The need for forgiveness and reconciliation that you have just mentioned is difficult in situations like this. I agree that it is good to forgive and that it was violence of that time (of the 2000s) that took my wife but if a person, such as in my wife's case, has been killed the thoughts keep coming. My cousin who was among the assailants did not even attend my wife's funeral as well as the *nyaradzo* (consolation ceremony). At the time of the funeral and even after the violence he stayed in the mountain as if he was a baboon. Now he has returned back home. No one has asked him why he killed my wife but he appears to be regretting now. I do not attend *mabira* [ceremonies in *chivanhu* performed for the dead] because of the doctrines of my church but I attend *nyaradzo*. When the assailants see me at *manyaradzo* in the village they immediately go back to their homes. Because they do not want us to meet how can we reconcile? If they want to consult *n'anga* they can do so but I will not consult *n'anga* or even prophets. I won't consult *n'anga* in connection with the fact that my wife was killed because my in-laws and I agreed not to do.
>
> *Mwari pamwechete nevhu ndinoona zvinotaura kudarika isu vapenyu. Muna 2007 ngoro yevamwe vaitungamira vaipfuura napamba pangu mombe yakamhanya dzakananga pamba. Mukuda kudzora mombe ngoro yakarova imba ikatsemuka. Vaiva nemombe vakashaya chokuita ndakavati vaende uye handidi zvekutaura nazvo nokuti chokwadi tose hatina kuziva kuti chii chakaita kuti zvidaro. Mombe dzeumwe aizviti mukuru dzakatanga kungofa dzoga. Ini ndinofunga kuti kudzorerana uye norumwe rutivi mucherechedzo wekuti vanhu tauriranai. Handidi kuti vanhu vazoti akapfuma nokuripirwa*

pakafa mukadzi wake. Ini pfuma yangu ndinoshanda ndega. Kukumbira ruregerero nomuromo kwakanaka fani. Kana pasina kutaurirana hapana rugare. Sokuona kwangu vanhu vakatorerwa zvinhu zvavo vanofanira kudzorerwa zvavo. Ini handioni kuti kubata huku kana mbudzi kwaive nechokuita ne politics. Kunzi munhu pachivanhu unenge uine musha nezvipfuyo. Zvino kana ongouya otora chokwadi kana bndiwe unopaona sei? Kupinda church *tingapinde hedu tose asi shoko kune anemhosva haripindi."* (God together with the soil [the murdered wife], I think can communicate more than us the living. In 2007 the scotch cart belonging to the leader in the violence that took my wife rammed into my hut. The leader did not know what to do after that but I told him I did not want to talk much about that with him so he had to immediately proceed to his home. The cattle belonging to one of the leaders in the violence began to die mysteriously. In my case I do not want other villagers to say that I got my riches by way of compensation from those who murdered my wife. I work in order to be rich. But requesting for forgiveness when one does wrong is a good thing. When there are no talks or negotiations there will not be any peace. I think villagers who lost their property to assailants should be compensated. I do not see the link between politics and the confiscation of goats and chicken belonging to other villagers. To be considered a person in *chivanhu,* one has to have a home and property. So if the assailants just come and take the property of others away, how do you see that? We can attend the same churches but the sermons will not be effective for those who did harm to others.)

These two sets of experiences by Peel and Hoto need to be considered together with the experiences of Nhunha, whose family was divided during the violence. Nhunha noted that

> *Muma*1990s *upenya hwemhuri hwaiva nani nokuti zvinhu zvaisadhura sezvazvave kuita mazuva ano* (life in the 1990s was better because things were different from what they are these days). My husband was a security guard in Harare and though he was getting a small salary we were able to buy food for the family. I have stayed in this village since the 1990s and my husband would always come every end of month. *Nyaya yemari yakaoma iyi* (The story about money is difficult to

recount), you know that with a dollar you would buy things; the Zimbabwean coin [dollar] could buy things in the 1990s. *Saka chero murume wangu aiuya ne Z$50 tairarama zvakanaka tichiwana mari yechigayo,* sugar *nezvimwewo. Muna 2000 kwakatanga kunetsana* MDC ne ZANU PF. *Mitengo yakashanduka zvikuru ichikwira zvisina nematuro ese. Takatanga kushoterwa nezvokudya nokupfeka. Yakazoti nzara ya 2002 yauya veduwee takanonga svosve nemuromo. Mitengo yainge yakukwira mari yaitambirwa yainge isisatengi zvinhu zvizhinji sekumashure.*

Nzara iyi yakatisukuta apa taive nevana four. *Taipona nemuriwo nokuti taive tisina kukohwa taiponawo nechakata.* Chimwe *chakazotiraramisa ibhinzi neupfu hweKenya zvaitambiriswa vanhu ne* Christian Care. (So even if my husband gave me Z$50 we could survive, being able to buy sugar and other items as well as take grain to the grinding mill. In 2000 the MDC and ZANU PF parties started opposing each other. The prices began to rise inexplicably. We ran short of basic food items and we could not even afford to buy clothes. When the drought of the year 2002 struck, we suffered very much. Prices kept on rising until the earnings we had could not buy anything. We suffered the droughts particularly because we had a bigger family, with our four children. We survived by eating vegetables and *chakata* fruits from *michakata* trees (also called *pari capensis*), mentioned in Chapter One. We also survived by on the beans and mealie [maize] meal that we received from Christian Care.)

Ini ndakapinda pfumvu kuma 2000s (I got into deep trouble in the 2000s). My husband was a member of the opposition party. In 2008 during the rerun of Presidential elections we felt unsettled because members of the ruling party were moving around the villages beating up every villagers suspected of supporting the opposition.

One night when I was asleep in the bedroom with my children, I heard a knock on the door. I estimated it was about 10 pm. I asked who it was when I heard many other knocks on the door. They did not disclose their names but only said 'open the door!' I was gripped with fear. The door was kicked with force and it swung open. Two men entered but I heard some more voices outside the house suggesting that they were more than two assailants present.

They threatened that if I made any noise they would kill me together with my children. I did not want to die for the sake of my children. The men had their faces covered with cloth that left only a small aperture for their eyes. Both of them raped me, taking turns such that while one raped me the other was pointing a knife at me. My children were asleep all this while. At day break I informed my mother-in-law and my sister-in-law that I had been raped. I also reported to the police and my husband who was then in Harare was invited and he came to the village. What pained me more was that my mother-in-law and sister-in-law (who were supporters of the opposition party like me and my husband) alleged that I had not been raped but that I had had sex with my boyfriends. The police have not apprehended the rapists. My husband was so pained by this experience that he decided not to go back to his workplace in Harare but has since stayed with me in this village.)

The notions of *mweya/mhepo* in *chivanhu*, the notion of the soil [in this case in reference to the deceased] and the idea by the *n'anga*, referred to above, that the Gombe Mountain is *hama yeva*Hera all suggest complications to the idea of immanence that is central to animistic portrayals of modes of engagement in other regions of the world. If one considers Fontein's (2006) argument that for the Shona people, ancestors and *Mwari* do not turn into place though they use certain objects in the environment as vehicles through which they exercise influence in the human world, one would be inclined to think that the mountains and the soil and other features in the environment are merely used, if temporarily, as vehicles to exercise influence without the deceased necessarily assuming immanence in the features. In this sense the deceased and *Mwari* can be understood to temporarily attach themselves, in Opoku's (1978) sense even from without the objects, in order to exercise influence in the human world. Considering the dead as turning into soil would be contrary to *chivanhu* modes of engagement whereby they perform rituals like *kurova guva* which are meant to *kudzora mufi* or bring back the deceased into the household and into the *Nyikadzimu* [this does not literally entail bringing back the soil at the grave-site]. The ritual among the villagers of *svitsa* that marks the arrival, after a year of death, of the deceased into the world of

Nyikadzimu underlines the significance placed on the deceased's *mweya/mhepo*, rather than on the *mutumbi* (body) which would have been buried, in *chivanhu*. In this ritual what is brought back into the family is the *mweya/mhepo* of the deceased and not necessarily the material remains that lie in the grave. In *chivanhu*, it is the *mweya/mhepo* of the deceased that is deemed to journey to the *Nyikadzimu* after rituals have been conducted. When villagers dream of the dead, they claim to see their [astral] figures identical with their appearances when still alive. When Hoto spoke about the "soil as speaking more than the living", it is important to take into cognisance the ambivalences, which indicate that the soil is not animated by the dead, because he contrasts it with the living rather the soil can be understood as temporarily used as a vehicle by, *mweya/mhepo*, to exercise influence. Therefore the statement that "the soil speaks more than the living" suggests that the soil is not inherently living, it opposes the soil to the living and suggest that the soil is not alive in the same way as human beings. Eeven if the dead corpses are buried in it of which deceased as in Hoto's wife also have *nyaradzo* conducted for them to go to Heaven. The *chivanhu* rituals that Godobori, referred to above, mentioned including *kusunungura vadzimu* (to release ancestors or to have them unlocked from the blocking, or *kutsipika*, by witches) imply that ancestors do not have to be locked up or imprisoned in matter but they have to be free to move back and forth from *Nyikadzimu*. In this sense *kutsipika vadzimu* or *kusunga vadzimu* that is locking up ancestors in places/in matter or disabling them to move freely is deemed an act of witchcraft that necessitates counter rituals. If in *chivanhu* the soil itself was considered to talk in the literal sense and the dead were considered to turn into place including into soil, one would have expected villagers including Hoto himself to consider the activities that they all did such as ploughing and walking on the soil to be violence, in the human sense, on that soil. Equally in the context of Hoto's statement, one would not have expected villagers to seek human mediums that they often pay, to mediate between the living and the dead. And in Hoto's case if the soil were animate just as human beings I would have as a researcher been expected to hear or to be assisted to talk to the soil just like I talked to other informants; but this was not the case.

In translating *chivanhu* one should avoid what I call the fallacy of immediacy which is related to the tendencies of conflating things. When mediums speak during possession it is not the voice of the mediums but the voice of the *mhondoro* possessing them. This may be likened to listening to news over the radio or television where one would not conflate the radio and the voice. In this case conflating the radio and the voice generates the erroneous perception that the radio is speaking, whereas in fact some persons will be speaking over the radio from a distance. Similarly one would not consider the phone to be speaking but some person speak over the phone from afar. The fallacy of immediacy that is sometimes evident in some Eurocentric epistemologies would consider the immediately visible object to be speaking and talking but in *chivanhu* distinctions are made between the immediately visible and present medium and the distant person or entity using the medium's mouth to speak.

In a context where some modes of resilience have, since the pre-colonial times, been more fluid than subsequently envisaged by colonial authorities and scholars who rigidified African modes of engagement (Jeater, 2007), to conceive things in *chivanhu* in terms of immanence risks overly rigidifying again the otherwise more fluid modes of life in everyday life. As noted by other scholars 'spirits' travel to various places (Lambek, 2010) and therefore they are not necessarily imprisoned or locked in one place or in particular features in the environment though they can use the features as their vehicles, even if temporarily or once in a while. So ancestors follow people and they are not tied to places. It is therefore possible to argue that ancestors and God are [deemed to be] benevolently near in times of crises, and that when they are near or in the human world, they seize not only human mediums but also attach themselves to other objects that are used as vehicles to exercise influence in the human world. This [presumed] nearness of ancestors and God during times of trouble could explain why the Zimbabwean nationalists came up with the *mwana wevhu/umtwana welilabati* (son of the soil), and the idea that the bones of the dead had arisen, (Kriger, 1992; Mudzengi, 2008; Ranger, 2004a cited in Fontein, 2006) during the *Chimurenga* war of liberation. It was this erroneous assumption that ancestors are necessarily interchangeable with their material remains that explains why the colonial settlers, as Ranger (1969, 136) observes, buried the bodies of Nehanda and Kaguvi (*mhondoro*s who led the war against colonist in 1980s) in secret places so that no 'native' could take away their bodies and claim that their spirit had descended to any other prophets or witchdoctors. Sadly for the colonial settlers, between the 1890s when they buried Nehanda and Kaguvi in the secret graves, and 1979 when the war of liberation ended, many Zimbabweans became mediums of Nehanda up to the current period understandably because it is the *mweya* of Nehanda that is for certain purposes, if more, important and not simply the buried remains.

While scholars like Werbner (1989) have argued that the human condition is an awakening of divinities, it is clear in this chapter that it is not only the awakening of divinities in the form of *vadzimu* but also the awakening of *mashavi*, *ngozi* and ideologies, all of which have the capacity to haunt others that explain the human condition. Between these categories there can be conflicts such that for instance when *midzimu* are preventing certain ideologies from taking root, they are labelled as demons or as belonging to the past; and this is an effective way of demobilising and disarming others as shown in the case of Nehanda and Kaguvi above. Equally when one has a *shavi* and would like to take hold of a family member, demobilising the *midzimu* would open up space for the *shavi*.

It has also been shown that presumptions of animism are out of place in *chivanhu* metaphysics. Animism as we may have to remember was conceived by Frazer (1926: 6, 17) in terms of 'primitive' people tending to attribute to everything not only to animals but to plants and inanimate objects a principle of life that of which they were themselves conscious. For Frazer, the worship of nature, in animism, is based on the personification of natural phenomena where primitive man attributes a personality akin to his own to all or most striking of the natural objects whether animate or inanimate by which he is surrounded.

The erroneousness of conflating objects and spirits attaching to or taking abode in them is best exemplified by British explorer, officer, hunter, and conservationist Frederick Courteney Selous (1881: 331) in a book entitled "A Hunter's Wanderings in Africa" (Abraham, 1966). Selous erroneously referred to the precolonial Zimbabwean medium of Chaminuka as Situngweesa, which was in fact the name of Chitungwiza hill on which he lived. The medium's real name was Pasipamire and not Situngweesa yet it took a long time for Frederick Selous to notice that he was mistaken in addressing that medium as Situngweesa (Wollacott, 1975). So, European travellers and scholars were indeed erroneous in attributing animism to Africans. Africans drew distinctions between hills and human beings that lived on the hills. Such conflation of objects and spirits is traceable to erroneous European narratives where for instance Socrates rebuked Phaedrus when he believed that the first prophetic utterance came from an oak tree that some Europeans at the Zeus temple contended they could listen to (Ophir, 1991: 3). This explains why (hau)ontology better portrays the shifts or the movements of entities and spiritual forces back and forth connecting places, spaces, temporalities and entities, and the ways in which they sometimes manifest in different forms. With all this it is necessary to return to key issues in this chapter.

A return to some key issues

The trips to the mountains and other places to pray to *Mwari* predate colonialism as supported by Ranger's (1969: 103) observation that the intelligence service of the *Mwari* cult was provided by regular visits to the central shrines of the intermediaries variously called the children of *Mwari*, the *wosana* or the *Manyusa* from various districts: they also provided the machinery for the transmission of advice and instructions from the cult centre to scattered worshippers. However the trips to the mountains do not presume animism because there are no presumptions of immanence of God in the mountains: rather God is deemed in *chivanhu* metaphysics as residing in Heaven and not imprisoned in the mountains and other features. Neither do the trips to the mountains in times of trouble presume absence of social organisation in *chivanhu* which has been under the onslaught of colonialism. As Bullock (1927: 10) laments less than forty years after colonisation,

> we are witnessing the break-up of the social system of the Mashona people, so far as the young generation is concerned. All those prohibitions which prevented the primitive man from being law unto himself are going, some at our direct bidding, and many from contact with Europeans and the economic system which they have introduced. They [young natives] now live not for the race but for themselves, individually, and for the pleasure of themselves.

Similarly, a few years after Bullock's above-mentioned book was published, Posselt (1935: 111, 113, 115-6) noted that among the Shona,

> reverence for chiefs, elders and parents was the general rule, but now it is rapidly falling into disuse. The disintegrating influences of Bantu institutions are also corroding all restraint and discipline born of traditional custom and enforced by traditional institutions, thus undermining the very foundations of family life and communal organisation. It is a painful reflection that primitive people is usually debased to a lower level by its first contact with European culture, that is debased to a lower level than the one it had attained. Why should the good contained in the social and ethical structure of such a people have to be destroyed before European ideals can take root? Is the process of destruction a necessary or unavoidable preliminary measure? Can we not enlarge and beautify the existing edifice without razing it to the ground? No real and lasting progress will be made until the mist of prejudice and misconceptions have been cleared, to permit a wider and more tolerant scheme. Nor should we permit a misguided solicitude to check every natural aspiration of the native to follow or develop ideas underlying his tribal traditions, merely because they appear in conflict with our conceptions of morality and right. We must learn to first appreciate the outlook of the native, to respect his ideals, and to gain a truer perception of his capacity before we attempt to apply the cramping effects of change. After all it is

surely better to let him grow up as a true child of African culture, than to change him into the spurious product of another civilisation. For the present, '*festina lente*' [make haste slowly] should be our guiding maxim.

The cases explored showed that in *ukama* it is not merely connections that matter but also the substantive entities often matter more as underscored by the accounts of pain and suffering. The *ukama* involves a careful balancing between the interests of individual substantive ontologies of the villagers and the *ukama* between the villagers. In *ukama* the individuals' own subjectivities and personal experiences of violence are not marginalised or neglected. In fact in *chivanhu*, there are proverbs such as *chida moyo hamba yakada makwati* (one should do what one's heart wants) and *ngoma inorira ichiti kwangu* (individuals always try to praise themselves); such proverbs emphasise the place of individual subjectivities and personal choices even though *chivanhu* also underscores *ukama*. Also underlining the role of the individual in *chivanhu* is the proverb *moyo muti unomera paunoda* (the individual has to decide what he/she wants). In *ukama* therefore, careful balance is often negotiated in weighing where and when connections are more important and when substantive beings assume primacy over connections. As indicated in certain of the cases, some connections are regarded as undesired and subject to exorcism. *Ukama* shows that the interdependence among human beings is multifaceted: there is material/economic interdependency between human beings for example that is satisfied when *hama* share material aspects. But *ukama* also implies physical, linguistic, spatial, marital, temporal, emotional and *mhepo/mweya* connections, all of which, though delineated, range from the immediate to the distant, the visible to the invisible. Though there are such connections in *ukama*, there are no presumptions of flatness presupposed in some theories that assume the absence of hierarchies and rhizomatic structures (Latour, 2005; 2006). As underscored in the cases and evident in the organisation of village and family life, there were hierarchies including chiefs, headmen, village heads, family heads and so on who were expected to play roles in abating violence. While other scholars intimate absence of boundaries, chiefs and headmen knew their boundaries. In fact as Palmer (1977: 17) argues citing Ranger, a chief (much as a family head in this case) may not occupy all of his land but would still know its limits and would be sensitive to invasion by strangers. And in *chivanhu* life is also regulated through rules and customs such as those that pertain to marriage, incest and etiquette.

Evidence in this chapter shows that arguments about there being no structured or regulated societies in pre-colonial Africa, that there were no hierarchies or centralised systems, that there was porosity and lack of sovereignty with no centralised authority and that therefore no entitlement to territorial integrity, cannot be supported. Equally, arguments and assumptions that there were no clear political boundaries and no settled ideas on who was outsider or insider, that Africans could not raise themselves unaided by Europeans, that they could be protected as individuals but could not have political equality, rendered equality as individuals and not as organised society and that the societies could therefore be dismantled (Parekh, 1995: 87) are not supported. Arguments such as these have a long history of supporting the colonisation processes in many parts of the world including Australia, North and South America, Africa, Asia, and the South Pacific where the inhabitants were portrayed as the absolute opposite of Europe and as similar to animals. It can therefore be argued that it is rather the colonial disruptions and postcolonial deconstructionism that have harmed African institutions that are subsequently paradoxically deemed by the same Eurocentric scholars to be now absent. The disruptions to such pre-colonial institutions impoverished African everyday life resilience. It can also be argued that such African institutions acted as walls against which Africans could lean in times of hardships as indeed it is said in Shona proverbs that *chirema ndechina mazano chinotamba chakazendama kumadziro* (a disabled person should be clever enough to dance while leaning on the wall). The individualism and other institutions privileged by colonialism have torn *ukama* apart, effectively removing the walls that the historically and colonially 'disabled' Africans could lean on in times of hardships. The insistence by villagers that they would consult *n'anga* should also be understood the context of colonial destruction of indigenous the religious institutions whereas, Mararike (2009) argues, Africans were placed by colonial interruptions into "zones of no network coverage" and the voices of ancestors became unreachable. For this reason, informants often complained that many of the contemporary *n'anga*s, who are not vetted by mediums and other senior spirits at *bira* ceremonies such as those conducted in the past, are hosts not of the benevolent and peaceful ancestors (*vadzimu*) but of *mashavi* and of *zvikwambo*. Though the vernacular adage that: "*ukama igasva hunozadziswa nekudya*" (*ukama* is half empty, it has to be filled up by feeding) was applied, as noted above, to encourage people with food and other material supplies to help others, the recipients of various forms of assistance were also encouraged to express gratitude as ways of generating and sustaining connections. The above adage is used together with *seka urema wafa*, meaning that one should never laugh at *hama*. Stressing the significance of *ukama* it is said that *ukama hautengwi nemari* (*ukama* cannot be bought using money). It is to aspects of *kutenda* (to thank) that I turn in the next chapter.

Chapter Four

On Economies of *Kutenda:* Agency, Action and Resilience Against Economic Adversities

While taking a rest at the village shopping centre on 31 May 2011, I met Sod, an old man of about seventy years, who was coming from one of the secondary schools in the district. He was taking a rest, apparently tired of cycling along the rugged and sandy village paths. After exchanging greetings, Sod bought a cool drink and sat on the shop veranda with me. Although the month of May in Zimbabwe often marks the end of summer, Sod had already run out of the staple maize meal. He pointed out that on account of insufficient rains he had harvested only five litres' worth of grain that season and so he was once again struggling to survive. That day he had just been to the school where his son was a teacher in order to seek his assistance. He noted that he expected NGOs to intervene again very quickly in order to avert the starvation of previous years.

As if to support himself physically before recounting the story of previous years, Sod shifted his position and leaned on the shop wall. He then told me that he had survived, along with other villagers, on *hacha [parinari capensis harv.]*. He and other villagers would walk over about twenty kilometres up to Nyazvidzi River where there were farms with many *mihacha* trees. Those close to the villages were claimed by other villagers and so competition for the fruit was very stiff. So Sod would wake up at one o'clock in the morning and walk to Nyazvidzi. In order to help carry the fruit, he always drove his donkey with him and on arrival he would wait for the ripe fruit to fall from the trees. He used the fruit to make thick porridge so that his family could eat, but other villagers used the fruits to brew beer which they sold. Though the villagers had many other fruit like *mazhanje [uapaca kirkiana]*, *hute [syzygium cordatum]*, *maonde [sycamarius]*, these were seasonal; when they were about to go out of season the chiefs petitioned NGOs to assist. The NGOs donated one bucket of maize grain per family per month, and Sod had therefore to supplement the maize meal with wild fruit for some time.

Sod stated that his sons in Harare could not remit anything because they were also facing challenges such as the absence of basic commodities, acute cash shortages and hyperinflation. Before he resumed cycling to his home Sod remarked: *"Mwari vakagona kuita kuti michero yacho ibereke maningi nguva iyoyo"* (God did us a great favour by ensuring that the trees have yielded a lot of fruit).

Like many of the villagers I subsequently interviewed, Sod accounted for economic matters not merely in terms of living human beings' interventions, but also in terms of the interventions of *Mwari* who was deemed responsible for abundance of fruit as well as for the droughts. Such beliefs suggest that for Sod the economy is not merely a secular human realm as opined in some economic theories since the eighteenth century (Schabas, 2005). While some theorists maintained that the economy was a distinct entity and subject not to natural processes but to the operations of human laws and agency, thinkers such as Adam Smith held that nature is wise, just and benevolent in ways that made wealth a gift of nature. Nature deified and viewed in Europe in animistic ways since the eighteenth century was used as a polite word for God in Adam Smith's 'Invisible Hand' (Evensky, 2005; Schabas, 2003): it was assumed to have a purpose, human welfare, and to be teleological. According to Schabas, Adam Smith had studied pneumatics, the science of spirits or spiritual beings. Pneumatics was also treated as speculative physics and concerned metaphysical questions about ethereal beings as well as the physics of the air and other plastic fluids. Though this teleological view of nature came to underpin the idea of the invisible hand of the market considered by Adam Smith to be the hand of the deity Jupiter, these views differ from cosmologies and metaphysics in Africa. The presumption that nature is God underpins notions of animism and relational ontologies with which I grapple in this book.

Though inhabitants of Zimbabwe sent delegates to visit the *Mwari* shrine in the Matopo Hills in times of want (McGonagle, 2007; Bullock, 1927; 1950; Gelfand, 1956; 1967), they did not consider the hills and other features of the environment to be God.

In spite of some connections between God and the spirit world to some features of the landscapes, the Shona (Fontein, 2006: 58) do not consider God and ancestors to turn into place. Thus in contrast to the eighteenth century European deism mentioned above, where nature was viewed as God, the spirit world and *Mwari* manifest on some parts of landscape, through rocks, caves, pools and trees, animals, birds and people, without conflating themselves with the features or mediums that they use as their vehicles. Instead of conceiving wealth and welfare as emanating from objects of nature (or from a God immanent in nature) as implied in the teleology of Adam Smith for instance, inhabitants of Zimbabwe were reported to view welfare as emanating from *Mwari/Nyadenga* and for some also from the ancestors (Bourdillon, 1976; Gelfand, 1966; 1967: 20-21; Bullock, 1927: 124-5) neither of whom was understood to be immanent in nature.

Much as in the economies where the invisible hand of market forces is deemed to regulate prices and availability of items, often in ways that appear miraculous (Comaroff and Comaroff, 2001; Sanders, 2003), accounts of the inhabitants of Zimbabwe show ways in which *mweya,* conventionally understood as spirits, and God were considered to provide for human welfare sometimes in miraculous ways. Though the food items could have been left by other supplicants under trees as well as in other places (McGonagle, 2007; Gelfand, 1966), worshippers/petitioners to shrines such as the Matopo Hills were deemed to be miraculously provided with food which they suddenly saw, "warm from a mysterious fire and ready for consumption upon opening their eyes" (Mutswairo, 1983; Gelfand, 1967: 21; Bullock, 1927: 24-5; Gelfand, 1966).

Sharing some logical connections with what Comaroff and Comaroff (2001) call millennial capitalism in which finance capital manifests its spectral enchantments, its modes of speculation based on less than rational connections between means and ends (in the stock exchange, insurance, gambling), modes of survival among the inhabitants underscore some openness of economies as well as the import of spectral presences with some closure, as will be explained in this chapter. While scholars like Comaroff and Comaroff emphasise these spectralities of capital, Homi Bhabha argues, in a foreword to Fanon (1963: 9, 17), that for the majority of colonised peoples the most essential value is land, which must provide bread and, naturally, dignity. For Bhabha, the primary purpose of decolonisation was to repossess the land and territoriality from colonisers. Globalisation on the other hand propagates a world made up of virtual transnational domains and wired communities that live vividly through webs and connectivities on line. Supporting Bhabha, Mignolo (2007: 9, 17, 44) argues that the logic of coloniality is the implementation of capitalist appropriation of land, exploitation of labour and accumulation of wealth in fewer and fewer hands. Decoloniality for Mignolo is delinking, undoing the logic of coloniality; it is delinking from the colonial matrix of power and it means not just changing the content, but also the terms of the conversation.

Because, for some scholars, economies in other parts of Africa are viewed as based on the 'cosmic processes' (Kassam, 1994), such economies can be understood to challenge the conventional renditions of the world in terms of linear time and of the contemporary classifications of the world into levels of development. Even though the notions of more worlds besides the human world are considered to exist in connection with Africa (Fardon, 1990; Bernard, 2003; 2007; Mawere and Wilson, 1995; Bullock, 1950; Devisch, 2001), they have not been taken into cognisance in formal and conventional classifications of the worlds. In a context where in everyday life, worlds such as those of the *njuzu* underworld and the *Nyikadzimu* of ancestors, also referred by some church members in the villages as *Goredema*, are deemed to exist (Fardon, 1990; Bullock, 1950; Burbridge, 1924; 1925; Mawere and Wilson, 1995; Mudege, 2008: 94-95; Bernard, 2003; Isichei, 2002; McGregor, 2003), the classification of worlds into developing and developed (Escobar, 1995; Sachs, 1997) appears to oversimplify the complexity of the geographies of everyday life.

Everyday life geography thus simplified was translated into categories of first, second, and third world countries in development parlance (Escobar, 1995); and, as instruments of control over the social and physical realities of Asia, Africa and Latin America, such notions of development precluded other ways of seeing and managing economies (Escobar, 1992; Gibson-Graham, 2004; 2005). Though such modes of colonising space and time through development discourses premised on *a priori* categorisations of space and temporal linearity have persisted, the development that they were deemed to yield has barely materialised, thus precipitating an impasse in development theory (Schuurman, 1993). In spite of attempts to tinker with economic rationalisations through structural adjustment programmes, economic woes have worsened (Bond, 2005; Mkandawire, 1995; Dashwood, 2003; Stiglitz, 2002; Bello, 2004; Gibbon, 1995; Amin, 2011).

While rationality is often deemed to mark formal economic theories, the empirical realities of Euro-modern economic policies in everyday life do not seem so rational given that the vicissitudes of the market sometimes play havoc on the quotidian domains, making markets seem irrational (Amin, 2011), and such economics have attracted demonstrations by the underprivileged on a world scale (Bello, 2004). Though such secular economics replaced the Christian morality of the European Middle Ages to which it was originally subordinate (Wilk and Cliggett, 2007), the enthronement of the 'Goddess of Reason' in the Cathedral of Notre Dame de Paris during the French Revolution meant that the rebellion was itself also framed in religious terms and that religion continued albeit in a different form (Bryne, 1996: 6). Although Euro-modernity has been understood to have championed autonomy and rationality, displacing religion (Coleman *et al.*, 2009: 6; Farmer, 2010; Maynes *et al.*, 2008), such views have been argued to be illusions as Euro-modern subjects are considered to be disciplined in unprecedented ways even as they begin to proclaim autonomy (Maynes *et al.*, 2008). Envisaged and experienced locally in Africa not as revealing, but as concealing the powers that animate their world, such Euro-modern economies are hardly regarded as rational, clear or comprehensible as they are moved by unseen powers much as in witchcraft (Sanders, 2003).

According to some thinkers, it is not just the failure to operate in accordance with market forces that accounts for suffering, but rather the 'demons of poverty' often embodied without consciousness of such embodiment (Meyer, 1998). For some it is participation in family and community rituals of possession, of rain, of first fruits ceremonies, or in sessions of divination or beer parties that invoke the 'demons of poverty' (Maxwell, 2006); for others, writing about various places in the world, it is failure to perform rituals to thank spirits considered to help the living that accounts for poverty (Baker, 2008; Colson, 1971; Ncube, 2004; Mudege, 2008; Gelfand, 1956; 1970; McGonagle, 2007; Verdery, 1999). Thus, the *midzimu* were considered responsible for the nation's prosperity, tranquillity and fertility, and so the markets established for trade with Europeans during the early period of contact were preceded by libations and offerings of cloths (Bhila, 1982: 75). The shift to 'secular market forces' has not alleviated the problems of inequality and poverty since markets have entailed hidden fists that serve to legitimise global inequalities (Bello. 2004; Stiglitz, 2002; Watts, 1991). Though for some, offerings to ancestors, placed under trees, could be enjoyed by passers-by who, after eating, also had to thank these ancestors and ask for plenty (McGonagle, 2007), for others, blessings were deliberately and explicitly detached from the kinship-based distributive economy, particularly if one's kin were not born again Christians (Marshall, 2009). What is seldom noted in such vilifications of ancestors is that, as Colson (1971: 210, 238, 239, 243) argues, *masabe/mashavi* possession dances appeared at the beginning of the nineteenth century with colonialism and they dramatised the desire of the *shave* spirits presumed to have invaded the bodies of the Tonga who fell one after the other as victims of new forms of possession attributed to the new spirits. The early *masabe/mashavi* [plural of *shavi*, homeless spirits of foreign deceased individuals] dances represented the essence of various foreigners encountered at that period, and under possession the victims spoke the language of the *shave* spirit. While some churches consider those who stick to ancestors to be prone to *mashavi/masabe*, Colson observed that the Siameja people of the Tonga were less prone to *masabe* than others because they showed a greater degree of adherence and respect to the cult of their ancestors, who continued to control their lineages. Colson's observations are supported by Gelfand (1956) and Bullock (1950: 59) who note for instance that when the host is possessed by a *mazungu shave* he may speak English,

Portuguese, or Afrikaans even if these languages are unknown to him. For Bullock (1950: 159, 160) the *mashave* are spirits of foreigners who died in Mashonaland and who wander until they find a host, or until the time when they would have died naturally, or are laid to rest. The *shave* are not, for Bullock, the visitations of a responsible family spirit but the alighting of the wandering spirit of a foreigner on a casually selected individual. Unlike family spirits, such *mashavi* are comparatively recent (Burbridge, 1938).

While ancestors are considered by some scholars as 'demons of poverty', others have shown that some groups of people relied on ancestors for their wealth. For instance, McGregor (2003: 96) notes that a medium called Siabumbe would immerse himself in a river only to emerge after seven days, arms laden with a variety of agricultural produce from a gorge below the Victoria Falls. McGregor's observation is supported by Alexander *et al.* (2000: 37) who note with reference to Tonga elders that a medium used to go into the pool called Lubimbi and come out later, without a scratch, carrying green mealies [maize cobs], sweet reeds and melons. For Gelfand (1970) *vadzimu* like the principle of equality and so for the Shona, prosperity, comfort and good living are derived from the spirits of his ancestors. But Gelfand argues that some people acquired talents as individuals from foreign spirits outside the family, or from spirits of a stranger who was a hunter or had some special talent and died far away from his home in a foreign land, without a burial.

Thus, on the bases of such explanations in terms of spiritual interventions in innovations, various precolonial societies have been noted to have had civilisations that included agriculture, pottery, pyramid building, written languages, astronomy, calendars, advanced arithmetic, mining, smelting, spinning and clothes, systems of law, medicine, religion, science and education (Debenham, 1960: 87-8; Jahn, 1961: 85; Ellert, 1984) Other scholars like Oswalt (1973: 3) observe that the American Indians' precolonial discoveries and inventions included potatoes, beans, tomatoes, tobacco, various drugs, pipes, hammocks and rubber syringes. For Oswalt, the early colonising Europeans who were established only precariously in America borrowed the entire maize complex from local indigenous populations they erroneously called Indians: they were taught by these inhabitants how to cultivate corn, process the harvest and prepare it as food. With respect to the Shona people, Palmer (1977: 13-4) notes that travellers to Mashonaland and other parts of Africa observed agricultural prosperity, including a variety of produce, together with local, regional and long distance trade, and the emergence of a wide range of entrepreneurs. The Shona produced finger millet (*mhunga*), sorghum (*mapfunde*), maize (*magwere/chibage*), rice (*mupunga*), cucumbers (*magaka*), pineapples, lemons, papayas, peas, beans, sweet potatoes, tomatoes, pumpkins, melons, cotton, tobacco, ground nuts, yams, and cassava. They also kept livestock, including goats, cattle, sheep, fowls and dogs, and engaged in production of agricultural tools and weapons, in basketry, wood carving, making clothes, nets and mats, and mining. Palmer (1977: 91) also notes that the Europeans initially obtained maize seeds from African farmers, and that Africans grew more agricultural products than White settlers during the colonial era; this realisation saw the colonial government introducing preferential measures for White settlers so as to help them withstand the competition from African farmers.

In spite of explanations of prosperity in term of spiritual forces, some people have tended to emphasise individual agency (Maxwell, 2006). However this, in Mamdani's (1996) terms, apparently "poststructuralist position emphasising agency" diminished the significance of "historical constraint in the name of salvaging agency, making agency appear as lacking historical specificity". Thus while conceiving blessings in terms of ancestors and God appears to strait- jacket agency within the iron laws of history, understanding wellbeing in terms of individual talent effaces historical contexts of dependency on others prior to the realisation of the talents. Emphasising individual talent occludes the contributions of others in the historical emergence of talent. And it ignores the debts to the past, some of which are deemed to keep returning to cause havoc in the form of *ngozi*, that is, the aggrieved dead who were not paid as servants, who were murdered or cruelly treated during their lifetime (Gelfand, 1970; 1967; Mudege, 2008; Fontein, 2010).

Thus, while missionaries sought to efface such practices, preaching about the devil and the possibility of possession by evil spirits (Colson, 1971: 234), such manifestations of the dead in the form of *ngozi* demanding compensation may simply be interpreted as cases of wronged persons demanding compensation, rather than as evil spirits. This is not to argue that there is no concept of evil spirits in *chivanhu,* since *mashavi* and *zvikwambo* [plural of *chikwambo*] are seen and experienced as evil and motivated by selfishness and individualism. Though ancestors, as distinguishable from *ngozi*, were misinterpreted by missionaries as evil spirits distracting men from God, some in Zimbabwe were convinced of their effectiveness. While missionaries' sermons preached that those who offered to the ancestors would go to Hell and burn forever, this clashed with the general Tonga conviction that the living would eventually become ancestors themselves and receive offerings in their turn. Aspirations to live in the *Nyikadzimu* (world of ancestors) with relatives after death (Mudege, 2008) explained the persistence of rituals as much as the aspirations to be in foreign territories explain rituals attendant to logics of border crossing (McGonagle, 2007). Deemed to be benevolent, to be richer and to live in invisible worlds that parallel human worlds (Westerlund, 2006; Fardon, 1990; Devisch, 2001; Bernard, 2003; 2007), ancestors have been counted as part of Shona individual families (Gelfand, 1956: 41). The fact that beer was brewed for *bira* ceremonies of thanksgiving to ancestors and that these ceremonies were conducted to celebrate the homecoming of migrant labourers (McGonagle, 2007) underscores the multiple borders that have to be navigated in everyday life (West and Luedke, 2006; Rutherford, 2008). Such commerce, as I understand it, between the world of ancestors and the world of living human beings, has been noted as significant in ensuring the wellbeing of human beings. Writing about Madagascar for instance, Verdery (1999: 43) notes that ancestors are "made" by remembering them, remembering creates a difference between the deadliness of corpses and the fruitfulness of ancestors. The ancestors respond by blessing their descendants with fertility and prosperity. For Verdery, the living must keep feeding their dead kin so as to ensure the ancestors' blessing and continued goodwill, both essential for the wellbeing of the universe.

While some writers emphasise the crossing of national borders by traders and by migrants who subsequently send remittances back home (Maphosa, 2009; Bracking, 2003; Bracking and Sachikonye, 2005; Muzvidziwa, 2005), others highlight healers' ways of maintaining and crossing 'cosmic' as well as terrestrial borders (West and Luedke, 2006; Bernard, 2003; 2007; McGregor, 2003). Yet others look at ways in which borders, whether cosmic or terrestrial, open up but often close off as citizens struggle to control resources and as immigrants are met with xenophobic violence as well as *zombiehood* in foreign workplaces where they are exploited as slave labour (Nyamnjoh, 2005; 2006; 2007; Isichei, 2002).

Although issues of openness and freeing the economies from state control have been pursued often with disastrous consequences for human welfare and security (Mkandawire, 1995; Bond, 2005; Stiglitz, 2002; Dashwood, 2003), little has been done to interrogate notions of openness and freeing economies in terms of popular epistemologies including the everyday life ideas of geographies and worlds. In spite of the fact that in Africa, informal governance by international institutions has intensified the loss of sovereignty by African states (Mkandawire, 1995; Stiglitz, 2002), other invisible entities conceived in popular epistemologies to govern economies have been sidelined often on summary condemnation as forms of witchcraft and sorcery (Jeater, 2007; Devisch, 2006; Kapferer, 2006). If the invisible hand of the market works with a hidden fist (Bello, 2004) and if international institutions pressure the rest of the world to accept their programmes and conditionalities even as they generate more poverty (Dashwood, 2003; Stiglitz, 2002), capital and Euro-modernity assume the role of apparatuses of capture, stifling local diversity and alternative ways of doing economies (Escobar, 2008).

Through the Shona concept of *kutenda* (to thank), this chapter focuses on villagers' understanding of the economy as governed not merely by human institutions but by entities such as *mhondoro*, for which libations are paid. The *mhondoro* to whom ceremonies of *kutenda* are often directed have been noted as having played important parts in Shona economic life. Bourdillon (1976) for instance notes that a boy was taught by the *mhondoro* in a dream how to smelt stones and extract ferrous metals. And Gelfand (1959) notes that the first seed known to the Mashona was *mapfunde* (*Sorghum bicolor*, formerly known as kaffir corn) and *rukweza* (millet), but as they did not know how to make *sadza* (thick porridge) or brew beer with *rukweza/mapfunde*, the *mhondoro* entered a young girl and taught her. *Mapfunde* was then growing wild in the forest. For Manungo (2014: 12) these were the *pasichigare* or halcyon days, the golden era when Shona and Ndebele economies went hand in hand with well-structured political systems. But for Moyana (1984: 172) the 1893 war of dispossession in Matabeleland saw the settlers loot and impound, via the Loot Committee of 1895, African cattle, so that out of the estimated 280,000 cattle the Ndebele were left with only 40,930. Some 73% of confiscated cattle left Matabeleland for Kimberley and Johannesburg, and more livestock were confiscated in default of paying taxes (Palmer, 1977: 42, 51, 101).

The belief that other entities such as *mhondoro* were controlling and governing the economies poses questions about agency. While as hinted above, Adam Smith regarded nature in terms of an active deity with a purpose in teleological terms to advance human welfare (Schabas, 2003; 2005; Evensky, 2005), scholars of Africa and Zimbabwe (Opoku, 1978; Rattray, 1927; 1969; Bullock, 1927; 1950; Fontein, 2006) emphasize that it is not objects of nature themselves that are deemed to have the agency but rather the spiritual entities temporarily abiding in or attaching to some of the objects. Writing about the Shona, Fontein (2006: 88) notes that the spirit world does manifest itself in the landscape through rocks, caves, pools, trees, but through people and animals that become vehicles for communication between the parallel existences or worlds of the people and spirits, particularly on those ritual and sacred occasions when these worlds do share temporal and spatial dimensions.

While some scholars discern the agency of the stones or objects themselves (Latour, 2005), others notice the deferred agency of human beings who infuse the objects such as the pebbles with desired forces/energies (Gell cited in Miller, 2005). For Gell, the primary reference point is to people and their intentionality behind the world of artefacts. In this sense the creative products of a person or people become their distributed minds that turn their agency into their effects as influences upon the minds of others. Though some see human social agency in the objects, others perceive spiritual energies of the dead human beings mobilised in the rituals and during the making of the objects. While Latour (2005; 2006) and others note the absence of hierarchies, other writers discern the presence of hierarchies including in spiritual terms where the High/Supreme God is worshipped (Opoku, 1978; McGonagle, 2007; Gelfand, 1956; Rattray, 1927; Aschwanden, 1987; Bullock, 1950; Bourdillon, 1976). And the market is deemed by others to be worth sacrificing for, within (neo)liberal economies, even though the development anticipated to follow sacrifices to the (neoliberal) market never materialised.

Although neoliberal economies have been vaunted as open and free, a number of scholars perceive them as mechanism in which many developing countries have been pressured by various international institutions to eliminate trade barriers while developed countries were allowed paradoxically to maintain their own barriers, resulting in inequalities and increased poverty levels despite repeated promises to reduce poverty (Stiglitz, 2002; Watts, 1991). In so far as the markets themselves are deemed to be controlled by those who set the prices, they operate through the hidden fists, mentioned above, of the developed countries that control these markets (Bello, 2004). In this sense, the IMF, the World Bank, the General Agreement on Trade and Tariffs (GATT) and the World Trade Organisation (WTO) are controlled by Westerners whose interests and views differ vastly from those of the poor in developing countries where they exercise influence without having been elected and therefore without having constituencies (Stiglitz, 2002). For this reason some scholars note that the accelerated flows of capital, goods, electronic information and migration induced by globalisation have only exacerbated insecurities, uncertainties and anxieties, bringing about an obsession with citizenship, belonging, and the building and reactivation of boundaries as manifested in xenophobia and other forms of intolerance (Nyamnjoh, 2005; 2006; 2007).

It is in the context of the debates about agency, openness, freedom in the market and broader economies that this chapter looks at ways in which Shona villagers were resilient in the face of material want. The notion of agency has been explicated in a number of works. For Jones and Cloke (2002: 47-49), by recognising the agency beyond the human domain albeit usually interrelated with human agency, it is possible to contest, fragment and dissolve the nature-culture divide which has dominated Western thought and action. The development of Latour's Actor-Network Theory (ANT) has valorised a perspective of agency which accentuates the relational, subjugating the importance of particular actors *per se* within networks in favour of a focus on the multiplicity of mutually constitutive and depositioning actants which together serve to 'hybridise' agency. Other scholars like Whatmore (1999: 29, 49, 52) have argued that agency should be seen as relational achievement involving the creative presence of organic beings, technological devices and discursive codes. Agency is seen as spun between different actors rather than manifested as solitary or unitary intent and it is conceived as decoupled from subject-object distinctions. These hybrids are then seen as mobilised and assembled into associative networks in which agency represents the collective capacity for action by humans and "nonhumans". Yet other scholars argue that it is the slave who is linked to action alone, rather than to the making of things (Armstrong, 2012: 10). In this sense, when Africans act within economies that they have not made, they can be interpreted in terms of enslavement.

It is through the practice of *kutenda* that the economies of the villagers can be understood as expressing interconnectedness not only within the visible realms but also between the visible and the invisible, the near and the far. In this sense the economies of *kutenda* underscore the existence of what other scholars have called conviviality (Nyamnjoh, 2002) in which different or competing agentive forces are recognised as needing negotiated understanding in ways that empower individuals and groups alike, not marginalising one for or by the other. As underscored in rituals of *kutenda*, conducted in *chivanhu*, where the living, the dead and some entities in the environment are all deemed to be connected (McGonagle, 2007; Gelfand, 1966), this kind of conviviality can be conceived as one where different worlds (of the dead and the living), and different spaces and temporalities play out in simultaneity and synchrony. *Kutenda* in its reckoning of ancestors and *Mwari* is akin to ways in which some individual business people have embraced spirituality, treating others as brothers and sisters, and God as an invisible shareholder in the business (Gold, 2004). This attitude does not describe, however, the behaviour of former colonial powers. As Fanon (1963: 53, 59) so potently argues, colonialism and imperialism may have withdrawn their flags, but they have not settled their debts to the colonised people on whose backs they built European opulence. And yet the victorious European nations demanded reparations from Germany for the looting carried out by the Nazis during World War II. Fanon writes that it is for this reason that formerly colonised peoples do not tremble with gratitude when European heads of state declare that they will come to the aid of the unfortunate people of the underdeveloped world. Though some scholars argue that ancestors are 'demons', others note some theologies such as the Catholic where Christian and non-Christian ancestors are deemed to be mediators between God and human beings, provided the latter obey "natural law" (Daneel, 2007). It has been pointed out that the early missionary Robert Moffat's use of the word demons to denote ancestors did violence to both Biblical and conventional Tswana usage. For Comaroff and Comaroff, describing ancestors as demons reflect missionary ideology, with long term effects on indigenous consciousness (Comaroff and Comaroff, 2005: 550).

While *kutenda* includes aspects of exchanges linking groups of people, as noted by Levi-Strauss (1970) and Keane (1994), it is not merely about exchanges but also about ways in which those exchanges are motivated, enhanced and retained. Though *chivanhu* and the attendant *kutenda* are considered by some scholars in terms of the traditional practice of relying on the dead, others suggest that even in 'modern' economies, there exists a reliance on [the economic ideas of] dead scholars whose ideas outlive their originators and return or are resuscitated from time to time [as neither dead nor alive nor as undead zombies] (Paul Krugman, 2009c cited in Quiggin, 2010). In fact the reliance by Africans on economies of Western colonial empires that have experienced social death since independence constitutes the old African logics of relying on the dead to enhance [or destroy] economies. Thus, contemporary economic exhortations to attract foreign investors involve specific ['secular'] ritual conjurations to reattract Western capital in spite of the social death of empire. The economy of *kutenda* is one in which worlds much more complex and numerous are envisaged in everyday life in ways that expose the simplicity of conventional dichotomies between developed and developing worlds.

A brief look at economic challenges

Zimbabwe's economic challenges were aptly portrayed in the Reserve Bank of Zimbabwe Governor's book entitled *Zimbabwe's Casino Economy: Extraordinary Measures for Extraordinary Challenges* (Gono, 2008), in which he expresses concern that the Zimbabwean economy has become a casino economy in which some citizens survive on speculation rather than on productivity. He attributes the hyperinflation of 231 million per cent, as of 2008, partly to the casino economy and partly to sanctions imposed by Western governments. Although the causes of the hyperinflation are attributed not only to lack of productivity but also to the invisible hands of the market, money laundering, profiteering including hording of commodities and other factors, the emphasis on productivity and the attendant efforts by the government to control the economy were particularly interesting for a number of reasons. Although productivity was emphasized, factories were closing down and relocating to other countries. As if this challenge were not enough, salaries earned by citizens, particularly in the formal sector, were eroded by hyperinflation even before they could be withdrawn from the bank. Although productivity was emphasised, inputs and technology were unavailable, in states of disrepair or vandalized during the on-going farm seizures. In short, the government's efforts to define and control matters resulted in companies, particularly big transnational corporations, relocating to other countries.

The government sought to control factories as well as commodity prices. These efforts led to the flight of capital beyond the national borders, resulting in formal sector unemployment levels rising to over ninety per cent, and in the proliferation of an informal sector over which the government had little or no control. Inevitably, some citizens engaged in speculation and money laundering.

The 2008 elections were held at a time when over 80 per cent of the population was living below the poverty line. According to the International Crisis Group's May 2008 update, over four million people were in desperate need of food. The Central Statistical Office failed to release official inflation figures for February through May, only to report in July that the figure had reached 231 million per cent. There were chronic shortages of foreign currency, fuel, electricity, water and basic commodities, and unemployment had reached levels in excess of 80 per cent. In spite of the fact that over 5.1 million people in Zimbabwe required food assistance between January and March 2009, the government restricted food distribution efforts of several humanitarian NGOs (Tarisayi, 2009; Coltart, 2008; Matyszak, 2009). The government had already banned some NGOs from distributing food in 2004, with President Mugabe saying that Zimbabweans did not want to choke on international food aid which they did not need (Coltart, 2008). On 4 June 2008 the Ministry responsible for social welfare issued a directive that all NGOs were to cease field operations with immediate effect, alleging that humanitarian NGOs were distributing food on a partisan basis. The exchanges or lack thereof between the Zimbabwean government and European governments have some parallels with events in the early colonial period. The government of Zimbabwe's rejection of humanitarian assistance parallels the refusal in the early colonial era by inhabitants of what is now Zimbabwe to accept the first famine relief by the colonial government because they alleged that the colonial troops had plundered and destroyed their grain during the first war that marked colonisation (Chigodora, 1997; Iliffe, 1990). During the crisis period in Zimbabwe, the Reserve Bank of Zimbabwe Governor was bitter about the fact that a German company, Giesecke and Devrient (G&D), which makes paper for printing money and from which Zimbabwe had been importing for 43 years, had been ordered by the German government to stop exporting paper to Zimbabwe as part of sanctions against the country (Gono, 2008: 118). Further complicating this was the allegation that neoimperialists were interfering in the country via NGOs allegedly purporting to be involved in humanitarian activities. For Gono (2008: 25, 33), American President Bush signed the United States of America Zimbabwe Democracy and Economic Recovery Act (ZIDERA) in 2001, declaring Zimbabwe's economic and land redistribution policies a threat to the objectives of American foreign policy. It directed American representatives in multilateral organisations such as IMF and WB and the African Development Bank to vote against any assistance to Zimbabwe. For Gono, there was interference by the invisible yet active hand of powerful nations which stirred up dirty politics in pursuit of an illegal regime change, often interfering through intergovernmental organisations led by the United Nations such as the United Nations Development Programme, the IMF and WB, which sometimes use their technical advice to advance political agendas. For Gono, these interferences including sanctions were forms of economic terrorism designed to coerce Zimbabweans to disown their government.

Similar arguments about NGOs conveniently neglecting crucial aspects of history such as the colonial land expropriations and effects of global power relations in their portrayals of African suffering have been raised by other scholars like Amutabi (2006) and Palmberg (2001: 16). Amutabi is critical about ways in which the neglect of history of Africa is designed to misrepresent, doctor and manipulate local scenes and images thereby simplistically and narrowly attributing problems on the continent to local conditions. For this reason NGOs that simplistically and narrowly portray African problems as local in origin are critiqued for posing as new missionaries repeating the old gospels that Africans are suffering merely because of their own backwardness or primitiveness that can be addressed via salvation from the Global North.

However, also of particular importance in this chapter are the modes of resilience relied on in contexts of hardships; such modes of resilience can best be described in terms of the vernacular adages *chaitemura chave kuseva/kugarika tange nhamo* (suffering often precedes better life) and *chitende chinorema ndicho chinemhodzi* (the heavy pumpkin is the one that has seeds) and *chidokodoko chirere, muviri chikuru chinozouya wakora* ([while there is] very little sustenance for the body, more will come later when it is fat, or, from small beginnings come great things). Other adages include *usafananidze nguo nedzaTarubva* (don't compare your apparel with those of people who have overcome problems). Such adages explain the resilience of Zimbabweans through the hardships brought about by the neoliberal economic system in which they were urged to be strong and hopeful that the economy would improve.

In line with Palmberg (2001), Zimbabwe's *Parliamentary Debates (Hansard)*, 37(11) of November 2010 notes that small to medium enterprises were running 80% to 90% of the Zimbabwean economy and providing in the process 95% of the jobs; but because the enterprises were small and indigenous they were not recorded, and thus invisible to the international community. An earlier issue of the same publication, dated 16 March 2010, 36(7), states that government has no problems with NGOs in general, but rather with those which at the inception of the land redistribution exercise in the year 2000 diverted their resources from developmental issues to what they called governance issues, where they operated parallel structures instead of working to complement government efforts. In the context of the economic challenges, it is appropriate to consider ways in which villagers deployed their agency in modes of resilience.

Agency, action and openness? resilience in everyday life economies

In the context of the crisis described above, villagers struggled to make ends meet. Mat, whom I interviewed on 5 June 2011, resigned in 2008 from his job as a teacher, which could no longer guarantee his survival. He expressed bitterness about hyperinflation and shortages of cash and basic commodities. He was exasperated by the fact that after walking twenty kilometres to the nearest bank, the cash he withdrew from his salary immediately became valueless. He noted that in 2008 his entire salary could buy only a two kilogram packet of sugar. In his trips to the bank, he was unsure whether he would be able to withdraw his salary because banks often ran out of cash. But even when he managed to withdraw some, he was unsure whether commodities would be available in the shops. Mat explained:

> Because of the ever present threats of starvation, teachers like me survived on wild fruits. One of the challenges we faced was that of acute cash shortages, the other was shortages of basic commodities like food, the third was political violence. All these problems contributed to the hunger and threats of starvation in the year 2008. Like in my case I did not have money because I often could not access it from the bank. I also did not have food, I did not even have clothes because my old clothes were torn and I could not buy new ones in the context of the challenges. Teachers like me sought assistance from villagers who were on donor lists: sometimes the villagers just gave us some food but other times they gave us pieces of work to do in exchange for the food. They assisted us with beans, cooking oil, maize grain and mealie meal.

Mat's exasperation was directed at the government which he considered to have unhinged the economy, deemed to have been much better in the period prior to the onset of the crisis. Other villagers who were retrenched in the 1990s partly blamed the IMF-imposed neoliberal economic reforms that entailed workforce retrenchments, removal of price subsidies, market deregulation and opening up the economy to global markets, the vicissitudes of which they considered to have set the national economic downturn. Some village church members attributed want to afflictions by the dead manifesting as *mashave*, considered to infect the living with poverty (Maxwell, 2006; Marshall, 2009). But, as will be shown below, other villagers like *mbuya* Noreen attributed the suffering partly to the neglect of rituals and to the privileging of individualism in some families, which she understood to cause rivalries and competition, thus making it difficult for members to perform necessary rituals together.

Mbuya Noreen's sentiments were exemplified by narratives about *ngozi* within some families which, because of lack of cohesion amongst their members, found it difficult to resolve their afflictions through collective rituals. The *ngozi* was emanating from the *mweya/mhepo* of a deceased unpaid servant, for example. It is important to underscore that in *chivanhu* as indicated by Noreen, payment for services rendered is also a form of *kutenda*. The case of Nuh; who walked about stark naked, was understood in terms of *ngozi*. When I met her she was standing still by a village path early in the morning and would not respond to greetings. By late afternoon when I returned home from my interviews with other villagers, I found her standing still naked and in the same place; still she would not respond to greetings. Baffled, I spoke to the villagers with whom I stayed, who laughed and explained that Nuh was a village woman afflicted by *ngozi* who would not let her look for employment or even get married. The story was that her paternal great-grandparents once employed a male domestic servant from Malawi whom they had failed to pay. When the servant died his *mweya* was observed to have returned as *ngozi* to demand that the debt be settled. But instead of paying up the debt, which they could not easily have done because they neither had the resources not knew the family of the deceased servant, her great-grandparents were advised by a healer to build a hut in the forest for the *mweya* to stay without afflicting the living. This worked for some time but when the great-grandparents died little was known within the family, which had also lost its cohesion, about how to maintain the hut and pacify the *mweya* of the servant which was then deemed to have taken over the faculties of Nuh. The logic of Nuh's nakedness has theoretical import in that it shows that openness can amount to vulnerability to the ramifications of *ngozi* or outside forces. It also shows that once one is open and vulnerable, the invasion by other forces can affect the body as well as the faculties, often with serious results. The theoretical import is therefore that to open up entails having one's vitality replaced by other vitalities and does not necessarily result in improvement and greater dignity. This case can be understood in terms of penetration by *ngozi* in the family and into the body and mind of one of its members. It can also be understood in terms of penetrations by ideologies and ideas that deny the existence of *ngozi*, and have encouraged people to throw caution to the wind, thus opening spaces for the invasion by *ngozi*. But the case can also be understood in terms of penetration and disruption of African economies during the colonial era, when dispossessed Africans who lost their cattle, land and labour to colonists no longer had resources to pay their own servants, thus opening themselves up for *ngozi* afflictions.

A *ngozi* deemed to be arising from unpaid debts (Gelfand, 1967; 1970) as in Nuh's case also poses complications to notions of agency. It speaks to constraints on ideas of autonomy due to the fact that individuals or families failed to *kutenda* their servants materially. In other words, a *ngozi* of such a kind can be understood as punishment by the deceased for failure to thank, in a material sense, the servants. In contexts where family and individual histories matter in struggles for survival, agency is best understood not merely in terms of the emergence or pre-eminence of the individual but in terms of historical contexts and embeddedness deemed to enable or disable the agency. By explaining their troubles in terms of the failures of the government to manage the economy, of the disastrous structural adjustment programmes of the IMF, of afflictions by the dead, as well as in terms of neglect of performance of rituals, villagers can be understood to be underlining such historicity of agency and action in so far as it impinges upon their contemporary contexts.

The significance of context was underscored by Mari, who said during an interview:

> My son, the money we had in Zimbabwe prior to the introduction of bearer cheques in the 2000s was valuable. Do you know the Z$10.00 which was red in colour? That one had value. The bearer cheques which the Governor of the Reserve Bank of

Zimbabwe (RBZ) printed during the recent years were really newspapers, worthless newspapers. But now this money [American dollars being used in multicurrency Zimbabwe since the 2009 Government of National Unity] from Obama has value so you can easily buy the commodities that you want. The only problem is that it is not ours. I went to my bank several times during the crisis but I was told that the bank had run out of cash. I survived through cross border trading, selling ground nuts in Botswana. I am also lucky because my brother-in-law who is in Australia sent me US$100.00 using moneygram; then he would phone me so that I collected the money in either Harare or Mutare.

Further stressing the economic challenges, Mari stated:

Madhora emuno aive neuremu kusiyana nemapepa akazouyiswa na Gono *aingonzi nhasi adhindwa mangwana a* expire, *fume abviswa mamwe mazero. Panguva yaGono ndaiti ndaendesa chibage ku* GMB *mari yaiuya ndayaura apa inenge isisatengi kana* two kilograms *dze*sugar. *Ma*bearer cheque *aingoita dutu izvo hapana zviripo nokuti chikoko chemachisa chainge choita* two billion *zvisingarevi chinhu*" (The Zimbabwean dollars initially had value unlike the mere paper notes that [RBZ governor] Gozo introduced, which were printed day in day out and expired as soon as they were printed, requiring the frequent striking off of some zeros on the notes as a way of revaluing them. During Gono's time, I sold maize grain to the Grain Marketing Board but I always got my cash late when it had become valueless, so that it could not even buy a two kilogram pack of sugar. The bearer cheques that Gono introduced would appear in the form of heaps of bank notes but they were useless notes because then a box of matches cost two billion Zimbabwean dollars.)

The fact that the RBZ Governor kept on printing money even though it expired soon after the printing echoes former British Prime Minister Tony Blair's (2011: 311) comment that "…sometimes in a crisis you have to demonstrate activity to keep spirits up, but the actual machinery is working away effectively. Sometimes the machinery itself is non-existent or inadequate and then you have to think first. Otherwise the activity is useless or even worse, counterproductive". The unproductiveness, and hence uselessness, of some actions and agency particularly in contexts of crises underscore the inadequacy of theories premised on action and agency in explaining everyday life. Action and agency alone cannot be eaten and in this instance villagers wanted to get things that they could eat to survive, rather than to merely act or exercise agency.

I will cite here two cases that showed the resilience of villagers in the context of the shortages of cash, commodities, and formal employment. One of the villagers who struggled to survive was Sende, whom I interviewed on 30 May 2011; he said:

> In 2007 I was dismissed from work because the company I worked for was relocating to Mozambique. Since then I stayed in this rural village but then there were droughts so I realized that my family was in trouble and could starve. I requested my young brother in the city of Harare to sell my bicycle which I had left there so that we could get money to buy maize grain. I borrowed money for bus fare to Harare but it was eroded by inflation before I used it. My wife advised that we could borrow some more and I would return the money on my return from Harare. We borrowed some Z$10.00 more and I was eventually able to travel to Harare. When I arrived in Harare I realized that my young brother had not managed to sell the bicycle because no one could buy it in a context where workers were allowed to withdraw only a maximum of Z$500.00 [sufficient to buy South African R50] from their bank accounts. There was an acute shortage of cash. I wondered what I could do since my family was without food back home. My family decided to sell our asbestos sheets and some of my clothes so that they could survive; they exchanged the items for maize grain. After some days, my young brother and I were informed that some farmers in Mutoko District were exchanging cows for maize meal. One cow was being exchanged for two 12,5 kg bags of maize meal. However when we arrived in Mutoko they wanted to charge us two 24 kg bags of maize meal for a cow. On our way back to Harare we happened to help a villager with transport and because he had no money he promised to pay with a calf. He gave us the calf and we exchanged it for a bigger cow which

we slaughtered so that we could carry the meat with us. Unfortunately our car had a fault so we spent days in Mutoko and during those days we dried the meat. I sent some of the meat back home and my family shared it. At one time during the crises my friends and I intended to go to Chiyadzwa but on the day in question we saw a bus that was overloaded with passengers some of whom informed us that we had better turn back home because there were police officers in Chiyadzwa who did not want villagers to mine for the diamonds, as we intended to do in that area. We subsequently tried again to go to Chiyadzwa and began walking at 1 a.m. but the other friend with whom we intended to go informed us that the situation was still bad in Chiyadzwa so we did not proceed with the journey. But we had walked a great distance already. We were also informed that in Chiyadzwa some miners were trapped in the mines and also that the fruitfulness of the mining activities depended on ones *rombo* (luck).

The second case is that of Movha, whom I interviewed on 25 August 2011, and who told me:

> I went to Chiyadzwa with other villagers because we wanted to mine diamonds there. We had syndicates with others who had experience in mining the diamonds in the area and so they knew which direction to take flight when things were bad with police in Chiyadzwa. The miners were beaten and some had dogs set on them. It required luck to get the diamonds because people like me went to Chiyadzwa and stayed there for two months but we did not get anything. I returned home when I realized I was failing to get diamonds. My friends and I carried food with us but it ran out without us getting anything. I did not call my family back home because there was danger in the bush [Chiyadzwa] so one does not have to inform one's family. Because of the economic crisis which accounted for shortages of fuel, I also used to walk to Murambinda which is tens of kilometres away to withdraw my salary. I eventually gave up withdrawing the salary because the earnings were eroded by inflation even before I withdrew them. I abandoned my job at the village school and decided to go to my home village. I have stayed in my village from May 2008. At home in my village, I grew vegetables

and tomatoes which I sold to schools and to other villagers. I am still growing the vegetables and tomatoes. I pick a bucketful of tomatoes daily. In Chiyadzwa were I used to go, some people could be digging very close to me and they would get the diamonds but, like I said, I failed to get even a piece. Other individual miners paid the officials that were guarding the place so that they could be allowed to get in and dig. They subsequently shared the proceeds. Food was very expensive in Chiyadzwa because the presence of diamonds pushed the prices up. I did not call my family when I went to Chiyadzwa. *Pachivanhu zvinonzi usataure uchienda kusango"* [in *Chivanhu* it is said that one should not tell one's family when one is going to the bush because they could immediately begin to grieve of the dangers].

He asked me to ask his wife, who was then preparing breakfast, to tell me how he appeared when he returned from Chiyadzwa as he could not describe it further himself. His wife simply said "now it is better because the currency has value. So he will not go to Chiyadzwa anymore".

In such challenging times, villagers survived partly by receiving donations from NGOs. The NGOs were accused by the government of being biased, of supporting and preferring members of the opposition MDC party which was, together with the NGOs, regarded as agents of 'Western neoimperialists'. Having read in the newspapers and in literature that the Zimbabwean government had proscribed some NGOs from distributing humanitarian assistance, I was keen to understand the villagers' own attitudes and views about NGOs and the work which they did in the villages, and decided to attend the session for the disbursement of food handouts. So at about 10 a.m. on 28 February 2011, I joined the other villagers who had gathered at Dananai where an NGO was set to distribute food handouts. Amid exhilaration and singing *ndiani waronga kudai, ndiMwari wakanaka, ndiyani waronga kudai ndiMwari wakanaka* x 5 (who has planned this, it is the good God, who has planned this, it is the good God x 5), villagers' names were called out. Each individual on the list of beneficiaries received ten kilograms of rice, five litres of cooking oil and a bag of mealie meal for porridge. And for all these donations the villagers expressed gratitude through the singing and dancing.

This scene underscores how the villages were connected to other places in the world. The shopping centre was a hive of activity with the villagers streaming in to receive their donations and walking off with what they had received. The NGO staff, whose offices were in Mutare about 300 kilometres away, were busy loading and unloading food stuff and dolling out the donations. Reflecting how different people and places in the world were connected to the villages, the tents in which the food was distributed were inscribed WFP [World Food Programme]. The containers of the cooking oil were marked USA, and on the mealie meal sacks was written Algeria Solidarity. On the NGO's vehicles was marked Africare, the organisation that managed the donations on behalf of WFP.

In spite of the benefits of such food handouts, villagers' narratives of such sessions underscored conflicts and variations of perceptions among themselves. NGOs had specific criteria to select beneficiaries, which often excluded some individuals. Village heads who compiled lists of beneficiaries for submission to NGOs also had their own criteria and they were alleged by some villagers to exclude their political rivals from the lists. Other villagers such as Mod and Manki whom I met just before the food handouts accused the beneficiaries of laziness, pointing out that NGOs' donations accounted for laziness among some villagers who had become accustomed to receiving handouts as they were afflicted by *mashavi enhamo*. Mod and Manki were not part of the beneficiaries as the donations were for villagers afflicted by HIV/AIDs.

Implied in the sessions and the narratives by the villagers is that agency or even action is interpreted in terms of motives and interests. The government's vilification of NGOs as agents of neoimperialism as well as the villager beneficiaries' own gratitude underscored moral issues in interpreting action or agency. Such interpretations in terms of moral questions not only import political issues into agency, but they also explain why villagers for instance expressed their gratitude to the NGO staff but not to other apparatuses such as trucks and wheelbarrows that scholars of relational ontologies would hold as actors and persons also. While some scholars have sought to interpret the actions of human and non-human beings symmetrically in terms of their being actants, the villagers' reactions indicated the pre-eminence of human beings and of God. The reactions of the villagers appear to support Alfred Gell's theory of natural anthropocentrism wherein our primary reference point is to people and their intentionality behind the world of artefacts (Miller, 2005); but among the villagers the reference points were also to *Mwari* and *midzimu* (ancestors). More importantly, the experiences among the villagers show that mere action is not what they wanted in order to survive. This implies that action is not sufficiently transformative and would not guarantee transition to better life; much more than action was expected.

Such reference points were present in Try's account of his life. I interviewed him on 3 June 2011. Some time in 2006 he was taken ill to the extent that he was unable to walk and had to be taken to hospital in a wheelbarrow:

> I was diagnosed with TB and AIDS and put on a free treatment course. Noting my diagnosis with AIDS and the criticalness of my condition, the NGO called Dananai added me to the lists of its beneficiaries so that I received porridge, beans, peas, maize grain, cooking oil, and mealie meal for porridge. *Ndakanga ndafa ini. Varungu kuvatuka zvedu asi vanetsitsi ndinovatenda. Dai vasiri ivo ndingadai ndakafa ini. Ndaitombotambura hangu kuwana mari yebhazi asi ndinotenda kuti mukoma wangu aindibatsira aiti akawana mari ondipawo. Muchiona kusimba kwandaita kudai ndavakuita basa rangu rekuvaka full-time. Ndakararama nenyasha dzaMwari. Ndinotenda Mwari vakatondigonera handisisina nhamo iye zvino handichapiwi chikafu hangu asi ndasimba zvekuti ndave kuzvishandira ndichidya* (I was dead. We shout at the Europeans but they are philanthropic, I thank them. If it was not for them I would have died. I sometimes had problems getting bus fare to go to the hospital but I thank my brother who assisted me with some money. You see me strong now so I can do my own job as a builder. I survived thanks to God. I thank God who assisted me so that now I have not many troubles, I can do my own work and earn some money.)

There are three instances in Try's statements where he used or alludes to *kutenda*): in one instance he is thankful to the Europeans at the hospital who provided him with treatment for TB and AIDS and the food donations, in another instance he is thankful to his brother who assisted him during the moment of illness, and in yet another he is thankful to God whom he considered to have made it possible for him to survive.

Further explaining ways in which inhabitants of Zimbabwe survived through *chivanhu*, that is, through relations of *kutenda* ancestors and *Mwari*, *mbuya* Noreen remarked that:

> *Vakuru vedu vaienda kuMabweadziva kunokumbira mvura kunaMwari uyo vaitendazve. Vaifamba mifambo mirefu saka vaiti kana vonzwa nzara vaikumbira chikafu pasi pemichakata vopiwa sadza raingonyuka. Asi ikozvino chikafu hachichabudi nokuti vanhu vakasvibisa nzvimbo dzacho netsvin uye nekutyora mitemo yemhondoro pamwe neyaMwari. Tave kutongorarama ne kupiwa chikafu nema*donor.*Vamwe vemumhuri vapandukirana nekuda kwemari havachabatsirani kana kuita mabira.* (Our forefathers went to Mabweadziva [now called Matopo Hills] to ask God for rain. They walked long distances and so when they were hungry they petitioned for food under *michakata* trees and *sadza* was provided by God who they thanked. Now, even if one requests such food it does not appear because people have defiled the places under such trees. We now have to simply survive on donors. Family members among some of us villagers have turned their backs on one another, they no longer assist one another and they do not even cooperate in ceremonies.)

Conceiving *kutenda* rather differently from Try, *mbuya* Noreen had this to say when I met her on 5 November 2011:

> *Mazuvano kukumbira sadza pasi pemuti hazvichaiti asi mumvura munonzwika ngoma kurira. Vakare vaive vakatendeseka, vaitenda, vaikumbirira Zimbabwe yese kuMabweadziva uko kwaienda masvikiro. Vaimboenda nembeu kunouchikwa vodzoka vanhu vopiwa. Vaikumbira sadza pasi pemuti kana vonzwa nzara vopiwa rakatobikwa kwete zvema*NGO-*itsitsi dzei tsvimborume kubisa mwana wemvana madzihwa- kubhururuka nazvo kubva mhiri kwamakungwa ivo vakaviga mari paMvuma apa tawana*

independence-vakafutsira mari. Bulgar *yemaNGO ini handidi ndinotokushira huku; ndinombozvibvunza kuti ndezvevanhu here kana mhuka izvi kana mishonga yavanorapisa vanhu handigutsikani nayo. Yavanoti* AIDS *sei iri yevatema-chikafu chavanotipa hachina kunaka dzimwe nguva chinodya muviri kwemakore wozoona zvonetsa.* (These days petitioning for *sadza* under trees does not yield desired results though we still hear drums being beaten under the water of some pools. The forefathers were more faithful and thankful to *Mwari* and ancestors, they petitioned on behalf of the whole of Zimbabwe at the Mabweadziva Hills where mediums resorted to appropriate ceremonies. They used to go there with seeds to be blessed before planting and on their return they distributed the seeds to the rest of the inhabitants. They petitioned for *sadza* under trees when they felt hungry and they were given the *sadza* already cooked, unlike the NGOs – what empathy is this that they pretend to show by flying all the way from overseas with food to donate to us when they refused to share the wealth of the country after independence? I do not even like the bulgar that the NGOs donate, I give it to chickens. I sometimes ask myself if the food they donate is for human beings or for animals, even the medicines they use to treat people I have doubts about its safety. What they call AIDS, why is it that it only afflicts the Blacks, is it not because of the kind of food they donate to us which is not good? May be the food slowly destroys the body for years before one notices.)

Scepticism such as expressed by *mbuya* Noreen is rooted in *chivanhu* where sayings such as *kuda chemungozva hubata mwana* (those who want assistance of mothers with young babies have to baby sit the child) also entail looking for deeper causes behind actions rather than satisfaction with apparent disinterested empathy. The adage exhorts one to consider ways in which for instance coloniality often thrives and justifies the relevance of colonists' interventionism by surreptitiously creating and sustaining problems for colonised peoples, for which it then claimed to singularly possess solutions. Similarly, in the vernacular proverbs *mwoyochena ndowei bere kurinda munhu akafa* (what good naturedness is it for a hyena to guard the corpse of a human being) and *hapana mhou inokumira mhuru isiri yayo* (no cow lows for a calf that is not its own) underline the need to search for deeper causes of apparent empathy. But in spite of her misgivings about the food being donated, villagers with few alternatives could not, as it were, forego eating the flesh of a polecat when they did not have that of a hare. It is also important to note that in *chivanhu* where ancestors are counted as family members, national and international food policies do not take such African metaphysics into consideration. Yet as I witnessed among the villagers, some prepare meals called *gunere* once a year in honour and commemoration of ancestors. This is particularly so in the case of healers such as *mbuya* Noreen, who organise *bira*s once every year for their ancestors, using food stuff and grain such as *rapoko* (finger millet). Besides, in African cosmologies of *chivanhu*, when food circulates among different households those who bring the food are expected to eat a portion of it in the presence of the people who are expected then to eat the meal. This is known as *kubvisa huroyi* (to show that the food is not poisoned or does not contain witchery substances). In such cosmologies food that has not been subjected to *kubvisa huroyi* is treated with suspicion.

Mbuya Noreen's scepticism about donated food is also underscored in discourses on genetically modified organisms (GMOs) where it is contended that the food being produced and donated is hazardous to health; this scepticism also exists with respect to efforts towards food sovereignty in developing countries (Sithole, 2011; Mulvany and Moreira, 2009, www.newzimbabwe.com, *'Zimbabwe's Minister Made defends GMO ban',* 10 June 2012). Casting doubts on food aid, some scholars note that during the colonial era poisoned bread was given to Australian Aboriginal families, and that the latter were treated as experimental animals, so that the Aboriginal settlements disappeared within fifty years (Yahya, 2001: 43). Similarly, *mbuya* Noreen's misgivings about whether donated food is for human beings or for animals underlines the important distinction in *chivanhu* between humans and animals that scholarship on animism fails to make by conflating the two. Though her misgivings about NGO donations have been similarly recorded in other places such as in Masvingo District (Gutu, 2004: 57 cited in Masunugure *et al.*, 2007) where villagers considered food aid as inferior and to be livestock feed in countries of origin, she did not appear to dislike people from other countries, as in fact her daughter was employed in Johannesburg by a Chinese businessman. Her dismay about the desecration of places under some trees where they petitioned for food can also be interpreted as an expression of disgust at the closure of worlds, in the absence of appropriate ritual performances, observances of taboos and customs, including the ancestral worlds which were understood to have facilitated modes of resilience. While her account of food petitioning under the trees is supported by Gelfand (1967: 21); Mutswairo (1983) and Bullock (1927: 24-5, 1950), other scholars have pointed out that villagers during their rituals often left food under such trees as *michakata,* and passers-by could eat the food and then thank ancestors who were deemed to have provided it (McGonagle, 2007). Though other scholars underline the suddenness of the appearance of the food, *mbuya* Noreen did not remark on this. While Bullock (1927: 24-5) for instance notes that the priesthood of *Mwari* made a feature of a feast of viands and beer which appeared suddenly on a bare rock, warm from some hidden fire, supposedly provided by God, *mbuya* Noreen simply stated that food appeared after petitions were made during pilgrimages to Mabweadziva. But in later work, Bullock (1950: 163-4) notes that colonial Zimbabwe had now changed for the new, as indigenous inhabitants said that *Mwari* could no longer manifest himself through and to his children as He had before because the land had now become *chirumbi,* that is, enveloped by the aura of the Europeans.

The remark by *mbuya* Noreen that nowadays food is not supplied by *Mwari* under trees because the places under them have been desecrated, and that taboos on purity are no longer observed, can also be understood in terms of the villagers' frustration with cashless banks. Possibilities of acting without getting connected to one's desires underlay the frustration with respect to failure by some villagers to access their salaries from banks that could not dispense cash during the crisis. To the extent that villagers expressed frustration at their failures to access cash and to buy commodities which were not available in the shops during the crisis, they indicated the need to pay attention to such dispositions including the personal anguish that attends privation as well as the jubilation that attends successful connection with desired ends. In this way the villagers' modes of engagement raise the issue of how one might conceive the action of human beings as symmetrical with the action of nonhumans as implied in Latour's ANT, without running the risk of ignoring or slighting the significance of feelings including the attendant frustrations and joys that are also crucial in understanding matters of resilience and survival. The theoretical insignificance of a focus on actors and action is captured in the vernacular phrases *kutambiswa bhora risina mweya* (to be made to act vacuously without achieving desired ends or without improvement) and *kuitwa chidhori* (to be treated like a doll, that is, manipulated). In this sense the vacuity of the neoliberal reforms which worsened instead of improving the conditions of the citizens, the vacuity of colonial forms of forced labour (*chibharo*) and enslavement, and the vacuity of working during the crisis period for earnings that were immediately eroded by inflation all amount to *kutambiswa bhora risina mweya*. Other villagers employ the phrase *kushandiswa* (to be used) as well as the proverb *mutsa worutsoka kuperekedza ziso* (it is stupidity of the foot to accompany the eye on an errand from which it cannot profit itself) to indicate those who are made to act or to do things for nothing. These ideas can be interpreted in terms of the English proverb 'if you made your bed with thorns then you must sleep on it'. However the challenge in African economies is that their foundations are not laid by Africans; rather, they have been laid for Africans by Europeans since the colonial period, while it is the Africans who are forced to sleep on the economic bed even if it is made of thorns, as it were.

The point here is not that villagers did not see the significance of other factors that aided their survival, but rather that struggles for survival are often matters of politics of survival in which what matters is not only action but also feelings and the possibility of imputing blameworthiness for action and inaction. In moments of such politics it is often human beings who are blamed for action or inaction including for certain results that may be deemed undesirable. The absence of cash for instance was blamed on bank officials as well as on government officials, including the Governor of the Reserve Bank of Zimbabwe: the absence was not blamed on the ATMs [automatic teller machines] machines which could not dispense the cash because officials had not loaded them. Similarly, the absence of commodities and the hyperinflation were blamed on government officials who in turn blamed the shop owners for profiteering: the commodities themselves were not blamed for disappearing. Even though money vanished in the banks due to hyperinflation, it was bank officials and government officials who were blamed for it; it was not the money that was blamed for vanishing. For instance, Fel, whom I interviewed on 28 June 2011, pointed out that although in the 1990s she could afford to buy commodities because the currency was relatively stronger than the bearer cheques which the Reserve Bank of Zimbabwe Governor introduced in the 2000s rendered things unaffordable (as when a loaf of bread cost Z$10 billion in the recent past).

What the above modes of engagement suggest are perceptions that there are things such as ATMs which, although they may be deemed in terms of Latour's ANT to act by dispensing cash, are not considered blameworthy; in such a scenario human beings look behind the machines to see human beings who attract the blame in their stead. The modes of engagement also suggest that human beings act and attract blame or praise. The third position is that of healers who consider the *mweya/mhepo*, which I will look at more closely below, to act and attract blame as well as praise. Arguably, these efforts to see causal human individuals behind things do not speak very well to the ANT which presumes flatness and symmetry between humans and nonhumans because the efforts underline perceptions of hierarchy even among human beings themselves. In this vein, a thing in *chivanhu* is not a *munhu* simply because it acts, even if, in similar ways to *munhu*, and statements such as *kuita semunhu* (to simulate a human being) underscore this clearly. The modes of engagement reflect hierarchies which, however faulty and often blameworthy, were a feature of the organization of everyday life in the villages as well as in the country. In view of such modes of engagement, it can be argued that the connections among the villagers were as much horizontal, in cases where villagers connected with their fellows, as they were vertical, with respect to the hierarchies.

Even though agency explains the villagers' modes of engagement including their connections with others, it can also be argued that in view of the privation, the frustration, the feelings of helplessness and the disablement of some modes of resilience, the villagers were more powerless patients than agents in the connections. The above-noted lamentation by Mat that even the village school teachers were reduced to begging for food by the crisis underlines the pitfalls of perceiving the villagers, in the context of the crisis, merely as agents, without also noting the ways in which they were rendered patients of their fellows from whom they begged for food. In this sense the switches from being a school teacher to begging and surviving on picking and gathering wild fruits can be understood as having been punctuated as much by agency as by moments of being patients. In this sense the deployment of agency can be understood in terms of efforts to take flight from being patients, but as seen with respect to the villagers such flights are not always a guarantee of success. It is the absence of such guarantees that often necessitate multipronged pursuits in everyday life struggles to survive. It is because one is not securely an agent that one petitions others, connects with others, engages with others in a variety of ways that call for appraisals, reappraisals and feedback, which in turn explains the endurance or otherwise of the connections. *Kutenda* (to thank) is one such way in which villagers offered appraisals and feedback on and about others with whom they were connected.

The notion of *kutenda* can be understood in terms of Levinas' (2001, 2003) argument on ethics that our being does not close in upon itself and sustain itself like a substance; it continually projects itself into the world of possibilities that answer to them. However other scholars have reservations about Levinas' arguments and this was the reason for which the Zimbabwean government resisted placing itself under the tutelage of what it termed the neoimperialist forces that it blamed for engineering the crises in the country. But for Levinas, the impossibility of being and the sense of there being nothing more to be done, as was the case in Zimbabwe, is the mark of the limit of the situation in which *uselessness of action* is the sign of the supreme instant from which humanity can only depart. Nausea, for Levinas (2003), coupled with malaise, that is, the fact of being ill at ease which appears as a refusal to remain in one place, as an effort to get out without knowing where one is going, qualifies the essence of this attempt to place our being in the tutelage of the outside. Yet this kind of ethics, founded on desperation, that forces one to deliver oneself to the tutelage of the outside, has been linked by other scholars to slavery where, faced with the possibility of starvation, individuals are forced to deliver themselves up (Pinfold, 2007: 261). This notwithstanding, a look at everyday life shows modes of resilience premised on *kutenda* where there is expression of gratitude for the other's import in sustenance.

Kutenda

Popo, whom I met and interviewed on 4 August 2011, narrated his struggles to survive thus:

> I started selling vegetables, potatoes and fruits in 2003. In 2008 I barter-traded in cooking oil and soap. I bought the cooking oil from Mozambique and exchanged it with maize grain at the Grain Marketing Board; now I have managed to buy six cows. I have tried my hand at a number of things like gold panning, switching over to informal trading again. Now I sell these clothes, batteries, shoes and oils. I did not go further than the General Certificate of Education 'O' level because my father died in 1997 and since my two brothers were already at university my mother decided to focus on them in her financial priorities. But now I am living well. I have learnt a lot from my experiences, so that even if you leave me to stay in a desert I will find means to survive. It is God who gives me the means to survive and I thank him for that, but sometimes as human beings we fail because of witches and *zvikwambo* [conventionally understood as goblins].

Zvikwambo zvinobata pfungwa dzevanhu asi vamwe vanokanganiswa nekudeketererwa. Zvikwambo zveluck zvinobira vamwe zvoshatirisa Mwari mvura yoramba kunaya. Tine maziso asi hationi zvemumhepo zvakaita sekubiwa kunoitwa pachishandiswa zvikwambo" (*Zvikwambo* arrest the minds of people but some people are disabled because others people perform rituals to arrest their success. *Zvikwambo* for luck steal from others making God angry, so that people are visited with droughts. We have eyes but we cannot see things in the wind like the fact that *zvikwambo* steal from others.)

Also noting the significance of *kutenda* partly with reference to *ngozi* to which I hinted above, *Mbuya* Noreen remarked that:

> *Ngozi yakaoma, munhu haaurayiwe. Mhepo dzakagara dziriko kubva kare paive nevaya vaigarira kuti vapiwe vakadzi vanhu vozoita ruchiva vozvarira vana paneupfumi uya ziso rake rinonga richingova paakaratidzwa. Anoroorwa hake asi haaiti mwana odzoka pamusha ozoita zitete risingaroorwi kana rafa rodzoka vave vaviri. Mudzimu unoda kucheneswa, Bira rinoita kuti udzoke mumusha kana risati raitwa anonzi ari kumashizha. Mamwe mabira ndeekutenda mudzimu. Bira ini ndichaita gore rinouya, gore rino handina mari. Panobikwa doro rebira uya akapondwa mutorwa anotopiwa yake hari inoiswa kunze kwemusha vanouya vatorwa vopfuura vachimwa. Vakuru vemisha vanototanga vapira kwaari kuti tinoziva kuti muri mumusha hari yenyu ndiyi musakanganise zvedu. Iyezvino vanhu vave kuti ukarimwa zvinotorana newe, kunyepa anotorana newe sei usina kumuuraya?* (A *ngozi* poses difficulties; a person should not be killed. Winds of the dead have always been in existence in history there were people who worked as servants so that they would be given wives but because the promises were not kept. After their death the servants continued to look forward to the fulfilment of the promises so they seized women in the families concerned, the women could get married but fail to conceive and return to their natal homes to stay as unmarried aunts possessed by the deceased unpaid servants. As far as the ancestors are concerned they need to be cleansed through rituals so that they become purified from dirty spirits. The *bira* is done so that the ancestors can return home; if it is not done the deceased stays in the bush. Other *bira* are done simply to thank the ancestors. I will be conducting my own *bira* next year; this year I have no money. When beer is brewed for the ancestors' *bira*, the person who will have been murdered by family members has to be informed and given his/her own pot of beer

which is placed outside the homestead so that passersby will drink the beer. This is a way of acknowledging the presence of the deceased strangers who may still be within the homestead. The elders of households must first inform the murdered that they know he/she is in their homestead so he/she should not disturb their ceremonies. But nowadays people claim that if one drinks the beer for the murdered the latter will leap onto you: this is a lie, why would the murdered leap onto one who did not kill him/her?)

Mbuya Noreen's observations were replicated in Rora's notes to me on 30 January 2011. Rora, a *n'anga* by profession reported that

> When villagers do not perform *kutenda* ceremonies for their ancestors, some get involved in accidents. Often for those who die, it is because they neglect *kutenda* in *chivanhu*; some villagers no longer perform *kurova guva* ceremonies for the deceased because they say they have joined churches. Beer for the *bira*s to thank *midzimu* is no longer brewed yet the *midzimu* would have been assisting for instance in making one pass at school or university. There is need to brew beer to inform the *midzimu* that you have passed. Even in marriages divorce rates have risen because villagers no longer perform ceremonies for *midzimu* and they also no longer compensate the *ngozi*, some of the villagers have assumed *chirungu* so they no longer perform all these ceremonies, thus they no longer have the protective walls of the ancestors. *Bira* involves brewing beer to thank the senior ancestors and you tell them, villagers should drink the beer and dance like the ancestors used to do when alive and in the human world. The wealth of some villagers vanishes because it is not connected to the *Nyikadzimu* of their ancestors. *Chivanhu hachife* (*chivanhu* does not die). The *Mashavi* exist, the *shavi* of poverty exists. The *shavi* of poverty is one that some villagers deflect, when they visit them, to their *hama*. The *shavi* of the foreign deceased brings poverty in families and it comes as *mbereka* (an attachment) behind the deceased family members who during their lifetime honoured it and so it continues to revolve within the family. It then shuttles between the different families in *ukama* and those who discover its existence consult *n'anga* requesting that he/she sends it away and to other families in the

ukama. The *n'anga* then goes to the forest and calls the name of the intended new victim of the *shavi* and then tells the *shavi* to go to that new victim. The *shavi* goes and stays with that person or new victim; the *shavi* of poverty is not destroyed by churches. Churches provide only temporary solutions or respite for five to ten years before the *shavi* resurfaces or returns again. Some *mashavi* are sent away after they have been asked to lodge in fowls or in goats. Others are left by victims, with the assistance of *n'anga,* at crossroads. Whoever is first to pass by the crossroads after that ceremony will be the *shavi*'s new victim and will carry it home. The *shavi* can be made, by the *n'anga,* to sit on a nice item and then the item is left at a crossroad or in a forest so that any person who picks it up will also pick up the *shavi* which will then begin to stay with the person in his/her home. If you remember the forefathers, that is, your *vadzimu* as distinct for *mashavi*, they will also remember you and ensure that you do not get into trouble and even the *mashavi* will not be allowed by your forefathers to trouble you. These days many of the rich people in Zimbabwe are those without high education but who perform the *kutenda* ceremonies. Europeans have retained their memorial services but we have abandoned our *chivanhu*.

While these statements by Rora support Colson's (1962) observation that among the Tonga in northern Zimbabwe, a man's successes and failures are not his alone but belong to the group which has supplied him with a guardian *muzimu* and share with him a ritual attachment, some villagers no longer observe such precepts.

Kutenda can be understood as a way of reckoning connections of *ukama* with others. It is a way of acknowledging the difficulty, or even the impossibility of exercising agency or acting in the world all on one's own. It can be understood as a way of recognizing the import of others, as in Try's case, where one is more of a patient than an agent, that is, when one's agency is debilitated by ill health and other forms of want. It is a way in which connections with others perceived to enhance life are acknowledged and fostered. *Kutenda* is considered among the villagers to be so important in maintaining connections of *ukama* that it is said that *kusatenda huroyi* (to fail to thank the other is witchcraft). This can be understood to emphasize to individuals that they do not live merely by asserting autonomy and that they should recognize the import of others, who may feel harmed by failure to be acknowledged. Conversely the Shona dissuade their members from *kudyira uroyi mukunyara,* that is, to acknowledge and accept poisonous food due to shyness. So while the English would enjoin one not to look a gift horse in the mouth, this *chivanhu* adage promotes forthrightness and frankness in exchanges.

Remarks linking failure to thank others with whom one is connected to *uroyi* (witchcraft) suggest that such failure risks breaking connections that render life much in the way that *uroyi* is understood to interrupt the flows of life. In other words, connections can be conceived in terms of variants of insurance from which individuals reap benefits through petitions, and conversely they invest in the connections that render life via *kutenda.* While such connections can be viewed in terms of Ingold's (2011: 63) meshworks of entangled lines of life, in times of crisis connections can be understood as much in terms of life as with lifelessness and death, that is with threats to life. To privilege life may be to ignore moments when life is interrupted, and lost; it would be to miss moments when life and death cohabit or share the same spatial and temporal domains. Yet as indicated above, even banks had moments during which they were punctuated by the life of clients, as well as when they were deserted for absence of cash; shops equally had moments when they were punctuated by the life of shoppers as well as deserted for want of commodities, and workplaces had moments when they were deserted for want of living wages in the hyperinflationary context. In view of such vicissitudes of the crisis and the unpredictability of life one can speak of moments of life rather than lines of life, for life during a crisis is lived for the moment. And as seen in the ceremonies in honour of the dead who were petitioned and thanked by some villagers, life is often articulated with death and with the dead who hover in the vicinity.

Such *kutenda* connections between the dead and the living, between life and death, can be interpreted from one ceremony which I attended in 2011. When I met Don in January of that year he indicated that he wanted to conduct a ceremony to thank his ancestors for the trading business he had established in Mozambique. I eagerly took it as an opportunity to participate in the ceremony and to learn how he conducted it. A few days later, I accompanied him to a healer who offered advice on how to proceed. Following instructions from the healer, Don bought some *rapoko* grain and put some in a small plate over which he uttered statements informing his ancestors about the oncoming ceremony. He then poured the *rapoko* back into a sack. I helped him carry the sack which weighed about 20 kilograms to a well where he soaked the grain for seven days, removing the water when it started sprouting. The *rapoko* was then dried on a rock where it was spread for some days before it was taken to the grinding mill. From the grinding mill Don secured a drum into which he poured water and mixed it with some *rapoko* and maize meal. He then poured the mixture into some clay pots and left it to ferment overnight. On the following morning he poured the mixture into a drum and boiled it until it had reduced by half, and started smelling like home brewed beer. He left it to cool, added some more *rapoko* meal, stirred, and set it aside to ferment overnight. The following morning he squeezed the mixture through a sack so that the beer was smooth.

Immediately after the beer was processed, Don sent word to the village head as well as to other villagers whom he could find to join him in the ceremony. They sat under the shade of a big tree which was not of ritual significance to the ceremony. Before he started issuing the beer, Don went into a hut and uttered statements informing his ancestors that the beer was ready for consumption. He then carried the pots of beer to the shade. As the villagers drank, stories including how other villagers had performed similar ceremonies were shared until the evening. Much as the villagers mobilized one another for the ceremonies, they deemed the ceremonies to mobilize the invisible realms of their ancestors who were considered to aid the modes of resilience of those who performed such ceremonies. Among the villagers, ancestors, though dead, were considered to be active in the human realm, remaining embedded in *ukama* connections with the living whose welfare they were deemed to influence.

Don's ceremony can be understood in the context of the broader engagements by the villagers between the visible and the invisible realms in their efforts to survive. In his case he petitioned the invisible realm of his ancestors as well as individuals in the visible realm including the healer from whom he had sought advice and the other villagers he had invited to participate in the ceremony. He understood his petitions to have import on his material resilience. But contrary to arguments that there is reliance on spectrality alone, Don's experiences show that he was also involved in productive work even as he was also thankful to his ancestors who were conceived not as providing but rather as aiding his work. Don is not an exception as in *chivanhu* terms like *nyope/simbe* are used as derogatory terms for those who are lazy and do not engage in productive work. While reliance for food on others, including NGOs, is sometimes viewed as overreliance on others, known in vernacular as *kusunza/kupemha,* it is regarded lowly as it is deemed to be a sign of laziness. The effect of Don's ceremony was a web of complex connections understood to engender feedback on different levels. Though the worlds of ancestors are dismissed using Euro-modernist lenses, paradoxically scientists are investing huge efforts to discover new worlds including engaging in expensive space explorations (see for instance Berlitz 1975, Bizony 2012). This paradox of course poses questions about whether the scientists or Euro-modernists simply want to perpetuate the notion that they alone can discover worlds, and if they have not yet discovered them, anyone else's knowledge about other worlds is dismissed with scepticism. Also arising from Don's ceremony, as well as from the fact that *midzimu* are counted in *chivanhu* as family members, is the question whether NGOs and other donors should count only living family members as beneficiaries and determine the quantity of food to be distributed on the basis of the basic needs of the living members only. Counting *midzimu* as family members entails costs but as Bhila (1982) notes, Europeans who initially brought gifts of cloth for *mhondoro*s immediately preceding colonisation knew that the Shona held the view that national wealth was premised on *midzimu* rather than on sacrifice to the invisible hand of the market. Similarly in African contexts where some food items are taboo in totemic terms, there are questions as to how the donations by NGOs would take such taboos into cognisance. Eating items that are totemically tabooed is understood as *kudya mutupo* (to eat one's totem) that would result in *kubva mazino,* literally to become toothless but meaning to become powerless. How such African ideas of powerlessness and empowerment can be considered in development and transformation should be part of future projects. Such taboos and expression of gratitude to ancestors are greeted with disapprobation among church members but then there is a paradox in it. The paradox is that colonial settlers justified racism and colonial projects on the pretext that the Africans were descendants of Ham, who is recorded as having mocked his father when he saw him naked; yet it is precisely via the colonial religious practices that Africans were encouraged to ignore their forefathers. As already noted in the preceding chapters, in pre-colonial Zimbabwe *Mwari*'s oracle advised Africans to respect their parents and ancestors and to accord them the rituals due to them. Yet the colonists expropriated the African assets some of which were used in rituals, making it impossible to perform rituals in honour of ancestors.

Among the villagers one notices some convergences as well as divergences premised on the different ways in which they deemed the invisible realm to be constituted. Members of the many churches that dotted the villages viewed ancestors as lying in the same realm of the malevolent dead such as the aggrieved deceased that return as *ngozi*. So they bunched ancestors together with the *ngozi* as in the category of *mweya yakaipa,* literally translated as bad air, for which one needed exorcism. For this reason they dissociated themselves from family ceremonies aligned with ancestors, and healers such as *mbuya* Noreen therefore decried what they considered the churches' role in pulling family members apart, making the performance of ceremonies difficult. Her own son who had joined an apostolic sect withdrew from it when the leaders pressured him to abandon his mother for a surrogate mother within the church. The church leader argued that her son had to sever connections with her because she was a healer. In the light of Shona adages such as *ziva kwawakabva mudzimu weshiri urimudendere* (be cognisant of your origins for if you are not so, your future is doomed), Noreen's son refused to let go of his mother. It is interesting to note ways in which churches have sought to retrench not only the institution of ancestors but also the institution of parenting, as in the case of Noreen. This is done on the basis of arguments that they can take better care than the ancestors and the parents, even yet prying Africans away from their families including their ancestors, and deeming *Mwari* responsible for generating conflicts where harmony is expected and required in *chivanhu* if one is to realise prosperity.

But church members relied on *tsvimbo* (rosaries), literally translated as knobkerries, which are also used by healers, as well as on prayers. Timo, who left his job at the height of the crisis, always carried his *tsvimbo* around his neck. I met Timo, aged about 25, on 3 August 2011. He said he had worked in a mine in Matabeleland up to 2008. He said the following:

> I deserted employment when it was not helping me survive in 2008 and I came back to Buhera while on leave. Bank withdrawals were limited at that time to Z$500.00. I was ferried by a company car to Bulawayo and my wife and I had all our belongings. I wanted to board a train from Bulawayo to Gweru but the train was already full. I did not have enough money for food and travel back home to Buhera. Fortunately I met my wife's friend who worked at the take away restaurant by the train station. She gave us *sadza* (thick porridge) and paid for our train tickets and made sure that our belongings were put on board the train. She also gave some money to my wife. A*kaita madhiri ake mukati akadzoka kwatiri (*she performed her tactics inside the railway offices and then came back to us). We arrived in Gweru but at that time I no longer had money enough for the journey from Gweru to Buhera. I went to CABS (Central African Building Society) to withdraw money. I presented my identity card as well as my bank card but because I was stressed I punched wrong numbers. My wife was in her first pregnancy and I had no money for my in-laws, for our food or for *kusungira* rituals [associated with marriage and first pregnancy] for my wife. I punched wrong numbers after which the bank teller asked whether I was all right. I informed her of my

troubles. At that time withdrawals could only be done inside banks. I eventually succeeded in punching the correct pin numbers. Buses did not want to ferry our belongings because I did not have enough money. A man I met at the bus stop [Timo intimated that the man was a member of a church] asked me if I wanted to go home in Buhera and I said yes. He said, 'let me then assist you carry you luggage to the bus stop'. I cast my eyes to the bus stop and realized that a long distance truck which was due to Buhera was just leaving. Upon arrival at the bus stop a taxi driver declined to ferry us because of our luggage. In the middle of pondering how we would get home, a vehicle belonging to sisters of the Roman Catholic Church which was bound for Chipinge was arriving and it stopped a distance away from where we were. I explained my troubles to the sisters and then they asked me where my *tsvimbo yevaRoma* was. I showed them the rosary which was around my neck. They then allowed me to board together with my wife and our baggage. We eventually arrived home in Buhera. My wife went straight home from the bus stop to inform our family that we had arrived. My brothers subsequently carried our baggage home. I cried as I could not believe that I had eventually arrived home. I have not yet returned to work. We stayed together at home, with my family, because some of them used to trouble me when I was working, they accused me that *hauna musoro* (you have no head/you are not wise with your money) so when we were together in the village and without means I wanted to see who among them would accuse me of not using money wisely. I will not abandon my Church, the Roman Catholic, because it helped me a lot. When we arrived at the shopping centre I showed the Catholic sisters the Buhera branch of our church as they were passing by on their way to Chipinge. I thank God and I also thank the sisters.

The ways in which invisible forces, some of which are subject of *kutenda* while others are subject of vilification, were deemed to impinge on everyday life can be exemplified by the case of Wita whom I met in June 2011. Her story exemplified ways in which some invisible forces were subject to vilification rather than *kutenda* among the villagers particularly if the invisible forces brought suffering even if for the benefit of a few. Her story also resembled many others I was told by different individuals in the villages and in many ways they parallel Comaroff and Comaroff's (2001) account on millennial economies particularly as involving spectral presences and as not premised on productivity but on speculation. The accounts among the villagers were of *zvikwambo* which were understood to be made by sorcerers in order to harm others, to acquire wealth and to be feared by others. Wita, whom I interviewed on 10 June 2011, pointed out:

> *Chikwambo mweya wemunhu akafa wakaipa unobuda uri pazvinhu zvakaita semaruva, kiti, chirume chipfupi kana mishonga chaiyo. Chikwambo chinotorwa kana kutengwa nechinangwa chekuda kubudirira muupenyu pazvinhu zvakasiyana zvinosanganisira kuda kupfuma kana kungoda kutyiwa munharaunda kana pabasa"* (a *chikwambo* is air of a deceased human being that is evil and that manifests on things such as flowers, cats, very short men, or herbs. It is acquired or bought with the aim of succeeding in life in a number of dimensions including riches, in order to be feared in the area or at workplaces).

Thus the *chikwambo* is similar to what is known in different cultures as *incubus* in Latin, *dab tsog* among the Homong in Vietnam, Laos and Thailand, *gui ya chuang* in China and *kanashibari* in Japan (Bizony, 2012: 223). For Bizony, in all these instances it is a male form that lies upon sleepers, especially women, the female equivalent being *succubus*, and it is an eerie entity of short to medium height.

Nau, who also spoke on the same topic, noted that she had miserable experiences with *chikwambo* which she alleged her husband acquired from a healer in South Africa with the aim of enhancing his luck during the crisis period. She further alleged that he was given the *chikwambo* in the form of a flower which he was told to feed with milk, by pouring it on the flower. The worries that led to her consulting healers arose from dreams which she frequently experienced, subsequent to her husband's acquiring the *chikwambo*. In the dreams, a very short man had sexual intercourse with her every night. Unaware that it was her husband who had acquired the *chikwambo* that was troubling her, she informed him about her dreams. Her husband merely shifted to another bedroom. Nau continued to experience the dreams and every morning woke up feeling very tired. She subsequently consulted a healer who disclosed that because the *chikwambo* needed a wife, it was taking her. Nau subsequently informed her husband about the healer's allegation and he confirmed that he had acquired the *chikwambo* for purposes of enhancing his luck. He further alleged that when he shifted from his bedroom he was fleeing the *chikwambo* which was beating him because it wanted Nau for a wife. Her husband died shortly after that and Nau consulted prophets who helped her remove the *chikwambo* by destroying the flower and the herb through which it manifested and by bidding its *mhepo/mweya* to leave the homestead. As noted above a *chikwambo* is not considered in *chivanhu* to be a *munhu* (person) but is deemed to be a *chinhu* (thing). For this reason different forms of the demonstrative 'this' are used for *munhu* and for *chikwambo*: this *munhu* is referred to as *munhu uyu*, while this *chikwambo* is referred to as *chikwambo ichi*. In both churches and *chivanhu* the *zvikwambo* are deemed to visit impurities and suffering on *vanhu* (plural of *munhu*) so they are destroyed. *Zvikwambo* and *mashavi*, as noted in Chapter Three, appear to be comparatively recent because in pre-colonial society Africans stayed together as closely knit groups of *hama* (relatives) and without having to travel so far and to mix so much as to fail to distinguish between on one hand *midzimu* and on the other hand *zvikwambo* and *mashavi*. As explained above *zvikwambo* are considered to be *mweya* of deceased from outside circles of *ukama* and often also from outside the country. Equally *mashavi* are from outside the circles of deceased *hama* – they are from foreigners whereas *midzimu* are from deceased *hama*. What this entails is that *zvikwambo* and *mashavi* are not integral aspects of *chivanhu* in the sense that they are deemed to be derived from outside *ukama* and from foreigners.

In interpreting such experiences it is important to note the ways in which in such everyday life dreams are conceived to bridge the wakeful and sleep time. One should also note how verification of connections between the visible and the invisible realms is done as ways of ascertaining articulations. In Nau's case she sought to verify her dreams by consulting a healer, and often in their verifications villagers consulted several healers and or prophets in different areas. In Nau's case her dreams were verified by the fact that sometime during the moments when she was troubled by the *chikwambo* her daughter who became a second victim started having similar dreams and experiences which she shared, including waking up feeling very tired. In these cases the visible is understood in terms of the invisible and vice versa, even as women made efforts to disentangle themselves from the rapacity of the *chikwambo* that troubled them. But at a theoretical level the notions of *chikwambo* signal opposition to circulation of herbs and migration to regions where migrants would possibly acquire the *zvikwambo*. The notions signal opposition to global economic slashing and burning, including by capital that relocates to other regions, thereby creating hardships in areas from which it relocates.

But villagers such as Mai T did not consider the *zvikwambo* to spread sexually transmitted diseases. She said that

> *Chikwambo hachiparadziri zvirwere zvepabonde zvinosanganisira* HIV/AIDS *nekuti ini ndakatanga kuita zvekurota ndichisangana nemurume ndichiri musikana asi ndakangoroorwa nemukomana wangu ndiri mhandara yakazara saka zvinoratidza kuti hapana physical contact asi ndezvepamweya chete. Hapana* physical contact *zvinonetsa kuti munhu awane umbowo hwakakwana. Vanotizve chikwambo hachioneki nemaziso saka mapurisa anoda umbowo hunoonekwa uye kubatika, unongokuvarira mukati (chikwambo* does not spread sexually transmitted diseases including HIV/AIDS because in my case I started dreaming of having sex with a man when I was still a young girl but when I was married I was still a virgin so there is no physical contact. It is difficult for a person to get full evidence of rape by *chikwambo*. They also say that *chikwambo* is not ordinarily visible and the police want tangible evidence of rape, so we women just suffer in silence without anyone taking notice.)

Though such cases of *zvikwambo* are conventionally disparaged as mere belief rather than empirical experiential realities, parallels can be drawn between Mai T's experiences with *zvikwambo* and some developments in virtual sexuality. For Hearm (2006) information and communication technologies (ICT) are developing what she calls democratic and diverse sexualities beyond the exploiter/exploited dichotomy, blurring binaries between sexual reality and sexual representation. She argues further that there is increasing domination of the virtual as the mode shifts in sexual space and place; there is a development of new forms of sexual citizenship within shifting transpatriarchies. Other scholars such as Clark (2003) note that research into a branch of virtual reality concerned with electronically mediated sexual contact has developed the sub-area known as teledildonics. Teledildonics research involves data sensing condoms and dildo-like vaginal inserts that communicate signals and motions between genitalia of distant [invisible] agents. For Clarke, the objective of teledildonics is to simulate many of the details of real bodily touch and sexual intercourse and thus create standard sexuality at a distance with telepresence adding moving activities full of multisensory high band real-time, two-way interaction (O'Farrel and Valone, 2002: 210). But similar transgressions of space and bodies, in virtual sexualities including the subversion of normal sexuality, are also underscored in Schimdt's (1997) observation that *chikwambo* manifests by making it impossible for a woman to marry – if she marries her lineage or in-laws will be punished by the spirit: she may not get along well with husband, she may remain barren or die.

Because some invisible forces manifesting as *mhepo/mweya* such as *ngozi* and *zvikwambo* are deemed to cause suffering in everyday life, it is necessary to draw distinctions between them and the world of *midzimu* that are considered benevolent and protective parents who continue their duties of protecting descendants even after death. Don's experiences indicate that *midzimu* differ from *zvikwambo* which other scholars (Shoko, 2007) describe as spirits of people raised by magic with an appetite for sex, money and blood, and who enter into contracts with the owners in terms of which the owners provide sex and blood, and the *zvikwambo* provide money which they steal elsewhere. Though a focus on agency/action would open space for different entities including invisible forces, what often matters in everyday life is not mere action/agency, but effectiveness of the action or agency. It is such effective or fruitful action or agency that is subject to *kutenda* as indeed evident in the proverb *totenda maruva tadya chakata* (we express gratitude after eating).

Such fruitfulness of action or agency also underscored the contestations between the Tonga in northern Zimbabwe and missionaries as noted by Colson (1971). Missionaries preached about the devil and the possibility of possession by evil spirits, but the Tonga held they had good evidence of the effectiveness of their ancestors whose offerings missionaries held would lead one to hell and burn forever. This clashed with the general conviction that people who offered to ancestors would become ancestors and receive offerings in their turn. Don's modes of engagement described above can be understood in terms of Colson's observations among the Tonga. The important theoretical import of such modes of engagement is that poverty is perceived partly in terms of misalignments between on the one hand the worlds of ancestors (*Nyikadzimu*) and (*Denga*) Heaven, and on the other hand the world of their living human descendants. Similarly, in the churches poverty is conceived in terms of misalignments between the world of living humans and Heaven. Yet other scholars like Richards (1994) attribute poverty to misalignments between the post-colonial local context and the global. In this sense the global has usurped logics and positions of gods even as it is paradoxically critical towards engaging with African ancestors. In *chivanhu*, the misalignments create openings for *ngozi*, *mashavi* and *zvikwambo* that explain poverty. In view of ways in which some villagers considered themselves to be suffering due to malevolent dead in the form of *zvikwambo*, it is necessary also to consider moral issues in relating with some of the others. For purposes of this book it should be noted that implied in *kutenda* is the historicity of agency, which is to say that agency is held to exceed the present or contemporaneous.

The way in which some villagers considered the worlds of the dead (to which *kutenda* was often directed) to influence the world of the living was also evident to me on 7 March 2011. On that day, I went to the *svikiro* medium and upon my arrival; she informed me that her mother had died a few days back. When her mother was seriously ill, the *svikiro*'s deceased father came from the *Nyikadzimu* world of ancestors (*vakauya*) and told her:

> *makanonoka mungadai makavapa mushonga wemudumbu nokuti ndimo maivarwadza. Chimbomirai kuenda navo kuchipatara kwamuri kuda kuenda navo motanga matsvaga mushonga wemudumbu* (you have not been quick enough; you should have given her medication/herbs for stomach troubles because it is her stomach that is painful. Can you postpone taking her to hospital where you want to take her to get some herbs for stomach troubles first)?

The medium's mother said to her husband, 'You'd better take me with you'. But he asked where to, and the dying woman answered 'to where you are staying'. The *svikiro* then said that her father was quiet for a while. When the *svikiro* went to collect *mushonga wemudumbu* [herbs for the stomach] from a woman who had some, she was followed and informed that her mother had just died. The *svikiro* ended her narration of her dying mother's experiences by telling me, '*vanhu vanotambirwa nevadzimu vavo kuNyikadzimu kana vafa* (when people die they are accompanied to the world of ancestors by their deceased *hama*)'. But she said she had just been to a *nhimbe* work party where villagers were being urged by leaders to reconcile, forgive and work together. She said the problem was that it is *vanhu* who are living who say these things about forgiveness yet they do not let the *vadzimu/vakuru* lead.

The medium added:

> The *vakuru* then just watch even if things are not being properly done; they will be asking, '*saka vanhu ava varikuti varikuitei* (so they just watch and ask one another whether the people involved know what they will be trying to do)'. It is necessary to invite the *vakuru* so that they talk and say what they want done, in order for progress to be made, and it is necessary to thank the elders when they have done us good things.

When accompanying me home the *svikiro* said, '*apa ndipo panzvimbo yenyu yemukwerera* (this is your place for the rain ceremonies)'. I asked her to tell me if the villagers had managed that year to perform *mukwerera* and she answered,

Makarambaka imi nekuda kwekushanja saka wakaitirwa kumwewo.Vanhu vanoramba midzimu vachitya kufumurwa. Umwe kwaMurambinda akanzi nevamwe mbuya (mudzimu) komusoro wemukwasha uri mudura urikuudiyi (you [referring to other villagers] refused to perform the *mukwerera* because you are not ritually clean so we performed the ceremony elsewhere. People refused to welcome and thank their ancestors because they feared that if ancestors intermingle with the living, the ancestors would reveal the secret bad dealings including about bad *mushonga,* which harm others, that some of their descendants would have acquired).

The everyday life of the villagers indicates that unqualified openness can result in vulnerability rather than resilience: for instance, in their metaphysics they envisage *ngozi* afflicting some who are then entered by the *ngozi* and lose their faculties. And openness of economies where some acquire *zvikwambo* is feared by villagers as that could lead to exposure and affliction of their families by the *zvikwambo* that would have entered them. Equally, openness in a (neo)liberal era, although coupled with closures in the form of privatisation of companies and the conditionalities of the Bretton Woods institutions, led to vulnerability and exposure of Africans to the vicissitudes of the global market economy and the rapacity of global capital. In the same logic, perceptions that Africa was open accounted for colonisation of Africa in the first place, including the systematic retrenchment of the control by African pre-colonial states, ancestors and other invisible entities deemed by colonisers to be demons, which were subsequently replaced by the invisible hand of the market. In the light of the vulnerabilities and vicissitudes visited by the conditionalities of the neoliberal era, those visited by colonisation as well as those of the recent global liquidity crunch, it is cause for wonder whether the openness involving the exit of the state would not exacerbate vulnerability and human insecurity. The logic behind the fact that Africans shun some of the dead even of their own family if they bring in their train avenging foreign deceased shows that what matters in Africa is not merely connections to others, because some might be coming to avenge and impose conditionalities. Rather, what matters is the quality of the connections that are then harnessed. It is not the mere existence of networks, meshworks or globalisation, but the quality of the import of such connections. The doubt by the healer as to whether the food donated by NGOs was for animals or for human beings underscores not only the significance of quality in global-local connections, but also that of avoiding conflating human beings and animals. While circulation is important, it is necessary to take into cognisance its historicity, that is to say the connections that notions of circulation have with colonialism and coloniality more broadly. The challenge is that global circulation cannot be divorced from antecedent colonial forcible expropriations of land, cattle and other resources from the Africans who were promised the benefits not only of subsequent circulation of wealth but also development and civilisation – all of which never materialised. The conflicts in Zimbabwe were indeed underpinned by exhortations by government to be resilient in reclaiming land from Whites; but conversely, globalisation and liberalism would exhort resilience so as to retain circulation of commodities albeit without such ownership and control of resources. Notions of circulation and flows imply a recycling of the logics of (neo)liberalism. By enforcing the radical opening up of economies to multinational corporations and to commodities from outside borders, neoliberalism reduced nations to global units of consumption where even inferior goods are dumped. Similarly, the liberalisation and opening up of pre-colonial economies deconstructed families and kingdoms as units of production, reducing them to units of consumption in the colonial context. Therefore circulation alone guarantees neither decoloniality nor development; rather, it guarantees the opposite if the historicity of the coloniality of power, of economies, of being and of epistemology is considered. The (neo)liberal deconstruction of economies within families, kingdoms and nations does not reduce, alleviate or eradicate poverty, but in fact increases vulnerability by eroding vestiges of entitlement and ownership. Thus notions of circulation alone have shortcomings in the sense that they enjoin the former colonies to reject and forget their past, in terms of control and ownership of resources, in order to take up the colonially defined past of dependence on the metropole. As noted in Chapter Two, the idea of inexorability of linearity of time privileged by Western notions of development legitimises the tyranny of temporality. It also serves to cloak colonial expropriations in that efforts to reclaim colonially expropriated resources would then be interpreted as retrogression belonging to the past that liberalism, in spite of its purported liberalism, would not allow underprivileged and disinherited sections of humanity to revisit. Thus, this tyranny of temporality in development discourses and practices serves to legitimise the tyranny or dictatorship of capital on a worldwide scale. The tyranny and dictatorship of capital is perhaps best exemplified with respect to transnational corporations which have assumed the role of global slash and burners, locating and relocating in different places of the world even as Europeans paradoxically condemned African shifting cultivators as primitive.

The unqualified deployment of notions of actors and stakeholders in development projects and other contemporary interventions circumvent the notion of ownership [in, *chivanhu huridzi*]. The *huridzi* has been increasingly eroded via these (neo)liberal conceptualisations of actors and stakeholdership that preach inclusion even as they exclude others from ownership and control. In *chivanhu*, there are adages such as *chawawana batisisa mudzimu haupe kaviri*, the logic of which is comparable to that of the English proverb 'a bird in hand is worth two in the bush'. Similarly, the adage *totenda dzadzoka dzaswera nebenzi* (we will be thankful if an unreliable person herding cattle returns home with all of them) underscores the uncertainties of relying on hopes of circulation. The uncertainties are pinned as much on the reliability of the people involved as on the reliability of that which is expected to circulate. So, all these adages stress the shortcomings of circulation and openness as these are understood to generate vulnerabilities and uncertainties in life.

Shortcomings of circulation notwithstanding, in the medium's narrative above, there are other invisible entities that help living human beings. Equally, in Try's experiences reported above, the agency of individuals is connected to the agency of others, and there are ways in which other individuals that have assisted one, even if subsequently absent, are congratulated. Try's illness had debilitated him in such a way that he could not operate as an individual and so he subsequently showed appreciation of the work on NGOs that helped him with food, doctors and hospital staff who helped him with medication, and his brother who helped ferry him to the hospital. A closer look, in the next chapter, at the ways in which villagers attend to their health challenges indicates complex ways in which they sense the presence of absent other beings that had import on their lives.

Chapter Five

Sensing Presences?
Health, Illness and Resilience

The night of the 5th of July 2011 was as quiet as one would expect in a village that is distant from the main roads and busy shopping centres. On this day I lay asleep in a hut. But I was not alone; there were two young boys on the other side of the hut deep in sleep. At about midnight I thought I heard knocking on the door loud enough to wake me up. Still lying on the bed, I checked to ascertain if it was not one of the children knocking on something but they were both fast asleep. Gripped with the fear that members of the political parties who were at each other's throats had for some reason decided to visit me in the middle of the night, I remained in bed. But before long I saw two figures enter the hut and one of them came straight up to me and then sat on me. I felt huge strength suddenly well up in me and I heaved the figure off me. I rose up and instantly both figures disappeared from the hut via the door which I was sure I had locked before going to sleep.

I had already been told many stories about experiences of villagers who were victims of midnight attacks by political party activists who sometimes broke down the doors when their intended victims refused to open them. Zimbabwe was at the time of my fieldwork gripped in interparty, interpersonal and witchcraft related violence.

As the figures that had entered the hut disappeared I was surprised to find that the door had not been broken down. The figures appeared to have simply slipped in and out undeterred by the locked door. I was not sure if I was merely dreaming, or having what psychologists define as 'paranormal experiences' or paranoia to explain experiences that differ from those conventionally understood as normal. Nor was I sure that I was not manifesting the signs of traumatic experiences that are ordinarily understood to occur when one has been exposed to stressful events such as the kind of violence that I was researching. In villages embroiled in such violence, uncertainty was an inevitable part of everyday life and had to be lived with. What I was sure about was that I was occupying a space where certainty and uncertainty often intersect and oscillate. What further complicated my experience was that during my preliminary fieldwork, about a year earlier, prophets in the churches that I participated in informed me that I was on my way to becoming a prophet and would experience and see things out of the ordinary, and which other people might consider strange.

Indeed the strangeness of things was part of what I was studying and the spaces which I sought to enter could themselves have been understood in terms of the strangeness of their violence and the resilience of the strengths to survive. Moving as I did from places of relative safety in towns and the university into violence ridden villages could itself have been interpreted as strangeness. Similarly leaving one's family in town to stay away from them to do fieldwork could have been interpreted as estrangement which in *chivanhu* is a form of strangeness. But to consider some things as strange *a priori* is often to demarcate space; it suggests contentment in the spaces of the familiar. It suggests unreadiness to move to the borders between spaces, between that which may be defined as strange and the familiar. But then it is often within the borders of spaces, of things, that one gets shaken and challenged including by the often unexpected and inexplicable presences that visit one. Indeed, there is often no guarantee that one's own presence in such border spaces does not itself constitute both strangeness and familiarity to others. So here I was in a village, in a hut, in the middle of the night, asleep in a context of violence where, like other villagers threatened by the violence, I often sensed that I was hovering on the borders of things. While ordinarily in *chivanhu* the worlds of *chokwadi/idi* (truth) and *nhema/manyepo* (falsehoods) are taken for granted, I sometimes felt that I hovered between the borders of risk/safety, certainty/uncertainty, and reality/unreality. While my experiences can be understood in terms of Victor Turner's (1969) explications on liminality of ritual subjects whose conditions are ambiguous and elude or slip through the classifications that normally locate state and position in cultural space, it can be argued, in the case of the villagers of my fieldwork, that life generally was liminally marked by violence and uncertainty. As indicated in reference to the riskiness that I sensed even from inside the hut, risk and safety were not necessarily located in separate territories. What I call sensing presences is an invitation to share such border spaces, the generative moments they offer to rethink what it means to inhabit/not to inhabit the border spaces marked by the presences of things ordinarily understood as opposites. I want to argue that the kind of everyday life about which I write involved inhabiting such border spaces, between things, in which sensing them was an important part of resilience. And this involved intermingling with the world in various ways, some of which entailed reversing the conventional order of senses. My experiences during the fieldwork can partly be understood in terms of Coole and Frost's (2010: 10) argument that in the 'new materialities' we find cosmic forces assembling and disintegrating to forge more or less enduring patterns that may exhibit internally coherent, efficacious organisation, objects forming and emerging within relational fields, and subjectivities being constituted, open series of capabilities or potencies that emerge hazardously and ambiguously within a multitude of organic and social processes. While conventional modes of sensing tend to be privileged in formal epistemologies, senses and sensing are for other scholars understood differently. For Serres (2008), they allow the body to mingle with the world. Understanding senses as intermingled and mixed in Serres' sense allows one to interrogate epistemologies which, for some historical reasons, often privilege and universalise the physical ocular senses in matters of knowledge. If, as Serres observes, with references to debates by philosophers such as Democritus, Aristotle and Socrates, the number of senses has not always been settled at the conventional five, it is unclear why humanity is often assumed invariably to have or stress this particular number of senses. As underscored by telepathy, clairvoyance, extrasensory perception and out of body experiences, some people are gifted with extra senses.

Among the few African scholars who have questioned the convention is Kathryn Linn Geurts (2002) whose research in Ghana indicates that some cultures recognise other senses, such as balance (physical and psychological) as essential components of what it means to be human. These findings highlight the error of assuming the universality of the five senses model. Geurts suggests the need to understand ways in which different senses play out differently in different contexts. I would argue that it is appropriate as well to consider how different ways of sensing play out in contexts of crisis such as the one I studied. In the context of the crisis that marked Zimbabwe, different senses were deployed in various ways in everyday life struggles for resilience.

But to speak of things as unstable is not necessarily to suggest binaries; rather, it is merely to underscore the shifting, or fluid character of things in everyday life. It is to note that ways in which villagers shifted from one mode of resilience to the other translated the complexity of comings and goings. Perhaps a good example of the prevalence of such comings and goings in everyday life is Chavunduka's (1978) observation that Shona patients went back and forth between biomedicine and traditional healing, often relying not only on their own decisions but on those of their kin (see also Simmons, 2012; Gelfand, 1959). While his study is useful in understanding the lack of secure moorings in the kind of everyday life that I observed, it does not explore ways of sensing presences that explain illness and health. Such switches between modes of health services, as I will show below, also prevailed in my research area; but what I want to focus on are ways of sensing things rather than merely the switches by patients from one form of service to the other. I also want to focus on the comings and goings as well as manifestations not only of patients but also of the different beings whose presences were often sensed differently.

This notion of presence upon which I wish to ground modes of resilience against illness in everyday life is well captured by Jean-Luc Nancy's (1993: 5) argument that presence is coming which is also a going away; it is a back and forth movement, the coming that effaces itself and brings itself back. This kind of presence is one that eludes ordinary modes of representation; it eludes being defined as a subject or object, or as purely present or absent. Here Nancy is grappling with the notion of representation that he attaches to modernist epistemology; but he then argues that there is no humanity or perhaps animality that does not include representation although representation may not exhaust what, in human beings, passes infinitely beyond humanity. And for Nancy, the irrepresentable, pure presence or pure absence, is also an effect of representation. So while Heidegger attempts to conceive and practice nonrepresentational thinking, an attempt that initially takes the form of rejecting representation (Stelladi, 2000: 218-228), it has been argued that there is no thinking that is nonrepresentational. Nonrepresentational thinking as a way that is not founded on representation that has nothing to do with it, that has no need to refer to something else in order to function properly, is problematised. For Stelladi, all we know, as opposed to representational thinking, is suspended thinking, which rests neither in representation nor anything else. This differs from Heidegger's dreams of phantomatic, nonlogical and nonrepresentational thinking. For scholars like Engelke (2007) who also think through issues of representation, the invisibility of the invisible world is not necessarily a problem because hearing the invisible may in some cases be more important than seeing it.

With respect to this chapter on health, I seek to render the idea of presence partly in terms of the back and forth movements of patients, of the context in which drugs and money to purchase them were often available but also unavailable, and illnesses were present but also absent. It is a kind of presence, I will argue, that is understood by situating oneself on the borders where many different things are ongoing without reducing themselves to being invariably present in the conventional representational sense of being ever-present. In this sense I wish to shift attention from studies that begin by seeking to understand what is (or deemed to be) present, to a mode of analysis that begins from presences. As I felt myself to be in a liminal space, I want to begin not necessarily from conventional variables such as social-cultural, biological, physical and psychiatric imperatives in health and illness (Kleinman, 1986; 1988; Kiev, 1972), but from the more labile everyday life modes of engaging issues of illness and health. Thus the focus is on presence; it is on the coming into presence of things. While other scholars have understood some matters of health in terms of mysticism and esoterism (Ahyi, 1997; Kiniffo, 1997), I wish to explore them in terms of the ways in which things come into presence. I wish to understand things in terms of their presences, that is, their comings and goings as well as manifestations, some of which may escape attention.

Understanding things in terms of manifestations, comings and goings would extend the work of other scholars that suggest the existence of mysticism in African health issues. For instance while Kiniffo (1997) notes that needles are held to be mysteriously placed in the bodies of patients and healers remove the needles by the magnetic laying of hands, the idea of mystery can be explained in terms of the comings and goings as well as manifestations of *mweya/mhepo* (air/wind). The *mweya/mhepo* in the Shona language is translatable as the way in which spiritual forces manifest themselves. The presence of *mweya/mhepo* is hinted at in Simmons (2012) who argues that *miti*'s (herbs) potency is not self-evident because it comes from external sources, that is, ancestors or the healing spirits, and it is given agentive power through men and women's intentions. The ability to use *muti* implies a moral relationship with an ancestor's healing spirit and/or God, without whose support the *muti* remains inert. The idea that I wish to develop is that it is necessary to move beyond preoccupation with, which is not to say abandon, the materialities that have characterises scholarship in the past. Green (1996) for instance focuses on Catholic medicines including holy water, blessed oils, ashes, amulets and palm branches placed above doorways at Easter; Catholic amulets include rosaries and medals worn to protect from witchcraft and misfortune. Whether or not these palpable medicines and *muti* should be regarded as fetishes has, as I will show below, been the subject of scholarly debates. For Jahn (1961: 156, 159) the respect is never for the wood itself but for the *muntu* (human being) who has chosen it as their seat: the object is a *kintu*, a thing and nothing more, it is not a fetish or god and so it is not worshipped. Other scholars such as Evans-Pritchard (1972: 89) argue that fetish implies the presence of an indwelling ghost or spirit, but he proceeds to note that objects are human creations and in their material selves have no significance. Evans-Pritchard further notes that objects acquire significance only when they are endowed with supernatural power through a rite which, also by human agency, infuses them with that power: an object and its virtue are thus distinct.

Understanding things in terms of ways in which they come into presence makes it possible to interrogate not only notions of placebo but also related notions of fetishism, in so far as they are connected to African religion, health and healing as well as to the ideas of absent presences that I grapple with here. Though some scholars have considered modes of engagement in terms of fetishism (Taussig, 1986), the term itself and its implications in the context of Africa have been critiqued. For instance Opoku (1978: 4) argues that the term fetishism has become a synonym for African religions with the implication that such religions amounted to nothing more than the use of worship of charms. The term 'fetishism' in this sense is considered imprecise because religions in Africa mean more than the word 'fetish' implies as there is in African languages a clear distinction made between man-made religious objects and spiritual beings or deities. Other scholars like Rattray (1927) have similarly argued that fetishism as the lens through which to describe African world views entails abandoning the Africans' own distinct classifications and divisions of beings into, for instance, ancestors and the Supreme Being since fetishism focuses on objects. This focus explains the scientific quandaries with respect to the use of placebos. As Harrington (1997) argues, placebos are the ghosts that haunt the house of biomedical objectivity; they are the creatures that rise up from the dark and expose the paradoxes and fissures in definitions of the real and active factors in treatment. Though some argue that healers use ineffective or placebo dosages (Shapiro and Shapiro, 1997), others contend that rationality and objectivity are not special characteristics of a single kind of knowledge-science; rather, they result from whatever institutional practices serve a particular culture or create self-evident validity (Turnbull, 2000). Recognition of different rationalities underpins Oliver Human's (2012) observation that there are exceptional cases in which in order to diagnose disease effectively, a doctor must often break with protocol and concede to the risk inherent in this divergence from authority. By relying on traces of evidence not modelled, and by diverging from protocols, doctors depend on a type of knowledge, a derogation from that which is considered central to thought process, and this challenges modernist ideas of classification.

A focus on presence may not be understood merely in terms of hybridity of the beings and objects that come into presence. Indeed if in everyday life things come and go, and life cannot be viewed merely in terms of hybridity, which would privilege the moments and products of conjugations of things. Yet when things come and go in everyday life they often miss as much as they meet one another. In its emphasis on the product, a focus on hybridity misses the goings and comings of things in everyday life. Presence may be inferred from what Ingold (2010) calls creative entanglements. Ingold's work is marked by his rejection of a focus on the materiality of things and by his insistence that they are in fluid becomings where the material things are enmeshed with the nonmaterial including the wind which, he argues, is understood in some societies to be life itself. Thus distinguishing objects from things, Ingold argues that the object stands before us as a *fait accompli*, presenting its congealed, outer surface to our inspection; the thing, by contrast, is a going on, or better, a place where several goings on become entwined. While Ingold's explication is useful in so far as it advises that the place to start is with the fluid character of things rather than materials, a focus on becomings risks occluding what I have called the 'unbecomings' that are also part of everyday life. Such a focus also occludes moments when some things cease flowing, which is when the flows are blocked for some reason. In other words a focus merely on flows neglects the existence of boundaries and closures including the ritual creation of space as ways to define territory (Thornton, 1980).

Some such unbecomings arguably had their presence in the state of the health services in Zimbabwe where hospitals and clinics were bedevilled by the absence of drugs, frequent strikes, brain drain, derelict equipment, and where some patients were often detained for failing to pay fees. These can hardly be defined as a becomings. Equally, the vilification of healers, who could have provided alternative health services, as archaic witchdoctors (Chavunduka, 1980; Jeater, 2007), can hardly be defined as becomings. For these reason I wish to understand the modes of engagement among the villagers in terms of (hau)ontology, that partly derives from Derrida (1993; 1994). (Hau)ontology makes it possible to understand life in terms of becomings and unbecomings, in terms of the various visitations and presences, and manifesting that feature as part of everyday life particularly in a context of crisis. It allows one to situate in the borders of the real/unreal, certain/uncertain, life/death, illness/wellness. By so doing, it allows one to dwell in the spaces where things are not necessarily settled in spite of the often effortful struggles to settle them. Such efforts to settle the health challenges were evident both at government level as well as that of everyday life. In order to appreciate the everyday life modes of engagement, I will therefore start by briefly noting a number of challenges at the government level highlighted by some Members of Parliament.

Some brief notes on health and resilience

The Parliamentary Debates of 16 May 2007 highlighted challenges in the Zimbabwean health sector including recurring industrial action, high staff attrition, inadequate funding, old equipment and infrastructure, incomplete projects, lack of drugs, inaccessibility of health services and the collapse of referral systems. The Minister of Health and Child Welfare noted during the debates that the majority of the citizens could no longer afford to buy drugs due to high prices. Further challenges noted included fuel shortages, poor road networks and aged fleets of vehicles, all of which made it difficult for stock to be moved to various health centres.

In the context of the challenges raised by the Minister, a debate ensued in which some Members of Parliament suggested that citizens should be encouraged to rely on traditional medicine. One MP, Betty Chikava, argued that traditional medicine is not dangerous as it is used worldwide. He urged the other MPs to take into cognisance the fact that modern medicines that they trusted so much come from the roots and barks of trees, from plants, from forests, though they are subsequently processed into capsules or tablets. She argued further that there was no reason why Zimbabweans should not use traditional medicines (ZPD 16 March 2010, HOA 36(27): 1732-1733). The binary between traditional and scientific medicine has been questioned by scholars including Karen E. Flint (2008: 10) who argues that "European discourse on African 'tradition' had been self-serving, leading white rulers […] to create a false binary that painted African 'tradition' as the antithesis to European 'modernity'." Flint (2008: 141) goes on to argue that "the professionalization of biomedicine needed a foil against which to protect itself as scientific, technologically advanced and the sole possessor of knowledge on the body, health and wellness". Notwithstanding these arguments by scholars, other Members of the Zimbabwean Parliament, such as Mr Sibanda argued that, with respect to traditional medicine, one of the questions was of efficiency with respect to dosage. He noted that traditional doctors were not well educated on the issue of dosage, so that dosage became counter effective and risk killing a lot of people. He argued further that in the technology age it was necessary to encourage the use of scientific medicines rather than resorting to the 'prestone' age. He went on to say that citizens had to be prevented from consulting 'witch hunters' and healers who would perform divination (*ZPD* 16 Mar 2010). This MP failed to recognise the existence of indigenous science and technology, including indigenous mathematics, in *chivanhu* (Chirikure, 2010; Ellert, 1984). He failed to recognise ways in which Western science relies on indigenous knowledge about plants and herbs, which it paradoxically neglects to acknowledge (Harding 1994). In his glorification of Western science, the MP equally failed to recognise ways in which Western science often uses Africans as guinea pigs in medical trials and experiments by global pharmaceutical companies.

The MP also failed to note was that Zimbabweans had for a long time relied on both biomedical health institutions and healers (Chavunduka, 1978). Many people took some of their illnesses to Western trained medical practitioners in hospitals, clinics and private doctors' surgeries, and others to healers such as diviners and herbalists (Ross 2010). Thus the Zimbabwean MP failed to note all these dynamics including the global resurgence of traditional medicines and the support it receives from global organizations such as the World Health Organisation (Gurib-Fakim and Kasilo, 2010; Mhame *et al.*, 2010). He also failed to note the fact that about eighty per cent of the population in developing countries including the African continent use traditional medicine for their primary health care needs. He failed to recognise the fact that the notions of traditional and scientific emerged in a context of contestations over medical and medicinal space (Flint, 2008). Finally, the MP failed to contextualise African medicine in the emerging literature, whereas Susan Reynolds Whyte (1989: 289) cited in Westerlund (2006: 133) notes that afflictions which were once dealt with in Monographs on African religion and cosmology now belong to the realm of medicine and medical anthropology. For Reynolds Whyte, what scholars knew as divination now appears as diagnosis, what they interpreted as ritual is now termed therapy, and a victim of supernatural forces is now called a patient while his/her relatives are the therapy managing group. While knowledge including the need to develop and apply scientific criteria and methods for proof of safety and efficacy of medicines is undoubtedly important (Gurib-Fakim and Kasilo, 2010) it is important to note that knowledge alone does not guarantee survival. Knowledge has not necessarily eradicated suffering and want in the world (Maxwell, 2007) and therefore it is necessary to think about survival not merely in terms of the presence/absence of knowledge but also in terms of the presence/absence of wisdom to enable survival.

While such everyday life modes of resilience against ill health, including consultations of healers (Waite, 2000) and prophets (Dube *et al.*, 2011) have often been judged in terms of lack of knowledge, the modes of engagement can be read to underscore the value of dynamism and diversity in everyday life. But it is not only the dynamism and diversity of modes of resilience against illness that are indicated; also implied in everyday life modes of engagement are different ways of sensing presences. Implied also are different ways of sensing the presence/absence of illness, and the presence/absence of factors responsible for illness and for recovery. Everyday life in the midst of such differences can be understood in terms of translation, in terms of movements back and forth during moments of navigating the differences. But unlike in studies by Chavunduka (1978), which focus on movements by human beings seeking treatments from different practitioners, this chapter also looks at the things much more broadly as constituted in manifestings including movement back and forth. It looks at some things that are responsible for illness as involved in processes of translation that enable them to have presence even where it might not be readily possible to represent such presence in conventional ways. In other words, this chapter looks at the shifts and flows of things in everyday life and the ways in which the things involved in the shifts and flows were sensed in so far as they were deemed to impact on matters of health.

The manifestations, comings and goings of everyday life

When I met Fasti, she had just joined another apostolic church in her village and she was happy about her decision. Although there were many apostolic churches in her village, some of them such as the Johanne Marange, of which she had been a member together with her in-laws, did not allow members to consult hospital medical staff. The church's allegation, according to Fatsi, was that the medicines used in hospitals are derived from traditional herbs and so the leaders ruled that the members of the church had to desist from consulting hospitals. Although she was unhappy with these rules, she had been forced into this church by her in-laws who were part of its leadership. The incident that saw her finally withdrawing her membership involved the illness of her four-year-old daughter. When the child was taken ill Fasti immediately consulted a prophet of the Mugodhi Church who, upon realizing the child's critical condition, advised Fatsi to consult the clinic immediately. The prophet advised her that if she did not consult the clinic that day her daughter would die at night. Fearful that her in-laws would not allow her to consult the clinic, [but also fearful that her daughter was going to die if she did not act] Fatsi decided to sneak to the clinic where injections were administered to her child. But unfortunately for Fatsi, she was advised by the nurses that her daughter had to spend the night at the clinic so that her condition could be monitored and treatments administered every few hours. She tried to convince the nurses that she did not have money to pay for the overnight stay and suggested she could instead return with her daughter the following morning. However the nurses maintained that she had to be continuously monitored throughout the night. So with dejection Fatsi eventually sent word to her husband to fetch some clothes for her and her daughter as well as some money.

The following morning Fatsi was advised by the nurses to take her daughter to a hospital called Murambinda which was about twenty kilometres from the clinic. Though she still had worries about the reprisals from her in-laws as well as about the fact that she did not have enough money for the travel, Fatsi agreed. Luckily a couple offered her a free lift insisting that she should use the little money she had for her daughter's treatment. Happy that the nurses had treated her with hospitality and that some fellow patients had assisted with food, Fatsi returned home to find out that her in-laws were already busy inviting one another for a meeting in which they wanted to accuse her of going to the clinic. But once again Fatsi noted that she was in luck because the in-laws failed to agree among themselves since some of them argued that she could not have simply watched her daughter die.

Salient in Fatsi's case are some assumptions about presence and absence that are often missed with a focus on things that are readily ontologically present. Because the nurses focused on Fatsi and her daughter whom they could see, they missed the presence of her in-laws who effectively were 'absent presences' during their discussions with the mother. Equally, in considering herself unable to take her daughter to the hospital for lack of money, Fatsi may be understood to have missed the possibilities that she would be assisted with money, which seemed to have been absent but were in fact present. In both instances the challenge was to avoid focusing merely on what was materially present as well as materially absent. The challenge was to focus on the shifts and flows that offered opportunities even when possibilities appeared to be non-existent. The challenge was to focus on the presence of things, which is to say, on their comings and goings that rendered them neither present nor absent. The challenge was to think not merely in terms of pure absence and pure presence but in terms of presence that was absence and vice versa. Suggested in all this is a need to focus not necessarily on the readily ontologically present but on how things manifest, come and go. As shown in the case, a focus on things as purely present and purely absent often generates and exacerbates hopelessness even in situations where possibilities for manoeuvre exist.

The challenges of focusing merely on biomedical explanations were best exemplified by Fatsi's other experience of illness in her family. When her son was taken ill she took him to the hospital so that he would be treated for the stomach pains that beset him. Fatsi noted that her son was examined by a doctor who explained the illness as a genetic disease the name of which she did not remember. Contrary to the doctor's explanation, Fatsi maintained that the reason why her son always relapsed into the illness as soon as he stopped taking the pills was that he had been made to lick some soil bearing worm eggs by a woman in the village with whom she did not have good relations. So for three years she consulted the hospital doctor, and the pain stopped each time her son took his medicine and reappeared once he stopped taking it. By the end of the three years Fatsi noted:

I heard my heart telling me to consult a prophet. I first went back to the clinic but I tore the part of the medical report which stated that it was a genetic disease that afflicted my son. When I went to the prophet I was given a *munamato* (prayer) comprising lemons that were prayed for. My son had to drink the *munamato* for three weeks during which I was consulting the prophet. After using the *munamato* my son passed out waste mixed with many long worms that could fill a cup. When he recovered the prophet gave me another *munamato* which comprised a red string which he prayed for and tied around my son's waist so that the illness would not revisit him. Although this illness occurred when he was five year old it has not recurred and now he is twelve.

Underscored in Fatsi's experiences are not only her comings and goings to and from the hospital but also the comings and goings of the illness, and the manifestations of the illness. Her vacillations can be read to imply that both decision and indecision inhabited her mind. The vacillations can also be understood in terms of the elusiveness of both truth and falsity in a context where things are often on the move. It is, as I show in this chapter, by paying attention in everyday life to such presences that are absences and absences that are presences, that it becomes clear that things are not necessarily what they appear to be. It is not invariably the materialities of such things that matter but often the ways in which they are deemed to be visited by other presences/absences. The presence of the string after the prayers was no longer that of the string, it became the presence of *munamato* (prayer) which is to say it became *munamato* rather than a mere string. The primacy in this sense was no longer given to the materiality of the string but to the connections it was embedded in, which is to say, its more fluid life-giving properties. Primacy was then given to the properties deemed to have assumed presence in the string. The challenge then is to sense (not just to see) such a string as a string but also not a string; it is to sense not only the material aspects but also the nonmaterial aspects that convoked its morphing into or manifesting as another presence. The experiences of Fatsi do not suggest that villagers had no notion of physical causation or specific organisms causing illness, as Snow (1977: 41) suggests, because Fasti clearly attributed the illness to the soil and worms that she saw coming out of her son's body. Equally, her experience does not imply that she had no concept of a mere string, but rather that she considered a string that had been prayed over to have become more than a string.

It might be called a mere string after the *munamato* by one who had not been present at the convocation and whose senses deny him or her the ability to sense it as not merely a string. But calling it a mere string as such could be a good way of saying 'I fail to sense other presences or that the presences are elusive to one's senses'. With the presence of things in motion, in this sense, it becomes possible for the true to become the false and *vice versa* in a manner that destabilises the dichotomies that are often assumed between them. Because some things are held to manifest in different forms and to be highly mobile, they assume the status of absent presences.

One might for instance consider the narratives among villagers that the *njuzu/madzimudzangara* [half human half fish entities that manifest as *mhepo/mweya*] do not want to be seen by some human beings and that, according to (Burbridge, 1924), they "quickly manifest as fish", wind/air, or simply vanish upon intrusion of their spaces by human beings. Such narratives highlight the propensities of some things to manifest in impermanent forms, thereby rendering dichotomies unclear.

If such ambivalences of things in everyday life are considered in the context of the crisis in the country which was marked by oscillations between presence and absences of drugs, medical staff, and cash, it becomes possible to conceive the ambivalences as part of the broader context where things were constantly oscillating and in flux. Within the broader national context where drugs were being sold on the streets and where hospitals kept in store drugs some of which were long past their expiry dates, these ambivalences are nothing surprising. A thing could be what it appeared to be but it could as well manifest as something else.

Implied in such ambivalences and often rapid turns in such everyday life, are the ways in which they sometimes elude representation even if they may have presence. When an entity is understood to vanish, elude glances and then reappear such as was done by the villagers in their modes of evading violence, representing it as purely present is often difficult where becoming absent is its other attribute. Conversely it becomes difficult to represent the entities as purely absent where becoming present is its other attribute. This suggests a kind of world where life is lived in terms of presences, in terms of the comings and goings rather than in terms of only that which can be readily conventionally represented as present.

A case that indicates how presences were conceived in everyday life is that of Grub whom I met on 27 March 2011. His narrative indicates how such presences were negotiated in the spaces between consulting healers and consulting hospitals. Grub remarked:

> There are some things that can be fixed by the hospitals: other things need *n'angas* (healers) or prophets. We consult *n'angas* or

prophets first. You may not be treated well at the hospital because there is *mhepo* (wind) that make it difficult for the doctors to diagnose well. Doctors may say after operation that they are not seeing any problem. The *mhepo* will be pushed (*kusundirwa*) so that you spend a long time without getting treatments. For prophets, they treat even if the one who is ill is absent, they see the problems even for family members who may not be present and they give water to drink or to use when bathing. After doing all this we go to the clinic and we do not encounter problems. First we fix our things here because *mhepo* will be present. There is need to continue to remove the *mhepo* until the patient feels that it has been removed. But the bad people sending the *mhepo* may continue sending it so that the illness is on and off. Even our homesteads, we cleanse them of the *mhepo*, the *mhepo* will be present sitting in the homesteads. The Prophets can give us water to spray so that witches do not get in. But the witches may continue to send the *mhepo*. The *n'anga* puts *midzi* (roots) in bottles which are planted during the night around the homesteads so that witches do not get in.

Comments similar to Grub's were also underscored by a *n'anga* called Dhodho, who said:

Tinorapa mumisha munenge mapinda mashavi ekuroya anongoda kuuraya vamwe. Misha inogadzirwa kuti varoyi vatadze kusvika kuroya vamwe. Pane hoko dzinoroverwa usati waisa bango rako, hoko dzemiti dzinochengetedza musha nokuti havachazokwanisi kupinda mumusha. Varoyi vanoramba vachiedza vachishevedzana kuti vabatsirane kubvisa hoko kuti vapinde. Vanozowana umwe pakati pavo anokwanisa kubvisa hoko iya. Hoko dzinoda kuiswa itsva kusati kwapera makore gumi kuti varoyi vasapinde. Kana musha usina kugadzirwa zviri nyore kupinda, vamwe vanotouita base rekuroya. Mudzimu haugoni kuchengetedza musha pasina hoko vanokurirwa.Ukaroora muroyi kana shavi rake ririguru vanouya voita base mumusha. Murume wacho pfungwa dzake dzinenge dzisisiri mushe, anongoteera mukadzi. Mudzimu haugoni kuchengetedza musha pasina hoko vanokurirwa (We treat homesteads so that witches will not be able to bewitch others or to kill them. There are sticks that have to be used as pegs when you build a house so that witches will not enter. The witches will however keep on trying to enter and they seek the assistance of other witches until one of them is able to undo the pegs. So, one has to renew the pegs once every ten years so that witches will not enter. If a homestead is not protected it is easy for witches to enter. But if you marry a witch the homestead will be used as a base for witches. The husband like a zombie will simply play to the wife's bidding. If there are no pegs ancestors will have difficulty protecting the homestead.)

In the light of Dhodho's remarks it is easy to understand why the Ndebele people were apprehensive when early colonial settlers drove pegs into the ground when they marked boundaries in Matabeleland (Palmer, 1977).

While it is often assumed that an individual is invariably an individual, here the model of an individual that is posed is one in which he/she is possibly accompanied by presences that may not be sensible to the doctor's treatment. The model in Grub's comment is one where the patient understands him or herself and the homesteads as visited by presences held to elude the senses of the medical personnel. Moreover, it is a model where the doctor is understood to begin by focusing on the individual patient, whereas people who are ill start by looking at and addressing the nonmaterial more fluid presences before going to the hospital. In this encounter between patient and doctor, the latter is portrayed as rather unaware of the kind of presences the patient understands him or herself to be visited by and meddling in the doctor-patient interactions. In other words, the remarks suggest that what matters is not just the presence of the doctor and the patient but the presence of other things as well, which are held to enhance or block processes of treatment. But the experiences above do not imply that there is no representation of everyday life. In fact, the physical plane that people inhabit, complete with structures such as churches, clinics, hospitals and so on, can be identified, located and described because people have in their minds coherent maps of their surroundings. It is important also to note that being sceptical or doubtful in everyday life does not necessarily mean abandoning representationalism. Rather, it is to represent a state or even a process of the mind. While the kinds of invisible entities the villagers envisaged could not be seen (or represented) by everyone, they could be if described by healers, mediums and prophets. In this way everyday life does not necessarily abandon representation; rather, there are some who are able to see, using their extra modes of vision, other ordinarily invisible entities much as a scientist endeavours to see ordinarily invisible microbes.

While personal difficulties and the ways in which things can be understood to enhance or block processes of treatment can be interpreted in the broader context of the national level vicissitudes generated by the crisis, they may also be interpreted as an inherent part of everyday life. Indeed, at a material level, the vicissitudes with respect to the intermittent absence of drugs, equipment and staff in hospitals constituted serious impediments to the treatment of patients. And at a nonmaterial level, the presence of a social context marked by acute shortages of basic commodities can be understood to have also constituted blocks to the treatment of patients. In this sense, the patient bearing such a model can be read to be importing the elusiveness of things in the broader national context to the particular doctor-patient situation where the doctor is held to fail to address, or even recognise, the presence of elusive phenomena that block his practice. And where the wind that Grub refers to is understood to manifest in other forms rather than being reducible to the *mhepo*, the model may be understood to underscore the lack of prioritized attention in formal health provisions to the vicissitudes, flows or comings and goings of things, be they material or nonmaterial.

Grub's allusion to witches and to the *mhepo* that causes illness can be understood to underline the significance of attention to flows in everyday life. But these flows have to be understood within the context where the wind morphs into and manifests as other things or entities. They also have to be understood within a context where witchcraft is not necessarily reducible to the occult but is also explained in terms of the broader absences and presences of everyday life. When in the context of the interparty violence some villagers used herbicides and pesticides to poison livestock belonging to their opponents for instance, they codenamed their exercise 'operation *chidhoma*' (ghost) because they operated by sneaking in during the night. By acting like ghosts, the villagers can be understood to have likened their operation to a kind of witchcraft that targeted the livestock of their opponents. This 'operation *chidhoma*' was parallel to reports in other parts of the country where political party activists often forced their opponents, some of whom were abducted to camps, to drink pesticides and herbicides. In these instances, the idea can be read to have been to be absent yet present: in their games of hide and seek, the opponents engaged in comings and goings that rendered them absent but also present. The idea was, as is implied in the term *chidhoma*, that the villagers used, to haunt people without necessarily becoming present to the gaze of others. Suggested in the modes of engagement marked by such comings and goings is the issue of how to sense the world without privileging the stable present whose preponderance often obscures the messiness of the lived world.

To designate the absence that is presence of things, that is to say the duplicities, of everyday life, I have borrowed from what Derrida (1994) calls hauntology to create the notion of (hau)ontology, discussed in Chapter Three. This concept allows a shift from privileging ontology and categories to a mode of writing that makes it possible to conceive things as coming and going in ways that often elude representation. In other words (hau)ontology makes it possible to write about the instabilities, duplicities and vacillations that often characterize moments of crisis while allowing one to recognise the fact that not all hauntings are deconstructive in the Derridean sense. Thus (hau)ontology makes it possible to conceive ways in which what is haunted sometimes retains its ontological structure even as it is enmeshed in complex comings and goings, flows, fluxes and manifestings. It makes it possible to rethink how the presences and absences of things are sensed without necessarily privileging what can be readily conventionally represented as present/absent. In this way it highlights the debatability of senses as conventionally understood yet it also underscores the temporality of sensing as sensing that which has temporal presence within the reach of one's senses. Focusing on dreams, divinations and prophecies, I now wish to show some ways in which different ways of sensing presences played out in everyday life.

(Hau)ontology: making sense of presences through dreams, divination and prophecies

The significance of dreams and other ways of sensing presences is indicated in the three related cases that I will detail below and then connect together.

The first case was that of Nod, a vendor whom I met in February 2011. She stated:

> I was assisted by some prophets this year. Last week a prophetess I did not even know visited me because she had had dreams about me. I was not feeling well when she came. The prophetess assisted me with *munamato* (prayer) which I was advised to use for bathing for nine days, now I am feeling ok. *Paive nechinhu chaivepo chakandiruma pamusana pachirema, kurwadza nekuzvimba.* (There was a thing that was biting me at the back which was also feeling heavy, painful and swollen).
>
> At my shop I was no longer having customers. Now I am receiving customers. Some people burnt their *mushonga* (herbs) in a drain by my shop just before I started feeling ill. They first wrapped the *mushonga* with papers and then set it alight producing bad smoke that also made me cough. The prophetess sprayed holy water from the three perennial rivers namely Mupfure, Nyaguwi and Mazoe. She prayed for the water from the three perennial rivers and then advised me to bathe using it. I only gave her money for bus fare to go to the rivers to collect the water; she helped me and so on the ninth day which was yesterday I started feeling well again. She also informed me that had I seen the thing which had bitten me I was going to die immediately.

The second case is that of Mari, who lived very close to where I stayed during the early part of my fieldwork in January 2011. One morning she came to fetch water from the borehole at the house where I stayed, but she looked disturbed. As she usually did when she came to fetch water, she pulled a mat and sat down for a while to discuss issues in the village with my informant's family. But this time she narrated dreams she had just had in which many people appeared at her homestead hunting for her. She said:

> I ran away and hid. One of the people chasing me then asked me 'so this is where you are hiding?' The man who asked me was peeping through the window to get a glimpse of me. I pinched him and then beat him as well as the others who were with him. They wanted to catch me and my daughter. After I beat them there came many creatures that looked like dolls that could walk. I beat them but they produced air which was smelly. I beat them using my church garment. They were resisting.

This dream shows some of the kinds of things villagers like Mari considered as engendering some illnesses. Some such things were deemed to be experienced first at the level of dreams and then translated into the wakeful lives. To note such things is not necessarily to imply that the villagers attributed illnesses solely to such moments: the villagers also had other ways of explaining illnesses like common cold, which generally did not occasion connection to such dreams. Rather, it was the kinds of illnesses that were deemed to be prolonged or resistant to cures that were often connected to such dreams. Now to appreciate some of the ways in which such dreams were considered to translate to the level of wakefulness, I will note a dream in which I was involved and how it was translated by a prophetess afterwards.

The third and last case I wish to note here is the dream that I had just after Zan visited my informant in January 2012. Zan was brother to Lee, my informant, and he had just visited him after a stint in the diaspora. Although his visit was short, lasting only about an hour, and although it was my first time to meet him, I had a disturbing dream the night Zan left my informant's homestead. In the dream, Zan walked west holding his car in his hands while his mother walked east. But in between them was a grinning man who hid from them. In the dream Zan's mother had been driven to a sea of dirty smelly water and my sense was that it was the grinning man who was doing this. Upon my asking him why he did such a bad thing, he immediately bolted away and manifested himself as what I thought was a drum. The dream generated worries on my part and upon waking up I told my informant about it. We discussed the dream as we usually did, and during the discussion I indicated to him that I had a sense that his brother Zan, his children and mother were likely to get into trouble. I had woken up that morning feeling that I had been struggling in the dream to assist them but I did not quite know what to do to assist.

Unknown to us was that Zan had failed to drive to his home the previous evening after his visit to my informant. Some thirty kilometres on my way to Harare that day, I saw Zan's car parked by the road side so I decided to drop off and have a chat with him. He was sitting beside the car and his two children were sleeping at the back. Immediately after our greetings, Zan informed me that his car had developed some electrical faults which nearly led him into an accident that evening. What surprised me was that during his narration of the incident he stated that from the time immediately before the incident he felt like some wind was blowing sand into his face so that he could no longer see properly. I decided to help him fix his car but then a few minutes after our meeting his five year old daughter fell ill and started vomiting.

After I had assisted Zan, we drove to his home, where his mother informed him that his two other children had also fallen ill just before our arrival. His mother also narrated what she considered an odd event in which she was nearly gored by cows that had been fighting that day. She had tried to intervene but the cows turned to her and chased her away: she was only assisted by other villagers. After taking his children to the clinic, Zan decided to consult a prophetess who stayed some five kilometres from his homestead. Keen to follow the events, I asked him to allow me to accompany him if it was convenient for him, to which he agreed. During our meeting with the prophetess I narrated my dream about Zan which she then interpreted as indicating that Zan was supposed to have been involved in an accident. She also hinted that what I saw as a grinning man in the dream was in fact a *chikwambo*, that is a manifestation of the air of the deceased raised by witches, also called a zombie in literature, sent to cause harm to Zan's family. She also noted that the fact that Zan and his mother were walking in opposite directions in the dream meant that the *chikwambo* was intending to create a rift between Zan and his mother so that they would quarrel and then when illness and death struck members of the family they would not assist one another. The prophetess advised that the *chikwambo* needed to be destroyed and removed from Zan's house so that his family would be well and he would not be involved in an accident when he travelled back to his workplace. She indicated Zan had to pay her some US$10 for removing the *chikwambo*.

Although prophets did not generally charge for their services, Zan agreed to pay her before we headed back that evening to his homestead, together with the prophetess and her husband. We went straight to his house where the ritual to catch the *chikwambo* was to be done. The prophetess sang for a while, prayed and then told everyone present including Zan's mother that the *chikwambo* was hiding in Zan's wife's bag in which she kept her clothes. She indicated that the bag, which was in a separate house, had to be brought to the homestead. Zan's wife rushed off and in a few minutes returned with the bag in hand. The prophetess then asked Zan to check if she or her husband had anything in their pockets which they might be suspected to use to trick the rest of us. Quickly, Zan checked and confirmed that the prophetess and her husband did not have anything with which they could have played tricks on us. The prophetess then knelt down, prayed and fumbled in the bag. She brought out something wrapped in a red-and-white-striped piece of cloth and then staggered around as if she was carrying something heavy. After some minutes she knelt down and asked those of us who wanted to have a look at the way the *chikwambo* manifested to wash our faces with water which had been prayed over. The explanation for washing the faces with the water was that if we did not do so the *chikwambo* would render us blind as we looked at it. The *chikwambo* manifested as an assortment of snail, herbs and some beads, all of which were burnt soon after the ritual.

Thus, in the case of Nod, she may be understood to have had presence in the dreams of the prophetess even though she was actually not present at the prophetess' house. Equally the people including the doll-like creatures that Mari dreamt were chasing her might have had presence in her dreams without being actually present. And in my case Zan can be understood to have had presence in my dreams even though he was not actually present when I dreamt about him. This hints at a scenario in which things that are not physically available are not necessarily absent as is often assumed in epistemologies that would dismiss as inconsistent suggestions that a thing can be absent but nevertheless present and *vice versa*. If things are understood in terms of becomings in which they can be absent but present, that is in terms of their goings and comings, it arguably becomes easier to understand why among the villagers being absent is not necessarily an opposite of being present. During the fieldwork, I was asked by some of the villagers: "*Asi murikuchikoro?*" (Are you at school?), even though I was clearly with them in the villages and therefore not at any school. What this means is that it is possible for one to be present but absent and to be at different places at the same time. It implies that we can be present where we are absent and therefore that presence is not necessarily measured on the basis of being fixed to a place but rather in terms of comings and goings that make it possible to have presence in many places at the same time.

What this then presumes is a theory of presence in which there is not necessarily pure presence or pure absence. It presumes a theory of presence in which things have different ways of registering presence and absence. When water is used as *munamato* (prayer) it can be understood as registering its presence as a prayer rather than merely as water. When illness manifests in dreams in the form of violent creatures it can well be registering presence as a mode of oncoming violence revealed in the dreams. The challenge in such a context where things vacillate is to shift focus from analysing things merely in terms of the mind to the various ways in which they come to be sensed as they come and go. The challenge is to avoid giving illness and associated violence a home either in the mind or in the social but to see them also in terms of their manifold comings and goings that come to be differentially sensed. It is a challenge to understand other things including dreams not merely as objects to be analysed and interpreted but as modes by which the presence of other entities is actively registered in a world where being physically present in a particular space is not invariably an imperative.

Apart from sensing the presence of things through dreams, villagers also relied on divination and prophecies that can be understood to have underscored the ways in which things, including illnesses, were connected to many different other kinds. My encounters with *n'anga* and prophets indicated that although they often noted particular things that engendered illnesses, they also stressed the connections between different kinds of things. In this sense what they underlined was not just the thing as an ontological object but the ways in which it was connected to many different things via their comings and goings as well as manifestings. So, contrary to scholarship that portrayed *n'anga* as witchdoctors with principal briefs to identify witches (Jeater, 2007; Gelfand, 1964), my sense was that *n'anga* dealt more with sensing connections, often also harnessing them, and the comings and goings of things, than with witches as discreet ontological entities. For instance during my participation in the churches, some illnesses were explained in terms of breaks in connections and flows rather than merely in terms of a witch being present in one's life. Madness and other forms of mischief, including witchcraft, were often explained as much in terms of absence as in terms of presence: to portray such absence villagers remarked: "*haana kukwana*" (literally he/she is not enough) or *dzakadambuka* (the brains are torn apart). In this sense '*kusakwana*' (being not enough, i.e. being incomplete) can be understood in terms of a lack of what is expected in the mode of life in the midst of others rather than merely in terms of possessing malevolence. However there are also statements such as *dzakatachana* (there are wrong connections) that are used to refer to madness and insanity. The ideas of *kukwana* and *kusakwana* were also linked to ways in which babies were treated with herbs in *chivanhu*. Geli, for instance, noted in an interview on 29 January 2011 that:

Pachivanhu vana vaitsengerwa kusvika kuma 1980s *kuitira mudumbu (ruzoka). Kutsengerwa uku kunoita kuti munhu agarisike, adzikame. Kana asina kudzikama munhu anonzi hauna kutsengerwa uye hauna kukwana* (In chivanhu babies had herbs administered to them to prevent stomach problems which are called *ruzoka*. This administration of herbs makes one stable. If one has not had such herbs administered villagers say that one is not enough).

For the reason that some villagers who did mischief were considered to be not enough, those who were identified as witches were sometimes not harassed but rather invited and informed of their lack and, within the churches, measures were prescribed to restore expected flows, in order to render the individuals enough. Such invitation might well have been influenced by the criminalisation of witchcraft accusation since the colonial period but then since 2004, the Criminal Law (Codification and Reform Act) has decriminalised accusations of witchcraft, provided the healers and prophets can render evidence. This then suggests a mode of engagement that is not preoccupied merely with sensing things as discreet but rather sensing their manifestations, comings and goings. If witchcraft is understood in terms of presences that are also absences, it becomes possible to conceive how a preoccupation with only fixed, stable and objectively present things assists in missing the nuances in the comings and goings of everyday life. It is appropriate to follow up on the illness, and to contextualise it in matters of health, that struck me during fieldwork.

The ways in which such nuances are often missed can best be exemplified by my own experiences during fieldwork in 2010-2011. At the beginning of the preliminary fieldwork in June 2010, I visited an old man in the village and attended a church service with him. Towards the end of the service the prophet in that church pointed at me and prophesied that I would experience acute pain in my feet at some point, but for a reason he did not explain he noted that the illness would arrive in the summer season. According to the prophet, some *varoyi* (conventionally understood as witches) who were envious of me had gathered soil from my footprints, mixed it with herbs, needles and other substances. They had then placed the concoction under cover on one path on which they knew I would walk.

When I met a *n'anga* towards the end of my fieldwork, she threw some carved sticks down onto a reed mat as a form of diagnosis. The six sticks fell in different directions leaving gaps between them. Zviko, the *n'anga* whom I interviewed and who did the diagnosis in December 2011, said "*Muri kuvhurirwa mhepo* (someone is opening up space for the wind to get to you) and that is why your feet are painful". She said it was because I had been trapped (*kutsikiswa*) so there was a need to *kutemerwa* (to have incision made and herbs rubbed in).

The *kutsikiswa* is causing pain in your back and in your chest. Some witches have put dirty stuff in your wife's stomach and in her kidneys so she needs herbs to cleanse the dirt in the mornings because that is when she feels the pain. Some villagers and other people lie that *midzimu* and *Mwari* are separated. *Handizvo, midzimu na Mwari murume nemukadzi vari pamwechete* (that is not it, ancestors and God are wife and husband, they are together). My *midzimu* told me to continue attending church services within the Roman Catholic Church when I had briefly stopped attending the church services. You have been bewitched by three villagers who allege that '*unoonesa*' (you see too much of our secrets in the village).

While the divination sticks that Zviko used may be interpreted by scholars whose theories are underpinned by animism as animate, they can also be interpreted in the logics of statistical manipulations where figures are manipulated to interpret things and entities that may not be present to be directly interrogated. It is a way of signifying the invisibles in a visual way without implying that the invisibles and the sticks become one another. If in interpreting my ancestors using the sticks she meant the two to become one then I would not have expected her to keep the stick that would have 'become my ancestors' as in fact there would not have been any point in her keeping them.

Zviko's diagnosis helps make sense of presence that is absence in that she noted that she was seeing the witches even in their absence when we were in her hut. It also helps to make sense of presence that is absence in the sense that my wife about whom she was talking in her diagnosis was not with me but in Harare, about 200 km away. Her diagnosis also helps make sense of absences that are also presences in the sense that while she noted that the witches alleged that I was seeing too much of what they were doing in the village, I had little physical contact with the three villagers whom she mentioned except when I met them during the day in the course of my fieldwork. Thus the *n'anga* helped me note various ways in which presence is sometimes made sense of even when a thing is not necessarily present. The presence of the illness when it was not present, the presence of the future when it was not present, my presence in the form of my footprints when I was not present and the presence of perforations in my feet even when the needles were not present all suggested modes of sensing where neither presence nor absence were deemed to be invariably pure.

Mindful of the fact that my illness resembled what Gelfand (1985: 32, 36) called a rheumatic state as well as what is known in vernacular as *chipotswa*, I needed to maintain the dialogue between the different ways of conceiving the illness as open. I did not want to lose out by prematurely discarding other possible explanations. What I was not happy about though was to characterize the illness merely as a rheumatic state when it appeared in many ways to be a process rather than a state. So for instance while Gelfand likens *chipotswa* to a rheumatic state, the *chipotswa* is more of a process than a state. His other observation which underscores process is that with *chipotswa* the witch plants the poison on the victim's path so that when he or she steps on it or comes into contact with it, it enters his/her body within which it then circulates to other parts. The reason why I was not happy to conceive my illness as a state or condition was that it clearly had a history which could not have been discarded without impoverishing the diverse ways of sensing the presences of things. In everyday life where things are often characterized more by processes than by stasis, emphasizing states and conditions would have made me lose the nuances about how things become as well as their regimes of presences and absences.

My encounters with *n'anga* suggested that what matters in treatment is not necessarily the naming of an affliction, whether as a rheumatic state or *chipotswa,* because different names can be given to the same thing. Pombi, whom I interviewed on 30 January 2011, noted this in the following manner:

*Unogona kupomerwa AIDS usina pane zvaitwa nevaroyi. Varoyi vave kuroya saizvozvo unoonda, unoshanduka ganda ma*Doctor *oti tiri kushaya chirwere asi apa panenge pane mishonga inenge ichitokanganisa* doctor *iyeye kuti asakuonere. Ma*doctor *mamwe ave kuti zvinoda chivanhu.*

Varoyi vanokudyisa vanhu. Kudyiswa kwehuroyi kudyiswa wakarara kana wakamuka. Kudyiswa nemukadzi kuti uuye nemari yese. Umwe mukadzi anenge achinzenzereka odyisa murume kuitira kuti mitauro isawande. Kudyisa murume kutsvaga mishonga wobikwa nebhurukwa mvura yacho yobikiswa muriwo netumidzi imwe ndeyekufukira, mukadzi anogara papoto utsi hwacho huchiwira mupoto hunova hunozobikiswa zvamuchadya mese. Munhu anenge asiri mukati mazvo anoti chivanhu hakuna (You can be considered to have AIDS when actually it will be witches' activities. Witches are now bewitching people so that they have symptoms like those of AIDS or they do so in such a way that doctors will say they are failing to have diagnosis and this can be because the witches' activities will be interfering with the diagnosis. Some doctors now advise patients to consult *n'anga*s in *chivanhu* way. Witches cause one to eat poisoned concoctions while one is asleep or awake. But other villagers are made to eat concoctions by their wives who will want their husbands to bring all the pay home. Some of the wives make their husbands eat concoctions because the wives will be engaging in adultery and so the herbs would render the husbands docile and reticent. Such wives surreptitiously consult *n'anga* for herbs which they cook together with the wives' underwear. Some of the concoctions involve the wives squatting over a pot with steam which falls into the pot and is used to cook food that the husband and wife will eat together. Some people say that there is no *chivanhu* simply because they are not in it).

While Pombi explained some of the aspects of witchcraft in terms of *chivanhu, chivanhu* does not tolerate witchcraft. In fact some contemporary *n'angas* who resort to witchcraft and to prescribing witchcraft related remedies for their clients are demonised as *n'anga varoyi* (combining witchcraft practices with treating clients). Some informants presented in Chapter Two lamented the fact that although in the past there were genuine *n'anga*, there are nowadays many fake *n'anga* who cheat people. But during the fieldwork I also met *n'anga*s who stated that they would not treat clients who consulted them in the absence of family members. They also stated that when a client wanted to bewitch a *hama* they would, as a way to dissuade the evil minded client, insist that he/she bring along the intended victim in the interests of full transparency.

Not much has been written about the *kudyiswa,* but Gelfand (1985: 36) mentions it when he notes that *chidyiso,* which is the same as *kudyiswa,* is caused by ingestion of food that has been bewitched. For Gelfand (1985) *chidyiso* is characterised by foreign bodies remaining stationary or moving in the victim's digestive tract. The poison is believed to have no immediate effect on the victim but the symptoms start to show after some weeks or even months. With all this about absent presences, it is necessary to turn back to key issues raised in this chapter.

A return to a few key issues about presences and absences

This chapter has argued that resilience against illness in everyday life involved navigating the terrains of biomedicine as well as the terrains of prophets and healers. The ways in which these were navigated depended on the kinds of material and nonmaterial presences that were sensed to show up, manifest and promote or disrupt processes of treatment/wellness. It has been noted that some objects such as soil, pebbles, strings and water are considered to assume presence in the healing sessions not necessarily as the object that they appear to be but as *munamato* once they are sanctified for use. In this sense human beings infuse agency into things some of which would be understood as natural in the kind of modernist understanding that Latour (1993; 2005) argues is founded on the nature-culture divide which is the basis of the 'binaries between humans and nonhumans' (such as animals, trees and other objects). To the extent that healers and prophets render agency to the things which they then advise their patients to use, they can be understood as rendering fuzziness such that things manifest as otherwise than they ordinarily would be understood. Therefore the villagers' conceptions are that such objects are rendered via the intercession of human beings with agency as in the case of *munamato,* for instance, when they have been prayed over. On the other hand, the conceptions that *mhepo* constitutes the nonmaterial presences around material objects underscore the need to consider not only the agency of material things but also the nonmaterial aspects that come and go, of which they are parts.

Taking cues from Ingold's (2007; 2010; and 2011) argument that there is a need to start from the flows rather than from congealed objects, this chapter has privileged the nonmaterial things deemed to have presence and to manifest in matters of health and illness. Following Ingold, it has been argued here that materials of different sorts with various and variable properties mix and meld with one another in the generation of things; however, some differences with Ingold's interpretation were noted. The chapter has focused also on *mhepo* in so far as it was deemed for instance to interfere with doctor-patient interactions. But to extend Ingold's argument about the ways in which things mix and meld with one another, I have looked at how in everyday life the presence of other things is sensed. In this way I have argued that things do not just mix and meld because there is also separation of things in rituals and in treatments for instance. So while Ingold emphasizes the mixing, melding and the becomings of things, this chapter has shown that there is much more than these issues in everyday life, where things become and also unbecome, things mix but they also unmix, so to speak. I have used the notion of (hau)ontology to characterize the lack (which is not necessarily absence of) of settledness of such things in the kind of everyday life studied. I have argued that in (hau)ontology there is the comings and goings of things, the manifestations of things in various forms of presence entailing complex interactions and intermingling that however do not invariably result in the Derridean deconstruction. In the (hau)ontology that I conceive there is no readily drawn binary between construction and deconstruction.

The switches from biomedical regimes to healers and prophets and vice versa can be understood to indicate such lack of settledness in the everyday life. The lack of faith in some medical diagnoses, which some villagers such as Fatsi contested, indicate the lack of settledness of matters of truth which are often assumed in conventional practices to be settled once tests are done. By switching from prophets and healers to medical institutions the villagers also indicated lack of trust in the modes of diagnoses and treatment that could otherwise be deemed to compete with or complement the medical provisions. What this implies is that the kind of truth that sometimes matters in everyday life is not necessarily formally given but rather located in the comings and goings of things or in the practices. Because it is truth that is partly lived on the basis of such comings and goings of things, it is not always readily available for ordinary representation and for epistemologies founded solely on such formal representationalism.

Whereas the Euro-modern representationalist epistemologies privilege understanding of things in terms of rigid subjects and objects in everyday life, where things are understood in terms of comings and goings, subject and objects cannot always be delimited as such. When villagers understand the *mhepo* to block the doctors' diagnosis, they can be understood to be noting that during the processes it is not only the doctor and patient as subject and object that matter but that there are other things that render the subject-object divide not as neat and pure. When the villagers note the presence of other things manifesting in various kinds of materialities and as nonmaterial aspects they can be understood to be underscoring the possibility of things to have presence without becoming subjects or objects in the conventional sense. To have presence without invariably registering in conventional objectivist ways of knowing as present is how some things in such everyday life may be characterized. But failure to register in a particular expected way as present does not invariably imply being absent or nonexistent as is assumed in those some representationalist epistemologies. Such Eurocentric representationalist epistemologies presumed absence of science and scientific representations in indigenous knowledge when in fact scientific knowledge existed. In *chivanhu* for instance there is knowledge of internal body parts such as *itsvo* (kidneys), *mapapu* (lungs), *chiropa* (liver), *moyo* (heart), *uropi* (brains), *dundira* (bladder) and *tsinga* (veins). And herbalists know their herbs on the basis of representing them via different names and properties. The experiences I had with my illness indicate that things often have their own ways of registering presence which may not be readily accessible to some senses. For this reason they may be subject to a variety of interpretations, which have different traction.

This chapter has shown that matters of senses and of what things have their presence are not invariably settled in everyday life as they appear to be in formal and institutional discourses. Bearing in mind the disparities in the senses and the aspects of sensing that are stressed (Serres, 2008; Geurts, 2002) one is persuaded in the light of this research to think that the domain of senses needs retranslation in ways that would democratize the modes of engagement in the world. When villagers use the vernacular term *kunzwa* (literally to hear) not only to refer to the auditory senses but also in reference to bodily feelings, they can be understood to be indicating the disparities in understanding senses in everyday life as well as in formal institutional renditions. The statement, '*ndanzwa kurwadziwa*' (literally, I have heard pain though it can also be read as I felt pain) underlines the different understandings of the sense of hearing. Equally when villagers use the terms *kuona* (literally to see) to refer not only to the sense of sight but also to the process of thinking such as in the phrases: '*ndaona kuti zvakanaka*' (which can be read, I have seen it in my mind's eye to be good or I have thought it good), they can be understood to be rendering different conceptualisations of senses from the institutional conventional. But as indicated in this chapter, sometimes one is not allowed to see the things that make one ill though they may have other ways of sensing the presences of such things as heaviness, biting pains and so forth. Equally, although I did not see the needles that were allegedly used to cast illness on me, when I fell ill I felt acute pricking pain as if needles were indeed being pushed into my feet, and after the treatment sessions my feet registered many small perforations the size of needles. The point here is to underline the fact that what often matters in everyday life is not always to see the things that are deemed to have presence: it is often to sense the things in a broader way.

In the context of the shiftiness of things, the different ways of sensing presences and the nomadism in seeking health services, one notices the lack of settledness of facts about health matters. Although translation constitutes ongoing [unfinished] business in everyday life, there are also terms such as *kuguma/kupera/kupeta* (to end/finish/conclude) that signify the end, which is also anticipated in the adage *chisingagumi chinoshura* (that which does not end portends ill fortunes). Translation underlies the movements from one mode to the other; it underlies the modalities of sensing presences and it underlies the epistemic shifts that are suggested by the switches in modes of health provision. If such ongoingness of modes of translation is rendered central in research on everyday life, it becomes possible to recognize why dichotomies are often not an enduring aspect. It becomes for instance possible to understand why a thing can be absent but present. In other words it becomes possible to reckon why phenomena such as illnesses often elude epistemological appropriation and representation even as their presence may be sensed.

When prophets and healers among the villagers remark that: '*pane chiripo*' (there is something in presence), or *pane mamhepo* (there are winds in presence) or *hapana chiripo* (there is nothing in presence) they can be understood to be alluding to things that come and go with illnesses and health. When such things are understood in terms of presences they suggest both temporal and spatial qualities and in this way they enable not only the histories of things but also ways in which they come to connect in order to be told. The presence may be registered via action but also via inaction. The commissions and omissions of the government and other institutions including the global which were understood to have rendered the presence of constraints in the provision of health services would best exemplify the double-edgedness of presence: things can have presence without necessarily acting, as in the case of my illness where it had been foretold a year and a half before it struck. In other words, presence cannot be understood merely in terms of becomings in Ingold's sense; it can also be understood in terms of moments of convergence when there is as much potential for unbecomings as there is for becomings. But for some things, it is for healers, mediums and prophets to sense for their clients as they have in Serres' argument, exceptional senses beyond the usual five.

But the experiences of the villagers are contrary to Levy Bruhl's (Willis and Curry, 2004) argument about mystical participation in a world where humans can assume animal form, or be in more than one place simultaneously, in a world of multiple and incommensurate powers, a world of flow rather than substance, of creative chaos rather than linear causality. As argued elsewhere in the book, villagers consider neither creation to emanate from chaos nor human beings to become animals. Creation among the villagers is understood to have been the work of *Mwari*. In everyday life, a human being is recognised as a human being and if he/she were to become an animal it would be taken as strange enough to require the intervention of healers and prophets. Equally, the everyday life among the villagers is not characterised by a desire to escape bodily limitations and become sorcerers, as suggested in Deleuze and Guattari's (Lee, 2003) work on becoming, which centres on man as a primary analytical category marked by a desire to escape the bodily limitation and resorting to sorcery. In fact sorcerers are ostracised and castigated by villagers and their possible presence is one reason why villagers attend church services where sorcerers are detected and dealt with if they happen to be present. As argued elsewhere, it is not that spirits, even of sorcery, become animals, but rather that some spirits may temporarily manifest as animals. It is therefore necessary to distinguish between becomings and manifestations.

Conclusion

This book has shown that villagers evince a number of everyday life modes of engagement including *mukwerera* or rain petitioning, relying on dreams, prophecies and divination, via *ukama*, through *kutenda* and a variety of ways of sensing and knowing. These modes of engagement were not invariably opposed to Western-modern modes of engagement, knowing, sensing, and acquiring and sharing information for example about weather forecasts or about violence through the use of cell phones and radios. This book therefore argues that *chivanhu,* which encapsulates the villagers' modes of engagement, is not invariably steeped in dichotomies.

Though *chivanhu* has been portrayed as tradition and consigned to the past, it speaks to connections between temporalities, spaces, things and beings. While the European Enlightenment portrayed time simply in terms of linearity of past, present and future, in *chivanhu* time is also experienced in terms of simultaneities that do not invariably occasion distinctions between temporalities. Because *chivanhu* recognizes these temporalities, the underlying implication is that *chivanhu* is not inimical to change but, as the medium indicated with respect to reconciliation noted in Chapter Three, [decent] change is engaged in with the consultation of elders (*vakuru*) and in terms of evaluations in the light of existing values and norms. The fact that Zimbabweans and Africans in general consult ancestors before making decisions about the future should not be misinterpreted as colonists did to mean ancestors are in the realm of the past. A more accurate interpretation is that Africans consult their ancestors because they regard them as existing in the realm of the future, that is, as being ahead of the living rather than in the past or behind their progeny, or even behind the temporal present. This view is clearly expressed in the Shona saying that '*nzira inobvunzwa vari mberi*' (to know your way, you ask those who are moving ahead of you). What was interpreted by colonists as resistance to change among indigenous people can be understood rather as resistance to expropriations of material and cosmological resources by colonists who sought to cloak these actions in the more neutral and innocent term of change. So the issue is not so much that *chivanhu* is resistant to change (*shanduko*) but rather that *chivanhu* has been prevented from relying on inbuilt dynamism and mechanisms of change that included broad consultations of the living and the *mhondoro* as well as *Mwari* – all significant in their metaphysics. In this vein, it can be argued that notions of modernity and tradition are actually political terms meant to deride and arm-twist those labelled as traditional so that they follow the tracks of the colonists deeming themselves to be "modern". If Euro-modernity is traceable to René Descartes in the 1600s and if Christianity goes back almost 2000 years, why would they be considered modern while African kings, chiefs and practices of the 1700s were considered traditional?

In view of the above argument I would rather conceive what are called traditions as 'repressed African modernities'. This makes it possible to think through the historicities of such repressed modernities and to view them not necessarily as backward but simply as possible to liberate. By conceptualising them as repressed modernities, one can envisage the historical politics and colonialities in the creation of alterities out of the colonial subjects' modes of engagement.

The modes of relating in *chivanhu* as indicated in *ukama* include connections between the visible and invisible realms, the realms for instance of human beings and of *midzimu* (ancestors) understood as manifesting in the form of *mhepo/mweya* as resident in *Nyikadzimu* while visiting human beings [in the human world] from time to time. They also include connections between the near and the far, deemed for instance to be interlinked through *mweya/mhepo* which are relied upon in divination, dreaming and prophecy. But the connections in *ukama* are also defined in terms of material exchanges such as means of survival, blood, and by other things such as language, that help bridge difference. The different forms of relating in *chivanhu* underscore the multifacetedness of relationships relied upon in struggles for survival. Wildman's (2006) contention that there is a variety of relations, differently valued, that need consideration in relational ontologies is vindicated in *ukama*.

Much as different scholars have emphasised different ways of relating, whether through Ingold's (2011) meshworks or through Latour's Actor-Networks, or through animism in some parts of the world (Viveiros de Castro, 2004; Bird-David, 1999; Descola, 1996), Buhera villagers conceived different forms of everyday life relationships that were valued differently. Healers and mediums emphasised connections via *midzimu*/ancestors also understood as *mweya/mhepo*, while prophets and church members emphasised direct connections with *Mwari* (God). These different forms of relationships, as well as different values attached to them, indicate ways in which relationships are subject to value judgments depending on context and time. But these value judgments also pertain to different ways in which the entities themselves are valued. Healers and mediums for instance allow their bodies to be entered by their deceased *hama* who manifest as *midzimu*, but conversely, bodies deemed to have been entered by *ngozi* aggrieved dead are held by healers to require exorcism. Similarly, prophets of apostolic churches allow their bodies to be entered by the [Holy Spirit]: they shun possession by *midzimu*, in spite of the fact that the Holy Spirit is also addressed as *mudzimu unoera* in the churches, as well as by *ngozi*. The villagers' ways of relating with *mweya/mhepo* show selectivity and complex processes of inclusion and exclusion much in the same way, as some scholars note that flows and circulation of information and capital goods are marked, in the global world, by intensification, building and rebuilding of boundaries (see Nyamnjoh, 2005; Blair, 2010).

Jahn (1961: 18, 102) recognizes the difference between *muntu/munhu* as a Bantu concept that embraces both living and dead human being(s), while *kintu/chinhu* refers to one or more animals, minerals or objects, none of which have wills of their own: this concept is at the core of *chivanhu* and shows that human beings are distinguished from animals. It also indicates that when a sacrifice, prayer or petition is made, it is never to the plant or animal or mountain but to the ancestors, that is the *muntu* force, attaching/presumed to be sitting on it or using it as its vehicle. Also supporting McGregor's (2003: 94, 97) findings elsewhere in Zimbabwe is the fact that in *chivanhu*, when mysterious voices are heard they are not assumed to be the voices of trees, mountains, rivers or pools but rather the voices of ancestors or of the dead human beings who may happen to be in the vicinity of the hearer. So while scholars such as Ranger (2000) have argued that in the Matopo Hills of Zimbabwe pilgrims and worshippers can hear 'voices of the rocks that speak', see 'messages of the rocks', understand and convey an African appreciation of rocky and sunny parts of Africa, the voices that church members and I heard were not of the mountains, or rocks or trees but those of church members and prophets prophesying on the mountains and in the caves. While Ranger (2000) argues as above, in Ranger and Ncube (1996: 40) it is noted that Dokotela Ncube, who had a farm about a mile away from Dula shrine in Matopo Hills, went into the cave and found two pieces of metal that an old woman who spoke as the voice of God struck together. It is noted that it was the old woman who spoke as God in Kalanga and in a foreign language. So, even as the prophets with whom I went to the mountains were prophesying, they were not understood to have become God, because clear distinctions were made between the prophets and God. And while the voice during prophecy could be understood as emanating from God, the prophet was merely the seat or vehicle of the voice. The failure by colonial authorities to distinguish between God and prophets led them to kill prophets in the erroneous belief that they were killing God himself. As Ranger (1966: 106-7) notes, native Commissioner Bonar Armstrong and the American Scout Frederick Russell Burnham tried to quell the uprising known as the Matebeleland Rebellion, or Second Matabele War, at the inception of colonialism in June 1896 "by shooting the *Mlimo* (God)", but what they did was to shoot the priest and to imprison his family and associates under the erroneous impression that they were killing God/*Mlimo*. This can be understood in terms of the fact that Europeans interpreted African phenomena in terms of European naturalistic metaphysics and the view that God was immanent in matter in the visible objects such that He could be killed or shot at. Disasters and forbearances occur; but when they do so, it is not nature that is speaking as is often assumed simplistically via naturalistic metaphysics. Rather, as noted elsewhere in this book, it is God and/or ancestors who could be communicating by using those objects as mere vehicles to exercise their influence in the human world. In fact, God and ancestors are not considered to be incarnate or immanent in human beings or in earthly objects.

It is the ability to see ephemeral mysterious appearances of the invisible dead (*madzangaradzimu* or *madzimudzangara*) that underlines the differences between naturalistic metaphysics and the metaphysics of *chivanhu* in which ephemeral mysterious appearances do not necessarily transform themselves into physical features on which they manifest. Such appearances seem to be widespread, and are not confined to *chivanhu*; for instance McGregor (2003: 96) notes of the Tonga that when you see at a shrine young girls, a whole village with women pounding and children crying, you clap your hands for permission to pass and everything disappears. Equally, Wiseman (2011: 193) notes that apparitions have an uncanny knack of looking like a normal person and 'their ghost-like nature' becomes apparent only when they do something impossible like suddenly vanishing or walking through a wall. Writing about Europe, Frede (2011) observes that the world of later antiquity was populated not only by all the things we could see and touch but also by myriads of transparent and intangible beings or even incorporeal beings of various kinds. I have argued that it is such *madzimudzangara* that naturalistic metaphysics sought to dispense with, to misinterpret and to conflate them with natural objects. In the 'new spirituality' that is being advocated by some scholars (Tacey, 2003), it is also such phenomena that are misinterpreted in terms of immanence of God; yet it is one thing to advocate new spirituality and another to write African metaphysics as they are. The colonial misinterpretations of African metaphysics in terms of immanence and naturalistic metaphysics can best be understood in terms of colonial quest for control: to control colonial subjects the colonists needed to interpret all aspects of Africans' modes of life in terms of what they could touch, define and harness in structural terms. This is why African ancestors were (re-)cast in terms of animism, as transforming into features of the landscape; this is why God as conceived by Africans was reduced by colonists to the earth and to immanence in the landscape features. When colonists failed to fathom African metaphysics they derided Africans. As Mungazi (1996) argues, Victorian-era Europeans shared the illusion that African societies lacked structure, and this illusion was also a result of what David Hapgood identified as a mythology of imperialism (which assumed that African culture and society were void of values and ideas, and spread the myth that African minds and society were disintegrated, disjointed and did not contribute to a cohesive and integrated social system). Yet it has been shown in this book that failure by colonists to understand African metaphysics was not the Africans' fault, but rather that of incorrect metaphysical assumptions founded solely on naturalised metaphysics brought by colonists to the business of trying to comprehend Africans' modes of engagement.

The flights by villagers from violence and from violent relations indicate that while some relations are important in surviving violence, others pose danger to individuals and are shunned. The individuals' flights indicate their preferences for their own lives (as substantive entities) over the kind of relational ontologies that accord primacy to relations. The arguments in relational ontologies that relations have primacy over substantive entities (Wildman, 2006; van Inwagen, 2011; Paul, 2013) legitimise the marginalisation of the lives of the individuals as substantive entities (in preference for relations) yet it is often the individuals who generate and sustain relations. In other words, giving primacy to relations rather than to substantive entities runs the risk of violating the integrity and senses of personhood/self of the individuals who provided accounts of the relations in the first instance. To argue that substantive entities have neither their own essence nor their own being would in fact be to legitimise the violence against others thereby considered to be of no essence: it would be to legitimise the murders and other offences against individuals who were being victimised. Relationality premised on immanence claims other people have no essence and denies their sovereignty; such denial of sovereignty was a justification of colonialism. Pagden (1993) captures this well when he notes that the Indigenous Peoples of the Americas were deemed by the Europeans who established colonies in the New World to be 'natural slaves' with no claim to sovereign authority over themselves or rights over the land on which they happened to reside, thus justifying the conquest and the exploitation of their labour. Notwithstanding colonists' assertions noted by Pagden above, human beings are deemed in *chivanhu* to have their own being and essence, as underscored in accounts where the *mweya/mhepo* of the murdered were understood to return to avenge. In this instance the *mhepo/mweya* as the essence of individuals is deemed to survive physical death and to constitute the phenomenon of *ngozi* that is held in *chivanhu* as possibly harmful to others. Also, as noted with reference to Butler in Chapter Three, there exists in *chivanhu* the notion of the 'I' and 'we', as in the vernacular terms *inin'* and *isusu*, even as there is also insistence on *ukama*.

It may well be possible to contest the reality of such phenomena as *ngozi* on the basis of Enlightenment rationalism which, as Davies (2007: 7) argues, sought to put an end to the phenomena of spirits and ghosts, although this simply displaced and internalised the world of spirits into the realm of psychology. From Davies' position, it can be argued that the psychological phenomenon of fear haunts us in the same way that ghosts do. Yet before the Enlightenment, what haunted people could be regarded as external to the mind and not merely a psychological problem. Interpreting God as immanent in nature as was done during the Enlightenment could have helped ease arguments about rationalism; but in *chivanhu*, phenomena such as *ngozi* underscore modes of engagement different from those of the Enlightenment (Reynolds, 1996; Schmidt, 1997; Gelfand, 1959 and Bourdillon, 1979). Since it was part of the Enlightenment, Eighteenth Century rationalism wherein nature became a polite word for God deemed immanent (Evensky, 2005), questioning modernist epistemologies involves questioning such ideas of immanence. The ideas of immanence appear to underpin notions of animism that were often attributed by scholars even to contexts with different cosmologies (Opoku, 1978; Stanner, 2005; Rattray, 1927; 1969; Fontein, 2006). But in so far as notions of immanence and animism fail to acknowledge invisible outside forces and powers that influence objects and things, they are blind to indirect influences including indirect rule such as exercised in coloniality. This the notions do by shifting attention entirely to what is immanent, and by so doing they conceal practices of transcendence by the empire as they also conceal causation emanating from outside the self.

In the context of *chivanhu*, there are indications that villagers did not [ordinarily] conceive objects as animate, in the same way as human beings are animate. Some particular entities and places including mountains, rivers, waterfalls and animals were considered to be the temporary abode of or manifestations of *midzimu* for instance, but the entities and objects themselves were not considered to be the *midzimu*. Rather the *mweya/mhepo* of the *midzimu* was deemed to temporarily attach to, rest or manifest in/on the features. Even though *Mwari* was deemed to manifest in particular mountains, caves and other places, He was not considered to have become the features or the things through which He manifested his presence. Whereas animism and the considerations of God as immanent in nature would suggest pantheism or polytheism, in *chivanhu* there is a recognition of God as the one Supreme Being as is clear in the various names for God such as *Nyadenga*/owner of Heavens, *Musiki*/ creator, *Wekumusorosoro*/the one who ranks highest, *Musikavanhu*/creator of human beings. In this sense there is, in *chivanhu*, evidence of ranking or hierarchy of things and beings that also relate or connect with one another.

Although *midzimu*/ancestors and *Mwari* are deemed to have shrines, not every feature of the environment constitutes a shrine: selected places and features are deemed to be shrines or places where villagers hold that they can interact with ancestors and God on ritual occasions. Such places can be understood as liminal spaces where, in Fontein's (2006: 88) terms, the worlds of human beings and those of ancestors share temporal and spatial dimensions. But the worlds that share spaces in everyday life are not merely the human and the ancestral worlds: everyday village life is also punctuated and affected by other places outside the villages. The ways in which food aid arrived and was distributed in village life indicated ways in which worlds were interwoven. The ways in which commodities and other remittances circulated in the villages in times of economic and political challenges underscored ways in which everyday village life could be understood in terms of liminal spaces where commodities from different places, and even currencies from different countries, circulated. It is in reckoning such liminality of everyday life that I have sought to understand the modes of engagement in terms of what I call (hau)ontology. This notion is derived from Derrida's (1994) notion of hauntology as discussed in chapters three and five. For Derrida hauntology is about a deconstructive figure hovering between life and death, presence and absence, and as a place where we can interrogate our relation with the dead, examine illusive identities of the living, explore boundaries between thought and unthought. (Hau)ontology, on the other hand, does not presume, privilege or prioritise deconstructive figures because life is not all about deconstruction. Indeed in what I call (hau)ontology there can be hauntings without deconstruction as indeed there can be haunting without (re)construction. In other words, an entity can be haunted and yet retain its ontological features, haunting does not necessarily result in ontogenesis or (onto)instability, understood here in terms of instability of prior ontological frames, or even atrophy or negentropy. It is these qualities of (hau)ontology that can be used to theorise and conceptualise resilience and distinguish it from sacrifice, where I conceive of sacrifice primarily in terms of deconstructing a figure and in the process generating its paralysis, fatality or petrification. While Derrida sought to resuscitate the figure of the ghost from the dustbins of the Enlightenment era, his conceptualisation of hauntology in terms of a deconstructive figure brings negative connotations to the spectral figural presences that he seeks to resuscitate. It is with the notion of (hau)ontology that I seek to navigate these negative connotations in the Derridean hauntology for in (hau)ontology it is not always possible to tell or foretell whether a spectral presence is deconstructive or (re)constructive as indeed the effects of the spectral presences are often subject to debates. The effects of the presence of NGOs in Zimbabwean politics, the effects of what I have called the absent presences, of European and American figures in Zimbabwean economics, politics and society, the effects of the absent presence of the state in everyday life and the effects of absent presence of the dead and of God in life cannot all be accounted for in terms of deconstructive figures in the Derridean sense as indeed such effects were hotly debated even in the Zimbabwean Parliament as well as in the media.

So what I call (hau)ontology includes visitations by social figures and the ramifications of media ideologies in everyday life. But in light of ways in which citizens in the diaspora remitted money and commodities, (hau)ontology in this book is not understood merely as deconstructive figures but also as constructive figures that helped to make life possible during the economic and political challenges in the country. (Hau)ontology in this sense also borrows insights from Gordon's (2004: 24-5, 2012: 1) argument about hauntology, that is, the instance of the "merging of the visible and the invisible, the dead and the living, the past and the present into the making of worldly relations and into our accounts of the worlds". Though Gordon's argument is important in understanding (hau)ontology, what mattered for the villagers in the context of everyday life struggles to survive violence was not necessarily world making or making accounts of the world but survival and resilience. In other words (hau)ontology as understood through *chivanhu* is not about world making because there are many worlds that are conceived in its metaphysics and also the worlds in Shona metaphysics are conceived as created by God. (Hau)ontology is about opening oneself to possibilities of survival and closing down possibilities of trouble. It is about action, about resistance, resilience and survival; but it is also about making and sharing meanings and values, rationalities, vitalities and so on. It is in this sense that villagers made value judgements about what relations and substantive entities they could engage in the context of threats to survival.

Thus (hau)ontology is about life giving or life terminating possibilities near or far, visible or invisible to which entities connect or get connected, depending on whether life or death is envisaged in the possibilities. Some connections, as they would be envisaged in (hau)ontology, are not given but they have to be made on the basis of protocols and etiquette, as indicated in the petitioning ceremonies in described in Chapter One. Some connections succeed while others fail, and some connections are more enduring while others are short lived; yet others are more valued and hankered for than others, as shown in the ways in which some villagers rely on churches and others on healers and mediums. Because (hau)ontology does not presume that all connections are inherently good, as some connect with covert agendas, it allows room for the rationalisations of entities wishing to connect or even disconnect. (Hau)ontology does not presume that it is mere action that is important or that life is determined by the ability to act, but rather that when acting or even before the action there is rationalisation of outcomes, that is of what is in the action; and this is what explains why some actions are terminated while others are retained. Entities are not necessarily inherently enmeshed or connected. As Lefebvre (2000) and Gardiner (2000) argue, everyday life cannot be deemed to be irrational, illogical or confused, as philosophers have historically misunderstood it to be. Indeed, as this book has shown, to petition invisibles in other worlds who constitute absent presences in everyday life is neither irrational nor illogical when considered in the context of petitions made to invisible corporate entities as well as distant invisible countries. In this vein (hau)ontology exposes the paradoxes of the colonial scholars who labelled such everyday life conceptions of invisible beings as irrational and illogical even as the colonial scholars and officials engaged with their home countries in the distant invisible lands away from the colonies where they were based. Indeed even in the contemporary era researchers continue to view such everyday life modes of engagement with the invisible worlds as irrational and illogical even as they themselves are busy engaging with invisible distant lands via various modes of communication at a distance. For (hau)ontology, ancestors are understood as living in another invisible world, and much as there are requests to other places that may not be readily visible, the ancestral worlds are also subject to petitions and requests.

(Hau)ontology as understood in the context of this book encompasses ways in which villagers were visited by spectres of violence, by violent others, by the *mhepo/mweya* and indeed by other villagers with whom they shared material means of survival as well as *ruzivo*. In this sense (hau)ontology does not presuppose that the entity that is haunted is always amenable to haunting as indeed there are also abatements and foreclosures including flights from possibilities of being haunted. Connections via *mhepo/mweya*, as is clear in the experiences of healers and mediums where the *mweya/mhepo* possess and release them after the divination sessions, indicate that hauntings are temporal as much as they are, at least, more frequent with particular beings, entities and spaces. This temporality and spatiality of (hau)ontology makes it possible, in everyday village life, for villagers to go about their lives without invariably presuming that everything around them is animate. For this reason, presuming that everything is animate risks taking exceptions for rules.

So it is mainly healers, mediums, prophets as liminal persons and liminal places or features where worlds are deemed to share space and temporality that appeared to be more open to the connections with others. But even as they occupy liminal spaces, healers, mediums and prophets insist on purity and cleansing rather than on hybridity, at least in an unqualified sense. In this sense, (hau)ontology is neither about hybridity or hybridisation nor about ontogenesis, particularly in view of the fact that healers, mediums and prophets do not profess to create things, which creation they attribute to *Mwari*. But in (hau)ontology it is also possible to understand Africa as in a liminal position partly as a result of the duplicities of Euro-modernity since colonial eras, where Africa was promised civilisation yet what was delivered by Euro-modernity was backwardness, Africa was promised development yet what was delivered was underdevelopment, African ancestors and cultures were vilified yet African ancestral artefacts were looted and taken to Europe, Africans were vilified as ignorant yet their knowledge was looted, Africans were promised humanitarian interventions yet this was a means to colonise them. (Hau)ontology makes it possible to theorise deterritorialisation at the periphery while there is territorialisation at the metropole; critiques of sovereignty at the periphery while there are affirmations of sovereignty at the metropole; demilitarisation at the periphery while there is increasing militarisation at the metropole; expropriations at the periphery while there are appropriations at the metropole. It makes it possible to theorise critiques of power at the periphery while there are affirmations of power at the metropole; critiques of patrimonialism at the periphery while there are affirmations of patrimonialism at the metropole. (Hau)ontology takes note of duplicities in the critiques of patriarchy at the periphery even when there is reliance on patriarchy at the metropole; it makes it possible to see duplicities where there is development at the metropole and underdevelopment at the periphery. Why there is critique of clientelism at the periphery while there are affirmations of clientelism at the level of the metropole can be understood via the lenses of (hau)ontology. Similarly critiques of nationalism at the periphery even as there are affirmations, extensions of nationalism and the creation of supranationalisms at the level of the metropole can be understood via (hau)ontology. (Hau)ontology enables theorisation of insistence on openness at the periphery while affirming closure at the metropole. Exhortations of more liberalism at the periphery while sustaining corporate hegemonies at the metropole can equally be understood via (hau)ontology. It makes it possible to see the duplicities when following cultures at the metropole is defined as convention while following cultures at the periphery is defined as oppression; it enables one to understand the duplicities when claims to help the poor are accompanied by the destruction of the cultural resources of the impoverished; it makes it possible to theorise duplicities in claims that people of the periphery have no essence while essence is acclaimed at the metropole; it makes it possible to theorise the duplicities in decentring the periphery while creating centres in the metropole. (Hau)ontology enables theorisation of insistences on humanism at the metropole while there are insistences on animism and posthumanism at the colonised periphery. The theory of (hau)ontology also enables understanding of the duplicities when the worlds of everyday life are dismissed even as the metropole spends millions looking for life in other worlds and planets. (Hau)ontology enables one to theorise the duplicities when there is insistence on democracy at the metropolitan home while practising imperialism at the periphery abroad. It enables one to view the duplicities in Euro-modernity that preached freedom and abolition of sacrifices even as it paradoxically enslaved Africans, expropriated African property including cultural artefacts, and introduced sacrificial forced labour for Africans in European industries. Such duplicities that positioned Africa in a permanent zone of liminality are well captured by Zine Magubane (2003: iv), cited in B.M. Magubane (2007: 25), who argues that Euro-modernity has from the outset been a discourse that practised darkness and violence even as it preached enlightenment; witchcraft even as it lay claim to the realm of scientific rationality; inhumanity even as it presented itself as the discourse of secular humanism.

While Lan (1985) and others argue that it was deemed dangerous in colonial Zimbabwe for mediums to wear Western style clothes, eat factory produced food, smoke cigarettes and use Western medicine, mediums and healers among the villagers I studied used items such as mobile phones, solar panels, fertilizer and radios. As Lan (1989) argues, mediums were not opposed to everything modern, as they accepted money which they and the *mhondoro* could claim, but rather to highly priced goods and extortionate prices. The relaxation of taboos against Western items after the war of liberation in the 1980s (Lan, 1985) indicates that the mediums' opposition to the items reflected their opposition to the colonial state; but in other places *mhondoro* also allowed mediums to use Western items including riding on buses and wearing trousers (Bourdillon, 1987). Thus opposition to European manufactured good can be understood in terms of the context of the liberation war in which Europeans also applied poison to clothing destined for use by the liberation fighters (see also Simmons, 2012).

The significance placed on *mweya/mhepo* in *chivanhu* underscores the role of fluidity and flows, however limited in other ways. But connections via the *mhepo/mweya,* as indicated in the chapter on petitioning for rain, appear to be more labile than what is presumed in notions such as rainmaking, or what Tsing (2000) calls 'world making'. Though scholars such as Latour (2005) present an approach they argue is intended to bridge the nature-culture divide, by conceiving both humans and nonhumans as actants (that deploy action), in *chivanhu* differences/distinctions are not bridged merely by actions, as some actions can actually widen differences. The presuppositions that modernity created and relied on nature-culture divides is erroneous in view of the fact that in colonial territories European colonists did not seek to separate their culture from nature; rather, the essence of colonialism was that colonists grafted their cultures on the nature or territories of the colonies. In this sense, the essence of colonialism was the appropriation of nature in colonies rather than separating such nature from European culture. This is why in land claims by Australian Aborigines, Europeans based their refusal to return the land on the pretext that they had improved it, that is, inscribed European culture on it. In Zimbabwe, the same arguments about improvement were raised during the land redistribution exercise as White farmers sought to dig in and resist the redistribution of land to Blacks. Indeed, seeking to bridge binaries between nature and culture on the basis of the historically troubled notion of animism, which is understood to have legitimised enslavement and colonisation of others, would be inimical to rethinking conflict and peace. In fact animism would again be a fresh writ of violence, exploitation and subjugation rather than a panacea to such violence. While other scholars have argued for the need to bridge divides on the premise that this would address violence, I want to argue here that attempts to bridge binaries that in the process create liminal persons and institutions in fact escalate violence. This is so because liminality, particularly when it is coupled with notions of impurity, poses danger to those in spaces of such liminality. Liminality often precedes sacrifice and so to the extent that some networks, meshworks and connections generate and legitimise liminality, they could in fact account for violence and sacrifice. Violence is sometimes infectious and so connection can serve as conduits. Thus violence is not only borne out of binaries and dichotomies: it also results from the liminal position into which coloniality positioned Africa as a way of maintaining it as a frontier where resources can be extracted while global liminal ritual violence [on the continent] distracts attention. It is more importantly the values (including moral and ethical) attached to particular actions that influence whether or not particular actions widen or narrow divisions. Being premised on orature, with stress on verbal utterances such as during performance of rituals of *kukumbira* and *kutenda*, differences in *chivanhu* are also bridged.

The reliance by villagers on *Nyikadzimu* and other worlds of *mweya/mhepo* underscores the fact that what matters in everyday life is not merely the global but the ways in which different worlds play out together. For villagers, conceiving the *Nyikadzimu* as inhabited by *midzimu* that are deemed to be wiser and richer than human beings, the implication is that everyday life cannot be understood merely in terms of the conventional classifications of worlds as developed and underdeveloped. Theories that do not take into cognisance such worlds as conceived in everyday life merely replicate the notions of globalisation that is troubled by inequalities even as it envisages connections, entanglement, networks or meshworks from which other scholars have proposed delinking. In a context that recognises other worlds, the question is why the global, which only gained prominence in the post-cold war era, must be the reference point even as knowledge democracy is gaining ground. The efforts by Zimbabwe to delink from IMF and World Bank programmes and conditionalities, and the current standoff between the International Criminal Court (ICC) and African states that are accusing it of targeting African leaders, flag the need to interrogate the logics of the variety of "alternative" worlds envisaged in everyday life and their import in rethinking resilience. So in the light of the implications of the existence of different worlds to which villagers in *chivanhu* resort, it can be argued that the reference points in *chivanhu* are not merely to the global but to different worlds, including the worlds of ancestors, as conceived in the quotidian. As noted above, the interconnections between these worlds including between the entities that are conceived to originate from them has been understood in terms of (hau)ontology. This (hau)ontology is not merely about flows: in it there are also [surreptitious] blockages, flights and other modes of mobility and manifestations not restricted to flows and becomings, as evidenced in the case of Zimbabwe flows in terms of investments ceased and flows imperilled by neoliberal stagnation and retrenchments. In a context where evolutionism is questionable, it would be important to interrogate the connections between becomings and such evolutionism and associated processes of development. In this sense becomings would imply reversion to the old logics of development and evolution even as there is evidence that Africa has not developed to the extent that it might have. Conversely, unqualified application of the notion of becomings would legitimise coloniality as it can encompass becoming colonies, becoming underdeveloped, becoming poor, becoming animal and other negative aspects. Such theories that rely on becomings need to pay attention to the contemporary thrust towards decoloniality as the objective of transformation processes. For instance it is necessary to question the import of theoretical assumptions about 'becoming an animal' for Africans struggling to decolonise themselves and acquire humanely means of survival.

One way to understand (hau)ontology is to consider Turner's (1969) notion of liminality and *communitas* and Van Gennep's (1960) work on rites of passage. In this logic, and as applied to (hau)ontology in this book, Africa can be envisioned as in a liminal position of betwixt and between since the colonial era when it was co-opted to become part of the empire: it was placed into a rite of passage. However, this has not resulted in an egalitarian community even after independence as coloniality of power has maintained its hold on the continent, keen to keep former colonies in such a liminal position where, as initiates, they are easier to control and discipline in the absence of their own structures and *communitas*. Liminality is exemplified in the portrayals and creation of frontierism in peripheral parts of the world – portrayals of such peripheral parts of the world as contested and hence as amenable to scramblings. Liminality is likewise perceived in the creation of frontierism and contestations of economies, modes of resource possession and ownership, politics, knowledge, governmentality, states, laws, sovereignty and cultures of the peripheries. Looked at this way, it is easier to understand the rise of deconstructionism, postmodernism and general aversion to structures and collectivism in the decolonising countries at the periphery since the late 1960s. It also becomes easier to understand other rising posts including posthumanism and 'cyborgism' that presuppose decentring the human as well as hybridising the human.

It is important for African scholars to remember that enslavement and colonisation were precisely about decentring the African humans [while at the same time centring the colonial settlers] so that they were reduced to the level of animals. For this reason, Africans whose agency is celebrated each time they decentre and deconstruct their own institutions need to be wary that colonial logics still reign in the context of global apartheid still premised on logics of colonialism. In other words, decoloniality need not entail decentring and deconstructing only African institutions because African precisely need their institutions in order to effectively seek redress from (neo-)colonists. A flat, fractured and decentred Africa will be ill-poised to effectively claiming redress. If *chivanhu* and Ubuntu were about claiming redress and restitution, and if claiming redress and restitution are about rising up, even if in the mode of avenging spirits or *ngozi*, then contemporary exhortation for Africa to be flat, animistic and rhizomatic are in effect antithetical to redress and restitution. Empire has always desired [haunted] Africa to be flat and to prostrate before imperial power, and so flatness does not speak to decoloniality, in fact it speaks to the opposite.

As Bizony (2012: 211) argues about cyborgs, when "we and our machines become one and the same thing […there can be] total bodily and mental integration, and the blurring of the line between us as individuals and we as a networked global info-species". Though other scholars would want to understand conflicts in terms of 'pathologies of the periphery' rooted in state crisis or partial exclusion from the global networks (Kaplan, 1994), the overall effect of all the coloniality of deconstructionism is liminality and what I have called (hau)ontology, particularly in the periphery where control of the whole process can be lost and technology, as Hornborg (2006) argues, becomes apparatuses of [global] machinations, in this case, of the decentred and deterritorialised peripheries. While it may be argued that Euro-modernism has relied on the secular in the age of re-enchantment, the social media including twitter, facebook, blogs and so on are deployed to facilitate interaction among invisible entities, and are used as well to stir revolts in the peripheries as ways of disciplining former colonies. For these reason, Herwig's (2009) argument about phases in social media where more powerful socioeconomic spheres impose their own logics and become the main drivers behind its growth is useful to consider.

In this vein, there is relevance in Vera's (2001) observation that Karen Blixen had written of Africans in her famous memoir *Out of Africa*, first published in 1937, that "When we really did break into the natives' existence they behaved like ants, when you poke a stick into their anthill they wiped out the damage with unwearied energy, swiftly and silently as if obliterating an unseemly action". More powerful socioeconomic spheres in Herwig's (2009) sense impose their own logics using social media to create liminality and control over the peripheries where they poke in Karen Blixen's sense. Sometimes the domination and control are concealed or partially concealed by 'generosity'. What one colonial lawyer in the then Rhodesia said in 1927 is insightful in conceptualising (hau)ontology. The lawyer, D.M. Stanely (reported by Palmer, 1977: 189), told a Legislative Assembly: "Camouflage it as we will, conquest, peaceful penetration, or by invitation, the fact remains that we have dispossessed the native of his land, and much he holds dear. Now for the sake of our honour, we must treat them as generously as possible, compatible with our retaining our supremacy". Such observations have justified critiques of 'humanitarian' projects and the imperial 'Responsibility to Protect', both argued to be mere cloaks by Euro-American powers to (re)legitimate imperial control, domination and intrusion into internal affairs of other nations around the world so as to exploit their resources (Boyle 2013: 156).

In (hau)ontology, the alternations between presence and absence of entities including NGOs in the villages, the alternations between moments when food was available and when it was not, and the fact that not all villagers were included on donors' lists of beneficiaries all indicate the inadequacy of explaining life merely in terms of flows. (Hau)ontology is also about the duplicities of life, the overt and covert modes of resistances as well as covert ways of offending, of deconstruction as well as (re)construction as exemplified by the violence and efforts to reconstruct society in the villages. Because, in (hau)ontology, entities sometimes manifest in the bodies of others, it can be understood not just narrowly in terms of becomings, but also about manifesting and manifestations (as much as it is about resisting these manifestings) in bodies of others, even if surreptitiously. Becomings and manifestations, as evident in the everyday life of villagers, need not be conflated because it is sometimes failure to become or to realise aspirations that one manifests in another entity. The cases of *ngozi* manifesting in the bodies of some living human beings is explicable in terms of the life force of the deceased having been terminated prematurely or in terms of that deceased not having been paid due credits during lifetime. Equally, the fact that some villagers retaliated by manifesting as ghosts and secretly poisoning cattle belonging to opponents who had confiscated their livestock underscores the difference between becomings and manifestings. When one's way is blocked, one fails to become and it is often at such junctures that one can manifest, often surreptitiously, in another form. These observations notwithstanding, it can also be argued on the contrary that some manifestations such as by *mweya mutsvene, mhondoro* and *midzimu* underscore not failure to become, at least in the eyes of some villagers, but victory, or successful struggles against, or over, finitude.

(Hau)ontology hints at the need to avoid forms of conflation such as those that conflated ancestors with demons or evil spirits (Comaroff and Comaroff, 2002), but the modes of engagement among the villagers also indicate the need not to conflate ancestors and *Mwari* with features in the environment, some of which they use as temporary vehicles to exert influence in the human world, particularly in terms of the notions of immanence. In this sense *vadzimu* as conceived among the villagers are neither conflatable with living human beings, whom they also use as vehicles or mediums, nor with features of the environment that can be conceived as nonhumans. In the same way it is an offence among the villagers to call a human being a dog or a baboon, as indicated in Chapter Three, it is deemed to be an offence to address a *mudzimu* in this manner. And, as reported in the same chapter, the *mhondoro* said, during my interview with him, that there were *vanhu* who also brew beer in the *Nyikadzimu* (also addressed in some churches as *Goredema*) where he was coming from. Contrary to conventional understandings of *vadzimu* as belonging to the past, there are indications among the villagers that they were deemed to be ahead of living human beings. The basis for consulting *vadzimu* is the Shona proverb that '*Nzira inobvunzwa varimberi*' (paths/directions are asked from those who are ahead not from those who are behind). This is to say that ancestors are ahead of their descendants and other living humans, who are conceived as coming into the human world from *Nyikadzimu*, so they are deemed to know both the human world and *Nyikadzimu* much better than those who come after them. In this logic what lodges in the past are the ancestors' buried bodies but not their *mweya/mhepo*, which is deemed to continue interacting with the living not from a position of pastness but of the futureness of the *midzimu and of Nyikadzimu*.

Though ancestors have been understood by some scholars in terms of 'bones that rise again' and other natural features (Fontein, 2010), one should exercise care not to conflate ancestors with materialities to which they attach themselves from time to time. This is to say that there is necessary to exercise caution not to over rely on naturalised (see Chakravartty, 2013) or scientific metaphysics in interpreting nonnaturalised metaphysical aspects of *chivanhu*. The risk in misinterpreting *chivanhu* in terms of naturalised metaphysics is that there could be a continuation of the earlier portrayals of such modes of engagement as *chivanhu*, in terms of the worship of nature, while in *chivanhu* distinctions are drawn between on the one hand the natural/material items, and on the other hand *vadzimu* and *Mwari*. Thus the nearness of *vadzimu* and *Mwari* to the human world at certain times and places has some parallels with what some scholars such as Tacey (2003) call 'new spirituality'. But contrary to the new spirituality, *chivanhu* does not to deny the existence of heaven and God as residing in heaven. This is to say that there are neither notions of immanence of *vadzimu* and God nor assumptions of the Spinozist notions of the univocity of Being. Also in *chivanhu*, unlike in the 'new spirituality', at least in Tacey's sense, there are mediators and mediums between *vadzimu* and *vanhu* and between *vanhu* and *Mwari*.

The challenge for scholars is to understand African modes of engagement with African lenses and this challenge is underpinned by the employment of theoretical frameworks whose primary goal is not to understand Africa but to model it. For this reason many theories erroneously presuppose that Africa had no essence prior to colonialism. When deconstructionist theories are employed the presupposition is that Africa did not have useful structures and institutions and so deconstructionism is taken to be synonymous with decolonisation when in fact it perpetuates colonially inspired destruction of African institutional and structural essence. Institutions and structures provide the housing within which one takes shelter in times of vulnerabilities yet the deconstruction and poststructuration of chiefs, kings, mediums, *mhondoros*, ancestors, African economies, cultures that started with colonialism seem not to have abated but have increased to include deconstructionism and poststructuration of the African states and bodies via for instance notions of cyborgism. The premise of cause right from the colonial era was that the institutions being deconstructed were not useful, but rather evil and demonic, or simply inadequate. In this light, African states have been targeted as inadequate and failed or collapsed. In advocacies of cyborgs the inadequacies of natural bodies is stressed in order to give way to the cyborged bodies purportedly improved via machine implants devised for global circulation of information. When it is deemed that we are in an era beyond modernity, it is also erroneously presupposed that there has been modernity in the singular, which Africa joined courtesy of colonisation.

Theories underpinned by the Hobbesian 'state of nature and states of war' similarly erroneously presuppose that Africa had no laws, no societies, no polities, no governments, no religion and no sovereignties prior to colonisation. Such theories that presuppose absence of institutional essence in Africa would not sit well with African modes of resilience because essence is central to resilience: if one has no essence one could not be resilient. Theories that assume openness in Africa miss the important point that just like every other body, African institutions, social structures and polities open up when danger is not in view and close off when danger is perceived. It is not that there is absolute openness and absolute closure, but there are alternations depending on perceptions of vulnerabilities and of opportunities. Such alternations of opening up and closing, depending on the exigencies, are fundamental aspects of processes of resilience of individuals and institutions. This is the premise of what I have called (hau)ontology in this book. It is therefore worthwhile to look beyond the surfaces of theories in order to understand deeper assumptions and presuppositions if theorisations on Africa are to be meaningful to the continent's aspirations.

Glossary of Terms

Chidhoma- conventionally witch familiar

Chikwambo- a *mweya*/'spirit' of a deceased person that is raised to generate a sorcerer's familiar or things he/she uses to harm others at a distance

Chinhu (plural *zvinhu*)- a thing as distinct from *munhu* (human being/person). In other African languages a *chinhu* is also known as a *kintu* while a *munhu* is also known as a *muntu*.

Chipotswa- a form of witchcraft/sorcery where a witch places poisons on the victim's path so that when he/she steps on it enters the body

Chishona/Shona/Chivanhu- vernacular language

Chivanhu- ways of life erroneously understood narrowly as traditions

Denga- Heaven

Guta- city

Haana kukwana- he/she is not enough in reference to behaviour considered wayward

Hama yevahera- relative of the *hera* clan

Hama- a blood relative but it is also sometimes used in a figurative sense to allude to connection

Hapana munhu- literally there is no person in reference to one deemed to lack *unhu* or the essence of a human being

Haya- a rain bird which survives on water that collects in tree trunks. With the approach of the rains, the *haya* bird sings. In English it is known as a cuckoo bird. It's a member of the cuculidae family

Hungwe- a bird known as fish eagle. It is a haliaeetus in Latin

Kutenda- to thank or to be thankful

Madendera- huge ground hornbill birds with black and red stripes which also sing with the approach of the rains

Mbuya- a honorific term also used to refer to female healers

Mhondoro- great grand-ancestor responsible for bringing rain

Muchakata- known as parinaricuratellifolia, it is the tree considered to be the village or resting place of ancestors under which people gather to petition for rain.

Mukombe- gourd used to share beer during the petitioning for rain

Homwe yevahera- pocket of the *hera* clan

Imhuka dzevanhu- they are mere animals used to distinguish between a person with *unhu* and one without *unhu*

Kukumbira mvura- to request/petition for rain from God and or from *mhondoro*

Kuona- to see

Kuonesa- to make one see

Mudzimu- an ancestor whose *mweya/mhepo* is deemed to shepherd living descendants. It is important to note that it is not all the deceased that become *mudzimu* but rather a specific deceased who then speaks through a living medium.

Kupfekwa nemweya- literally to be worn by the air/spirits/to be "possessed" and used as a vehicle by 'spirits'

Kurira nendimi- literally to sound with the tongue/ understood conventionally as speaking in tongues

Kusakwana- to be wayward/to be not enough

Kusatenda huroyi- to fail to thank is witchcraft

Kusundira- to push: often used in reference to sending bad wind/air/ spirits to others

Kusunungura mweya- literally to free the air in reference to freeing one's 'spirit' or soul from encumbrances

Kutenda- to thank

Madzimudzangara- 'spiritual' manifestations such as *njuzu* or mermaids/mermen

Mashavi- 'spirits' from outside one's clan ancestral circle/including 'spirits' of foreigners that came to and colonised Africa

Masvikiro edzinza- mediums of the clan

Masvikiro enyika- mediums of the country

Masvikiro enzvimbo- mediums of the area

Mhepo- wind: also deemed to manifest as 'spirits/deities'

Mhuka yesango- literary animal of the forest/conventionally understood as "wild" animal
Midzi- roots
Mishonga- medicines/herbs
Munamato- prayers
Munhu- a human being but often refers to a human being with *unhu*/African *chivanhu* ethics
Mushonga- singular of *mishonga*
Musikavanhu- God as deemed to have Created human beings
Musiki- Creator [ex nihilo] of the entire world
Muuya- air/spirit in Tonga of northwest Zimbabwe
Mwanangu- my child
Mwari- God or Creator ex nihilo
Mweya- air [in meteorological sense or spiritual sense] also deemed to sometimes manifest as 'spirits/deities'
N'anga- healers or African doctors
Ngozi- the deceased considered to return to avenge
Njanja- one of the groups of African people that settled in Buhera
Nyadenga- God as deemed to stay in and own the Heavens
Nzvimbo dzinoera- sacred places that are the resting places or abodes of spirits
Pungwe- political gatherings throughout the night
Ruzivo- knowledge
Sadza- thick porridge which is the staple diet in Zimbabwe
Samatenga- God as deemed to own the Heavens
Tsika- morals/ethics
Ukama- a mode of relating among *hama*
Unhu- ethics in *chivanhu* that are used in reference to *munhu* or *vanhu* [people who live in terms of ethics of chivanhu]
Uroyi- acts of bewitching
Vanhu- human beings but often also refers to human beings considered to have *unhu*
Varatidzwi- Church members who are deemed to be shown otherwise hidden things
Varoti- dreamers
Varoyi/umthakathi- conventionally understood as witches

Wekumusorosoro- God as deemed to rank highest

Bibliography

Abraham, D. P., 1966.The Role of Chaminuka and the Mhondoro Cults in Shona Political History, in Stokes, E. and Brown, R., eds. *The Zambezian Past: Studies in Central African History.* Manchester: Manchester University Press: 28-46

Adeleke, T., 2009. *The Case Against Afrocentrism.* Jackson: The University Press of Mississippi

Ahyi, G., 1997.Traditional Models of Mental Health and Illness in Benin, in Hountondji, P., ed. *Endogenous Knowledge: Research Trails. Dakar:* CODESRIA: 217-246

Ajei, M. O., 2007. *Africa's Development: The Imperatives of Indigenous Knowledge and Values*, PhD Thesis, UNISA

Akerlof, G. A., and Shiller, R. J., 2009.*Animal Spirits: How Human Psychology Drives the Economy and Why it Matters for Global Capitalism.* Princeton and oxford: Princeton University Press

Albert, E., 2001. Deleuze's Impersonal Hylozoic Cosmology, in Bryden, M., ed. *Deleuze and Religion.* London: Routledge: 184-195

Alexander, J., and Ranger, T., 1998. Competition and Religious Integration in the Religious History of North-western Zimbabwe. in *Journal of Religion in Africa.* Vol 8 Fasc. 1: 31

Alexander, J. et al., 2000.*Violence and Memory: One Hundred Years in the "Dark Forests" of Matabeleland.* James Currey, Heinemann

Amin, S., 2011. *Ending the Crisis of Capitalism or Ending Capitalism.* Dakar: CODESRIA

Amutabi, M. N., 2006.*The NGO Factor in Africa: The Case of Arrested Development in Kenya.* New York: Routledge

Andersen, J. A., 2002. *Rural-Urban Connections and the Significance of Land in Buhera district. Zimbabwe.* PhD Thesis: Wagenigen Universiteit

Anderson, D. M. *et al*, 1995. Revealing Prophets, in Johnson, D. H., and Anderson, D. M., eds. *Revealing Prophets.* London: James Currey: 1-27

Anderson, J. A., 1999. "The Politics of Land Scarcity: Land Disputes in Save Communal Areas, Zimbabwe", in *Journal of Southern African Studies*, Vol 25 No 4: 553-578

Anderson, J. A., n.d. "Sorcery in the Era of Henry IV: Kinship, Mobility and Mortality in Buhera District, Zimbabwe". *The Journal of the Royal Anthropological Institute* Vol 8 (3): 425-449

Ansu-Kyeremeh, K., 2005. Introduction, in Ansu-Kyeremeh, K., ed. *Indigenous Communication in Africa: Concepts, Application and Prospects*. Accra: Ghana

Aquina, M., 1967. The People of the Spirit: An Independent Church in Rhodesia, in *Journal of the International African Institute* Vol 37, No 2: 203-219. http://www.jstor.org/stable/1158255

Arendt, H, 1958. *The Human Condition*. Chicago: Chicago University Press

Arhim, K, 1994. The Economic Implications of Transformations in Akan Funeral Rites, in *Africa* 64 (3): 307-322

Asante, M. K., 2000. *The Egyptian Philosophers: Ancient African Voices from Inhotep to Akhenaten*. Chicago: African American Images

Artigas, M., 2001. *The Mind of the Universe: Understanding Science and Religion*. Pennsylvania: Temple Foundation Press

Atwood, A., 2010. Kubatana in Zimbabwe: Mobile Phones for Advocacy in Ekine S., ed, *SMS Uprising: Mobile Activism in Africa*. Cape Town: Pambazuka Press

Auge, M., 2012.*The War on Dreams*. London: Phito Press

Badiou, A., 2001. *Ethics: An Essay on the Understanding of Evil*. London: Verso

Badza, S., 2009. Zimbabwe's Harmonised Elections: Regional and International Reactions, in Masunungure, E. V., ed. *Defying the Winds of Change*. Avondale: Weaver Press: 149-175

Bahre, E., 2002. Witchcraft and the Exchange of Sex, Blood and Money Among Africans in Cape Town, South Africa. *Journal of Religion in Africa* vol 32, Fasc 3: 300-334

Baker, D., 2008.*Korean Spirituality*. Honolulu: University of Hawaii Press

Barnes, M. H., 1984, *In the Presence of Mystery: An Introduction to the Story of Human Religiousness*. Connecticut: Twenty-third Publication

Baron, A. A., 2005, *Empire and Imperialism: A Critical Reading of Michael Hardt and Antonio Negri*, London, Zed Books

Barret, C. B., and Maxwell, A., 2005. *Food Aid After Fifty Years: Recasting its Role*. London and New York: Routledge

Basu, K., 2011. *Beyond the Invisible Hand: Groundwork for a New Economics*. Princeton: Princeton University Press

Beach, D., 1980.*The Shona and Zimbabwe 900-1850*. Gweru: Mambo Press

Beach, D. N., 1994. *The Shona and Their Neighbours*. Oxford: Blackwell Publishing

Bellah, R N., 2005. Civil Religion in America, in Lambek M., ed, *A Reader in the Anthropology of Religion*. Blackwell Publishing Ltd: 512-522

Bello, W., 2004. *Deglobalisation: Ideas for a New World Economy*. Dhaka: The University Press

Ben-Yehuda, N., 1985. The Sociology of Moral Panics: Towards a New Synthesis, in *The Sociological Quarterly* vol 27, No 4: 495-513

Bergson, H., 2002. *Key Writings*. New York: Continuum: London

Berlitz C., 1975. *The Bermuda Triangle*. St Albans: Granada Publishing Limited

Bernard, P., 2007. Reuniting with the Kosmos. *Journal for the Study of Religion, Nature and Culture*.1.1: 109-129

Bernard, P. S., 2003. Ecological Implications of Water Spirit Beliefs in Southern Africa: The Need to Protect Knowledge, Nature and Resource Rights. *USDA Forest Service Proceedings. RMRS-27*: 148-154

Bhila, H. H. K., 1982.*Trade and Politics in a Shona Kingdom: The Manyika and Their Portuguese and African Neighbours 1572-1902*. Essex: Longman Group Ltd

Bickerton, C. J. *et al.*, 2007. Introduction: The Unholy Alliance Against Sovereignty, in Bickerton, C. J. *et al*, (eds), *Politics without Sovereignty: A Contemporary International Relations*. London and New York: Routledge. p 1-18

Bird-David, N., 1999. Animism Revisited: Personhood, Environment, and Relational Epistemology. *Current Anthropology* 40: S67-S91

Bizony, P., 2012. *The Search for Aliens: A Rough Guide to Life on Other Worlds*. London: Rough Guides Ltd

Blair, T., 2011. *Tony Blair: A Journey*. London: Arrow Books

Blaser, M., 2009. Political Ontology. *Cultural Studies*, 23: 5, 873-896

Bloom, H., 1997. *Omen of the Millennium: The Gnosis of Angels, Dreams and Resurrection*. London: Fourth Estate Ltd

Boddy, J., 1989.*Wombs and Alien Spirits: Women, Men and the Zar Cult in Northern Sudan*. Wisconsin

Boddy, J., 2005. Spirit and Selves in Northern Sudan: The Cultural Therapeutic of Possession and Trance. in Lambek, M., ed *A Reader in the Anthropology of Religion*. Oxford: Blackwell Publishing

Bodin, J., 1992.*On Sovereignty*. Cambridge: Cambridge University Press

Boidourides, M., n.d. The Relational Ontology of Social Network Theories,
http://nessiepkilo.com/files/moses_boundaries_the_relationalontology_of_social_network_theories_pdf

Boissevain, J., and Mitchell, J. C., 1973. *Network Analysis: Studies in Human Social Interaction*. Paris: Mouton

Bond, G. C., and Ciekawy, D. M., 2001. Introduction: Contested Domains in the Dialogues of "Witchcraft", in same, eds, *Witchcraft Dialogues: Anthropological and Philosophical Exchanges*. Athens: Ohio University Press: 1-29

Bond, P., 2005. Zimbabwe's Hide and Seek with the IMF: Imperialism, Nationalism and the South African Proxy, in *Review of African Political Economy* Vol 32, (106): 609-619

Boonzaier, E. et al., 2000.*The Cape Herders: A History of the Khoikhoi of Southern Africa*. Athens: Ohio University Press

Bourdillon, M. F. C., 1976.*The Shona People: An Ethnography of the Contemporary Shona with Special Reference to their Religion*. Gweru: Mambo Press

Bourdillon, M.F.C., 1987. Guns and Rain: Taking Structuralist Analysis too Far? *Africa Journal of the International African Institute* Vol 57, No 2: 263-274

Bourdillon, M., 1990. *Religion and Society: A Text for Africa*. Gweru: Mambo Press

Bourdillon, M.F.C., 1991.*The Shona People*. Gweru: Mambo Press

Bourdillon, M.F.C., 1999. The Cults of Dzivaguru and Karuva amongst the North Eastern Shona Peoples, in Schoffeleers, J., ed, *Guardians of the Land*. Gweru: Mambo Press

Boyle, F. A., 2013, *Destroying Libya and World Order: The Three Decade U.S Campaign to Terminate the Qaddafi Revolution*. Atlanta: Clarity Press

Bracking, S., 2003. Sending Remittances Home: Are Remittances Always Beneficial to those Who Stay Behind? *Journal of International Development* 15: 633-644

Bracking, S., and Sachikonye, L., 2005. Remittances, Poverty Reduction and the Informalisation of Household Well being in Zimbabwe. *Global Poverty Research Group*-WPS-045

Bredekamp H C., and Newton-King S., 1984. *The Subjugation of the Khoisan During the 17th and 18th Centuries, Conference on Economic Development and Racial Domination*. University of Western Cape

Brennan, F., and Packer, J., 2012. *Colonialism, Slavery, Reparations and Trade: Remedying the Past?* Abingdon: Routledge

Brown, B., 2001. Things Theory, Critical Inquiry Vol 28, No 1: 1-22, http: //linksjstor.org/sici?sici=0093-1896%28200123%2928%3A1%3c1%3ATT%3E2.0.Co%3B2-4

Brown, S. D., and Capdevila, R., 2006. Perpetuum Mobile: Substance, Force and the Sociology of Translation. in Law, J. and Hassard, J., eds. *Actor-Network Theory and After*. Oxford: Black well Publishing

Brown, S. L., 1997. The Free Market as Salvation from Government: The Anarcho-Capitalist View.in Carrier, J. G., ed *Meanings of the market: The Free market in Western Culture*. Oxford: Berg

Bryan, C. *et al.*, 1998. Electronic Democracy and the Civic Networking Movement in Context.in Tsagarousianou, R. *et al.*, eds, *Cyberdemocracy: Technology, Cities and Civic Networks*. London and New York: Routledge: 1-17

Bryant, L. R., 2012. Questions for Flat Ethics, *Hosted by the Philosophy Department at University of Texas* Arlington 18 October 2012: 1-23

Bryden, M., 2001. Introduction, in Bryden, M., ed, *Deleuze and Religion*. London: Routledge: 1-6

Buchanan R., and Pahuja S., 2004. Legal Imperialism: Empire's Invisible Hand?, in Passavant P A., and Dean J., eds. *Empire's New Clothes: Reading Hardt and Negri*. London and New York: Routledge: 72-92

Bullock, C., 1927.*The Mashona (The Indigenous Natives of Southern Rhodesia.* Cape Town: Juta and Co

Bullock, C., 1950. *The Mashona and The Matabele.* Cape Town: Juta and Co Ltd

Burbridge, A., 1923. How to Become a Witchdoctor, *NADA: The Southern Rhodesian Native Affairs Department Annual* Vol 1: 94-100

Burbridge, A., 1924. In Spirit Bound Rhodesia: *NADA* vol 1-6: 17-28

Burbridge, A., 1925. The Witchdoctor's Power: A Study of its Source and Scope: *NADA*: 22-31

Burnett, J. *et al*., 2009. Introduction. in same, eds, *The Myth of Technology: Innovation and Inequality.* New York: Peter Lang: 1-29

Byrne, J. M., 1996. *Religion and the Enlightenment from Descartes to Kant.* London: SCM Press Ltd

Callon, M., 2006. Actor-Network Theory-the Market Test, in Law, J., and Hassard, J., eds. *Actor-Network Theory and After.* Oxford: Blackwell Publishing: 181-195

Campbell, M. B., 2008. Dreaming, Motion, Meaning: Oneiric Transport in Seventeenth Century Europe.in Hodgkin, K. *et al.*, eds *Reading the Early Modern Dream: The Terrors of the Night.* New York: Routledge

Carrington, J. F., 1949.*Talking Drums of Africa.* London: The Carey Kingsgate Press

Cavendisch, W., 1999. The Complexity of the Commons: Environmental Resource Demands in Rural Zimbabwe" *The Centre for the Study of African Economics Working Paper* 92

Cavendisch, W., 2000. "Empirical Regularities in the Poverty-Environment Relationship of Rural Households: Evidence from Zimbabwe", *World Development* Vol 28, (11): 1979-2003

Chabal P., 2005. Violence, Power and Rationality: A Political Analysis of Conflict in Contemporary Africa in Chabal P., ed, *Is Violence Inevitable in Africa: Theories of Conflict and Approaches to Conflict Prevention.* Leiden: Koninklijke Brill. N.

Chakravartty, A., 2013. On the Prospects of Naturalise Metaphysics, in Ross D. *et al.*, eds, *Scientific Metaphysics*. Oxford: Oxford University Press: 27-50

Chatters, C. M. *et al.*, 1994. Fictive Kinship Relations in Black Extended Families, *Journal of Comparative Family Studies* Vol 25, (3), http://www.question.com/library/191-16988742/fictive-kinship-relations-in-black-extended-families

Chavunduka, G., 1978.*Traditional Healers and the Shona Patient*. Gweru: Mambo Press

Chavunduka, G. L., 1980. Witchcraft and the Law in Zimbabwe. *Zambezia*, VIII (ii): 129-148

Chavunduka, G. L., 1994. *Traditional Medicine in Modern Zimbabwe*. Harare: UZ Publications

Chavunduka, G. L., 2001. Dialogue among Civilisations: The African Religion in Zimbabwe To-Day, *occasional Paper No 1* Crossover Communication

Chigodora, J., 1997. Famine and Drought: The Question of Food Security in Zimbabwe, *Drought Network News* 1994-2001), Paper 40: 1-6, http://digitalcommons.un/.edu/droughtnetnews/40, (9), No1

Child H., 1965. *The History and Extent of Recognition of Tribal Law in Rhodesia*. Ministry of Internal Affairs Rhodesia

Chinyowa, K. C., 1997.Orality in Shona Religious Rituals,.in Vambe, T. M., ed, *Orality and Cultural Identity in Zimbabwe*. Gweru: Mambo Press: 9-17

Chipika, J. T. *et al.*, 2000. *Effects of Structural Adjustment in Southern Africa: The Case of Zimbabwe's Manufacturing Sector during Phase 1 of ESAP: 1991-1995*. Harare: SARIPS of SAPES Trust

Chirikure, S., 2010. *Indigenous Mining and Metallurgy in Africa*. Cambridge: Cambridge University Press

Chitando, E., and Manyonganise, M., 2011.Voices from Faith-Based Communities, in Murithi, T., and Mawadza, A., eds., *Zimbabwe in Transition: A View from Within*. Auckland Park: The Institute for Justice and reconciliation: 77-111

Chitehwe, S. S. M., 1954. Rainmaking in Mashonaland: *NADA the Southern Rhodesian Native Affairs Department Annual* 31: 24-26

Chitiyo, T. K., 2004. Land Violence and Compensation:

Reconceptualising Zimbabwe's Land and War Veterans Debate, in Batchelor P., and Kingma K., eds, *Demilitarisation and Peace building in Southern Africa* vol 1,

Chivaura, V. G., n d. Hunhu/Ubuntu: A Sustainable Approach to Endogenous Development, Biocultural Diversity and Protection of the Environment in Africa, http: //www.bioculturaldiversity.net/downloads/papers%20participants/chivaura.pdf: 229-240

Chung, F., 2006. *Re-living the Second Chimurenga: Memories from Zimbabwe's Liberation Struggle.* Stockholm: The Nordic Africa Institute: Weaver Press

Clark H., 2003. *Natural Born Cyborgs: Minds, Technologies and the Future of Human Intelligence.* Oxford: Oxford University Press

Classen, C., 1993. *Worlds of Sense: Exploring the Senses in History Across Cultures.* London: Routledge

Clercq, E. D., 2013.*The Seduction of the Female Body: Women's Rights in Need of a New Body Politics.* Basingstoke: PALGRAVE MACMILLAN

Coleman, W. D. *et al.*, 2009. Introduction. In Streeter, S. M. *et al.*, eds, *Empires and Autonomy: Moments in the History of Globalisation.* Vancouver UBC Press: 1-23

Collier, P., n.d. *Poverty Reduction in Africa, Centre for the Study of African Economies.* University of Oxford

Collins, S. L., 1989. *From Divine Cosmos to Sovereign State: An Intellectual History of Consciousness and the Idea of Order in Renaissance England.* Oxford: Oxford University Press

Colson E., 2006. *Tonga Religious Life in the Twentieth Century.* Lusaka Bookworld Publisher

Colson, E., 1971.*The Social Consequences of Resettlement: The Impact of the Kariba Resettlement upon the Gwembe Tonga.* Manchester: Manchester University Press

Colson E., 1962. *The Plateau Tonga of Northern Rhodesia: Social and Religious Studies.* Manchester: Manchester University Press

Coltart, D., 2008. A Decade of Suffering in Zimbabwe: Economic Collapse and Political Repression under Robert Mugabe in. *Centre for Global Liberty and Prosperity Development Policy* Analysis

Comaroff, J., and Comaroff, J., 2005. The Colonisation of Consciousness, in Lambek, M., ed, *A Reader in the Anthropology of Religion*. Oxford: Blackwell Publishing: 493-510

Comaroff, J., and Comaroff, J. L., 1999. Introduction, in Comaroff, J. and Comaroff, J. L., eds, *Civil Society and the Political Imagination in Africa: Critical Perspectives*. Chicago: University of Chicago Press: 1-43

Comaroff, J., and Comaroff, L., 2001. Millennial Capitalism: First Thoughts on a Second Coming., in Comaroff, J. L., and Comaroff, J., eds, *Millennial Capitalism and the Culture of Neoliberalism*. Durham and London: Duke University Press: 1-56

Comaroff, J. L., and Comaroff, J., 1993. Introduction, in same, eds, *Modernity and its Malcontents*, Chicago, University of Chicago Press: xi-xxxvii

Comaroff, J. L., and Comaroff, J., 2006. Law and Disorder in the Postcolony: An Introduction.in Comaroff, J. L., and Comaroff, J., eds, *Law and Disorder in the Postcolony*. Chicago: University of Chicago Press: 1-56

Conford, F. M., 1964. *Plato's Theory of Knowledge*. London: Routledge and Kegan Paul Ltd

Coole D., and Frost S., 2010. Introducing the New Materialism, in Coole D., and Frost S., eds, *New Materialism, Ontology, Agency, and Politics*. Duke: Duke University Press: 1-46

Cooper, G. et al., 2002. Mobile Society? Technology, Distance and Presence, in Woolgar, S., ed, *Virtuaal Society? Technology, Cyberbole, Reality*. Oxford: Oxford University Press

Crawford, J. R., 1967. *Witchraft and Sorcery in Rhodesia*. London: Oxford University Press

Crosson J B., 2013. Anthropology of Invisibilities: Translation, Spirits of the Dead and The Politics of Invisibility, *Cultural Fieldnotes,* http://prodn.culant.org/fieldsights/346-invisibilities-translation-spiritsof-the-dead-and-the-politics-of-invisibility

Curry, P., 2006. *Ecological Ethics: An Introduction*. Cambridge: Polity Press

Dagmar, M., and Herman, W., 2003. "Income and Labour Productivity of Collection and Use of Indigenous Fruit Tree

Products in Zimbabwe", *Agro-forestry Systems* 59: 295-305

Dah-Lokonon, G. B., 1997. 'Rainmakers': Myth and Knowledge in Traditional Atmospheric Management Techniques. Hountondji, P., ed, *Endogenous Knowledge: Research Trails*. Dakar: CODESRIA: 84-112

Daneel, M., 2007. *All Things Hold Together: Holistic Theologies at the African Grassroots*. University of South Africa

Daneel, M. L., 1970.*The God of the Matopo*. Leiden: Afrika-Studiecentrum

Daneel, M. L., 1987. *Quest for Belonging: Introduction to a study of African Independent Churches*. Gweru: Mambo Press

Daneel, M. L., 1998. *African Earthkeepers* Vol 1. Pretoria: University of South Africa

Das, V., 2002.*Critical Events: An Anthropological Perspective on Contemporary India*. Oxford: oxford University Press

Das, V., 2004. The Signature of the State: The Paradox of Illegibility, in Das, V. and Poole, D., eds, *Anthropology in the Margins of the State*. Oxford: James Currey: 225-252

Das, V., and Kleinman, A., 2001. Introduction. in Das, V. *et al*., eds, *Remaking A World: Violence, Social Suffering and Recovery*. California: University of California Press: 1-30

Das, V., and Poole, D., 2004. State and its Margins: Comparative Ethnographies. in Das, V., and Poole, D., eds., *Anthropology in the Margins of the State*. Oxford: James Currey: 3-34

Dashwood, H. S., 2003. Economic Justice and Structural Adjustment in Zimbabwe. in Ranger, T., ed, *The Historical Dimensions of Democracy and Human Rights in Zimbabwe, vol 2, Nationalism, Democracy and Human Rights*. Harare: University of Zimbabwe: 150-161

Davetian, B., 2009.*Civility: A Cultural History*. Toronto: University of Toronto Press

Davies O., 2001. Thinking Difference: A Comparative Study of Giles Deleuze, Plotinus and Maister Eckhart, in Bryden M., ed, *Deleuze and Religion*. London: Routledge: 76-86

Davies, C. A., 2009. *Reflexive Ethnography: A Guide to Researching Selves and Others*. Abidon: Routledge

Davis, C., 2007. *Haunted Subjects: Deconstruction, Psychoanalysis and the Return of the Dead*. PALGRAVE: MacMillan

de Castro E., 2013, Economic Development and Cosmopolitical Reinvolement: from Necessity to Sufficiency, in Green L., ed, *Contested Ecologies: Dialogoues in the South on Nature and Knowledge*. HSRC Press

de Castro, E. V., 2004. Perspectival Anthropology and the Method of Controlled Equivocation. *Tipiti Journal of the Society for Anthropology of Lowland South America* 2 (1): 3-22

de Certeau, M., 1984. *The Practice of Everyday Life*. Berkeley: University of California Press

De la Cadena M., 2013. About Mariano's Archive: Ecologies of Storiers, in Green L., ed, *Contested Ecologies: Dialogues in the South on Nature and Knowledge*. Cape Town HSRC Press: 55-68

de la Cadena, M. 2010. Indigenous Cosmopolitics: Conceptual Reflections beyond "Politics", *Cultural Anthropology* vol 25, (2): 334-370

Dean J., 2004. The Networked Empire: Communicative Capitalism and the Hope for Politics, in Passavant P A., and Dean J., eds, *Empire's New Clothes: Reading Hardt and Negri*. London and New York: Routledge: 265-286

Dear, P., 2006.*The Intelligibility of How Science Makes Sense of the World*. Chicago and London: The University of Chicago Press

Debenham, F., 1960. *Discovery and Exploration: an Atlas-history of Man's Journey into the Unknown*. London: Geographical Projects Limited

Delaney, C., 2004. *Investigating Culture: An Experiential Introduction to Anthropology*. Malden, M A: Blackwell

Derrida, J., 1993. *Spectre de Marx: L'Etat de la dette, le travail du devil et la nouvelle international*. Paris: Galilee

Derrida J., 1994. *Spectres of Marx: The State of the Debt, the Work of Mourning, and the New International*. Psychology Press

Derrida, J., 2006. *Spectres of Marx*. New York: Routledge Classics

Descola, P., 1996. Constructing Natures: Symbolic Ecology and Social Practice.in Descola, P., and Palsson, G., eds. *Nature and Society: Anthropological Perspectives*. London and New York: Routledge: 82-102

Devisch, R., 2001. Sorcery Forces of Life and Death among the Yaka of Congo, in Bond, G. C., and Ciekawy, D. M., eds, *Witchcraft Dialogues: Anthropological and Philosophical Exchanges*. Athens: Ohio University Press: 101-128

Devisch, R., 2006. Maleficient Fetishes and the Sensual Order of the Uncanny in South-West Congo.in Kapferer, B., ed, *Beyond Rationality: Rethinking Magic, Witchcraft and Sorcery*. Oxford: Berghahn Books: 175-196

Dobos, N., 2012. *Insurrection and Intervention: The Two Faces of Sovereignty*. Cambridge: Cambridge University Press

Douglas, H. et al., 1995. Revealing Prophets, in Douglas, H. et al., eds, *Revealing Prophets*. London: James Currey: 1-27

Douglas M., 2002. *Purity and Danger: An Analysis of the Concepts of Purity and Taboo*. New York and London: Routledge and Kegan Paul Ltd

Dube, L., 2011. Agness Majecha and the Zvikomborero Apostolic Faith Church. in Dube, L. et al., eds, *African Initiatives in healing Ministry*. Unisa Press: 73-96

Eisenstadt, S. N., 2000. Multiple Modernities. *Research Library Core*: Daedalus 129, No 1

Eliav-Feldon M., 2009, Vagrants or Vermin? Attitudes Towards Gypsies in Early Modern Europe, in Eliav-Feldon M et al., eds, The Origins of Racism in the West. Cambridge: Cambridge University Press: 276-291

Ellert, H., 1984.*The Material Culture of Zimbabwe*. Longman Zimbabwe Ltd: Harare

Endfield, G. H., and Nash, D. J., 2002. Missionaries and Morals: Climate Discourse in Nineteenth Century Central Southern Africa. *Annals of the Association of American Geographers* 92: (4): 727-742

Engelke, M., 2005. Sticky Subjects and Sticky Objects: The Substance of African Christian healing, in Miller, D., ed, *Materiality*. Durham and London: Duke University Press: 118-138

Engelke, M., 2007. *A Problem of Presence: Beyond Scripture in an African Church*. California: University of California Press

Englund, H., 2006. *Prisoners of Freedom: Human Rights and the African*

Poor. Berkeley: University of California Press

Eppel, S., 2004. Gukurahundi: The Need for Truth and Reparations. in Raftopoulos, B. *et al.*, eds, *Zimbabwe: Injustice and Political Reconciliation.* Cape Town: Institute for Justice and Reconciliation

Erlman, V., 2004. But What of the Ethnographic Ear? Anthropology, Sound and the Senses, in Erlman, V., ed., *Hearing Cultures: Essays on Sound, Listening and Modernity.* Oxford: Berg: 1-20

Escobar, A., 2002. Worlds and Knowledges Otherwise: The Latin American Modernity/Coloniality Research Program, Presented at the Tercer Congreso internacional de latino-americanistas en Europa, Amsterdam

Escobar, A., 1992. Imagining a Post development Era? Critical Thought, Development and Social Movements, in Social Text No 31/32, *Third World and Postcolonial Issues:* 20-56

Escobar, A., 1995. *Encountering Development: The Making and Unmaking of the Third World.* Princeton: Princeton University Press

Escobar, A., 2002. "Worlds and Knowledges Otherwise" Latin American Modernity/Coloniality Research Program. *Presented at the Tercer Congreso Internacional de Latin Americanistas en Europa*, Amsterdam, July 3-6, 2002

Escobar, A., 2008. *Territories of Difference: Place, Movements, Life, Redes*: Duke University Press

Evans-Pritchard, E. E. 1939.Time and Space, in Lock, M., and Farquhar, J., eds, *Beyond the Body Proper: Reading the Anthropology of Material Life.* Durham: Duke University Press

Evans-Pritchard, E. E., 1972. *Theories of Primitive Religion.* Oxford: Clarendon Press

Evensky, J., 2005. *Adam Smith's Moral Philosophy: A Historical and Contemporary Perspective on Markets, Law, Ethics and Culture.* Cambridge: Cambridge University Press

Fanon, F., 1963. *The Wretched of the Earth.* New York: Grove Press

Fardon, R., 1990. *Between God, the Dead and the Wild: Chamba Interpretations of Ritual and Religion.* Edinburgh: Edinburgh University Press

Farmer, P., 2005. *Pathologies of Power: Health, Human Rights and the New War on the Poor*. Berkeley and Los Angeles: University of California Press

Farmer, R. E. A., 2010. *How the Economy Works: Confidence, Crashes and Self-Fulfilling Prophecies*. Oxford: Oxford University Press

Farriss, N. M., 1987. Remembering the Future, Anticipating the Past: History, Time and Cosmology among the Maya of Yucatan, in *Comparative Studies in Society and History*, vol 9, (3): 566-593

Feuerman, S., 1990. *Peasant Intellectuals: Anthropology and History in Tanzania*. Madison: The University of Wisconsin Press

Fitzpatrick, P., 2004. The Immanence of Empire, in Passavant P A., and Dean J., eds, *Empire's New Clothes: Reading Hardt and Negri*. London and New York: Routledge: 31-53

Fontein, J., 2004. Traditional Connoisseurs of the Past: The Ambiguity of Spirit Mediums and the Performance of the Past in Southern Zimbabwe, University of Edinburgh Press, *occasional Paper*

Fontein, J., 2006. Language of Land, Water and Tradition around Lake Mutirikwi in Southern Zimbabwe, *The Journal of Modern African Studies* Vol 44, (2): 223-249

Fontein, J., 2006. *The Silence of Great Zimbabwe: Contested Landscapes and the Power of Heritage*. Abingdon: University College London Press

Fontein, J., 2010. Between Tortured Bodies and Resurfacing Bones: the Politics of the Dead in Zimbabwe, *Journal of Material Culture* 15: 423-448, http://mcu.sagepub.com/content/15/4/423

Formoso, B., 1996. Hsiu-Kou-Ku: The Ritual Refinement of Restless Ghosts Among Chinese of Thailand, *The Journal of the Royal Anthropological Institute* vol 2, (2)

Fortune, G., 1975, Form and Imagery in Shona Proverbs, in *Zambezia*, 4 ii: 25-55

Fowler, M. R., and Bunk, J. M., 1960. *Law, Power and the Sovereign*. University Park: The Pennsylvania State University Press

Fox, R., 1967. *Kinship and Marriage: An Anthropological Perspective*. Middlesex: Penguin Books Ltd

Frazer, J. G., 1926. *The Worship of Nature*. London: Macmillan and Co Ltd

Frede, D., 1996. The Philosophical Economy of Plato's Psychology: Rationality and Common Concepts in the Timaeus, in Frede M *et al*, eds, *Rationality in Greek Thought*. Oxford: Clarendon Press: 29-58

Frede, M., 2011. *A free Will: Origins of the Notion in Ancient Thought*. Berkeley and Los Angeles: University of California Press

Freeth, B., 2011. *Mugabe and the White African*. Oxford: Lion Hudson P/L

Freud, S., 1999.*The Interpretation of Dreams: A New Translation*. Oxford: Oxford University Press

Friedson, S. M., 1996. *Dancing Prophets: Musical Experience in Tumbuka Healing*. Chicago: University of Chicago Press

Fudge, E., 2008. Onely Proper unto Man: Dreams and Being Human, in Hodgkin K *et al.*, eds, *Reading the Early Modern Dream: The Terrors of the Night*. New York: Routledge

Furrow, D., 2006. *Ethics: Key Concepts in Philosophy*. London: Continuum

Garbett, K., 1977. Disparate Regional Cults and a Unitary Ritual Field in Zimbabwe, in Werbner R P., ed, *Regional Cults: A S A Monographs 16 Academic Press*. London New York: 55-92

Garbett, G. K., 1966. Religious Aspects of Political Succession Among the Valley Korekore (Northern Shona), in Stokes, E., and Brown, R., eds, *The Zambezian Past: Studies in Central African History*. Manchester: Manchester University Press: 137-170

Gardner, M. E., 2000.*Critiques of Everyday Life*. London and New York: Routledge

Garner, R., 1997. Ecology and Animal Rights: Is Sovereignty Anthropomorphic? In Brace L *et al.*, eds, *Reclaiming Sovereignty*. London: Bookends Ltd Royston, Horts: 188-200

Garuba, H., 2013. On Animism, Modernity/Colonialism, and the African Order of Knowledge: Provisional Reflections, in Green, L., ed, *Contested Ecologies: Dialogues in the South on Nature and Knowledge*. Cape Town: HSRC Press: 42-51

Gasela, R., 2009. "2009-Another Bleak Farming Season" in Metro Zimbabwe 11 January 2009.

Gbadegesin, S., 2002. Eniyan: The Yoruba Concept of a Person, in Coetzee P, H. and Roux, A. P. J, eds, *Philosophy from Africa*. Oxford: Oxford University Press

Gelfand, M., 1962. *Shona Religion with Special Reference to the Makorekore*. Cape Town: Juta and co Ltd

Gelfand, M., 1956. *Medicine and Magic of the Mashona*. Cape Town: Juta and Co

Gelfand, M., 1959a. *Shona Religion with Special Reference to the Makorekore*. Cape Town: Juta and Co Ltd

Gelfand, M., 1959b. *Shona Ritual with Special Reference to the Chaminuka Cult*. Cape Town: Juta and Co

Gelfand, M., 1964. *Witchdoctor: Traditional Medicine Man of Rhodesia*. London: Harvill Press

Gelfand, M., 1966. *An African's Religion: The Spirit of Nyajena: Case History of a Karanga People*. Cape Town: Juta and Co Ltd

Gelfand, M., 1967.*The African Witch: with Particular Reference to Witchcraft Belief and Practices Among the Shona of Rhodesia*. London and Edinburgh: E & S Livingstone Ltd

Gelfand, M., 1970. Unhu-The Personality of the Shona, *Studies in Comparative Religion* Vol 4, (1), www.studies in comparative religion.com

Gelfand, M., 1981. *Ukama: Reflections on Shona and Western Cultures in Zimbabwe*. Gweru: Mambo Press

Gelfand, M., 1985.*The Traditional Medical Practitioner in Zimbabwe*. Gweru: Mambo Press

Gelfand, M., 1988.*Godly Medicine in Zimbabwe*. Gweru: Mambo Press

George, G. M. J., 2009. Stolen Legacy: Greek Philosophy is Stolen Egyptian Philosophy, in *The Journal of Pan African Studies e-book*

Geschiere, P., 1997.*The Modernity of Witchcraft: Politics and the Occult in Postcolonial Africa*. London: University of Virginia Press

Geschiere, P., 2006. Witchcraft and the Limits of the Law: Cameroon and South Africa, in Comaroff, J. and Comaroff, J. L.. eds. *Law and Disorder in the Postcolony*. London: The University of Chicago Press: 219-246

Geschiere, P. and Fisiy, C., 1994. Domesticating Personal Violence: Witchcraft, Courts and Confessions in Cameroon, *Africa*. 64 (3): 323-341

Geurts, K. L., 2002. *Culture and the Senses: Bodily Ways of Knowing in an African Community.* Berkeley: University of California Press

Gibbon, P., 1993. 'Introduction: Economic reform and Social Change in Africa' in Gibbon, P., ed, *Social Change and Economic Reform in Africa,* Nordiska Afrikainstitutet, Uppsala: 11-27

Gibbon, P., 1995. 'Introduction: Structural Adjustment and the Working Poor in Zimbabwe' in Gibbon, P., Ed, *Structural Adjustment and the Working Poor in Zimbabwe,* Nordiska Afrikainstitutet, Uppsala: 7-37

Gibson-Graham, J. K., 2003. Surplus Possibilities: Postdevelopment and Community Economies, *Paper presented at a Special Session of the Institute of Australian Geographies Conference in Adelaide, Australia 16 April 2004*

Gibson-Graham, J. K., 2005. Surplus Possibilities: Postdevelopment and Community Economies, *Singapore Journal of Tropical Geography* 26 (1): 4-26

Gifford, A., 2012. Formulating the Case for Reparations, in Brennan F., and Packer J., eds, *Colonialism, Slavery, Reparations and Trade: Remedying the Past?* Abingdon: Routledge: 77-96

Gilhus, I. S., 2006, *Animals, Gods and Humans: Changing Attitudes to Animals in Greek, Rome and Early Christian Ideas.* Abingdon: Routledge

Gingrich, A., 1994. Time, Ritual and Social Experience. In Hastrup, K. and Hervik. eds *Social Experience and Anthropological Knowledge.* London and New York: Routledge: 166-179

Goddard, M., 2001. The Scattering of Time Crystals: Deleuze, Mysticism and Cinema, in Bryden, M., ed. *Deleuze and Religion.* London: Routledge: 53-64

Gold, L., 2004. *The Sharing Economies: Solidarity Networks: Transforming Globalisation.* Burlington: Ashgate

Gomart, E. and Hennion, A., 2006. A Sociology of Attachment: Music, Amateurs, Drug Users., in Law, J. and Hassard, J., eds, *Actor-Network Theory and After.* Oxford: Blackwell Publishing: 220-246

Gono, G., 2008. *Zimbabwe's Casino Economy: Extraordinary Measures for extraordinary Challenges.* Harare: ZPH

Goodman, E. D., 1988. *How About Demons: Possession and Exorcism in the Modern World*. Bloomington and Indianapolis: Indiana University Press

Gordon, A. F., 2004. *Ghostly Matters: Haunting and the Social Imagination*. London: University of Minnesota Press

Gordon, D. M., 2012. *Invisible Agents: Spirits in Central African History*. Athens: Ohio University Press

Goredema, C., 2004. "Whither Judicial Independence in Zimbabwe" in Raftopoulos, B. *et al.*, eds, *Zimbabwe: Injustice and Political Reconciliation*, Cape Town, Institute for Justice and Reconciliation: 99-118

Green, M., 1996. Medicines and The Embodiment of Substances Among Pogoro Catholics, Southern Tanzania, *The Journal of Anthropological Institute* vol 2, No 3

Gumplova, P., 2011. *Sovereignty and Constitutional Democracy*. New York: Nomos

Gupta, A. and Ferguson, J., 1992. Beyond "Culture", Space Identity and the Politics of Difference, *Cultural Anthropology* vol 7, (1): 6-23, http://www.jstor.org/stable/656518, accessed 1/9/2010

Gurib-Fakim, A. and Kasilo, O. M. J., 2010. Promoting African Medicinal Plants through an African Herbal Pharmacopoeia, in *The African Health Monitor: Special Issue, African Traditional Medicine*, Brazzaville: 63-66

Hadebe, S., 1997. The Role of Orature in the nationalist Struggle in Zimbabwe, in Vambe, T. M., ed, *Orality and Cultural Identity in Zimbabwe*, Gweru, Mambo Press: 3-8

Hadebe, S., 2001.*Orality and Cultural Identities in Zimbabwe*. Gweru: Mambo Press

Halbestam, J., and Livingston I., 1995. Introduction: Posthuman Bodies, in Halberstam J., and Livingston, I., eds, *Posthuman Bodies, Bloomington and Indianapolis*. Indiana University Press

Hallen, B., 2006. *African Philosophy: The Analytic Approach*. Trenton: Africa World Press Inc.

Hansen, H. B., 1995.The Colonial Control of Spirit Cults in Uganda, in Anderson, D. M. and Johnson, D. H., eds, *Revealing Prophets*. London: James Currey: 143-163

Hansen, T. B. and Stepputat, F., 2005. Introduction. in Hansen, T. B. and Stepputat, F., eds, *Sovereign Bodies: Citizens, Migrants and*

State in the Postcolonial World. Princeton: Princeton University Press: 1-36

Harding, S., 1994, Is Science Multicultural? Challenges, Resources, Opportunities, Uncertainties, Configurations 2.2: 301-330

Harrington, A., 1997. Introduction. in Harrington, A., ed, *The Placebo Effect: An Interdisciplinary Exploration*. London: Harvard University Press: 1-11

Harvey, H., 2006. *Animism: Respecting the Living World*. New York: Columbia University Press

Hastrup, K., 1995. *A Passage to Anthropology: Between Experience and Theory*. London and New York: Routledge

Hawkins, T., 2004. The Zimbabwean Economy: Domestic and Regional Implications, in Hough, M., Du Plessis, A., eds, *State Failure: The Case of Zimbabwe, Ad hoc Publication No 41,* Institute for Strategic Studies, University of Pretoria: 61-79

Hayashida, N. O., 1999. *Dreams in the African Church*. Amsterdam Atlanta: Rodopi B V

Hearn J., 2006. The Implications of ICT for Sexualities and Sexualised Violence: Contradictions of Sexual Citizenship, in *Political Geography* vol 25, (8): 944-963

Heathecote-James, E., 2009. *Seeing Angels: True Contemporary Accounts of Hundreds of Angelic Experiences*. London: John Blake Ltd

Heller, A., 1990. *Can Modernity Survive?* Cambridge: Polity Press

Helliker, K. *et al.*, 2008. Introduction, n Moyo, S. *et al.*, eds *Contested Terrain: Land Reform and Civil Society in Contemporary Zimbabwe*. Pietermaritzburg: S & S Publishers: 1-47

Henderson, P. C., 2005. Mortality and the Ethics of Qualitative Research in a Context of HIV/AIDS, *Anthropology Southern Africa* 28 (3 & 4): 78-87

Herodotus, D., 1942. *The Persian Wars*. New York: The Modern Library

Herva, V. P., 2009. Living (with) Things: Relational Ontology and Material Culture in Early Modern Northern Finland. *Cambridge Archaeology Journal* Vol 19, Issue 3: 388-398. http://journals.Cambridge.org/CAJ

Hinton, R. and Groves, L., 1998. The Complexity of Inclusive Aid, in Groves, L. and Hinton, R., eds, *Inclusive Aid: Changing Power and Relationships in International Development*. London: Earthscan: 1-20

Holleman, J. F., 1952. *Shona Customary Law with Reference to Kinship, Marriage and the Family*. London: Oxford University Press

Holling, C. S. *et al.*, 2002, Resilience and Sustainable Development: Building Adaptive Capacity in a World of Transformations, Ambio vol 31, (5): 437-440

Hornung, E., 1983. *Concepts of God in Ancient Egypt: The One and the Many*. London: Routledge and Kegan Paul

Hromnik, C. A., 1980. *Africa Before Livingstone*, UCT Centre for Extra-Mural Studies

Huffman, T. N., 1980. Linguistic Affinities of the Iron Age in Rhodesia, in Hromnik, C. A., ed, *Africa Before Livingston* UCT Centre for Extra Mural Studies: 1-5

Hugo, H. C., 1925. The Spirit World of the Mashona, *NADA*: 14-17

Human, O., 2012. The Rings Around Jonathan's Eyes: HIV and AIDS Medicine at the Margins of Administration, in Levine, S., ed, *Medicine and the Politics of Knowledge*. Cape Town: HSRC Press

Huwelmeier, G. and Krause, K., 2010. *Travelling Spirits: Migrants, Markets and Mobilities*. Oxford/New York: Routledge

Huwelmeir, G., 2010. Mediating the Apocalypse-Disaster of the Titanic in Vietnamese Pentecostal Discourse, *MMG Working Paper* 11-01.ISSN 2192-2357. www.mmg.mpg.de/workingpapers Gottingen

Ingarden, R., 1960.*Time and Modes of Being*. Illinois: Charles C Thomas Publishers

Ingold, T., 1993. The Art of Translation in a Continuous World, in Palsson, G., ed, *Beyond Boundaries: Understanding, Translation and Anthropological Discourse*. Oxford: Berg: 210-248

Ingold, T., 2006 Rethinking the Animate, Reanimating Thought. *Ethnos* Vol 71: 1: 9-20

Ingold, T., 2007. Earth, Sky, Wind and Weather. *Journal of the Royal Anthropological Institute 13 (S1): S19-S38*

Ingold, T., 2007. Materials Against Materiality. *Archaeological Dialogues* 14: 1: 1-16

Ingold, T., 2008. Point, Line and Counterpoint: From Environment to Fluid Space, in Berthoz, A., Christen, Y., eds, *Neurobiology of Umwelt: How Living Beings Perceive the World, Research and Perspectives in Neurosciences* (c) Springer-Verlag. Berlin Heidelberg: 141-155

Ingold, T., 2010a. *Bringing Things to Life: Creative Entanglements in a World of Materials, ESRC National Centre for Research Methods:* Realities Working Paper # 15

Ingold, T., 2010b. Footprints through the Weather-World: Walking, Breathing, Knowing, *Journal of the Royal Anthropological Institute* (NS): S121-S139

Ingold, T., 2011. Introduction, in Ingold, T., ed, *Redrawing Anthropology, Materials, Movements, Lines.* Surrey: Ashgate Publishing Ltd: 1-20

Inwagen, P. V., 2011. Relational Vs Constituent Ontology, Philosophical Perspectives. 25, *Metaphysics:* 389-404, http://andrewmbailey.com/pri/Relational.pdf

Isaac, B *et al*, 2009, Introduction in Eliav-Feldon M and Isaac B and Ziegler J, eds, *The Origins of Racism in the West.* Cambridge: Cambridge University Press: 1-31

Isichei, E., 2002.*Voices of the Poor in Africa.* Rochester: University of Rochester Press

Itandala, A. B., 2001, European Image of Africa from Early Times to the Eighteenth Century, in Mengara, D. M., ed, *Images of Africa: Stereotypes and Realities.* Trenton: Africa World Press: 61-79

Jackson, L., 2005. *Surfacing up: Psychiatry and Social order in Colonial Zimbabwe 1908-1968.* New York: Cornell University Press

Jacobson, M. F., 2000. *Barbarian Virtues: The United States Encounter Foreign Peoples at Home and Abroad, 1876-1917.* New York: Hill and Wang

Jahn, J., 1961. *Muntu: The New African Culture.* New York: Grove Press Inc

James, E. O., 1957. *Prehistoric Religion: A Study in Prehistoric Archaeology.* London: Thames and Hudson

James, W., 2005. Pragmatism's Conception of Truth, in Medina, J. and Wood, D., eds, *Truth: Engagements Across Philosophical Traditions.* Oxford: Blackwell Publishing: 26-38

Jamieson, M., 2009. Contracts with Satan: Relations with "Spirit Owners and Apprehensions of the Economy among the Coastal Miskitu of Nicaragua. *Durham Anthropology Journal*, vol 16 (2): 44-53

Janko, J., 1997, The Concepts of the World in Greek and Roman Thought: Cyclicity and Degeneration, in Teich M *et al*, eds, *Nature and Society in Historical Context*. Cambridge: Cambridge University Press.

Jean-Luc, N., 1993.*The Birth of Presence*. Stanford: Stanford University Press

Jeater, D., 2007. *Law, Language and Science: The Invention of the "Native Mind" in Southern Rhodesia*, 1890-1930. Portsmouth: Heinemann

Johnson, D. H. and Anderson, D. M., 1995. Revealing Prophets. in same., eds *Revealing Prophets*. London: James Currey

Jones, O., and Cloke, P., 2002. *Tree Cultures: The Place of Trees and Trees in Their Place*. Berg

Kalder, M., 2003. *Global Civil: An Answer to War*. Polity Press: Cambridge

Kane, N. S., 1954. *The World's View: The Story of Southern Rhodesia*. London: Cassell and Co Ltd

Kapferer, B., 2006. Introduction: Outside All Reason: Magic, Sorcery and Epistemology in Anthropology, in Kapferer, B., ed, *Beyond Rationalism: Rethinking Magic, Witchcraft and Sorcery*. Oxford: Berghahn Books: 1-30

Kapferer, B., 2006. Sorcery, Modernity and the Constitutive Imaginary: Hybridising Continuities, in Kapferer, B., ed *Beyond Rationality: Rethinking Magic, Witchcraft and Sorcery*. Oxford: Berghahn Books: 105-129

Kaplan, R., 1994. The Coming Anarchy: How Scarcity, Crime, Overpopulation and Disease are Rapidly Destroying the Planet, in *Atlantic Monthly*, February: 44-76

Karen, E. F., 2008. *Healing Tradition: African Medicines, Cultural Exchange and Competition in South Africa 1820-1949*. Scottville: University of KwaZulu Natal Press

Kasfir, N., 1998. Introduction: the Conventional Notion of Civil Society: A critique, in Kasfir, N., ed, *Civil Society and Democracy in Africa: Critical Perspectives*. London: Frank Cass and Co Ltd: 1-20

Kassam, A., 1994. The Oromo Theory of Development, in Osaghae, E., ed, *Between the State and Civil Society in Africa*. Dakar: CODESRIA: 16-38

Katiyo, W. 1976. *A Son of the Soil*. London. Rex Publishers

Keane, W., 1994. The Value of Words and The Meaning of Things in Eastern Indonesian Exchange, in *MAN* vol 29, No 3: 605-629

Keen, D., 2008.*The Benefits of Famine: A Political Economy of Famine and Relief in South West Sudan 1983-89*. Oxford: James Currey

Kendall, L., 2003. Gods, Markets and the IMF in Korean Spirit World, in West, G. H. and Sanders, T., eds, *Transparency and Conspiracy: Ethnographies of Suspicion in the New World Order*. Durham and London: Duke University Press: 38-58

Kiev, A., 1972.*Transcultural Psychiatry*. New York: The Free Press

Kincaid, H., 2013. Introduction: Pursuing a Naturalist Metaphysics, in Ross, D. *et al.*, eds, *Scientific Metaphysics*. Oxford: Oxford University Press

Kiniffo Henry-Valere, T., 1997. Foreign Objects in Human Bodies: A Surgeon's Report, in Hountondji, P., ed, *Endogenous Knowledge: Research Trails*. Dakar: CODESRIA: 247-263

Klassen, C., 2003. Cybercoven: Being a Witch online, *Studies in Religion/Sciences Religiousness* 31/1: 51-62

Kleinman, A., 1986. *Social origins of Distress and Disease: Depression, Neurasthemia and Pain in Modern China*. New Haven and London: Yale University Press

Kleinman, A., 1988. *Rethinking Psychiatry: From Cultural Category to Personal Experience*. New York: The Free Press

Knauft, B. M., 1998. Creative Possession: Spirit Mediumship and Millennial Economy among Gebusi of Papua New Guinea, in Lambek, M. and Strathern, A., eds, *Bodies and Persons Comparative Perspectives from Africa and Melanesia*. New York: Cambridge University Press: 197-207

Kramer, F., 1993.*The Red Fez: Art and Spirit Possession in Africa*. Verso: London

Kriger, N., 1992. *Zimbabwe's Guerrilla War: Peasant Voices*. Cambridge: Cambridge University Press

Kriger, N., 1995. *Zimbabwe's Guerrila War*. Cambridge: Cambridge

University Press

Krog, A. et al., 2009.*There was this Goat: Investigating the Truth Commission Testimony of Notrose Nobomvu Konile*. Scottville. University of KwaZulu-Natal Press

Kroker, A., 2004.*The Will to Technology and the Culture of Nihilism: Heidegger, Nietzsche and Marx*. Toronto: University of Toronto Press

Kuriyama, S., 2002.*The Expressiveness of the Body and the Divergence of Greek and Chinese Medicine*. New York: Zone Books

Kwon, H., 2010. The Ghosts of War and the Ethics of Memory in Lambek, M., ed, *Ordinary Ethics: Anthropology, Language and Action*. New York: Fordham University Press: 400-414

Laclau, E., 2004, Can Immanence Explain Social Struggles? in Passavant P A and Dean J., eds, *Empire's New Clothes: Reading Hardt and Negri*. London and New York: Routledge: 21-30

Lai, W. W., 2004. The Earth Mother Scripture: Unmaking the neo archaic, in Olupona, J. K., ed, *Beyond Primitivism: Indigenous Religious Traditions and modernity*. New York and London: Routledge: 200-213

Lambek, M., 2008. Travelling Spirits: Unconcealment and Undisplacement, *Huwelmeier and Krause 2nd Pages.indd*.17

Lambek, M., 2009. How to Make Up One's Mind: Reason, Passion and Ethics in Spirit Possession. Paper Presented at the University of Cape Town Sawyer Seminar Series

Lambek, M., 2009. Persons, Personages and Ethical Life from the Ethnography of Malagasy Speakers in Mayotte and Mahajanga, *Prepared for the UCT Sawyer Seminar on the Person*, August 2009: 11-24

Lambek, M., 2010. Introduction, in Lambek, M., ed, *Ordinary Ethics: Anthropology, Language and Action*. New York: Fordham University Press: 1-38

Lan, D., 1986.*Guns and Rain: Guerrillas and Spirit Mediums in Zimbabwe*. Berkeley and Los Angeles: University of California Press

Lan, D., 1989. Resistance to the Present by the Past: Mediums and Money in Zimbabwe, in Parry, J. and Block, M., eds, *Money and the Morality of Exchange*. New York: Cambridge University Press: 191-208

Latour, B., 1993. *The Pasteurisation of France*. Cambridge: Harvard University Press

Latour, B., 2004, Whose Cosmos? Which Cosmopolitics: Comments on the Peace Terms of Ulrich Beck, *Knowledge Commons* vol 10, Issue 3: 450-462

Latour, B., 2004. *Politics of Nature: How to Bring the Sciences into Democracy*. Cambridge: Harvard University Press

Latour, B., 2005. *Reassembling the Social: An Introduction to Actor Network Theory*. Oxford: Oxford University Press

Latour, B., 2006. On Recalling Actor Network Theory, in Law, J. and Hassard, J., eds, *Actor-Network Theory and After*. Oxford: Blackwell Publishing: 15-25

Law, J., 2006. After ANT: Complexity, Naming and Topology, in Law, J. and Hassard, J., eds, *Actor-Network Theory and After*. Oxford: Blackwell Publishing: 1-14

Lawrence, P., 2000. Violence, Suffering: The Work of Oracles in Srilanka's Eastern War Zone, in Das, V. *et al.*, eds, *Violence and Subjectivity*. California: University of California Press: 171-202

Lefebvre, H., 2000.*Critiques of Everyday Life*. Paris: Grasset

Lefort, P., 2001. Sierra Leone: Food at the Heart of the Conflict, in *Action against Hunger, 2000-2001, Hunger and Power*. London: Lynne Rienner Publishers

Lentz, C., 1995. "Tribalism" and Ethnicity in Africa: A Review of Four Decades of Anglophone Research. *Cali.Sci.hum*, 31 (2): 303-328

Levin, D. M., 1993. Introduction, in Levin D .M., ed, *Modernity and the Hegemony of Vision*. Berkeley, Los Angeles: University of California Press: 1-29

Levinas, E., 2001. *Existence and Existents*. Pittsburgh: Duquesne University Press

Levinas, E., 2003. *On Escape: De l'evasion*. California: Stanford University Press

Levi-Strauss., 1969.*The Elementary Structures of Kinship*. Boston: Eyre and Spottiswode (Publishers) Ltd

Iliffe, J., 1990. *Famine in Zimbabwe 1890-1960*. Gweru: Mambo Press

Louisiana State University. 2008. Evidence of Rainmaking Bacteria Discovered in Atmosphere and Snow, in *ScienceDaily*. http://www.sciencedaily.com/releases/2008/02/080228174801.htm

Lovemore, F., 2003. Medical Evidence of the Use of Organised Violence and Torture in Zimbabwe 2000-2003, in Lesizwe, T., ed, *Civil Society and Justice in Zimbabwe*, Proceedings of a Symposium held in Johannesburg 11-13 August 2003

Low, C. and Hsu, E., 2008. Introduction, in Same, eds, *Wind, Life, Health: Anthropological and Historical Perspectives*, Oxford, Blackwell Publishing: 1-15

Lyons, T., 2004. *Guns and Guerrila Girls:* Africa World Press Inc

MaCarthur, J., 2008, A Responsibility to Rethink? Challenging Paradigms in Human Security, International Journal vol 63, (2): 422-443

Macedo, D., 1999. Decolonising Indigenous Knowledge, in Semali, L. M., Kinchelve, J. L., eds, *What is Indigenous Knowledge: Voices from the Academy*. New York and London: Falmer Press: XI-XVI

Mackenzie, D., 1998. *Knowing machines: Essays on Technical Change.* Cambridge: The MIT Press

Mafuranhunzi, G., 1995. *Guerrilla Snuff.* Harare: Baobab Books

Magubane, B. M., 2007. *Race and the Construction of the Dispensable Other.* Pretoria: University of South Africa

Makumbe, Mw., 1998. Is there a Civil Society in Africa?", *International Affairs* Vol 74, (2): 305-317

Maldonado-Torres, N., 2008. *Against War: Views from the Underside of Modernity.* Durham and London: Duke University Press

Malin, B., 2006, Resilient Society, Vulnerable People: A Study of Disaster Response and Recovery from Floods in Central Vietnam, Uppsala: Department of Urban and Rural Development, Faculty of Natural Resources and Agricultural Sciences PhD Thesis

Mamdani, M., 1996. *Citizen and Subject: Contemporary Africa and the Legacy of Late Colonialism.* Princeton: Princeton University Press

Mammo, T., 1999.*The Paradox of Africa's Poverty*. Eritrea: The Red Sea Press

Mandela, N., 2013. *No Easy Walk to Freedom.* Cape Town: Kwela Books

Mandova, E. and Chingombe, A., 2013. The Shona Proverbs as an Expression of Unhu/Ubuntu, *International Journal of Academic Research in Progressive Education and Development* Vol 2, No 1. ISSN: 2226-6348: 100-107

Mangena, F., 2014, The Ethics Behind the Fast Track Land Reform in Zimbabwe, in Mararike C G., ed, *Land: An Empowerment Asset for Africa: The Human Factor Perspective.* Harare: University of Zimbabwe Publications

Mangena, F. and Makova, M., 2010. Shona Epistemology and Plato's Divided Line, *The Journal of Pan African Studies* vol 3, (9): 63-76

Mano, W. and Williams, W., 2010. Debating "Zimbabweaness" in Diasporic Internet Forums: Technologies of Freedom, in McGregor, J. and Primorac, R., eds, *Zimbabwe's New Diaspora: Displacement and the Cultural Politics of Survival.* New York: Berghahn Books: 183-201

Manyame-Tazarurwa, K. C., 2011. *Health Impact of participation in the Liberation Struggle of Zimbabwe by ZANLA Women Ex Combatants in the ZANLA operational Areas.* Central Milton: Authorhouse UK Ltd

Manzungu, E. *et al.*, 1996. Continuity and Controversy in Smallholder Irrigation, in Manzungu, E. *et al.*, eds, *The Practice of Smallholder Irrigation: Case studies from Zimbabwe.* Harare: University of Zimbabwe Publications

Maphosa, F., 2005. The Impact of Remittances from Zimbabweans in South Africa on Rural Livelihoods in the South Eastern District of Zimbabwe" *Forced Migration Studies Paper* no 14, University of the Witwatersrand

Maphosa, F., 2009. *Rural Livelihoods in Zimbabwe: Impact of remittances from South Africa.* Dakar: CODESRIA,
http://www.codesria.org/spip.php?article.13115

Mararike, C. G., 2009. Attachment Theory and Kurova Guva, in *Zambezia* xxxvi (i/ii) p 20-35

Mararike, C. G., 1999. *Survival Strategies in Rural Zimbabwe: The Roles of Assets, Indigenous Knowledge and Organisations.* Harare: Mond Books

Marcus, G. E., 1998. *Ethnography through Thick and Thin.* Princeton,

New Jersey: Princeton University Press

Marongwe, N., 2005. Traditional Authority in Community Based Natural Resource Management (CBRM): The Case of Chief Marange in Zimbabwe, in Dzingirai, V. and Breen, C., eds, *Confronting the Crisis in Community Conservation: Case Studies from Southern Africa:* University of KwaZulu Natal Press

Marshal, R., 2009. *Political Spiritualities: The Pentecostal Revolution in Nigeria.* Chicago and London: The University of Chicago Press

Maschio, T., 1998. The Narrative and Counternarrative of the Gift: Emotional Dimension of Ceremonial Exchange in South Western New Britany, in *The Journal of the Royal Anthropological Institute* vol 4, (1)

Masunungure, E. V., 2009. *Defying the Winds of Change: Zimbabwe's 2008 Elections.* Harare: Weaver Press

Masunungure, E. V. *et al.*, 2007. Summary of results of the Economic and Survival Strategies Survey (NED): *Mass Public Opinion Institute*, http://www.mpi.ref/index& PhP

Matikiti, R., 2007. Environmental Management: Karanga Ecotheology in Charumbira Communal Lands, in *Swedish Missiological Theme* 95, (3): 217-226

Matson, W. I., 1982. *Sentience.* Berkeley: University of California Press

Matt Lee., 2013. Memoirs of a Sorcerer, Notes on Giles Deleuze-Felix Guattari, Austin Osman Spare and Anomalous Sorcerers, Academia.ed. http://www.academic.ed/1819931 memoirs-of-a-sorcerer-notes-on-Giles-deleuze-felix-guattari-osman-spares-and-anomalous-sorcerers, accessed 25/6/2013

Mattei, U., and Nader, L., 2008. *Plunder when the Rule of Law is Illegal.* Blackwell Publishing

Matyszak, D., 2009. Civil Society and the Long Election, in Masunungure, E. V., ed, *Defying the Winds of Change: Zimbabwe's 2008 Elections.* Harare: Weaver Press: 133-148

Maurer, B., 2004. On Divine Markets and the Problem of Justice, in Passavant, P. A. and Dean, J., eds, *Empire's new Clothes: Reading Hardt and Negri.* New York and London: Routledge: 57-72

Maurer, B., 2005. Does Money matter? Abstraction and Substitution in Alternative Forms, in Miller, D., ed, *Materiality*. Durham and London: Duke University Press: 140-162

Mawere, A. and Wilson, K., 1995. Socio-Religious Movements, the State and Community Change: Some Reflections on the Ambuya Juliana Cults of Southern Zimbabwe, *Journal of Religion in Africa*, vol 25, XXV, 3, 252

Maxwell, D., 1999. *Christians and Chiefs in Zimbabwe*. Edinburgh: Edinburgh University Press

Maxwell, D., 2006. *African Gifts of Spirit: Pentecostalism and the Rise of a Zimbabwean Transnational Religious Movement*. Oxford: James Currey Ltd

Maxwell, N., 2007. *From Knowledge to Wisdom: A Revolution for Science and the Humanities*. London: Pentire Press

Maynes, M. J. et al., 2008. *Telling Stories: The Use of Personal Narratives in the Social Sciences and History*. Ithaca and London: Cornell University Press

Mbembe, A., 2000. On Private Indirect Government: *State of the Literature Series* 1/2000

Mbembe, A., 2001. *On the Postcolony*. Berkeley and Los Angeles: University of California Press

Mbembe, A., 2006. On Politics as a Form of Expenditure, in Comaroff, J. L. and Comaroff, J., eds, *Law and Disorder in the Postcolony*. Chicago: University of Chicago Press: 299-336

Mbiti, J. S., 1970. *Concepts of God in Africa*. London. SPCK

Mbofana, W., 2011. Incising an Unripe Abscess: The Challenges of Community Healing in Zimbabwe, in Murithi, T. and Mawadza, A., eds, *Zimbabwe in Transition: A View from Within*. Auckland Park: The Institute for Justice and Reconciliation: 191-222

McCandless, E., 2011. *Transformation in Zimbabwe: Social Movements, Strategy: Dilemmas and Change*. Maryland: Lexington Books

McGonagle, E., 2007. *Crafting Identity in Zimbabwe and Mozambique*. Rochester: University of Rochester Press

McGregor, J., 2003. Living with the River: Landscape and Memory in the Zambezi Valley, North West Zimbabwe, in Beinart, W. and McGregor, J., eds, *Social History and African Environments*. Oxford: James Currey Ltd: 87-106

McGregor, J., 2010. The Making of Zimbabwe's Diaspora, in McGregor, J. and Primorac, R., eds, *Zimbabwe's New Diaspora: Displacement and the Cultural Politics of Survival*. New York and Oxford: Berghahn Books: 1-36

McKay, J. P., 1983. *A History of Western Society: From Antiquity to Enlightenment*. Boston: Houghton Mifflin Company

McLean, G. F., 2004. *Persons, Peoples and Cultures: Living together in a Global Age*. Washington DC: The Council for Research in Values and Philosophy

McNeish, J A., 2005. Overview: Indigenous People's Perspectives on Poverty and Development, in Eversole, R. *et al.*, eds, *Indigenous Peoples and Poverty: An International Perspective*. London and New York: Zed Books: 230-238

Mcneish, J. A. and Eversole, R., 2005. Introduction: Indigenous Peoples and Poverty, in Eversole, R. *et al.*, eds, *Indigenous People and Poverty: An International Perspective*. London: Zed Books: 1-26

Mengara, D. M., 2001. Introduction: White Eyes, Dark Reflections, in Mengara D M., ed, *Images of Africa Stereotyping and Realities*. Trenton, Africa World Press: 1-19

Meyer, B., 1998, Make a Complete break with the Past: Memory and Postcolonial Modernity in Ghanaian Pentecostal Discourse, in Werbner R., ed, *Ritual Passage Sacred Journey*. Washington: Smithsonian

Mhame, P. P. *et al.*, 2010. Clinical practices of African Traditional Medicine, in *The African Health Monitor: Special Issue, African Traditional Medicine*, Brazzaville: 32-39

Mhame, P. P. *et al.*, 2010. Collaboration between Traditional Health Practitioners and Conventional Health Practitioners: Some Country Experiences, in *The African Health Monitor: Special Issue, African Traditional Medicine*, Brazzaville: 39-46

Mignolo, W. D., 2007, Globalisation and De-colonial Thinking, Special Issue of Cultural Studies (21-2/3

Mignolo, W. D., 2007, Delinking: The Rhetoric of Modernity, the Logics of Coloniality and the Grammar of Decoloniality, in Globalisation and Decolonial Thinking *Special Issue of Cultural Studies* 21-2/3

Mignolo, W., 2007. The Splendors and Miseries of "Science": Coloniality, Geopolitics and Knowledge, and Epistemic Pluriversality, in de Sousa Santos, B., ed, *Cognitive Justice in a Global World,* Plymouth, Lexington Books: 375-395

Miller, D., 2005. Materiality: an Introduction, in Miller, D., ed, *Materiality.* Durham and London: Duke University Press: 1-47

Mills, J., 2005. *Relational and Intersubjective Perspectives in Psychoanalysis: A Critique.* Maryland: The Rowman and Littlefield Publishing Group, Inc

Mills, J., 2012. *Conundrums: A Critique of Contemporary Psychoanalysis.* New York: Routledge

Mithofer, D. and Waibel, H., 2003. Income and Labor Productivity of Collection and Use of Indigenous Fruit Tree Products in Zimbabwe, *Agroforestry Systems* 39: 295-305

Mkandawire, T., 1995. Adjustment, Political Conditionality and Democratisation in Africa, in Chole, E. and Ibrahim, J., eds, *Democratisation Processes in Africa: Problems and Prospects.* Dakar: CODESRIA: 81-99

Moyana, H., 1984. *The Political Economy of Land in Zimbabwe.* Gweru: Mambo Press

Moore, S. F. and Myerhoff, B. G., 1977. Introduction: Secular Rituals: Forms and Meanings, in Moore, S. F. and Myerhoff, B. G., eds. *Secular Rituals.* Assen: Van Gorcum and Comp B. V: 3-25

Moreno, A. O. P., 1970. *Jung, God and Modern Man.* Notre Dame and London: University of Notre Dame Press

Morgan, M. H., 1901, Greek and Roman Rain Gods and Rain Charms, Transactions and Proceedings of the American Philological Association vol 32: 83-109
http: www.jstor.org/stable/2826/2, Accessed 25/5/2010

Morris, D. B., 1997. Placebo, Pain and Belief: A Biocultural Model, in Harrington, A., ed, *The Placebo Effect: An Interdisciplinary Exploration.* London: Harvard University Press

Motz, L. and Hane, J., 1995. *The Story of Astronomy.* New York and London: Planum Press

Moyana, H., 1984.*The Political Economy of Land in Zimbabwe.* Gweru: Mambo Press

Moyo, S., 2008. *African Land Questions, Agrarian Transitions and the State: Contradictions of Neoliberal Land Reforms.* Dakar: CODESRIA

Moyse, A., 2009. The Media Environment Leading up to Zimbabwe's 2008 Elections, in Masunungure, E. V., ed, *Defying the Winds of Change.* Avondale: Weaver Press: 43-60

Mudege, N. N., 2008. *An Ethnography of Knowledge Production: the Production of Knowledge in Mupfurudzi Resettlement Scheme, Zimbabwe.* Boston. Leiden

Mudzengi, E., 2008. Expropriation is Not Enough, Rights and Liberties is What Matters, in Moyo, S., *et al.*, eds, *Contested Terrain: Land Reform and Civil Society in Contemporary Zimbabwe.* Pietermaritzburg: S & S Publishers

Mulvany, P., and Moreira, M. A., 2009. Food Sovereignty: a Farmer-led Policy Framework, in Scoones, I., and Thompson, J., eds, *Farmer first Revisited: Innovation for Agricultural Research and Development.* Warwickshire: Practical Action Publishing Ltd p 174-179

Mupepi, M G., 2010, A Crisis with an Origin: Proposing a Framework for Local and International Engagements in Zimbabwe, in Mangara J., ed, *New Security Threats and Crises in Africa: Regional and International Perspectives.* Palgrave MacMillan: 247-271

Muphree, M. W., 1969.*Christianity and the Shona.* New York: The Athlone Press

Murove, M. F., 2009. African Environmental Ethics Based on the Concept of Ukama and Ubuntu, in Murove, M. F., ed. *African Ethics: An Anthology of Comparative and Applied Ethics.* Scottville: University of KwaZulu Natal Press: 315-331

Murphy, I. and Wannenburgh, A., 1978. *Rhodesian Legacy.* Cape Town: C Struik Publishers

Musoni, F., 2005. *Internal Displacement and Ethnicity in North West Buhera, Zimbabwe 1927-1979*, Five Colleges.edu

Mutasa, M., 2010. Zimbabwe's Drought Conundrum: Vulnerability and Coping in Buhera and Chikomba Districts. *MSc in Development Studies: Norwegian University of Life Sciences*

Mutowo, M. K. K., 2001. Animal Diseases and Human Populations in Colonial Zimbabwe: The Rinderpest Epidemic of 1896-1898, in *Zambezia*, XXIII, (i): 1-22

Mutswairo, S., 1983.*Chaminuka: Prophet of Zimbabwe*. Washington D C: Three Continents Press

Muzondidya, J., 2009. From Buoyancy to Crisis 1980-1997, in Raftopoulos, B. and Mlambo, A., eds. *Becoming Zimbabwe: A History from the Precolonial Period to 2008*. Harare: Weaver Press

Muzondidya, J., 2010.*The Zimbabwean Diaspora: Opportunities and Challenges for Engagements in Zimbabwe's Political Development and Economic Transformation*: 112-158

Muzvidziwa, I. and Muzvidziwa, V. N., 2012. Hunhu (Ubuntu) and School Discipline in *Africa*, vol 37, No 1 January-March 2012, Dharmaram Journals: 27-42\

Muzvidziwa, V. N., 2005. *Women without Borders: Informal Cross-Border Trade among Women in the Southern African Development Community Region (SADC)*. Addis Ababa: OSSREA

Muzvidziwa, V. N., 2009. Marriage as a Survival Strategy: The Case of Masvingo, Zimbabwe. *Zambezia* XXVII (ii): 147-164

Nabokov, I., 1997. Expel the Lover, Recover the Wife: Symbolic Analysis of a South Indian Exorcism, *The Journal of the Royal Anthropological Institute* vol 3, (2)

National Geographic News. 2009. Rainmaking Bacteria Ride Clouds to "Colonise" the Earth? http://news.nationalgeographic.com/news/2009/01/090112-clouds.bacteria.html

Ncneish, J., 2005. Overview, Indigenous People's Perspectives of Poverty and Development, in Eversole, R. *et al.*, eds. *Indigenous Peoples and Poverty: An International Perspective*. London: Zed Books: 230-238

Ndlovu-Gatsheni, S. J., 2006. Conflict, Violence and Crisis in Zimbabwe, in Matlose, K. *et al.*, eds. *Challenges of Conflict, Democracy and Development in Africa*. Johannesburg: ELSA

Ndlovu-Gatsheni, S. J., 2013. *Coloniality of Power in Postcolonial Africa: Myths of Decolonisation*. Dakar: CODESRIA

Newman, S., 2011. *The Politics of Post-Anarchism*. Edinburgh: Edinburgh University Press

New Zimbabwe.com, 10 June 2012, Zimbabwe's Minister Made

defends GMO ban. http://www.newzimbabwe.com/news.aspx?newsD=6863

Nhemachena, A., 2016. Double-Trouble: Reflections on the Violence of Absence and the 'Culpability' of the Present in Africa, in Mawere, M., *et al.*, ed, *Violence, Politics and Conflict Management in Africa: Envisioning Transformation, Peace and Unity in the Twenty-First Century*. Bamenda: Langaa RPCIG

Nhemachena, A. and Mawere, M., 2017. Introduction: Theorising Fundamentalisms and Fetishisms in the 21st Century, in Nhemachena, A. and Mawere, M., eds, *Africa at the Crossroads: Theorising Fundamentalisms and Fetishisms in the 21st Century*. Bamenda: Langaa RPCIG

Nightingale, A., 2010. Plato on Aporia and Self-Knowledge, in Nightingale, A. and Sedley, D., eds, *Ancient Models of Mind: Studies in Human and Divine Rationality*. Cambridge: Cambridge University Press: 8-26

Noble, M., 1973. Social Network: its Use as a Conceptual Framework in Family Analysis, in Boissevain, J. and Mitchell, J. C., eds, *Network Analysis: Studies in Human Social Interaction*. Paris, Mouton and Co

Norris, C., 2010. *Badiou's Being and Event*. London: Continuum Publishing Group

Ntholi, L. S., 2006. *Contesting Sacred Space: A Pilgrimage Study of the Mwali Cult of Southern Africa*. Eritrea: Africa World Press Inc

Nyamnjoh, F. B., 2005. *Africa's Media: Democracy and the politics of Belonging*, London: Zed Books Ltd

Nyamnjoh, F. B., 2006. *Insiders and Outsiders: Citizenship and Xenophobia in Contemporary Southern Africa*. London and New York: CODESRIA Books

Nyamnjoh, F. B., 2012. Potted Plants in Greenhouses: A Critical Reflection on the Resilience of Colonial Education in Africa, in *Journal of Asian and African Studies*, 47 (2): 129-154

Nyamnjoh, F. B., 2015. *"C'est l'homme qui Fait l'homme": Cul-de-sac Ubuntu-ism in Cote D'Ivoire*. Bamenda: Langaa Research and Publishing CIG

Nyamnjoh, F. B., 2007. "Ever-Diminishing Circles": The Paradoxes of Belonging in Botswana, in de la Cadena, M. and Starn, O., eds, *Indigenous Experience Today*. Oxford: Berg

Nyamnjoh, F. B., 2010. Racism, Ethnicity and the Media in Africa: Reflections Inspired by Studies of Xenophobia in Cameroon and South Africa, *Key-Note Address for Racism, Ethnicity and the Media in Africa Conference*, 25-26 March 2010, London

Nyamnjoh, F. B., 2011. Cameroonian Bushfalling: Negotiating Identity and Belonging in Fiction and Ethnography, *American Ethnologist* vol 38, (4): 701-713

Nyathi, P., 2001.*Traditional Ceremonies of Amandebele*. Gweru: Mambo Press

O'Farrell, M. A., and Vallone, L., 2002. Virtual Gender: Fantasies of Subjectivity and Embodiment, The University of Michigan Hausman BL, Virtual Sex, Real Gender: Body and Identity in Transgender Discourse: 190-213

Oakley, F., 2005. *Natural Law, Laws of Nature, Natural Rights: Continuity and Discontinuity in the History of Ideas*. New York Continuum Press

Oberleitner, G., 2005, Human Security: A Challenge to International Law? in *Global Governance* vol 11, No 2: 185-203

Offe, C., 1996. *Modernity and the State*. Cambridge: Polity Press

Ogbaharya, D. G., 2008, (Re) building Governance in Post Conflict Africa: The Role of the State and Informal Institutions, in *Development in Practice* vol 18, (3): 395-402

Okazaki, A., 2003. Making Sense of the Foreign: Translating Gamk Notions of Dream, Self and Body in Palsson, G., ed, *Beyond Boundaries: Understanding, Translation and Anthropological Discourse*. Oxford: Berg: 152-171

Okri, B., 1997. *A Way of Being Free*. London. Phoenix House

Oliver, H. H., 1981. *A Relational Metaphysics*. London: Martin Nijhoff Publishers

Omoweh, D. A., 2012. *The Feasibility of the Democratic Developmental State in the South*. Dakar: CODESRIA

Ong, A., 1988. The Production of Possession Spirits and the Multinational Corporation in Malaysia, *American ethnologist* Vol

15, No 1: 28-42, http://www.jstor.org/stable/645484, accessed 22/8/2008

Onyewuenyi, I. C., 2006. *The African Origins of Greek Philosophy: an Exercise in Afrocentrism:* University of Nigeria Press

Ophir A., 1991. *Plato's Invisible Cities: Discourse and Power in the Republic.* Maryland: Barnes and Noble Savage

Opoku, K. A., 1978. *West African Religion.* Accra FEP International Private Limited

Oswalt, W. H., 1973. *This Land was Theirs: A Study of the North American Indians.* London: John Wiley and Sons

Pagden, A., 1993. *European Encounters with the New World: From Renaissance to Romanticism.* New Haven and London: Yale University Press

Palmer, R., 1977. *Land and Racial Domination in Rhodesia.* Berkeley: University of California Press

Parekh, B., 1995. Liberalism and Colonialism: A Critique of Locke and Mill, in Pieterse J N and Parekh B, eds, *The Decolonisation of Imagination: Culture, Knowledge and Power.* London and New Jersey: Zed Books: 81-100

Pargament, K. I., 2007. *Spiritually Integrated Psychotherapy: Understanding and Addressing the Sacred.* New York: The Guilford Press

Parrinder, J., 1967. *African Mythology.* London: Paul Hamlyn

Parish, J., 2005. Witchcraft, Riches and Roulette: An Ethnography of West African Gambling in the U K, in *Ethnography,* Vol 6 (1): 105-122

Patel, V. *et al.,* 1995. Stressed, Depressed or bewitched: A Perspective on Mental Health, Culture and Religion. *Development in Practice,* Vol 5, (3): 216-224

Paul, L. A., n.d. Category Priority and Category Collapse, http://lapaul.org/papers/categorical-priority-and collapse.pdf

Pearce, C., 1990. Tsika, Hunhu and the Moral Education of Primary School Children, *Zambezia* XVII (ii): 145-159

Pearson, K. A., 2001. Pure Reserve: Deleuze Philosophy and Immanence, in Bryden, M., ed, *Deleuze and Religion.* London: Routledge: 141-155

Perera, S., 2001. Spirit Possession and Avenging Ghosts: Stories of Supernatural Activity as Narratives of Terror and Mechanisms of Coping and Remembering, in Das, V. and Poole, D., eds *Remaking A World: Violence, Social Suffering and Recovery*. California: University of California Press: 157-200

Peron, J., 2000. *Zimbabwe: The Death of A Dream: Lessons for South Africa*. Saxonworld: The Natal Witness Printing and Publishing Co (Pty) Ltd

Pfukwa, C., 1997. Unwritten Ethics and Moral Values: The Human Face of Chimurenga II, in Vambe, T. M., ed., *Orality and Cultural Identity in Zimbabwe*, Gweru, Mambo Press: 25-36

Phillips, J., 2000.*Contested Knowledge: A Guide to Critical Theory*. London: Zed Books

Pieterse, J. N., 2000. My Paradigm or Yours? Alternative Development, Post-Development, Reflexive Development, in *Development and Change* Vol 29: 343-373

Pignarre, P. and Stengers, I., 2011.*Capitalism Sorcery: Breaking the Spell*. New York: PAGRAVE MACMILLAN

Pigou, P., 2003. Executive Summary in Lesizwe, S., ed, *Civil Society and Justice in Zimbabwe, Proceedings on a Symposium Held In Johannesburg 11-13 August* 2003: 1-34

Pikirayi, I., 2001. *The Zimbabwean Culture: Origins and Decline of Southern Zambezian State*. Oxford: A Hamira Press

Pinfold, J., 2007. *The Slave Trade Debate: Contemporary Writings For and Against*. Oxford: Bodleian Library

Popke, J. E., 2003. Poststructuralist Ethics: Subjectivity, Responsibility and the Space of Community *Progress in Human Geography* 27, (3): 298-361

Posselt, F. W. T., 1935. *Fact and Fiction*. Salisbury: Government House

Potter, J., 2003. Negotiating Local Knowledge: An Introduction, in Potter, J. et al., eds. *Negotiating Local Knowledge: Power and Identity in Development*. London: Pluto Press: 1-29

Pottier, J. et al., 2011. Navigating the Terrain of Methods and Ethics in Conflict Research, in Cramer, C. et al., eds. *Researching Violence in Africa: Ethical and methodological Challenges*. Boston: Leiden: Brill: 1-22

Powers, E., 1891 Rain-making Science ol 18 No 456: 249 http://www.jstor.org/stable/1765516 Access 26/05/2010

Poxon, J., 2001. Embodied Anti-Theology: the Body without Organs and the Judgement of God, in Bryden, M., ed, *Deleuze and Religion*. London: Routledge: 42-50

Prah, K. K., 2011, Culture: The Missing Link in Development Planning in Africa, in Keita L., ed, *Philosophy and African Development: Theory and Practice*. Dakar: CODESRIA

Prey, R., 2012. The Network's Blind Spots: Exclusion, Exploitation and Marx's Process-Relational Ontology. *Triple C*. 10 (2): 253-273; http: www.triple-c-at

Putnam, H., 2004. *Ethics Without Ontology*. Cambridge: Harvard University Press

Quiggin, J., 2010. *Zombie Economics: How Ideas Still Walk among Us*. Princeton and Oxford: Princeton University Press

Raftopoulos, B., 2002. Briefing: Zimbabwe's 2002 Presidential Elections, *African Affairs*, 101: 413-426

Raftopoulos, B., 2009. Crisis in Zimbabwe 1998-2008, in Raftopoulos, B. and Mlambo, A., eds, *Becoming Zimbabwe: A History from the Precolonial Period to 2008*. Harare: Weaver Press

Ramose, M. B., 2002. I Conquer therefore I am the Sovereign: Reflection upon Sovereignty, Constitutionalism and Democracy in Zimbabwe and South Africa, in Coetzee P H and Roux APJ, eds, *African Philosophy Reader*. London: Routledge: 463-500

Ranger, T., 1969. The Role of Ndebele and Shona Religious Authorities in the Rebellion of 1896 and 1897, in Stokes E and Brown R., eds, *The Zambezian Past: Studies in Central African History*. Manchester: Manchester University Press: 94-136

Ranger, T., 1979. *Revolt in Southern 1896-7*. London: Heinemann Educational Books Ltd

Ranger, T., 1994. Religious Pluralism in Zimbabwe: A Report on the Britain-Zimbabwe Society Research Day, St Anthony's College, Oxford, *Journal of Religion in Africa* xx, 3: 226-251

Ranger, T., and Ncube, M., 1995. Religion in the Guerrilla War: the case of southern Matabeleland, in Bhebhe, N., and Ranger, T., eds, *Society in Zimbabwe's Liberation War* vol 2 Harare: University of Zimbabwe Publications: James Currey Ltd: 35-57

Ranger, T., 2000, African Views of the Land: A Research Agenda, in *Transformation* 44 ISSN 0258-7696

Ranger, T., 1966. Traditional Authorities and the Rise of Modern Politics in Southern Rhodesia 1898-1930, in Stokes, E. and Brown, R., eds, *The Zambezian Past: Studies in Central African History*. Manchester: Manchester University Press: 171-193

Ranger, T., 1977. The People in African Resistance: a Review, in *Journal of Southern Africa Studies* vol 4, No 1 Special Issue on Protest and Resistance

Ranger, T., 1985.*The Invention of Tribalism in Zimbabwe*. Harare: Mambo Press

Ranger, T., 1989. Missionaries, Migrants and the Manyika: The Invention of Ethnicity in Zimbabwe, in Vail, L., ed, *Creation of Tribalism*. Berkeley: University of California Press: 118-150

Ranger, T., 1999.*Voices from the Rocks: Nature, Culture and History in the Matopo Hills of Zimbabwe*. Oxford: James Currey

Ranger, T., 2003. Women and Environment in African Religion: The Case of Zimbabwe, in Beinart, W. and McGregor, J., eds, *Social History of African Environments*. Oxford: James Currey Ltd: 72-86

Ranger, T., 2010. The Invention of Tradition in Colonial Africa, in Grinker, R. R. *et al.*, eds, *Perspectives on Africa: A Reader in Culture, History and Representation*. West Essex: Wiley-Blackwell

Ranger, T. O., 1979. *Revolt in Southern Rhodesia 1896-7*. London: Heinemann Educational Books Ltd

Rasmussen, C. E., 2011.*The Autonomous Animal: Self-Governance and the Modernist Subject*. Minneapolis: University Of Minnesota Press

Rattray, R. S., 1927. *Religion and Art in Ashanti*. Oxford: Clandon Press

Rattray, R. S., 1969. *Ashanti*. New York: Negro University Press

Reeler, T., 2003. Crimes against Humanity and the Zimbabwe Transition

Reeler, T., n.d. Subliminal Terror? Human Rights Violations and Torture in Zimbabwe during 2008, *Centre for the Study of Violence and Reconciliation*, Braamfontein

Reeler, T., *et al.*, 2009. *The Tree of Life: A Community Approach to Empowering and Healing Survivors of Torture in Zimbabwe*. Torture Volume 19, No 3: 1-14

Reid, H., 1999. *In Search of Mortals: Mummies, Death and the Afterlife*. London: Headline Book Publishing

Reynolds, P., 1996.*Traditional Healers and Childhood in Zimbabwe*. Athens: Ohio University Press

Richards, D., and Ellis, A. D., 1982. *Medieval Britain*. Essex: Longman Group Limited

Richards, D., 1990. The Implications of African-American Spirituality., in Asante, M. K. and Asante, W. K., eds, *African Culture: Rhythms of Unity*. Trenton: Africa World Press

Richmond, O. P., 2007. Emancipatory Forms of Human Security and Liberal Peacebuilding, in *International Journal* vol 62, (3): 458-477

Robben, A. C. G. M. and Mordstrom, C., 1995. Introduction: The Anthropology and Ethnography of Violence and Sociopolitical Conflict, in Nordstrom, C. and Robben, A. C. G. M., eds, *Fieldwork Under Fire: Contemporary Studies of violence and Survival*. Los Angeles: University of California Press: 1-23

Roberts, T., 2005. Sacrifice and Secularisation: Derrida de Vries and the Future of Morning, in Sherwood Y and Hart, K., eds, *Derrida and Religion: Other Testaments*. New York and London: Routledge

Roseman, M., 1993. *Healing Sounds from the Malaysian Rainforest*. Berkeley: University of California Press

Ross, F. C., 2001. Speech and Silence: Women's Testimony in the First Five Weeks of Public Hearings of the South African Truth and Reconciliation Commission, in Das, V. *et al.*, eds, *Remaking A World: Violence, Social Suffering and Recovery*. California: University of California Press: 250-279

Ross, F. C., 2003. *Bearing Witness: Women and the Truth and Reconciliation Commission in South Africa*. London: Pluto Press

Ross, F. C., 2003. On Having Voice and Being Heard: Some After Effects of Testifying Before the South African Truth and Reconciliation Commission, *Anthropological Theory* vol 3 (3): 325-341

Ross, F. C., 2005. Codes and Dignity: Thinking about Ethics in Relation to Research on Violence, in *Anthropology Southern Africa*: 28 (3 & 4): 99-107

Ross, F. C., 2010. An Unacknowledged Failure: Women Voice, Violence and the South African Truth and Reconciliation Commission, in Shaw, R. and Waldorf, L., eds, *Localising Transitional Justice: Interpretations and priorities After mass Violence.* Stanford: Stanford University Press: 69-92

Ross, F. C., 2010. *Raw Life, New Hope: Decency, Housing and Everyday Life in a Postapartheid Community.* Cape Town: University of Cape Town Press

Rutherford, B., 2008. Zimbabweans Living in the South African Border Zone: Negotiating Suffering and Surviving, *Concerned African Scholars Bulletin* No 80: 36-41,
http: //concernedafricanscholars.org/does/acasbulletin.80-6pdf

Sachs, W., 1997. *The Development Dictionary: A Guide to Knowledge as Power.* London: Zed Books Ltd

Samkange, S., 1973. *Origins of Rhodesia.* London: Heinemann

Samkange, S. J. T. and Samkange, T. M., 1980. *Hunhuism or Ubuntuism: A Zimbabwe Indigenous Political Philosophy.* Graham Publishers

Sandage, A., 1987. Cosmology: The Quest to Understand the Creation and expansion of the Universe, in Asmov, I. *et al.*, eds, *The Universe.* Visual Publications Inc: 248-276

Sanders, T., 2003. Invisible Hands and Visible Goods: Revealed and Concealed Economies in Millennium Tanzania, in West, G. H. and Sanders, T., eds. *Transparency and Conspiracy: Ethnographies of Suspicion in the New World Order.* Durham and London: Duke University Press: 148-169

Sanders, T., 2008. *Beyond Bodies: Rain(making) and Sensemaking in Tanzania.* Toronto: University of Toronto Press

Schabas, M., 2003. Adam Smith's Debt to Nature, in Schabas, M. and Neil de March., eds, *Oeconomies in the Age of Newton.* Durham and London: Duke University Press: 262-281

Schabas, M., 2005.*The Natural Origins of Economics.* London: University of Chicago Press

Scheper-Hughes, N., 2007, Violence and the Politics of Remorse: Lessons from South Africa, in Biehl, J. *et al.*, eds, *Subjectivity: Ethnographic Investigations*. Berkeley: University of California Press

Schimdt, A., 1995. "Penetrating Foreign Lands: Contestation over African Landscape: A case Study from Eastern Zimbabwe, in *Environment and History* vol I, (3): 351-376

Schmidt, H., 1997. Healing the Wounds of War: Memories of Violence and the Making of History in Zimbabwe's Most Recent Past, *Journal of Southern African Studies,* vol 23, No 2: 301-310

Schmidt, H. I., 2013. *Colonialism and Violence in Zimbabwe: A History of Suffering*. Suffolk: James Currey

Schmidt, V. H., 2006. Multiple Modernities or Varieties of Modernity. *Current Sociology* 54, No 77

Schimmel, A., 1993. *The Mystery of Numbers*. New York and Oxford: Oxford University Press

Schuurman, F. J., 1993. *Beyond the Impasse: New Directions in Development Theory*. London: Zed Books Ltd

Scott, J. C., 1985. *Weapons of the Weak: Everyday Forms of Peasant Resistance*. New Haven and London: Yale University Press

Serres. M., 1995. *The Natural Contract*. University of Michigan Press

Serres, M., 2008.*The Five Senses: A Philosophy of Mingled Bodies*. London: Continuum Publishing Group, Trans, Margaret Sankey and Peter Cowley

Setiloane, G. M., 1975.*The Image of God Among the Sotho-Tswana*. Rotterdam: A.A Balkema

Shapiro, K., 2004. The Myth of the Multitude, in Passavant, P. A. and Dean, J., eds, *Empire's New Clothes: Reading Hardt and Negri*. New York and London: Routledge

Shapiro, A. K. and Shapiro, E., 1997. The Placebo: Is it Much Ado About Nothing?, in Harrington, A., ed, *The Placebo Effect: An Interdisciplinary Exploration*. London: Harvard University Press: 12-36

Sheridan, T. B., 1999. Descartes, Heidegger, Gibson and God: Towards an Eclectic Ontology of Presence, *Presence* Vol 8, (5): 551-559

Shildrick, M., 2002.*Embodying the Monster: Encounters with the Vulnerable Self.* London: SAGE Publications

Shoko, T., 2007. *Karanga Indigenous Religion in Zimbabwe: Health and Wellbeing.* England: Ashgate Publishing Ltd

Shoko, T., 2011. Healing in the St Elijah Church, in Dube, L. *et al.*, eds. *African Initiatives in Healing Ministry.* Unisa Press: 117-126

Shoko, T., 2012. Teaching African Traditional Religion at the University of Zimbabwe, in Adogame, A. *et al.*, eds, *African Traditions in the Study of Religion in Africa.* Surrey: Ashgate Publishing Ltd: 53-66

Simmons, D., 2012. *Modernising Medicine in Zimbabwe: HIV/AIDS and Traditional Healers.* Nashville: Vanderbilt University Press

Singer, P., 1994. *Practical Ethics.* Cambridge: Cambridge University Press

Sithole, W. W., 2011. A Critical Analysis of the Impact of Food Aid on Internally Displaced Persons: the Case of Manicaland Food Aid Intervention in Zimbabwe, MA in Disaster Management, University of the Free State

Smith, C., 2009. Does Naturalism Warrant a Moral belief in the Universal Benevolence and Human Rights? In Schloss, J. and Murray, M., eds, *The Believing Primate: Scientific Philosophical and Theological Reflections on the Origins of Religion.* Oxford: Oxford University Press: 292-318

Smith, D. W., 2001. The Doctrine of Univocity: Deleuze's Ontology of Immanence, in Bryden, M., ed. *Deleuze and Religion.* London: Routledge: 167-183

Smith, M., 2011. *Against Ecological Sovereignty: Ethics, Biopolitics and Saving the Natural World.* Minneapolis: University of Minnesota Press

Snell, B., 1948. *The Discovery of the Mind: The Greek origins of European Thought.* Oxford: Basil Blackwell

Snow, L. F., 1977. Popular Medicine in a Black Neighbourhood, in Spicer, E. H., ed, *Ethnic Medicine in the South West.* University of Arizona Press

Solomon, R. C., 1970. Hegel's Concept of 'Geist', *The Review of Metaphysics* vol 23, (4): 642-661, http://www.jstor.org/stable/20125667

Spierenburg, M., 2004. *Strangers, Spirits and Land Reforms: Conflicts about Land in Dande,* Northern Zimbabwe. Boston: Leiden

Stanner, W. E. H., 2005. Religion, Totemism and Symbolism, in Lambek, M., ed, *A Reader in the Anthropology of Religion.* Oxford: Blackwell.: 90-98

Starr, C G., 1984. *The Ancient Greeks:* New York: Oxford University Press

Stelladi, G., 2000. *Heidegger and Derrida on Philosophy and Metaphor: Imperfect Thought: Philosophy and Literary Theory.* New York: Humanity Books

Stengers, I., 2010. Comparison as a Matter of Concern, in *Common Knowledge* 17: 1: 48-63

Stiglitz, J. E., 2002.*Globalisation and its Discontents.* London: Penguin Books

Stoller, P., 1989.*The Taste of Ethnographic Things: The Senses in Anthropology.* Philadelphia: University of Pennsylvania Press

Stoller, P. and Olkes, C., 1987. *In Sorcery's Shadow: A Memoir of Apprenticeship among the Songhay of Niger.* Chicago and London: The University of Chicago Press

Stolow, J., 2009. Wired Religion: Spiritualism and Telegraphic Globalisation in the Nineteenth Century, in Streeter, S. M. *et al.*, eds. *Empires and Autonomy: Moments in the History of Globalisation.* Vancouver: UBC Press: 79-92

Szalay, M., 1995. *The San and the Colonisation of the Cape 1770-1879.* Conflict, Incorporation, Acculturation, Koln, Rudiger koppe Verlag

Tacey, D., 2003. *The Spirituality Revolution: The Emergence of Contemporary Spirituality.* Sydney: Harpercollins Publishers

Tarisayi, E., 2009. Voting in Despair: The Economic and Social Context, in Masunungure, E. V., ed, *Zimbabwe's 2008 Elections.* Harare: Weaver Press: 11-24

Taussig, M., 1986. *The Devil and Commodity Fetishism in South America.* Chapel Hill: The University of North Carolina Press

Taussig, M., 2005. The Genesis of Capitalism amongst a South American Peasantry: Devil's Labour and the Baptism of Money, in Lambek, M., ed, *A Reader in the Anthropology of Religion.* Oxford: Blackwell: 472-492

Temples, P., 1959. *Bantu Philosophy*. Paris: Presence Africane

Thompson, J., 2009. *Nature's Watchmaker: The Undiscovered Miracle of Time*. Dublin: Blackhall Publishing

Thondhlana, J., 2011. The Role of the Zimbabwean Media in the Transition Process, in Murithi, T. and Mawadza, A., eds. *Zimbabwe in Transition: A View from Within*. Auckland Park: Institute for Justice and Reconciliation: 223-254

Thornton, R. J., 1980. *Space, Time and Culture among the Iraqw of Tanzania*. London: Academic Press

Tsing, A., 2000. The Global Situation, *Cultural Anthropology* 15, 3: 327-360

Turnbull, D., 2000. *Masons, Tricksters and Cartographers: Comparative Studies in the Sociology of Scientific and Indigenous Knowledge*. Amsterdam: Harwood Academic Publishers

Turner, E., 1993. The Reality of Spirits: A Tabooed or Permitted Field of Study? *Anthropology of Consciousness*, 4 (1): 9-12

Turner, E., 1998. *Experiencing Ritual: A New Interpretation of African Healing*. Philadelphia: University of Philadelphia Press

Turner, V. W., 1968. *Schism and Continuity in an African Society*. Manchester: University of Manchester Press

Turner, V. W., 1969.*The Ritual Process: Structure and Antistructure*. London: Rutledge and Kegan Paul

Tuso, H., 2006. Indigenous Processes of Conflict Resolution in Oromo Society, in Zartman, I. W., ed., *Traditional Cures for Modern Conflicts: African Conflict Medicine*. Colorado: Lynne Rinner Publishers

United Nations Environment Programme. 2008. *Indigenous Knowledge in Disaster Management in Africa*, UNEP, Nairobi

Van Binsbergen, W., 2003. *Intercultural Encounters: Africa and Anthropological Lessons Towards a Philosophy of Interculturality*. Munster: Lit Verlag

Van Gennep, A., 1960. *Rites of Passage: Structure and Antistructure*. New York: Aldine De Gruyter

Van Zyl, D. H., 1991. *Justice and Equity in Greek and Roman Legal Thought*. Pretoria: Academic

Vera, Y., 2001. A Voyeur's Paradise....Images of Africa, in Palmberg, M., ed, *Encounter Images in the meeting Between Africa and Europe*. Uppsala: Nordiska Afrikainstutet.: 115-120

Verdery, K., 1999. *The Political Lives of Dead Bodies: Reburial and Poststructuralist Change*. New York: Columbia University Press

Verran, H., 2013. Engagements between Disparate Knowledge Traditions: Towards Doing Difference Generatively and in Good Faith, in Green, L., ed, *Contested Ecologies: Dialogues in the South on Nature and Knowledge*, Cape Town, HSRC Press: 141-161

Vuifhuizen, C., 1997. Rainmaking, Political Conflict and Gender Images: a Case of Mutema Chieftaincy in Zimbabwe. *Zambezia* XXIV (i): 31-49

Waelbers, K., 2011. *Doing Good with Technologies: Taking Responsibility for the Social Role of Emerging Technologies, Springer*. London: New York

Waelbers, K. and Derstewitz, P., 2013. Ethics in Actor Network, or What Latour could Learn from Darwin and Dewey. Science and Engineering Ethics, *Springer,* Netherlands, DOI. 10.1007/s11948-012-9408-1

Waite, G., 2000.Traditional Medicine and the Quest for National Identity in Zimbabwe. *Zambezia* (2000) XXVII (ii): 1-33

Ward, C., 2008. *Anarchy in Action*. London: Freedom Press

Warwick, K., 1998. *In the Mind of the Machine*. London: Random House UK Ltd

Watts, M., 1991. Heart of Darkness: Reflections on Famine and Starvation in Africa, in Downs, R. E. *et al.*, eds, *The Political Economy of African Famine: Food and Nutrition in History and Anthropology* vol 9. Pennsylvania: Gordon and Breach Science Publishers

Weatherall, D. J., 2012. Philosophy for Medicine, *Journal of the Royal Society of Medicine* 105 (9): 403-404

Weaver, J. C., 2006. *The Great Land Rush and the Making of the Modern World 1650-1900*. Quebec: McGill-Queen's University Press

Weinstone, A., 2004. *Exposure to the Posthuman Other*, Book Reviews. Minneapolis: University of Minnesota Press

Weitzer, R., 1984. Continuities in the politics of State Security in Zimbabwe, in Schatzberg, M. G., ed, *The Political Economy of Zimbabwe*. New York: Praeger Publishers: 81-118

Wennerlund, C., 2003. Coinage in 17th Century England, in Schabas M and de Marchi N, eds, *Oeconomies in the Age of Newton*. Durham and London: Duke University Press

Werbner, R. P., 1977. Continuity and Policy in Southern Africa High God Cult, in Werbner R P, ed, *Regional Cult A SA Monographs 16 Academic Press*. London New York: 179-217

Werbner, R., 1977. *Regional Cults A.S.A Monographs* 16. London: Academic Press

Werbner, R., 1989. Regional Cult of God Above: Achieving and Defending the Macrocosm, in Werbner, R.., ed, *Ritual Passage, Sacred Journey*. Washington: Smithsonian

Werbner, R., 1991.*Tears of the Dead: The Social Biography of An African Family*. London: Edinburgh University Press

Werbner, R. P., 1995. In Memory: A Heritage of War in South Western Zimbabwe, in Bhebhe, N. and Ranger, T., eds, *Society in Zimbabwe's Liberation War,* vol 2, Harare: University of Zimbabwe Publications: 192-205

West, H. C., 2003. Who Rules Us Now? Identity Tokens, Sorcery and other Metaphor in the 1994 Mozambican Elections, in West, H. G. and Sanders, T., eds, *Transparency and Conspiracy: Ethnographies of Suspicion in the New World Order*. Durham and London: Duke University Press: 92-117

West, H. G. and Luedke, T. J., 2006. Introduction: Healing Divides: Therapeutic Border Work in South East Africa, in Luedke, T. J. and West, H. G., eds, *Borders and Healers: Brokering Therapeutic Resources in South East Africa*. Bloomington and Indiana Polis: Indiana University Press

West, H. G. and Saunders, T., 2003, *Transparency and Conspiracy: Ethnographies of Suspicion in the New World Orders*. Durham and London: Duke University Press

Westerlund, D., 2006. *African Indigenous Religions and Disease Causation: From Spiritual Beings to Living Humans*. Boston: Brill

White, H., 2001. *Tempora et Mores*: Family Values and the Possession of a Post-Apartheid Countryside. *Journal of Religion in Africa*. XXI (4): 457-479

White, L., 1994. Blood Brotherhood Revisited: Kinship, Relationship, and the Body in East and Central Africa, *Africa*, Vol 64, (3): 359-372

Whitworth, B., 2007. *The Physical Wold as a Virtual Reality, Centre for Discrete Mathematics and Theoretical Computer Science,* Massey University, Albany, Auckland

Wildman, W. J., 2006. An Introduction to Relational Ontology, http: //people.bu.edu/wwildman/images/does/72%202010%20-%

Wilk, R. R. and Cliggett, L. C., 2007. *Economies and Cultures: Foundations of Economic Anthropology.* Westview Press

Willis, R. and Curry, P., 2004. *Astrology, Science and Culture: Pulling Down the Moon.* Berg: Oxford and New York

Willis, R., 1999. *Some Spirits Heal, Others Only Dance: A Journey into Human Selfhood in an African Village.* Oxford: Berg

Windrich, E., 1981. The Mass Media in the Struggle for Zimbabwe. Gweru: Mambo Press

Wiseman, R., 2011. *Paranormality: Why we See What isn't There.* London: MacMillan

Wiseman, S. J., 2008. Introduction: Reading the Early Modern Dream, in Hodgkin, K. *et al.*, eds. *Reading the Early Modern Dream: the Terrors of the Night.* New York: Routledge: 1-14

Wittman, N., 2012. International Legal Responsibility and Reparations for Transatlantic Slavery, in Brennan F and Packer J., eds, *Colonialism, Slavery, Reparations and Trade: Remaking the Past.* Canada: Routledge: 3-22

Wolfe, C., 2010. *What is Posthumanism?* Minneapolis: University of Minnesota Press

Woollcott, R. C., 1975. Pasipamire-Spirit Medium of Chaminuka, the Wizard of Chitungwiza, *NADA* Vol XI (2): 154-169

Yahya, H., 2013. *The Disasters Darwinism Brought to Humanity.* Ontario: Al-Attique Publishers Inc

Yolton, J. W., 2000. *Realism and Appearances: An Essay in ontology.* Cambridge: Cambridge University Press

Zaffiro, J., 2002. *Media and Democracy in Zimbabwe 1931-2002*. Colorado: International Academic Publishers Ltd

Zimbabwe Parliamentary Debates, House of Assembly. 16 March 2010. Vol 36, No 27; First Report of the Portfolio Committee on Health and Child Welfare on drugs and Medicines

Zuesse, E. M., 1979 *Ritual Cosmos: The Sanctification of Life in African Religion*. Ohio: Ohio University Press

Zunga, L., 2003. *Farm Invasions in Zimbabwe: Is Zimbabwe a Democracy?* Truth House Publishing

Zysk, K. G., 2008. The Bodily Winds in Ancient India Revisited, in Hsu, E. and Low, C., eds, *Wind, life, Health: Anthropological and Historical Perspectives*. Oxford: Blackwell Publishing: 99-107

Printed in the United States
By Bookmasters